KILMARNOCK

KILMARNOCK

James A. Mackay

A history of the Burgh of Kilmarnock and of Kilmarnock & Loudoun District

First published, 1992

ISBN 0-907526-52-7
Alloway Publishing, Darvel, Ayrshire

Printed by
Walker & Connell Ltd
Hastings Square
Darvel

Contents

To the Memory
of the late
J.F.T. 'Jock' Thomson

FOREWORD

When I was approached to consider writing a history of Kilmarnock as part of the celebrations marking the quatercentenary of the burgh, I must confess that I found the prospect rather daunting. To me, Kilmarnock meant whisky and Robert Burns—often combined, as I attend Burns Suppers all over the world and am confronted by the seemingly ubiquitous square bottles, so often used in the toast to the 'Immortal Memory' from Manitoba to Melbourne. But I could not recall a single epoch-making event which took place in the town, nor a single famous Kilmarnockian other than that sprightly chap in the tight breeches and top-boots 'born in 1820 and still going strong'.

As the headquarters of the Burns Federation, Kilmarnock is known to countless Scots in every part of the world and hyphenated Scots many generations removed from their native land. Similarly Kilmarnock is familiar to those who take the trouble to read the gilt lettering on those red and black labels so idiosyncratically aslant; and as there are only three countries in the entire world where whisky cannot be openly and legally sold I imagine that Kilmarnock brings a glow to the hearts of people of discernment and taste everywhere, from Abu Dhabi to Zimbabwe.

But, of course, Burns and fine blends are only two of the things for which Kilmarnock is famous, as I have since discovered. Killie's carpets, locomotives and water-valves have penetrated every corner of the globe. Textiles and engineering have long been the backbone of the town's prosperity and their vicissitudes have been reflected in Kilmarnock's recent history. So many of the textile mills, the forges and foundries, the footwear factories and the engineering shops have come and gone, old-established family firms have been taken over by multi-national conglomerates, sold and resold, or subject to receivership or management buyout, that the traditional industries have, in many respects, lost their specifically Kilmarnock identity. In the same way the Burgh Police and Fire Brigade, the Kilmarnock Infirmary and other services have merged their identity in larger bodies so that the sense of belonging to the town has been diluted. Similarly many people who work in Kilmarnock live in Kilmaurs or Hurlford or even farther afield; and conversely many Kilmarnockians now commute to jobs in Glasgow.

Even Kilmarnock itself has lost something of its individuality. Strictly speaking, the burgh whose quatercentenary we are celebrating this year no longer exists, having merged its identity with the surrounding district in 1975. But these problems of identity are common to all towns; regardless of where civic boundaries are drawn, or the superficial overlay of local and national administration, a town is still, at heart, not just the bricks and stones but the people who live and work there. This is their story. Within these pages is the narrative of hopes and disappointments, ambitions and achievements, triumphs and failures, but always the human dimension is foremost.

At the end of the day Kilmarnock and its inhabitants have a great deal to be proud of. Perhaps a better understanding of the past will help to engender a more positive attitude about the present and instil optimism for the future. Kilmarnock has had its share of good and bad fortune over the years, but it has always bounced back. Of course we can all find plenty to grumble about nowadays, but the overall pattern has been one of steady progress and improvement. Those who yearn for the good old days will learn herein that, for most of the working classes, conditions were harsh and life was one long grind of unremitting toil. Yet I cannot help thinking with admiration about the men and women who, lacking the educational opportunities we take for granted nowadays, succeeded in rising above the squalor and poverty of their lives to achieve great things and materially improve the lot of their fellows.

The story of Kilmarnock is the story of all provincial towns, originally the commercial centre of a country district, rising to prosperity in the wake of the Industrial Revolution, suffering from industrial decline and now coping in a largely post-industrial environment. No one knows what the next four hundred years have in store; but we may rest assured that Kilmarnock and its people will show that same spirit of resilience and resourcefulness which has been the hallmark of its past.

In compiling this history I have been indebted to James Hunter, Curator of Dean Castle Museum, to William Anderson, Chief Librarian, David Bett, Charlie Woodward and the staff of the Dick Institute in Kilmarnock, as well as the staff of Glasgow University Library and the History and Topography department of the Mitchell Library, Glasgow. I should also like to express my thanks to Douglas Campbell and his staff in Kilmarnock and Loudoun District Council Offices, to Sergeant David Bell of Strathclyde Police (Kilmarnock Division), Andrew Boyle, John Inglis, Joan Jones, Karon McKnight John Malkin, Kevin Collins, Jim Grugan, Janette Thomas, S.J. Todd, Betty Dunlop, John Moodie, Mungo Douglas, Sam Gilbert, Hugh Dick, Tony Vollum, Pat McGill, Janette Young, Joan Jones, Grace Wilson, Bill Service, Valerie Andrew, Fr. Quinlan, Jim Hill, Arnold Thomson, Andrew Baird, Frank Donnelly, Bill McGregor, C. Potter, Gillan Knox, John Knox, Frank Beattie, Sharon Callaghan, Bob Murray, Alec Marshall, Jim Potts, Bill Fitzpatrick, Ian McVey, Matt Spiers, Jim Mair, Ian Young, Jim McCallum, Frank Tocher and William Morton.

A special word of thanks is due to the staff of Alloway Publishing and to Jim Hyslop and Bobby McBride who did so much of the editorial work involved in this project and coped with all my queries with unfailing good humour.

James A. Mackay

1 EARLY HISTORY

People have lived in the Kilmarnock and Loudoun area for at least six thousand years, but tantalisingly little is known of early human settlement. From scanty archaeological finds we know that hunters roamed the district in the Middle Stone Age and that primitive farming was established by the New Stone Age. The remains of an Iron Age hill fort have been discovered at Fenwick 8km (5 miles) north of Kilmarnock, but remarkably little evidence of early settlement has so far come to light in Kilmarnock itself. Admittedly, very little archaeological excavation has taken place within the town, although it has been ascertained that the present street level near the Cross is seven feet (two metres) above the medieval level.

Few relics of Neolithic man have been found within the burgh, but about 1900 an urn containing three arrowheads was excavated opposite Mack's Corner, near the site of the present-day Gas showroom. In 1914 a wooden object was recovered from the river silt at the Glenfield Works. At the time this was believed to be a canoe paddle, which it closely resembled, however this is now known to be part of an ard - a primitive type of plough used in the Neolithic and Bronze Ages and perhaps later. Only one other example has been found in Scotland and indeed few anywhere in Europe, so this is an important item despite its poor preservation.

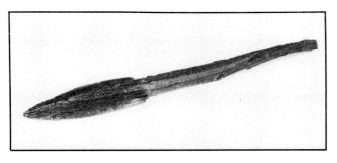

Neolithic Ard

Yet the location of the present town at the intersection of east-west and north-south roads would seem to presuppose the development of a hamlet where ancient trackways met near the confluence of the River Irvine and one of its principal tributaries (now known as the Kilmarnock Water). The route from Glasgow to Ayr runs through Kilmarnock, and the town straddles the Irvine Valley which would have been an important trade route from time immemorial. The Romans recognised the importance of the area by building a fort opposite Loudoun Hill at the head of the valley, shortly after the occupation of north Britain by Agricola about 80 AD. Capable of housing an entire cohort of 500 troops, this strategic outpost would have protected the cross-country trade route to the Clyde coast and policed the district. There is evidence to suggest that the fort was abandoned after Agricola returned to Rome in 85

AD, but it was re-occupied and expanded in the Antonine period (138-61 AD).

The name Kilmarnock is Celtic and literally means the monastic cell (or, in the archaeological sense, the 'developed cemetery') of St Marnoc or Mo-Ernoc. This and other names such as Kilmaurs, Kilbride and Kilwinning, suggest the spread of Christianity some time after Ninian established his church at Whithorn (Candida Casa) in 397. Early writers on Kilmarnock placed the foundation of Marnock's cell in 322 but this was doubted by Archibald McKay who, just as erroneously, considered that Christianity had come to Ayrshire in the wake of the Columban mission in the 6th century. Until such time as archaeological evidence pinpoints the earliest Christian settlement in the area historians are inclined to the view that Kilmarnock's first church was probably founded in the first half of the 5th century. There is, of course, nothing to suggest that St Marnoc himself occupied the first ecclesiastical site, merely that the cell was named after him. No fewer than 22 saints bore this name, or some variant of it,

Bronze Age Axe-head

so it is impossible to say which one of them was connected with the area. The name is found in places as far afield as Inchmarnock (Dunbartonshire) and Portmarnock (Ireland). James Hunter derived the name from Earnoc or Earnock while Francis Croome (1883) went further and gave the etymology of the name as Celtic *Mo Ernin occ* - 'my little (or young) Ernin' and suggested that the saint in question was one Ernin or Ernene referred to in Adamnan's *Life of St Columba* as a preacher renowned for his eloquence, but without a shred of evidence to support this. J. Kevan McDowall, in *Carrick Gallovidian* derived the name more prosaically (and incorrectly) as *Cill mor cnoc* which he thought meant 'Cell of the great cairn'; but *cnoc* means 'hill' and appears in many placenames as Knock or Crock. The cell or church of the big hill, if this derivation is correct, would suggest a location for the chapel on the eminence where the railway station now stands; although tradition, perpetuated by generations of antiquarian writers, has placed the earliest cell of St Marnock on the site of the present Laigh Kirk.

All traces of the labours of St Ninian and his followers disappeared during the centuries that followed the withdrawal of the Roman legions from Britain in 407. In the ensuing centuries the district formed part of the kingdom of the Britons of Strathclyde. The Scots (from Ireland) established a colony at Dalriada in Argyll between 498 and 503 and sixty years later the arrival of Columba on Iona marked the beginning of the re-introduction of Christianity. Whether Marnoc or Ernene belong to this later period cannot be determined, but it is more probable that the work of converting the Strathclyde Britons was carried on by Kentigern (St Mungo) early in the seventh century. Mungo, the founder of Glasgow is, at best, a rather shadowy figure and there is no chronicle or biography of him to link him definitely with mid-Ayrshire. In the eighth century Strathclyde fell under the sway of the Scottish king Angus MacFergus and it was his descendant, Kenneth Mac Alpin (844-60), who brought the Scots, Picts, Britons and Angles of Lothian together into a single kingdom.

Fossils of fish teeth from Dick Institute Museum collection

The process of consolidation was slow and painful, and it was not until the reign of David I (1124-53) that a pattern of local government began to emerge. During this period the king used Norman mercenaries to keep the native population in order. David introduced the feudal system and made grants of land to these Norman knights and barons. Thus the feudal bailieries of Cunninghame, Kyle and Carrick came into being. In 1205 King William the Lion curbed the independent power of his barons by welding these bailieries into the Sheriffdom of Ayr. The River Irvine formed the boundary between Cunninghame and Kyle and thus the burgh of Kilmarnock, for most of its history, lay within the territory of the former. When it expanded south of the river it straddled both Cunninghame and Kyle, and the present district incorporates portions of both bailieries. In the thirteenth century Cunninghame was governed (from Irvine) by Hugh de Morville, the Great Constable of Scotland, while Kyle came under the control of Walter Fitzalan. In this period Riccarton, now a suburb of Kilmarnock, developed as a separate town, deriving its name from Richard Loccart. The Loccarts were vassals of Hugh de Morville and according to Chalmers' *Caledonia* they founded the church of Kilmarnock as a dependency of the monastery of Kilwinning. This was based on a passing reference by Timothy Pont (1609) who is believed to have examined the records

of the monastery (no longer extant) and who says that the church 'bulte by the Loccarts, was dedicat to a holy man, Mernock, as vitnesses ye records of Kilvinin Abbey.'

The great magnates of Cunninghame and Kyle, in turn, granted lands to their principal followers and in this manner the landed families of the area emerged. These were the Craufurds of Craufurdland Castle, the Campbells of Loudoun, the Mures of Rowallan, the Cunninghames of Caprington and last, but by no means least, the Boyds of Dean Castle which stood about a mile north of the ancient town of Kilmarnock. A witness to a charter of 1205 between Bryce de Eglingstoun (Eglinton) and the town of Irvine was one *Dominus Robertus de Boyd, miles* (Lord Robert Boyd, knight). There is a tradition that this surname was derived from the Gaelic word *buidhe* (yellow-haired), but it may equally have been of Norman origin. The son of this knight, also Sir Robert, distinguished himself at the Battle of Largs in 1263. A local tradition maintains that in the mopping-up operations after Haco's defeat, Sir Robert Boyd and his companions defeated a Norwegian force at a place called Goldberry Hill. The words Gold Berry were later adopted as the motto of Kilmarnock in commemoration of this feat of arms.

For centuries Kilmarnock must have been no more than an insignificant hamlet. There is no mention of it in any medieval charters still extant, and the earliest written reference to it occurs in John Barbour's epic poem *Brus* composed in the late fourteenth century:

> Therefore the ways forth took he then
> To Kilmarnock and Kilwinnyne,
> And to Ardrossan after syne.

This refers to the flight of the English knight, Sir Philip de Mowbray, who was defeated by Douglas somewhere in the Cunninghame district after the outbreak of the insurrection in 1306.

It is with the Wars of Independence that Kilmarnock begins to emerge from the mists of antiquity. A decade before the Bruce, William Wallace of Ellerslie conducted a guerrilla campaign against the English. The old tradition that Wallace hailed from Elderslie in Renfrewshire no longer seems tenable. He was, in fact,

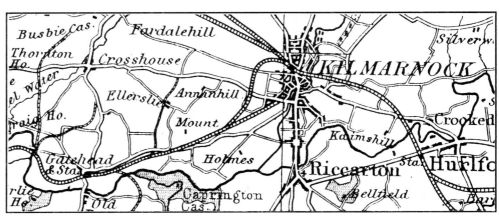

Early Map showing location of Ellerslie, ancient seat of the Wallace family

the son of Margaret de Craufurd and Sir Malcolm Wallace who held the lands of Riccarton. Ellerslie was, in fact, the name of an ancient seat near the Mount, about a mile west of Kilmarnock, and it appeared on Ordnance Survey maps till 1920. Although most of Wallace's exploits took place in other parts of the country his first confrontation with the English is said to have taken place on the banks of the River Irvine at Riccarton. A party of soldiers seized the fish which he had caught; Wallace slew three of them, the other two fled, and he retrieved the fish which had been impounded. Traditionally the place of this affray was marked by a hawthorn, known as the Bickering Bush. By 1822 the tree was in decay and it was then cut down and broken into small pieces by souvenir hunters, but the name survived in a local pub until it was demolished in the 1980s. At least one other skirmish took place in the 1290s within the district when Wallace ambushed an English convoy near Loudoun Hill. Among the Scots on that occasion was another Sir Robert Boyd, son of the victor of Goldberry. Blind Harry, in his stirring account of the battle, mentions Robert Boyd among the Scottish cavalry, and goes on to recount that Boyd played a notable part in the assault on Ayr shortly afterwards.

A decade later, on 10 May 1307, Robert Bruce defeated an English army in the same locality. Sir Robert Boyd was one of the first noblemen of Ayrshire to rally to the Bruce and remained a faithful supporter throughout the vicissitudes of that long campaign for Scottish liberty. He was assigned by the King to assist his brother Edward Bruce, and for services rendered to the Crown he was later granted (by charters of 1308 and 1316) the lands of Kilmarnock, Bondington (Bonnyton) and Hertschaw which had been forfeited by John Baliol. Sir Robert left three sons, Thomas, Allan and James. Nothing is known of them, other than that Thomas Boyd accompanied David II in his ill-fated expedition into England and was captured with him and Andrew Campbell of Loudoun and Robert Wallace at the Battle of Durham in 1341.

The eldest son of Thomas Boyd was Sir Thomas, styled *Dominus de Kilmarnock*. He is chiefly remembered for being embroiled in a feud with Neilson of Dalrymple whom he slew in one of those interminable squabbles that bedevil Scottish history. In 1409, however, he was pardoned by Robert, Duke of Albany. His son, Thomas, Lord Kilmarnock, was a man of great accomplishments who played a major role in the court intrigues surrounding James I. The King spent nineteen years in English captivity and when the Scots failed to raise the full amount of the ransom, Thomas Boyd was one of the noblemen who agreed to become a hostage for the remainder. The same Thomas was later accused of corruption and misappropriation of funds during the regency of the Duke of Albany; he spent some time in prison at Dalkeith, but was released on payment of a stiff fine into the royal exchequer. He died on 7th July 1432 and was commemorated by a fine monument in the old church of Kilmarnock. The memorial to Thomas and his wife Julia de Montgomery was still in existence

when Timothy Pont visited the town in 1609; but forty years later Irvine Presbytery reminded the then Lord Kilmarnock of the Act abolishing 'monuments of Idolatrie' and insisted that he 'demolish it and ding it doun' forthwith.'

The oldest document pertaining to Kilmarnock itself is dated 17th-20th November 1547 and deals with the election of a new parish priest in the presence of the parishioners, some 300 in number. Interestingly young Alexander Boyd was elected to fill the vacancy left by the death of Thomas Boyd of Lyne. Two of the four witnesses were Robert Boyd, son of Patrick Boyd of Hungryhill, and John Boyd of Nairstoun, while the notaries who subscribed the document were George Boyd and John Parker. The names of the 300 parishioners were also given in this document which shows that the commonest surnames at that time were Brown (20), Smith (16), Boyd (15), Paton (12) and Adam (11). Of the 76 other surnames on the list, all of them will be found in the local telephone directory to this day, a remarkable testimony to the stability of the population over the past four centuries.

The power of the great landowning families waxed and waned in the fifteenth and sixteenth centuries. While the De Morvilles died out, their lands passing to the Craufurds in 1189, the Fitzalans attained immense power as the progenitors of the Royal Stuart line, and their vassals prospered in their wake. Alexander Cunninghame was created Lord Kilmaurs by James III and then became Lord Glencairn in 1488.

Meanwhile the Boyds went from strength to strength. Sir Thomas, who died in 1432, left two sons named William and Thomas. The elder son became Abbot of Kilwinning, so the estate passed to the younger son. Nothing is known of this Sir Thomas other than that he murdered Sir Allan Stewart of Darnley at Polmaise between Linlithgow and Falkirk and was himself slain in revenge by the murdered man's brother,

16th Century ceremonial helmet

at Craignaucht in Dunlop parish. This vendetta was quaintly described by the chronicler, Lindsay of Pitscottie: 'In this mean tyme, quhill the countrie was walterrand to and fro in this maner, thair was nothing but murther, thift and slauchter in the south and wast of Scotland.' The fight in which Sir Thomas met his death at the hands of Alexander Stewart was 'a plaine batle, quhair the said Sir Thomas was cruellie slain with manie valient men on everie syd.'

Bloody feuds of this sort were, unfortunately, a common occurrence in the lawless Scotland of the fifteenth century. There is a local tradition that Lord Soulis, an English nobleman, was slain by one of the Boyds at Kilmarnock in 1444. No trace of this incident can be found in contemporary documents, and the story must be confused since the Soulis were an important Scottish family who died out in the fourteenth

Full suits of armour c 1530

century. Indeed, according to Timothy Pont the Soulis owned Kilmarnock Estate and Dean Castle after the Lockharts but before Balliol - who had it before the Boyds. Pont also says that the Soulis Cross marked the spot where Soulis was killed - but this event would have been nearly 200 years *before* 1444. Certainly the Soulis family gave its name to Soulis Street, and to the Cross which stood on it. Prior to 1825 the Cross was a slender stone pillar eight or nine feet high, but of very rude appearance, being entirely without architectural finish or ornament, except a small cross fixed on top. By that date, however, it was in a dilapidated condition and was replaced by a memorial more in keeping with the sentiment of the period. A niche was formed in the wall of the burying ground and a fluted pillar, surmounted by an urn, was placed within it. Over the niche was placed a pediment with a three-line description: 'To the memory of Lord Soulis AD 1444. Erected by Subscription AD 1825. The days of old to mind I call'.

Robert, son of Sir Thomas Boyd, was raised to the peerage in 1459 and was one of the regents of Scotland during the minority of James III and served as Ambassador to England in 1464-5. In 1466, however, he gained control over the boy-king and was appointed sole Governor of Scotland. The following year he added the high offices of Chamberlain and Lord Justiciary, consolidating his power by effecting the marriage of the King's sister Margaret to his eldest son Thomas, together with the earldom of Arran, despite the fact that she had already been promised to the Prince of Wales. It was Lord Boyd who negotiated the treaty between Scotland and Denmark whereby James III married the daughter of King Christian I and brought as her dowry the Orkney Islands. Such a powerful man inevitably made enemies and in 1470 they conspired against him. It was alleged that, in removing the young King from Linlithgow to Edinburgh, Lord Boyd had committed an act of high treason. He was arrested, tried and found guilty and condemned to death, but he escaped to England and died shortly afterwards at Alnwick. Thomas Earl of Arran, although out of the country on the mission to Denmark at this time, was tried and condemned in his absence. He went into exile and eventually died at Antwerp, where a memorial to him was erected by the Duke of Burgundy. His young bride, the King's sister, was sentenced to close confinement within her home at Dean Castle until her husband's death. The sister of the Earl of Arran, Lady Elizabeth Boyd, married Archibald Douglas, Earl of Angus and was the mother of Gavin Douglas, Bishop of Dunkeld and one of the celebrated medieval poets.

After this doleful episode the Boyds lost their national power, but managed to regain their estates and local influence. On the death of the Earl of Arran his son James was restored to the lordship of Boyd, together with the lands of Kilmarnock. James Boyd, however, was slain in 1484, while still a young man, in some petty squabble with Hugh Montgomery of Eglinton, and his estates then reverted to the Crown. Eventually they passed to Alexander, younger son of the Lord Boyd who had died at Alnwick. Nothing is known of this nobleman, except that he was a great favourite of James V who constituted him Bailie and Chamberlain of Kilmarnock. His eldest son Robert had the estates and lordship restored to him in 1536. The third Lord Boyd played a prominent part in Scottish politics during the turbulent period following the death of James V in 1542 and fought in the Battle of Glasgow Field between the Earl of Lennox and the Regent Hamilton (1543). The intervention of Lord Boyd with a party of cavalry at a crucial stage of the battle gave victory to the Regent and for this deed he was restored to the earldom of Arran in 1544. He died six years later.

He was succeeded as fourth Lord Boyd by his son Robert, a young man who had already earned notoriety from the murder, in 1547, of Sir Neil Montgomery of Lainshaw, to avenge the death of his kinsman James Boyd at the hands of Hugh Montgomery in 1484. For several years the Master of Boyd, as he was then known, had to go into hiding in fear of reprisals by the Montgomery faction. On succeeding his father he came out into the open and attained some prominence as a supporter of John Knox and the religious reformers.

Later he changed sides and became a trusted adviser to Mary Queen of Scots whom he accompanied to the Battle of Langside in 1568. During the Queen's captivity he was often employed on diplomatic missions, and was suspected of taking part in the murder of the Regent Moray. In great favour under the Regent James Douglas, Earl of Morton, he was banished in 1583 for his part in the Raid of Ruthven, a plot to kidnap James VI. He fled to France, but was later allowed to return to Scotland where he died on 3rd January 1590. His epitaph can still be seen in the interior of the Laigh Kirk, Kilmarnock. The stone, part of the original church, was preserved by being set into the wall of the present building at its erection in 1802. The epitaph bears the date 1589 (until 1600 the calendar year did not end till 24th March) and eight lines of verse, believed to have been composed by the celebrated poet, Alexander Montgomery. If this were Montgomery's composition, then it would be a poetic irony indeed, bearing in mind the feud which had existed between the two families for over a century.

During the fifteenth and sixteenth centuries the scattered hamlets and ferm-touns gradually developed into towns of some importance. Ayr had been a royal burgh since the beginning of the thirteenth century and Irvine was established not long afterwards. The towns in the present-day

Italian long necked lute c 1570

Kilmarnock and Loudoun District lagged behind the coastal towns in this respect. The first town to receive its charter was Newmilns, in 1490/91, and Kilmaurs followed in 1527. It is a measure of the relative unimportance of Kilmarnock at this time that it did not receive its burgh charter until 12th January 1592. The reference in many historical works to 1591 may be explained by the use of the Old Style calendar.

Thomas, fifth Lord Boyd, suffered 'ane vehement dolour in his heid' and sundry other ailments, for which he sought remedies at Spa in Flanders. As a young man, therefore, he was granted a passport (dated 15th July 1579) enabling him to go abroad for the good of his health. Evidently he recovered sufficiently for he lived long enough to succeed to the lordship, and

it was through his good offices that the charter creating Kilmarnock a burgh of barony was granted by James VI and ratified by Parliament on 5th June 1592. This charter created 'a free lordship and a free barony' of Kilmarnock and went on to state

> ... in consideration of the policies and buildings in the Kirktown of Kilmarnock, lying under the said barony... do, for the convenience and entertainment of our lieges frequenting the same, by the tenor of our present charter, infeu, erect, and create and make the said town, called the Kirktown of Kilmarnock, and the lands of the same with their pertinents, into a free burgh of barony for ever, to be called in all time coming the burgh or town of Kirktown of Kilmarnock: and we give and grant to the inhabitants and indwellers of the said burgh, present and future, plenary power, faculty and free power of buying and selling, in the same, wine, wax, cloth, woollen and linen, broad and narrow, and other merchandises whatsoever; and of having and holding in the said burgh bakers, brewers, butchers, venders of flesh and fish, and all other tradesmen belonging to a free burgh of barony...

The free burgesses were given the right of annually electing bailies and officers for the governing of the burgh. The burgesses were allowed to hold a weekly market on Saturdays and a free fair annually on 20th October, to last for eight days. Subsequently Stewarton, Fenwick and Galston in 1707, obtained by Act of Parliament the right to 'hold fairs and mercats'. Riccarton claimed to have been granted a charter in 1638, but this was never recorded in the Register of the Great Seal.

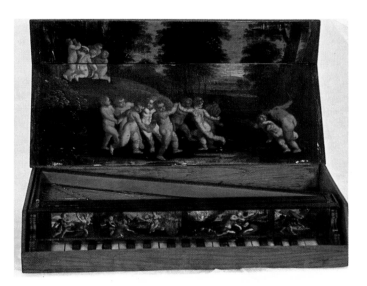

Seventeeth century spinet

2 THE BURGH OF KILMARNOCK, 1592-1974

'Kilmarnock from near Riccarton' Oil Painting by D.O. Hill, S.A. engraved by W. Richardson

The burgh of barony created four centuries ago was a small village of perhaps several hundred souls. In view of the fact that the *parish* had 300 parishioners in 1547, taking in the parish of Fenwick as well, the total population of the district may well have been three or four times that number; but those residing within the burgh boundaries would have been only a proportion of that figure.

Kilmarnock in the seventeenth century

The earliest description of the town was provided by Timothy Pont, the famous mapmaker, who visited the area in 1609 while making a survey of Cunninghame. He quaintly described Kilmernock-toune and Kirk as

> a large village and of grate repaire. It hath in it a veekly market, it hath a faire stone bridge over the river Marnock vich glydes hard by the said toune, till it falls into the river Irving. It hath a pretty church from vich ye village castell and lordschipe takes its name... The Lord Boyd is now Lord of it, to quhosse predicessors it hath belonged for maney generations...

Almost half a century later the Cambridge cavalry officer and angler, Richard Franck, compiled his *Northern Memoirs*. A devoted disciple of Izaak Walton, Franck was making a fishing tour of Scotland when he visited the town in 1658, but he was an acute observer who has left us with a rather unflattering picture of Kilmarnock as

> an antient corporation, crowded with mechanicks and brewhouses... a place through the midst of whose crazy, tottering ports [streets], there runs a river

replenished with trout. Step into her dirty streets that are seldom clean but on a sun-shiny day, or at other times, when great rains melt all the muck, and forcibly drive it down their cadaverous channels into the river Marr, whose streams are so sullied then, that the river loses its natural brightness, till the stains are washed out, and so become invisable. All which to examine is enough to convince you that the influence of planets is their best scavenger... These inhabitants dwell in such ugly houses, as, in my opinion, are little better than huts; and generally of a size, all built so low, that their eaves hang dangling to touch the earth... And that which is worse than all the rest, is their unproportionate, ill contrivance... Not one good structure is to be found in Kilmarnock; nor do I remember any wall it has, but a river there is, as I formerly told you of, that runs through the town; over which there stood a bridge so wretchedly antient, that it's unworthy our commendations.

Dean Castle c 1790

It seems strange that Franck noticed neither the Church nor Dean Castle. The latter, standing apart from the town and even then well screened by trees, may have escaped his notice, but he could scarcely have ignored the Church; perhaps it was too humble an edifice to deserve his attention. Regarding the inhabitants, however, Franck was rather kinder.

> Part of their manufacture is knitting of bonnets and spinning of Scottish cloth, which turns to very good account. Then, for their temper of metals, they are without compeer—Scotland has not better; and as they are artizans in dirks, so are they artists in fuddling, as if there were some rule in drinking, so that, to me, it represents as if art and ale were inseparable companions. Moreover their wives are sociable comers [kimmers], too, yet not to compare with those of Dumblain, who pawn their petticoats to pay their reckoning. Here is a jolly crew of ale-men, but very few anglers, crowded together in the small compass of a little corporation, curiously compacted.

From these quaint observations we may form the impression that the town was a small, congested place, a warren of narrow, mean streets with thatched huts of wattle and clay and overhanging eaves. The congested nature of the town and the extensive use of wood and thatch in the construction of its buildings made fire a major hazard. On 22nd May 1668 the entire town was destroyed by fire. The huts and hovels of 120 families comprising the entire population were destroyed, and from this it may be inferred that the population of Kilmarnock at this period was about 600. This calamity could not have come at a worse time, for the town had already been reduced to 'great misery and affliction' by having a large garrison forcibly quartered on them to suppress the Covenanting rebellion. The inhabitants 'being all poor tradesmen and having no other means of livelihood but their daily employment' were turned out into the surrounding countryside absolutely destitute and on the verge of starvation. These facts may be gleaned from the minutes of Kirk Sessions up and down the land which took up collections on behalf of the victims of this tragedy.

As a fisherman, Franck was particularly interested in the state of the river, virtually an open sewer when heavy rains cleansed the streets. The filthy state of the town is hardly surprising as, for upwards of a century after its incorporation, Kilmarnock had no magistrates or town council. The Boyds governed the town through a baron-bailie, but the townsfolk seem to have been left largely to their own devices.

From Franck's account we note that Kilmarnock was already noted for its textiles in general and its bonnets in particular. This is confirmed by the Town's Books wherein there is a reference to hose or stockings being made in 1603. On 21st December 1647, at a court held by Lord Boyd, about thirty bonnetmakers attended and complained of various abuses having crept into the craft. Consequently Lord Boyd tightened up the rules for the conduct of the craft in order to maintain the high quality of the product.

More interesting is the reference to the skill of the inhabitants in the manufacture of cutlery and other steel articles. This is corroborated by the anonymous *A Journey through Scotland* (London, 1723) which mentions the town as 'famous for all kinds of cutler's ware'. This probably also included horn spoons; in this period Kilmarnock supplied much of Scotland with these indispensable items.

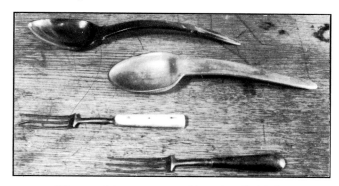

Kilmarnock horn spoons and horn-handled forks

That the inhabitants were pastmasters in the art of 'fuddling' (boozing) is borne out by the numerous references in the Council records to drunkenness and the various measures taken to curb it. In 1695, for example, it was enacted that 'no ale be sold by vintners after ten o' clock on Saturday nights'. In 1702 a proclamation was issued 'strictly requiring all vintners, taverners, and other retailers of Liquors, to shut their doors nightly at the tolling of the bells at ten hours throw the week, and at the tolling of the nine hours bell at the Saturday's and Sabbath's night, and to allow none to drink in their houses after the said times, under the penalty of six shillings Scots, for each person, to be payed by the master or mistresse of the house.'

The Kirk Session minutes of 12th December 1689 appointed the Elders 'in their respective quarters to go through and search the several ale-houses and other suspect places each Saturday night, immediately after

The Old Brig

nine o' clock, and that they take exact notice of such as they find drinking there, after the said hour, or any way deboshing'. It also appointed those Elders who took up the collection at the church doors, immediately after the commencement of public worship to 'go through the town, and search for such as absent themselves from the publick ordinances, or are drinking, or otherwyse profaneing the Lords Day...'

The bridge mentioned by Pont and Franck was probably situated between Cheapside and Sandbed Streets. There is no record of its original construction and it first appeared in the Town's Books in 1753 when it underwent extensive reconstruction to make it 'more safe for all sorts of traffic'. Nine years later it was severely damaged by floods and was subsequently rebuilt. In the course of time this structure, running from the Laigh Kirk to Titchfield Street, came to be known as the Old Bridge to distinguish it from later bridges linking Duke Street and London Road.

Of the original church of Kilmarnock, no trace now remains except the tower attached to the Laigh Kirk. As late as 1840 a stone bearing the date 1410 was

Dean Castle

attached to it although parts of the church may have been much older. It was considerably repaired and re-roofed in 1770 and the original bell was replaced in 1853. With commendable economy, the Kirk Session sold the old bell to a church in Stewarton. The lower part of the steeple is said to have been used as a prison during the Covenanting period. Following an appalling tragedy (see Chapter 7) the old church was demolished in 1802 and replaced by the present Laigh Kirk.

Dean Castle, ancient stronghold of the Boyds, is believed to have derived its name from the dene or hollow in which it was situated. It is flanked by two streams, the Borland and the Craufurdland, which come together to form the Kilmarnock Water. According to Pont, Dean Castle was originally the stronghold of the Loccarts, then briefly in the possession of Lord Soulis, before passing to the Boyds early in the fourteenth century. Pont described it as 'a staitly faire

ancient building' consisting of two great towers and a cluster of lower buildings. The walls of the higher tower were up to ten feet thick, with several vaulted rooms on the ground floor and, below, a great dungeon accessible only by a trap-door. The smaller tower was the main dwelling in later times. There is no record of this veritable fortress having withstood siege but, as previously mentioned, it was the enforced home of Princess Margaret, Countess of Arran during the lifetime of her husband. At a later period it was garrisoned by Captain Inglis and his troopers during the Covenanting times. Pont speaks of the gardens being well planted and ornamented.

William, the ninth Lord Boyd was fined £1,500 by Oliver Cromwell for his support of the Royalist cause. Following the Restoration of the monarchy, however, he was created Earl of Kilmarnock by Charles II on 7th August 1661. A second charter, conferring further rights and privileges on the town, was granted by the King in 1672 in favour of the first Earl who died in 1692. His eldest son, who succeeded to the estate and the earldom, died towards the end of the same year. He left two sons, the elder of whom became the third Earl and was served heir to his father in 1699. The following year this nobleman gave a grant to the town of the whole Common Good, comprehending 'the common greens of the said town, shops under the tolbooth yr' of, the weights, pocks and measures, the troan and weights yr' of, and the customs of the faires and weekly mercats, and all other customes belonging to the sd burgh and barony.' The 'troan' (tron) was the municipal weigh-house which, until about 1820, stood near the town cross. It was a simple wooden structure, consisting merely of a room supported by four pillars. Up to this time the magistrates were appointed by the lord of the manor from a list submitted to him annually. From 1700, however, the magistrates were to be elected, in the absence of the superior, by the bailies and council meeting at Dean Castle in the presence of a notary public and witnesses. An election of this kind took place in 1723 when Mungo Moor, Adam Boyd and others from the Council went to the Castle with the 'leit' (or list of proposed names).

By the grant of 1700 the Council was empowered by the Earl to hold courts and decide both civil and criminal actions, to collect fines and apply them to 'the use, utility and profit of the town and community'. The Council was also given the right of creating burgesses, 'secluding and debarring all others from any merchandising, trade, or mechanisme, except them that shall receave burgess tickets from them for that effect'. This grant and the charters of 1592 and 1672 served as the constitution of the burgh until the passage of the Burgh Reform Bill in 1832.

The First Jacobite Rebellion

The third Earl was a staunch supporter of the House of Hanover and when George I was proclaimed at Kilmarnock in August 1714 the Earl appeared with the bailies and other civic dignitaries on the stairhead of the Council-house where the ceremony was conducted with great solemnity. The stairway was carpeted for the occasion and the entire population of Kilmarnock attended at the Cross where a large bonfire was lit in celebration. The Earl's loyalty was soon put to the test. The following year the Earl of Mar raised the Jacobite standard in aid of the Old Pretender and marched south with an army of 12,000. The Earl of Kilmarnock raised a well-disciplined and equipped force of 500 men and mustered them, with the other fencibles of the south-west, at Irvine in August 1715. In his *History of the Late Rebellion* Peter Rae mentioned that the Earl was accompanied on this expedition by his son and heir.

> That which added very much unto it, was the early
> blossoms of the loyal principle and education of my
> Lord Boyd, who, though but eleven years of age,
> appeared in arms with the Earl, his father, and
> graciously behaved himself to the admiration of all
> the beholders.

In September, when the Jacobite forces advanced to Perth, the Duke of Argyll mustered the Hanoverian faction at Glasgow. The townspeople of Kilmarnock rallied to the call to arms and some 220 of them marched north on 19th September, followed a day later by the Earl himself and a force of 120 horsemen. The Kilmarnock contingent were second only to Paisley in mobilising to meet the Jacobite threat. The Kilmarnock men did garrison duty in Glasgow till 1st October and were then despatched by the Duke to deal with the lawless freebooter, Rob Roy MacGregor who was then harrying west Perthshire. The Kilmarnock contingent was based at Gartartan till 13th October when they were relieved by the Stirlingshire militia and thereafter held in reserve at Glasgow again. Thus they missed action on 13th November when the Hanoverian and Jacobite forces clashed inconclusively at Sheriffmuir near Dunblane. The Duke's troops numbered only about a third as many as the Jacobites but the battle was judged to be a draw. Both sides lost about 500 men, but effectively it marked the end of the rebellion. The defeat and surrender of the English Jacobites at Preston the following day dashed the hopes of the House of Stuart for three decades. The Hanoverian forces were demobilised on 21st November.

The Last Earl of Kilmarnock

The third Earl died in 1717 and was succeeded by his son William, then aged thirteen. The Boyd fortunes had been eroded and the fourth Earl seems to have been unduly extravagant. A memoir published at London in 1746 mentions that the estate was 'pretty much alienated' when he succeeded to it, and that his income 'was infinitely short of what the generosity, or rather the profuseness of his temper, would tempt him to spend'. In 1724, at the age of nineteen he married a girl four years his junior. Lady Anne Livingstone was the daughter and heiress of James, Earl of Linlithgow and Callander, who had been attainted for his part in the Jacobite Rebellion of 1715. Lady Anne was also heiress presumptive to the earldom of Errol. By the

time he attained his majority Earl William was the father of two sons, James and Charles. It might be supposed that fatherhood would have had a settling effect on him, but his own inability to manage his finances was now compounded by the recklessness of his mother, the Dowager Countess Euphemia, who was an inveterate gambler. When Euphemia married John Murray in 1727 it seemed as if her new husband would shoulder financial responsibility; but the marriage immediately ran into difficulties and poor Murray was compelled to resort to the law to prevent her running up gambling debts in his name. Lady Euphemia died barely two years afterwards.

The memoir of the fourth Earl of Kilmarnock states that he

> discovered an early genius not unworthy the dignity
> of his birth; but his father's death leaving him too
> soon at liberty to be his own master, and the
> indulgence that is generally given to young
> noblemen, added to the natural sprightliness of his
> temper, soon gave him an aversion to a rigorous
> study of letters, though he had made some progress in
> classical learning, and had acquired some tolerable
> notion of philosophy and mathematics; but there was
> too much of the volatile in his disposition to continue
> long at his exercises that required application; he was
> more happy in acquiring those which are called
> genteel accomplishments, such as riding, fencing,
> dancing, and some music; in all of which he excelled,
> and was justly esteemed by men of taste a polite
> gentleman.

What comes across in this encomium is a picture of a rather wayward, self-indulgent young playboy; but in fairness to the Earl it was also noted that he displayed a deep interest in the town and its manufactures. 'He was frequently present at the meetings of council, and was much esteemed by the inhabitants.' The truth of the matter is rather different. On one occasion when he delegated the task of selecting bailies from the Council Leit to Lady Anne the Council questioned the validity of this. Thereafter the Council pursued an increasingly independent line.

The fourth Earl was the last of the Boyds to reside in Dean Castle. In 1735 the Castle was partially destroyed by fire, caused when some flax was accidentally ignited while in the process of being cleaned or spun by one of the maid-servants. The Earl was actually touring the Continent at the time of the conflagration and happened to read in an English newspaper an account of the destruction, by fire, of a Scottish mansion called the Dean, the particular locality of which was not specified. Fearing that it was his own residence, he hurried home and found it reduced to a ruinous shell. Just as calamitous was the loss of a very fine library which had been amassed by Dr James Moor, an eminent classical scholar, who was tutor to the Earl's family and accompanied his lordship on his European tour. The estate was too encumbered by debt for any money to be available to rebuild the castle. Parts of the roof survived well into the nineteenth century, but it was roofless and desolate by 1879 when Archibald McKay described it. Prophetically he wrote, 'Its great strength may yet enable it to stand many centuries, an object of interest to the admirer of the picturesque, the historical inquirer, and the lover of hoary antiquity.'

After this accident, the Boyd family resided in Kilmarnock House, an old mansion situated between

Kilmarnock House

St Marnock and Nelson Streets. It had been built towards the end of the 17th century but a west wing was added between 1735 and 1745 and was still under construction when the fourth Earl became embroiled in the second Jacobite Rebellion. Ironically, in view of his youthful participation in the preparations to meet the Jacobite threat in 1715, the Earl had changed sides, doubtless influenced by his Catholic wife to some extent, although the chief reason given by Tobias Smollett is that the Earl was resentful of the fact that he had recently been deprived of a state pension which had been secured by Sir Robert Walpole. His help in the election of 1741 (which returned Sir Robert as Prime Minister but with a greatly reduced majority) earned him a pension of £400; but Walpole was defeated almost as soon as Parliament met and shortly afterwards went to the House of Lords as Earl of Orford, bringing to an end a premiership which had lasted 21 years. Only two payments, totalling £300, had been made from the Privy Purse before Lord Wilmington had the pension terminated.

Prince Charles Edward, on his progress south, lodged with the Earl and Countess at Callendar House on the outskirts of Falkirk and was promised armed support. The Earl is said to have visited Kilmarnock shortly afterwards and urged the inhabitants to join forces with the Young Pretender. Tradition has it that the townspeople were singularly unmoved. The 'Killie wabsters' preferred their looms to the battlefield, while the bonnetmakers would not exchange their shears for swords in the destruction of their fellow creatures. Some went so far as to state that they would more willingly take up arms against the Earl himself than take part in such a foolish and unnatural rebellion.

Memories of the persecution suffered during the Killing Times (see chapter 7) died hard in Kilmarnock.

This story is, of course, apocryphal and it is contradicted by the Earl's own statement, in a petition later presented on his behalf to King George II and the Prince of Wales. In this he claimed that

he influenced neither tenant nor follower of his to assist or abet the Rebellion; but, on the contrary, that, between the time of the battle of Preston[pans] and his unhappy junction with the rebels, he went to the town of Kilmarnock, influenced the inhabitants as far as he could, and by their means likewise influenced their neighbouring boroughs to rise in arms for his Majesty's service, which had so good an effect that two hundred men of Kilmarnock appeared very soon in arms, and remained all the winter at Glasgow, or other places as they were ordered.

Be that as it may, the facts are that the Earl joined Bonnie Prince Charlie and was appointed colonel of hussars and accompanied the Jacobite army in its advance south into England. He won the esteem of the Prince and was rapidly promoted to colonel of the Guards and then to the rank of general. He remained steadfast after the Jacobites turned back at Derby on 6th December 1745 and began their long retreat back to Scotland, with the Duke of Cumberland and General Wade in hot pursuit. Discipline in the Jacobite army was now very relaxed and the Highlanders pillaged as they went. The countryside which had, at best, been lukewarm towards the Prince, was now actively hostile.

The Jacobites occupied Glasgow on Christmas Day and rested there about a week, sending marauding parties into the surrounding districts in search of booty. A raiding patrol got as far as Stewarton and rumours flew ahead of this column that it intended to attack Kilmarnock. The town drummer patrolled the streets warning the inhabitants of the imminent attack and announcing a public meeting to be held at the Netherton for the purpose of devising measures to protect life and property. A large number of men rapidly mustered with every available weapon. After several rousing speeches about the rapacity and cruelty of the Highlanders, it was decided to march out to meet the rebels before they reached the town. Meanwhile the womenfolk dumped valuables in the wells and concealed clothing and footwear (both in great demand by the Highlanders) about the hedgerows.

The men of Kilmarnock marched up Soulis Street and Townhead, thence to the highway leading to Glasgow. At Craigspout, a little waterfall two and a half miles from the town, they learned from some travellers that the report had been a hoax, and that the Jacobites had left Glasgow and were marching towards Stirling. The intrepid volunteers marched back into the town and, on arriving at the Cross, discharged their muskets in the air, gave three hearty cheers for King George and, unscathed by dirk or broadsword, returned to their respective dwellings.

The Earl, on this occasion at any rate, hedged his bets. While he took his second son Charles into battle on the Jacobite side, his eldest son served in the Hanoverian Army and his youngest son, William, served in the Royal Navy. Apart from the Earl and his son Charles, only one inhabitant of Kilmarnock inclined to the Jacobite cause. This worthy was habitually known as Auld Soulis, because his house was next to the Soulis monument. In January 1746 the Jacobite army converged on Stirling, whose castle was garrisoned by Hanoverian troops. Meanwhile the Hanoverian forces under General Henry Hawley had advanced as far as Falkirk with a view to relieving the beleaguered garrison at Stirling. Prince Charles at first drew up his army to meet this menace at Bannockburn but was later advised by Lord George Murray to attack the Hanoverians where they were encamped. Two days before the battle, Auld Soulis left Kilmarnock and travelled to Falkirk, to gratify his curiosity and see the Prince and his army. When he arrived at Falkirk he was arrested by some Highlanders who asked him his business. Auld Soulis claimed that he was acquainted with the Earl of Kilmarnock for whom he had a letter. The Highlanders promptly and forcibly enlisted him in their ranks. He was therefore a somewhat reluctant witness of the battle. The following day he was put in charge of a horse carrying two wounded men, but he contrived to give his charges the slip and turned southwards, only to be robbed by other Highlanders of his shoes. He eventually got back to Kilmarnock, and doubtless had many a drink on his wonderful adventures with the Jacobite army at Falkirk.

In this encounter the Jacobites lost 40 men whereas Hawley lost over 400. Falkirk was a dramatic victory for the Prince, largely due to the overweening arrogance and ignorance of Hawley who had little regard for the fighting abilities of Highlanders. No small part in the outcome of this engagement was played by none other than the Countess of Kilmarnock. On the very morning of the battle Hawley was entertained to breakfast by the Countess at Callendar House. Hawley was so enchanted by the elegant appearance and engaging demeanour of the Countess that he passed several hours in her company, during which time Charles found ample opportunity for choosing the most favourable position for his troops. Hawley so far forgot his duty that he had ultimately to be told of the situation by a messenger, and he left Callendar House in such a tearing hurry that he forgot his bonnet. He clattered off bareheaded and reached the battlefield in time to see his troops in great disarray.

The victory at Falkirk on 17th January delayed, but could not affect, the outcome of the campaign. The Duke of Cumberland was now heading north with an army that grew in numbers by the day, whereas Charles's army was rapidly melting away. After several days the siege of Stirling was abandoned and the retreat north into the Highlands began. The Earl of Kilmarnock remained loyal to the bitter end, and at Culloden he commanded the Jacobite foot-guards. He was wounded in the battle, taken prisoner and paraded bareheaded along the Hanoverian ranks. His eldest son was an ensign of the Scots Fusiliers in the King's service and was so overcome at his father's bedraggled appearance that he broke ranks to cover him with his own hat. Many eyes, it is said, filled with tears on witnessing this impulsive act by young Lord Boyd. The same nobleman showed compassion to a Highland officer named Fraser who, with eighteen others, was summarily executed by firing squad soon after the battle. Fraser survived the bullet as well as the *coup de grace*—a blow from a musket-butt to his head—and some time later was found grievously wounded by Lord Boyd who got him conveyed to a safe place where he eventually recovered from his injuries.

News of the Battle of Culloden was received at Kilmarnock with great rejoicing. An entry in the Treasurer's Book notes a payment of £17 Scots to William Walker on account of entertainment at rejoicing on the victory at 'Colodin fight'. About the same time, the birthday of the Duke of Cumberland was royally celebrated by the bailies and councillors, £7.10s Scots being expended on that occasion. Meanwhile the Earl was taken to London and lodged in the Tower. On 28th July 1746 he was brought to trial with other distinguished Jacobites at Westminster Hall. The Earl pled guilty and recommended himself to the King's mercy. Two days later the court reconvened and the Earl made a plea in mitigation, citing the devotion of his father and his eldest son to the Hanoverian cause, and that he himself had bought no arms and raised not

Anti Jacobite Cartoon at the expense of the Earl of Kilmarnock

a single man for the cause of the Pretender. Despite his obvious contrition, the Earl found no favour from the court. With the other rebel lords (the Earl of Cromartie and Lord Balmerino) he was sentenced to be hanged, drawn and quartered, the singularly barbaric punishment then meted out for high treason. In the time between sentence and execution a petition was sent to the government by the Town Council of Kilmarnock. The Countess and Dr Moor, the family tutor, travelled to London to intercede with the King and Prince of Wales, but to no avail.

In the days immediately before sentence was carried out, the Earl was constantly attended by the Rev. James Foster, an eminent dissenting clergyman who has left an interesting and illuminating account of the unfortunate Earl. When asked by Foster what could be his motive for engaging in rebellion against his conscience, the Earl said 'that the true root of all was his careless and dissolute life, by which he had reduced himself to great and perplexing difficulties; that the exigency of his affairs was in particular very pressing at the time of the Rebellion; and that, besides the general hope he had of mending his fortune by the success of it, he was also tempted by another prospect of retrieving his circumstances, if he followed the Pretender's standard.'

On 18th August he went to the scaffold. The more gruesome aspects of the execution were omitted because he was a person of quality. He was spared the customary slow strangulation, to be cut down while still alive, disembowelment and ritual burning of his entrails before his face. Instead the execution was confined to beheading. Colonel John Walkinshaw Craufurd of Craufurdland, an old friend of the Earl, was by his side on the scaffold and held the red cloth into which the severed head fell. Later he had the mortal remains interred in the Church of St Peter. For these acts of friendship he was censured by the Army and demoted to the bottom of the army list. He later rose to the rank of major and latterly lieutenant-colonel and died in 1793 at the age of 72. There is a curious story concerning the Earl and Colonel Craufurd. They were walking one day near Dean Castle when they encountered David Rankine, known as the rhyming blacksmith of Kilmarnock, coming towards them with a bundle of straw. Wishing to draw from him some witty saying (for he was always ready with his answers), they cried 'Boo!' as he approached. The blacksmith looked at them for a moment, and then without the least effort, declaimed the following verse extempore:

There goes Craufurdland and Lord Boyd,

Of grace and manners they are void;

For, like the Bull among the kye,

They boo at folk as they gang bye.

He then threw the straw at them, exclaiming, 'Hae, beasts! There's a buttle o' strae to ye!' Archibald McKay, recounting this story, adds that 'His lordship and the colonel were so well pleased with this extemporaneous effusion that they instantly gave a piece of money to the author, who, after thanking them

for their kindness, trudged on his way, inwardly congratulating himself on his good fortune.' One cannot help wondering what Rankine really thought of their boorish behaviour.

Part of the ritual of public executions in the eighteenth century was the publication of broadsheets, often containing the confessions or last statements of the condemned, or gory illustrated accounts of the execution itself. These gruesome tracts found a ready sale. A hawker came to Kilmarnock with a stock of such broadsheets giving the details of the Earl's execution, but the populace, indignant at hearing their late lordship's name bawled through the streets in such an ignominious manner, mobbed the poor hawker so ferociously that he was compelled to flee for his life.

The Countess returned to Kilmarnock soon after the execution. Work on the west wing of Kilmarnock House had come to an abrupt end when the Earl joined the rebels. Many years later, when ingress was made into the large hall which had been closed up as a consequence, brand new window frames, wood-shavings and joiner's tools were discovered, exactly as they had been left when the work was stopped. The grounds of this house were remarkable for their large,

The Lady's Walk

stately trees. Most of them were removed when St Marnock Street was being laid out, but a magnificent beech, upwards of ten feet in girth, survived until 3rd May 1859 when it was cut down in consequence of it being much decayed. Other trees formed part of a wooded avenue long known as the Lady's Walk. This path derived its name from the last Countess of Kilmarnock who was accustomed to take her daily exercise there. The death of the Earl weighed very heavily upon her and she died of grief at Kilmarnock on 16th September 1747. She was in her 39th year and outlived her tragic husband by barely a year.

The Lady's Walk was a sweet rural retreat for more than a century, following the west bank of the Kilmarnock Water to the south of the town. In the course of time, however, as the town expanded, the house itself was engulfed by larger and more imposing buildings. Its quaint rooms, once the abode of the titled and the great, were later occupied by the burgh's Ragged School. In 1879 the Lady's Walk was greatly improved by the planting of ornamental shrubs and trees. Park benches and a drinking fountain were installed and Barbadoes Green, a field to the south, was laid out as a recreation ground.

Eighteenth century developments

The heritable jurisdictions of the Boyds over Kilmarnock were abolished in 1747, giving greater power to the Town Council. The Boyd estates were forfeited, but Lord Boyd succeeded in recovering them in 1752. He then sold them to William, thirteenth Earl of Glencairn. On the death of his great-aunt, the Countess of Errol in her own right, Lord Boyd succeeded to the title of Earl of Errol in 1758. The earldom of Kilmarnock, however, terminated with the execution of his father. The last Earl of Kilmarnock was one of the founders of St John's Lodge in 1734 and was its first Right Worshipful Master. He later held the Chair of the mother lodge Kilwinning and in the same year (1742) attained the Mastership of the Grand Lodge of Scotland. His son followed in his footsteps. In January 1761 the Earl of Errol was elected Master of Kilmarnock St John's.

By 1700 the population of Kilmarnock was about 1,000. Half a century later it had trebled, rivalling Irvine and surpassing the county town of Ayr. By-passed by the upheavals of the two Jacobite rebellions, Kilmarnock's dramatic growth and commercial progress in this period were due to its role as a market town serving a prosperous agricultural community, as well as its increasing importance as a textile centre. To Kilmarnock came the farmers of round about to have their corn ground. The original town mill was located near the Cross, its wheel powered by a lade or stream that flowed through the same spot. Shilling Hill (near the railway station) alludes to this, for the *sheeling hill* was a knoll on which the grain kernels were separated by the wind from the husks. This mill, occupied by a family named Rankin, appears to have been discontinued in 1703, to judge by references to it in the past tense in the Town Treasurer's Book of that year. The Rankins thereafter occupied the Newmill erected some way south of the town on the bank of the River Irvine. During renovation in the nineteenth century the then miller, Gavin Walker, discovered a stone bearing the date 1703 which confirms this as the year in which the mill changed its location.

Kilmarnock in 1750 presented a mean and slovenly appearance. The streets had not improved much since Franck's visit almost a century earlier and were crooked and narrow. The houses were generally single-storey thatched huts. The few two-storey stone buildings had outside staircases which not only obstructed the thoroughfare but gave the houses a clumsy aspect. The chief streets in the mid-eighteenth century were the High Street, Fore Street, Back Street (otherwise known as Smiddieraw or smithy row), Croft Street, Strand Street and Sandbed Street. Together with some buildings at the Cross, Nethertonholm and a few back tenements and lanes, they formed the entire town. The Cross was a narrow, confined space and access to the Kilmarnock Water was mainly provided by narrow paths through closes. The old town had developed haphazardly and as a result it was both compact and congested. Carts were quite unknown at this period, being first recorded in 1726 and then only for the purpose of conveying the blocks of stone required in the construction of the bridge over the River Irvine to Riccarton; consequently the civic authorities never had to consider wheeled traffic when the old streets were being laid out.

The town only really began to develop in the 1730s with the establishment of woollen manufactures. In 1743 the woollen manufactory obtained a grant of land, and the right to quarry stone for the erection of buildings. A waukmill was erected in 1746 and a dam constructed near 'the foot of the Path leading to the Meal Mercat'. The only public buildings in this period were the Church and the Town House, located west of the Cross. The latter was a gloomy structure, two storeys high, with a small belfry and several little shops on the ground floor. The shops were little more than booths, judging by the paltry rents charged by the Council. In 1720, for example, one was let to a cooper named William Aitken for a mere £8 Scots a year (eight shillings sterling or 40p in modern currency). Down a narrow lane at the west end of the building was the Thieves' Hole, a loathsome dungeon, above which stood the Tolbooth or town gaol. At its stairhead hung the jougs or iron collar in which petty delinquents were confined and exposed to public ridicule. Part of the upper storey contained the Hall or Court-house, nothing of which has survived apart from an elaborately carved mantelpiece which was preserved in one of the rooms of the Council Chambers but is now in Dean Castle. The entrance to the Court-house was approached by an outside staircase faced with a parapet. The stairhead commanded the market-place and provided a platform for public announcements of all kinds and the loyal toast on the occasion of the monarch's birthday. The Council minutes contain numerous references to these celebrations. The old Tolbooth was demolished about 1800.

The Meal Market in the High Street was built in 1705, a severely plain structure designed for the sale of grain to the inhabitants. On certain days of the week, however, the farmers of the surrounding countryside came into town and sold their produce from stands in this market. The Market was substantially rebuilt in 1840.

Until 1731 there was only one church in Kilmarnock, the parish church, otherwise known as the Laigh Kirk or Low Church, located west of the Cross. The expansion of the population meant that a single church was no longer adequate, so a second charge, known as the High Church, was created. This church was erected at the top of Soulis Street, the cost being defrayed by public subscriptions and a grant of £30 from the Council, together with generous donations from the Earl of Kilmarnock and Mr Orr of Grougar. The cost of construction amounted to £850, excluding the steeple which was not completed till 1740. The two collegiate ministers of the town preached by turns in the new church. Technically it was classed as a chapel of ease or relief church, but in 1811 it was constituted a separate parish church and had a separate district assigned to it under the name of the High Kirk Parish. In 1764 the system of alternate preaching was scrapped and the Rev. James Oliphant was appointed. The High Kirk was greatly improved internally in 1868-9 when stained glass windows by Keir of Glasgow were installed. One of these was dedicated to the memory of the last Earl and is particularly conspicuous. A fine pipe-organ was subsequently placed in the church.

Several bridges were constructed over the Kilmarnock Water to improve communication between one part of the town and the other. The Green Bridge was erected in 1759 and provided an exit for the town to the east. The Timmer Brig (timber bridge) was built in 1762 and the Flesh Market Bridge in 1770. The beginnings of the street later known as Waterloo Street were laid down in 1752.

The first major development, however, took place in 1765 when the Earl of Glencairn laid out a new line of street between the town and Riccarton. Unlike the original twisted, narrow thoroughfare, the new road was broad and ran straight as a die for about half a mile. Two thirds along the road heading south there was an intersection which widened to form Glencairn Square. This separated High and Low Glencairn Streets, the names given to the two sections of the road. By charging only moderate feu-duty the Earl encouraged the feuars to lay out extensive gardens, many of which have survived to this day. The original houses were humble in appearance and mostly single-storey, but in the late nineteenth and early twentieth centuries many of them were replaced by more substantial buildings and shops.

Archibald McKay's history includes a map, drawn in the mid-nineteenth century to give a rough idea of what the town must have looked like in 1783. This shows that, apart from the ribbon development along Titchfield and Glencairn Streets, the town had not expanded much beyond the area of fifty years earlier. Most of the inhabitants still lived in the area formed by the bend in the Kilmarnock Water, between the High Church and the Cross. Titchfield Street was approached by a narrow lane that followed the curve of the river and east of this there was still a maze of mean alleys running towards the Back Lane. Beyond that lay Mill Lane and Mill Road traversing open countryside. From the Low Green a bridge led on to the Mauchline road, south of which lay the woods and policies of Elmwood Bank and beyond the Manse of the parish church. West of the Kilmarnock Water, Bank Street ran southwesterly to Nelson Street which, in turn, led to the Irvine road. On this bank there was Kilmarnock House and its

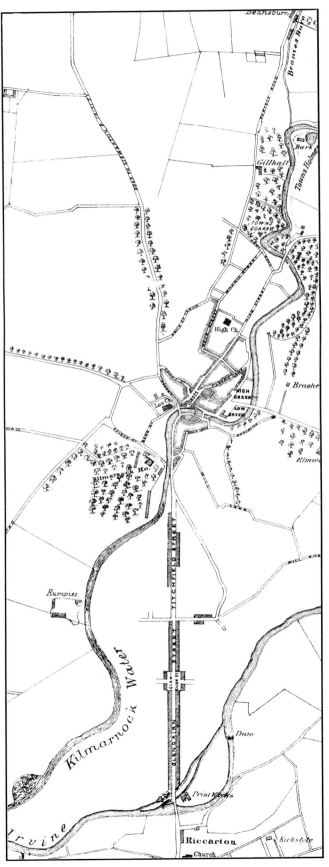

Town plan of Kilmarnock 1783

grounds and, to the south, the farm of Rumpie, held of the Earls of Kilmarnock at an annual rental of half a crown (12.5p) an acre, payable in hens and chickens. In the nineteenth century this 40 acre farm was absorbed into the lands of Holmes.

By 1790, when James Mackinlay and John Robertson compiled their account of the parish for Sir John Sinclair's *Statistical Account*, the population had risen to 6,776, of whom 5,670 resided in the town. Females outnumbered males by 3,075 to 2,586 and this was explained by the rise of the textile industry which provided ready employment to girls who flocked into Kilmarnock from the surrounding countryside. By now the town was governed by two bailies, a treasurer and sixteen councillors.

In 1791 James, fourteenth Earl of Glencairn died without issue and his place as the leading landowner of the parish was taken by Miss Henrietta Scott who had made very extensive purchases in the neighbourhood the previous year, including the right of patronage over the parish churches. Miss Scott was only a teenager at the time, and her coming of age in 1795 was celebrated in the town by a public rejoicing. Later she married the Marquis of Titchfield, later fourth Duke of Portland, who thus became the chief landowner of the district. In the closing years of the eighteenth and early part of the nineteenth centuries new streets were laid out which reflect this interest: Portland, Titchfield, Bentinck and Welbeck.

Two tragedies

Mention has already been made of the disastrous fire of 1668 which virtually destroyed the town. Another serious conflagration occurred on 26th April 1800. Originating in a malt-kiln which had become overheated, the fire spread with appalling rapidity, engulfing the houses in Nethertonholm (now Glencairn Street). The weather had been exceptionally dry for several weeks and the thatched houses went up like tinder. The accident took place around mid-day, so there was no loss of life, but 76 families, numbering upward of 300 souls, were rendered homeless and destitute in the space of an hour and a half. A public subscription led by the Marquis of Titchfield (who donated £100) soon raised a large sum for the rebuilding of the devastated street and this time slated roofs replaced the traditional thatch.

On Sunday 18th October 1801 disaster struck again in particularly bizarre circumstances. At that time the High Church happened to be vacant and its congregation crowded into the Laigh Kirk which was consequently filled to capacity. The morning service passed off without incident, but as the congregation was assembling for afternoon worship a chunk of plaster suddenly fell from the ceiling. Fearing that the roof was about to collapse, the worshippers already seated in the gallery stampeded for the stairs, knocking down those who were still ascending. The second *Statistical Account* (1839) described the heart-rending scene.

> Such a mass of human bodies were heaped on one another, that it was impossible, from the superincumbent weight, to render immediate assistance to those who were in the greatest danger. One layer of bodies after another was removed, until the passages were cleared; but alas, it was too late, for it was found that twenty-nine of the sufferers had already expired. A number of them died from suffocation; and others who survived were so severely bruised, that they never recovered their former health.

Some of the dead were so disfigured that their friends could only identify them by their clothing. The bodies of two women, in particular, were shockingly injured, their breasts being deeply imprinted by the heavy boots of an individual whose brutal hurry during the calamity was spoken off for many years thereafter. The Rev. James Mackinlay in the pulpit was powerless to quell the panic and, clasping his hands in an attitude of devotion, he cried out with a pitying voice, 'My people! Oh, my people!'. News of the disaster spread like wildfire, and as crowds gathered outside the church, anxious for news of friends and relatives, there was a danger of civil disturbance. The Royal Kilmarnock Volunteers, a militia regiment raised during the Napoleonic Wars, was rushed to the scene to restore order.

Ironically, the church was quite sound structurally; but there was apparently a prophecy in the locality that the roof was destined to fall upon the congregation. Just how impressionable people could be is testified by the story which got about soon after the catastrophe that several persons had seen a hearse drawn by six black horses passing through the centre of the burial ground that very day, driven by the Devil himself. This prompted one wag to remark that His Satanic Majesty was surely improving in his circumstances, when he could afford to ride about in his carriage and six. Not surprisingly, the heritors decided to allay public apprehension and immediately resolved to rebuild the church. The foundation stone was laid on 20th April 1802.

Civic improvements

In 1802 the population of the town and parish was estimated at 8,079. Trade and industry, stimulated by the wars with France, were booming and a taste for civic improvement resulted in an Act of Parliament for developing the town and its amenities. Many of the ancient tenements were demolished and the narrow lanes rapidly gave way to wide streets. In 1804 the New Bridge, as it was called, was erected; and later the same year King Street was laid out from the south end of the bridge to Titchfield Street. The following year the Council Chambers were built on the arch of the New Bridge, effectively covering the Water in the town centre. Widely regarded as a big improvement at the time, the building was being criticised as 'incommodious for the present business of the burgh' by McKay as long ago as 1848. Yet the Town House, with its undistinguished entrance on King Street, continued to serve Kilmarnock until the 1970s when it was demolished to make way for the redevelopment of the town centre. McKay thought that the Town House bespoke 'in various respects, the good taste and liberal views of its projectors'.

In the first decade of the nineteenth century further redevelopment of the old town led in 1812 to the laying out of Portland Street, running north from the Cross and thence to Wellington Street (1816) and Dean Street. More than anything else, the formation of these streets running almost due north from the town centre, transformed the appearance of Kilmarnock from a village to a minor city. Apart from improving the appearance of the town out of all recognition, the new thoroughfare provided a direct route for traffic passing from Glasgow to Ayr. Hitherto the main road had run along the steep and narrow path called Dean Lane, thence along the High Street, Soulis Street and Fore Street and, passing through the Cross, had then awkwardly diverged into Waterloo Street and abruptly turned along the Old Bridge at the Flesh Market into Market Lane. 'A more tortuous and inconvenient thoroughfare could scarcely be devised,' wrote McKay, 'and, in those days of stage-coaches and similar vehicles, the lives of the passengers, and even of the inhabitants dwelling along the route, must have been greatly endangered.'

The crux of this redevelopment was the Cross, arguably the most spacious public forum anywhere in Scotland in its heyday, ornamented by lofty and elegant freestone buildings which imparted an air of opulence and prosperity to the town. By 1811 the population of the town had risen to 10,148. Three years later the Tontine buildings were erected, adding considerably to the splendid appearance of the Cross. This provided the business community with meeting rooms and a library.

Kilmarnock in 1819

A map of Kilmarnock, published by Wood in 1819, shows the dramatic expansion of the town in the previous two decades. Both Low and High Glencairn Streets were now fully developed on both sides, and houses had also been erected along East and West Shaw Streets, running at right angles from Glencairn Square and named after Sir James Shaw, a native of Riccarton who became Lord Mayor of London and a member of Parliament. Farther north, Netherton had been redeveloped and Douglas Street laid out. A brewery, an abattoir and a print works had brought industry to the southern part of the town. Titchfield Street was not fully developed on its west side, and parts of King Street on its east side consisted of open fields, but there was more infilling on the banks of the Water. North of the Water the main development lay along Fore, Soulis and High Streets, but Boyd Street had also been developed, while Bank Street was rapidly developing as the commercial district of the town.

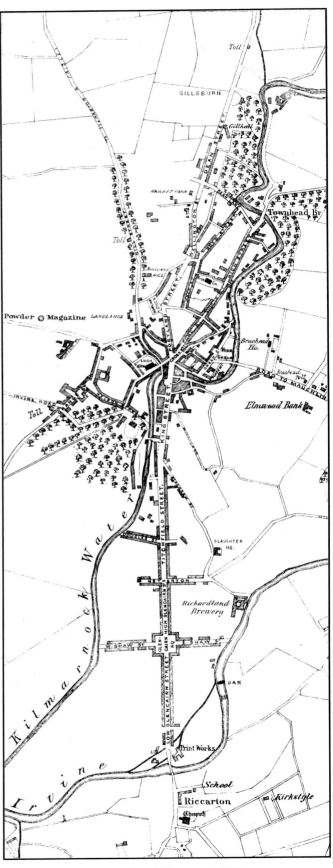

Town plan of Kilmarnock 1819

Townhead Bridge gave access to the east bank of the Water and led to Kilmarnock Foundry. Significantly, the town had now begun to spread westward, with recent development on Morton Place and Grange Street. The policies around Kilmarnock House were still heavily wooded, but nearby was the terminus of the horse-drawn railroad from Troon, opened in 1812 and providing Kilmarnock with a rapid and relatively inexpensive mode of transport to the nearest seaport. Tollgates had been erected on the turnpike roads from Glasgow, Stewarton, Mauchline and Irvine. Situated well away from the town, on the Busby road, was a powder magazine, where the powder and ammunition of the militia regiments were stored.

In 1818 there were five John Thomsons in the burgh, distinguished by their nicknames which tell us something about their personal appearance, habits or antecedents. They were known as Greasy Jock, Ploukit Jock, Lick the Spune Jock, Sodger Jock and London Jock—all Jock Tamson's bairns.

Agitation for Political Reform

The boom of the Napoleonic war years was followed by a slump which hit Kilmarnock's textile workers very hard. Almost overnight, thousand of handloom weavers, hitherto the aristocrats of labour, were thrown out of work. By the nature of their work, weavers were people of some education and independence of thought. From this section of the working class sprang the radical politicians who were eventually to transform the entire country. Industrial recession and economic distress went hand in hand with talk of parliamentary reform and even revolution. The first great public meeting (attended by upwards of 5,000 people) was held in Dean Park on 7th December 1816 for the purpose of organising a petition to the Prince Regent for the redress of grievances, and the principal speaker on that occasion was John Kennedy, formerly a weaver but now a schoolmaster, who argued for reform by constitutional means. Alexander Maclaren railed against the sufferings of the country and the narrow-minded policies of the government, while Archibald Craig warned of the increasing burden of taxation arising from the war. John Burtt, though unable to attend in person, sent a speech condemning the use of corporal punishment to cowe the working classes.

In 1819 when insurrection was in the air, the government took swift action to suppress dissent. Kennedy's house was searched for evidence of treason and sedition. Among his papers were several chapters of *Geordie Chalmers*. These the worthy magistrates seized, thinking that they might be treasonable communications from some dangerous radical of that name, and despatched them to Ayr for closer examination by the sheriff. Fortunately it was then realised that Geordie was a fictitious character and the manuscript merely part of a novel which later became a best-seller.

After brief detention at Ayr, Kennedy was released, but was less fortunate on a subsequent occasion. In mid-April 1820, along with other radicals, he was seized and sent under military escort to the county jail at Ayr. After nineteen days in detention, however, he was released, no evidence being found to justify his imprisonment. Kennedy took the hint, however, and promptly left the district, settling at Kilsyth. Here he spent the rest of his life as a schoolmaster and eventually completed his novel, but unfortunately did not live to see its success, for he died shortly after correcting the final proof sheets.

The population had good grounds for railing against injustice. Kilmarnock now had a population of almost 13,000, yet only *one man* (Major Parker of Assloss) possessed a parliamentary vote. In Ayrshire there were only 156 voters in a population of 170,000, and in Scotland as a whole over two million people were represented by just 2,700 voters—a situation which made for widespread corruption. Agitation for parliamentary reform had begun in 1792 and numerous bodies, of which the Friends of the People were the best-known, sprang up to demand a fairer system of representation; but the government of the day, fearful of the spread of Jacobinism from revolutionary France, suppressed this movement with great brutality and injustice. Although the government could justify its repressive attitude while the country was engaged in war, this argument was no longer valid once peace returned. Nevertheless, the government responded to renewed agitation with even more repressive legislation, culminating in the notorious Six Acts of 1819. Even before this time, the authorities in Kilmarnock were taking vigorous action against the radicals. Although John Kennedy escaped relatively lightly, others were less fortunate. Alexander Maclaren, who had chaired the meeting of 1816, and Thomas Baird who published the speeches from that occasion as a pamphlet, were both arrested and brought to trial in March 1817 on charges of sedition before the High Court in Edinburgh. They were found guilty and sentenced to six months imprisonment in the Canongate Tolbooth. Conditions in this ancient prison were so foul that both men died a few years afterwards, still relatively young.

On Saturday 19th September 1819 a meeting for parliamentary reform was held in a field at the back of Morton Place. Despite the small space available, no fewer than 7,000 men congregated there, drawn from Galston and Newmilns as well as Riccarton and Kilmarnock. At this meeting the agitators had the temerity to demand universal adult suffrage as the only way to reform the House of Commons and mitigate the distresses of the country. This meeting was conducted in an orderly fashion and passed off without incident. A second meeting was held in the same place on 20th November that year and attracted a crowd of up to 16,000 from all over the Irvine Valley. A Covenanting banner which had flown at the Battle of Drumclog in 1679 was waved on this occasion. The radical movement gathered momentum and, having failed to gain an audience in Parliament itself, the radicals now advocated armed insurrection. 1st April 1820 was scheduled as the day on which the people were to rise in arms against their oppressors. Placards to this effect were produced by the Committee of Organization for forming a Provisional Government and posted throughout Kilmarnock and other towns in the west of Scotland. When the great day dawned the insurrection did not materialise. Everyone seemed to expect that his neighbour would take the lead in the enterprise, and none having the hardihood to do so, the whole affair proved abortive. Although the uprising was a damp squib, the proposal was sufficient for the authorities to take firm action. Known ring-leaders of the radical movement were swiftly rounded up, and the populace cowed by a display of force. A squadron of cavalry was sent down from Edinburgh with a cannon which they erected at the Cross on 14th April. The troopers patrolled the town and enforced a curfew, while the magistrates, with a detachment of soldiers, rounded up the ring-leaders. The chief radical, Archibald Craig, was captured and held in the county jail for seventeen weeks, but released without being brought to trial. Afterwards he migrated to the United States and became a minister of religion in Indiana. John Burtt, a native of Riccarton, fled to America in 1817 to escape persecution and after studying at Princeton College, New Jersey had a distinguished career as a Presbyterian minister, professor of ecclesiastical history in Cincinnati and the editor of newspapers in that city and Philadelphia. On 17th October 1885, following the successful passage of the third Reform Act, a monument was unveiled by Lord Rosebery in the Kay Park to the Kilmarnock Martyrs— Baird, Maclaren, Burtt, Kennedy and Craig 'and other Kilmarnock pioneers of Parliamentary reform who, in the early part of the century, devoted themselves with unselfish zeal to the cause of the people.'

A regiment of volunteers, pledged to put down insurrection, was formed. Ironically, it was placed under the command of Major Parker, the one man who had a vote. Although no further popular demonstrations for parliamentary reform took place, the reasonableness of the demands eventually sank in. To its credit, Parliament effected reform from within. The Reform Act of 1832 swept away the so-called rotten and pocket boroughs and extended the franchise to many towns.

Martyrs Monument, Kay Park

Kilmarnock joined forces with the burghs of Renfrew, Rutherglen, Port Glasgow and Dumbarton to send a member to Parliament, the Liberal candidate, Captain John Dunlop of Dunlop being duly elected in 1832. To be sure, the electorate was very limited but successive Liberal governments gradually extended it. In 1832 the five burghs had a total electorate of 1,154; by 1874 the number of men on the electoral roll had risen to 8,020. Throughout that period, with the exception of the years 1837-41, Kilmarnock consistently returned a Liberal candidate.

Municipal progress

The slump of the post-Napoleonic period gradually decreased and the commerce of Kilmarnock improved in the 1820s. To help regulate the flow of the Kilmarnock Water a weir was constructed across the stream at Sandbed in 1821. The Sandbed Dam just downstream from the Town Bridge, was a familiar sight until the 1960s. In 1822 a joint-stock company was formed for the purpose of supplying the town with coal gas. Interestingly, it was an Ayrshireman, William Murdock (1754-1839) who discovered the technique of distilling gas from coal. His early experiments were carried out at Bello Mill, Lugar and continued after he moved to Redruth, Cornwall. In 1792 he succeeded in lighting his cottage and offices by gas, but it did not become a commercial proposition till 1803. By that date Alexander 'Sandy' Alexander, a cabinetmaker with premises in the Strand, is said to have illuminated his house and workshop by coal gas conducted inside by means of wooden pipes. The gasworks, erected in 1823, were located in Park Street. At first the gasworks were operated by a private company but they were taken over by the Town Council in 1871.

One of the prominent citizens of the early nineteenth century was Robert Rodger, landlord of the Turf Inn who took a leading part in the campaign for parliamentary reform. He is best remembered, however, for making the first aerial ascent over Kilmarnock, in the summer of 1830. Charles Green, the celebrated English balloonist (1785-1870), made his first ascent in 1821 from the Green Park, London as part of the celebrations marking the coronation of King George IV. He was the first balloonist to use coal gas instead of hydrogen and subsequently made numerous ascents all over the country. Thousands of people gathered at the Cross to witness the flight. Rodger, clad in light-coloured trousers and blue jacket specially made for the occasion, took his seat in the car of the balloon without the least symptom of dread. The day was a fine one, with very little cloud, and the ascent took place without mishap amid the cheers of the spectators who had demolished the barriers erected by the Town Council (with a view to charging an admission fee). The balloon glided away in a north-easterly direction and ultimately alighted in a hay-field near Eaglesham. Rodger was clearly an adventurous spirit, and on another occasion he went to the bottom of the sea off Portpatrick in a diving-bell.

One of the consequences of the political reforms of 1832 was a re-definition of the burgh boundaries and the addition of a provost, or chief magistrate; the first to hold this august office was John Andrew who had been among those responsible for securing the transfer of the Kilmarnock Bowling Club to its present location near the Kay Park in 1827. In preparation for burgh reform a new map of the town was surveyed in 1831 and published the following year as part of the

Britain in May and broke out at Kilmarnock in July, the first victim being one of the family of Petrie, a carrier in Low Church Lane, who is believed to have brought the infection from Paisley. Kilmarnock got off much more lightly than many other towns, although some 250 people succumbed to the terrible disease. In the second *Statistical Account* (compiled in March 1839) the Rev. Andrew Hamilton stated rather complacently that the mortality rate was 'nearly the same as in towns

'King Street, Kilmarnock 1840' from a drawing by Robert Johnstone, jnr Architect

parliamentary report. The new boundaries were defined in red, connecting ten points: the junction of the Kilmarnock Water and River Irvine (1), Irvine Road near the Grange Farm roadend (2), the Hillhead roadend on Old Kilmarnock Road (3), the Kilmarnock Water east of Bonfire Knowe (4), the Mauchline Road at the Mill Burn bridge (5), the confluence of the Mill Burn and River Irvine (6), Bellsland Bridge (7), Witch Knowe (8), the Ayr Road at the Maxholm Bridge (9) and the confluence of the Maxholm Burn and the River Irvine (10). Thus Kilmarnock burgh now incorporated the village of Riccarton. The map shows the Bullet Road (now Dundonald Road) which took its curious name from a game called bullet which was then very popular. 'Bullet' was also known as boules, and was similar to the French game petanque. The stone or iron boules were thrown to land beside a jack. This game went out of fashion as green bowls became popular.

Like everywhere else in the country, Kilmarnock was hit by the dreadful cholera epidemic of 1832. It first appeared in central Russia in the spring of that year and spread rapidly to the Baltic area. It reached

of equal magnitude in other parts of Britain. The health of the parish is as good as can be looked for amidst a population of so mixed a character.' McKay (1879) echoed the temperance sentiments of his own age when he commented that 'many of the sufferers were persons of irregular and dissipated habits, such as were reduced to a state of extreme indigence by their own folly and want of circumspection'. In truth, the town wells were badly polluted, notably by effluvia

Memorial to those who died in the Cholera epidemic of 1832

'Sandbed Street, Kilmarnock'   Oil Painting by James M. Mackay

from the tanyards. Drinking water in those days was drawn from springs in West Shaw Street and at Douglas Bridge, and from a number of wells: Haw's Well, Nelson Street Well, the Hole in the Wa' Well, Bicket's Tea Well (famous for its coldness and purity), the Flesh Market Well, Dr McLeod's Well and Mack's Well (over 40 feet deep). In 1849 cholera struck again and on this occasion 130 people died. Matters improved considerably the following year when a private company was formed to install a proper system of gravitational water supply from a reservoir on the Rowallan estate. Significantly, when cholera last visited the town (in 1854) only 34 people died.

The Great Flood

To fire and pestilence must be added flood, which on several occasions in times past has caused great hardship particularly in the congested south-western districts of the town. Even today, as one looks at the course of the Kilmarnock Water through the town, it is possible to visualise the problems which could arise when this stream was in spate. In the nineteenth and earlier centuries inundation in the crowded downtown areas was not unknown when the level of the water could rise with horrifying suddenness following heavy rainfall. On one occasion in the late eighteenth century the Kilmarnock Water rose to such a height that the road at Haw's Well was rendered impassable. In the early nineteenth century Glencairn Square and the adjoining streets were twice flooded by the rising of the Irvine and Kilmarnock Waters and once by the overflowing of the Irvine alone.

The worst flood, however, occurred in the space of a couple of hours on 14th July 1852. The weather in the previous weeks had been very hot and sultry, and the conditions were ripe for a severe thunderstorm; but no one could have foreseen the immensity of the torrential downpour nor the sudden ferocity of the flood-water. Early on the morning of the calamity thunder of unprecedented loudness was heard rolling over the town; and as it continued it increased in depth and solemnity until its peals became terrifying. This was accompanied by vivid flashes of lightning and then excessively heavy rain. The level of the Kilmarnock Water, fed by innumerable tributaries and the ditches that drained the moors and mosses to the north, rose dramatically to a record height, leading many to think that Lochgoin Reservoir had burst its banks, or that a waterspout had fallen on Fenwick Moor. In point of fact, the Croilburn and Craufurdland streams in particular were in spate and brought down vast quantities of timber as well as washing away the soil. A potato field at Hairshaw Mill on the Croilburn was so severely gouged out that a loch took its place. A stone weighing six tons and countless other boulders of lesser size were washed away. Two stone bridges over the Croilburn were completely swept away. On the Craufurdland Water, Alexander's carding and spinning mill two miles above Fenwick was severely damaged and pieces of machinery, some weighing up to two tons, were hurled into the torrent. Dalraith Bridge was demolished and at Sandbed Spinning Mill a boiler weighing a ton and a half was lifted into the current. This debris, gathering momentum as it went, smashed through the Parker estate at Assloss, destroying gardens and orchards, the trees either flattened or uprooted. The Duke's Bridge near Dean Castle vanished in an instant. Below, the flood was augmented by the swollen waters of the Borland Water and large tracts of the riverbank were ripped away and added to the maelstrom. The Bonnet-maker's Dam and Sluice were torn from their foundations, as was the Kilmarnock Foundry Dam. The foundry-workers' cottages were engulfed though luckily without loss of life. Farther downstream other factories and mills were either destroyed or substantially damaged, each adding its quota to the detritus forced into the narrow channel of Kilmarnock Water. The flood-water roared on with increasing velocity. By the time the flood hit the town itself the level had risen seven feet (more than two metres) above the mean street level.

The crucial point was in the network of bridges at the town centre, where several important structures, such as the Council Chambers, the police station (whose cells then contained 21 prisoners), banks, shops and other buildings were actually erected on the arches above the Water. At this point the channel was constricted into a flattened tunnel. At the entrance to this tunnel the water reared up, overturning the retaining walls and the parapet of the bridge, and rushed into Green Street, Waterloo Street, the Cross, Guard Lane, Market Lane and King Street. It was just after dawn when the main force of the water struck the town, and many of the inhabitants were still in bed. They were roused from their slumbers by screams and shouts 'The water is flooding the town!'

Archibald McKay, who was an eye-witness of this catastrophe, later wrote vividly:

Men, women and children started from their slumbers, and, almost in a state of nudity, ran in all directions seeking the more elevated spots; while others, terror-stricken, were unable to move from their position. As if to add to the horror of the scene, the large boiler floated into Waterloo Street, striking and injuring the walls of some of the houses. For a short time it was turned round and round by the eddying waters, and was again borne back into the river and dashed against the bridge, which many thought would fall to pieces before it. At last, on the water subsiding a little, it went crushing beneath the arch, emitting, as it disappeared, the most terrific sounds.

In the town centre the torrent divided and ran down several streets, to rejoin again and roar along King Street, presenting an awesome spectacle as it bore everything before it. Some 221 families were rendered homeless when their houses were swept away; of these, almost half were of the poorest class, the value of whose clothing, furniture, possessions and dwellings was put at £300. A public subscription taken up on behalf of these destitute families speedily raised over £550. Many other houses, shops and factories suffered extensive damage and inundation, the total loss sustained being put at around £15,000. This may not seem a large amount, but it was the equivalent of about

The Fleshmarket Bridge

£3,000,000 in present-day currency. Had the Flesh Market Bridge collapsed and blocked the channel of the river, the extent of the flooding would have been considerably greater and the loss of life as well as property might have been immense.

Afterwards marks were chiselled on the walls of several houses in the town to show the level attained by the flood waters. They ranged from a mere ten inches, indicated on the doorway of Finnie's ironmongery in Regent Street, and 7 feet 4 inches (2.4m) on the house of Mr Neill in Townholm.

Victorian splendour

Such was the resilience of Kilmarnock and its inhabitants that the damage was soon made good and further improvements in the inner district were made within a year or two. In the year of the Flood, in fact, Kilmarnock got a splendid new Sheriff Court, belatedly providing the Sheriff-Substitute (appointed in 1846) with commodious buildings worthy of his high office. The Court-house departed from the customary penchant for the Gothic and had a decidedly classical appearance, with triangular pediments and Corinthian pillars. It was erected on St Marnock's Street next door to Kilmarnock House. When the latter was demolished in 1935 the site was levelled to provide a car-park for the Court.

Sheriff Court

In 1855 a crenellated tower standing 80 feet high was erected on a hill 500 feet above sea level two miles south of Craigie village. On this hilltop Wallace is said to have watched the barns of Ayr burning as a reprisal for the murder of his uncle and other noblemen. Archibald Adamson (1875) says that Wallace exclaimed, 'The barns of Ayr burn weil'. This is an apocryphal tale, probably the invention of 18th or 19th century romanticists, for Barnweil is a very ancient name, recorded in documents at least as far back as 1177—more than a century before William Wallace. The Barnweil Monument was typical of its period, with its fairy turrets and Gothic arches, and reflects the Victorian romanticisation of one of the brutal periods in Scottish history.

Barnweil Monument

One of the most important developments of that decade was the opening of Duke Street, linking the Cross to Green Street. It was formally opened by Provost Archibald Finnie in November 1859. The following year another considerable improvement was wrought by the opening of Union Street in the upper quarter of the town. This was an era in which Victorian businessmen took enormous pride in their town and many of the architectural splendours of Kilmarnock were erected in this period. The Corn Exchange, (now the Palace Theatre) situated at the corner of what was then known as the Low Green, was erected in 1862-3 from designs by James Ingram, on Green Street and London Road. The Italianate structure was surmounted by a fine tower named in memory of Prince Albert, the Prince Consort, who died a few months previously. The upper storey accommodated the Athenaeum and Kilmarnock library while commodious shops occupied the ground floor. Eleven mascarons (sculptured stone heads) decorated the projecting keystones and included portraits of the

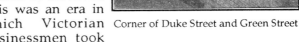

Corner of Duke Street and Green Street

'Waterloo Street'   Oil Painting by Andrew Law

Prince Consort, Colin Campbell, Lord Clyde (hero of the Indian Mutiny) and Sir James Shaw. In the main hall within, the business of the Corn Exchange was conducted; by contrast, there was a covered market outside the south end of the building dedicated to the sale of butter, eggs and other farm produce. Adjoining the Corn Exchange the Town Council erected the Agricultural Hall which was used for agricultural exhibitions as well as serving as the drill hall used by the Volunteers and later the Territorial Army.

One of the chief thoroughfares of the present day was projected in 1864 by the Town Improvement Trustees. The money for this scheme was donated by a native of Kilmarnock, John Finnie of Bowden Lodge, Kilmarnock and his generosity to his birthplace was recognised by naming the new street after him. It ran straight from Langlands Brae in the north to the Court House. Along this imposing street were erected many fine buildings in the 1870s. The Theatre or Opera House, with accommodation for 1,500 persons, was opened in March 1875. Unfortunately, it had a rather chequered career, being converted into a church in the 1920s and later reverting to business use before it was accidentally burned down in 1989. The elegant building erected by Provost Archibald Finnie housed the offices of the family firm as well as the registrar's office of James Gregory. Farther along the street a handsome block was erected by Bailie Matthew Muir and housed the head post office, the Town Chamberlain's office and the police station.

The Opera House

John Finnie Street

Expansion and consolidation

In the 1860s and 1870s there was a great deal of in-filling, as subsidiary streets were laid out and developed between the main thoroughfares that radiated from the Cross. Kilmarnock obtained a Municipal Extension Act in 1871 which considerably added to the size of the town. The new boundaries were defined as running 'from the point at which Kilmarnock Water joins the River Irvine, in a straight line to a point on the Irvine Road, where the road to Loanfoot Farmhouse leaves the same; thence in a straight line to the point at which the road to Hillhead leaves the Kilmaurs Road; thence in a straight line to a point on the Glasgow Road, where the road to south and north Knockinlaw leaves the same; thence in a straight line to a point on the Kilmarnock Water, which is distant seventy-five yards northwards from the point where the road from Beansburn to Darkpath Toll crosses the Kilmarnock Water; thence in a straight line to the bridge over the Millburn on the Mauchline Road; thence down the Millburn to the point at which the same joins the River Irvine; thence in a straight line to the Bellsland Bridge, on the road from Riccarton to Galston; thence in a straight line to the point called Witch Knowe, at which two roads meet; thence in a straight line to the bridge over the Maxholm Burn, on the Ayr Road; thence

down the Maxholm Burn to the point at which the same joins the River Irvine; thence down the River Irvine to the point first described.' This left the boundaries south of the river unchanged, but added considerably to the burgh in the north and west.

By 1879 Kilmarnock consisted of over 70 streets and 20 lanes and side-streets. The Municipal Extension Act gave powers to local authorities to make compulsory purchases of property for slum clearance, street improvements and the provision of sewerage systems. In Kilmarnock the Town Council used its powers under this Act to acquire and demolish the dilapidated properties in Strand and Bank Streets. These streets were subsequently widened and fine modern buildings erected along them, most notably the offices and bonded warehouse of John Walker & Son, spirit merchants. Many old buildings of considerable historic interest were lost in this redevelopment, but it must be admitted that they were in an extremely insanitary condition. The burgh slaughter-house, an insalubrious structure in St Andrew Street, was demolished and a new abattoir erected near the confluence of the Kilmarnock Water and the River Irvine. Handsome freestone dwellings and shops were constructed on St Andrew Street and Kirktonholm Street. Many beautiful and imposing villas, accommodating the well-to-do citizens, were built in the 1870s especially along London Road, Dundonald Road, Howard Street, Portland Terrace and Witch Road.

The outer fringe of the burgh at that time lay to the east of the railway line to Troon. Between this and the Kilmarnock Water Hamilton Street was laid out in the late 1870s but was not fully developed till the end of the century. Outside the burgh boundary, however,

Kilmarnock Cross

railway workshops were erected in the Bonnyton area and rapidly this developed as a suburb, with the cottages of the railway workers. Between the main line of the Glasgow and South Western Railway and West Langlands Street much of the heavy industry of Kilmarnock developed in the late nineteenth century. In this area were located sawmills, the Portland Forge, the Vulcan Foundry, the Britannia Works and the Titchfield Foundry among other similar enterprises.

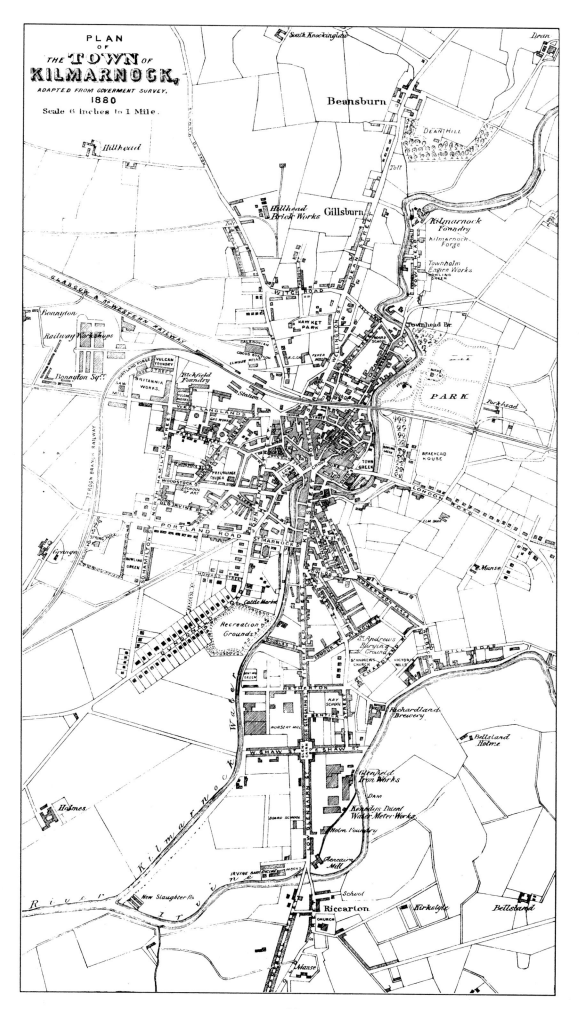

PLAN
OF
THE TOWN OF
KILMARNOCK,
ADAPTED FROM GOVERMENT SURVEY,
1880
Scale 6 Inches to 1 Mile.

Dean Street expanded northwards to Gillsburn and Beansburn and housing was developed out along the Kilmaurs road in the same period.

To the south, the district between Glencairn Street and the River Irvine was also built up at this time. Here were located many of the breweries and mills, as well as the Glenfield ironworks, Kennedy's Patent Water Meter works and the Irvine Bank engine works. Riccarton had become a suburb of Kilmarnock and also expanded enormously in this period. The town had now become the regional centre of north Ayrshire and many of the inhabitants of Hurlford and Galston, Mauchline and Catrine, Crosshouse and Kilmaurs, Stewarton and Fenwick travelled from their villages into Kilmarnock to work. Their labour and their spending power contributed materially to the prosperity of Kilmarnock at the turn of the century and beyond.

In 1811 the population of the burgh had stood at 10,148. By 1851 it had more than doubled, to 21,283, but after that date the rate of increase slowed down. At the 1871 Census the population had risen to 24,071. New housing of varying density was erected at the turn of the century. McLelland Drive was developed in the early 1900s, the terrace of two-storey houses, flats and maisonettes being constructed of red sandstone from Ballochmyle Quarry. Two-storey terraced and semi-detached houses were built on Rennie Street, while small villas and bungalows spread inexorably along the Glasgow, London and Kilmaurs roads.

Early twentieth century developments

Kilmarnock Corporation at the beginning of the present century was nothing if not go-ahead. In 1903 it obtained an Act of Parliament enabling it to embark on an ambitious electric lighting and traction scheme. This project flew in the face of public and expert opinion, although a plebiscite of the ratepayers was couched in such terms as to make the outcome ambiguous. Furthermore, the Corporation rejected overtures from the Irvine Valley towns to participate in the venture. A power station was erected on the north bank of the Irvine opposite Riccarton and by October 1903 both tramlines and overhead power lines were in

Kilmarnock Corporation tram at Glencairn Square

place. On 10th December Lord Howard de Walden inaugurated the service by himself driving the first tram. The story of this service, which lasted till 1926,

King Street, 1890

will be found in Chapter 9.

In the postwar period there was a resurgence of the social and economic upheavals which had caused so much hardship a century earlier, in the aftermath of the Napoleonic Wars. Ex-servicemen returned, not to 'a fit Britain for heroes to live in' but to unemployment, poverty, hunger and disease. There was an echo of the radicalism of the 1820s when, on 1st December 1922, an army of 400 unemployed Glasgow hunger marchers passed through Kilmarnock on their way to London to petition the prime minister. Three and a half years later Kilmarnock felt the effects of the General Strike. When the strike was called off, hundreds of strikers gathered in the town centre and refused to disperse, blocking the egress of the Scottish Transport Company's buses from the station in Portland Street. A rumour circulated that the TUC's demands had been met by the government and the strikers hailed this as a victory. Disillusionment set in later when the truth emerged in a BBC bulletin that evening. But by that time the strike was over—apart from the coal-miners who continued the struggle on their own for several months.

The electorate was considerably expanded as a result of the Act of 1918 which gave the vote to women over the age of 30. Because this brought a tremendous influx into the electorate the government decided to revise constituencies on the principle of areas with about 70,000 inhabitants. Hitherto Kilmarnock had been lumped together with several other burghs with which it had little in common, but now the political boundaries were redrawn and the Kilmarnock Division of Ayrshire was created instead. This embraced Catrine, Craigie, Crosshouse, Darvel, Dundonald, Fenwick, Galston, Hurlford, Kilmaurs, Mauchline, Newmilns, Riccarton, Sorn and Symington, an area of 5,810 acres with a population of 72,399. The electorate of 32,298 consisted of 19,813 men and 12,485 women. In the Khaki Election of December 1918 the Hon. Alexander Shaw, previously MP for the Kilmarnock Burghs, was re-elected under the Coalition Liberal ticket. He resigned in 1923, but Parliament was dissolved before a by-election could take place. In the election of December 1923 ex-Bailie Robert Climie, who had been the unsuccessful Labour candidate in 1918, won the seat in a three-cornered contest with a Liberal and a Unionist. Another general election took place a few months later and this time the Liberals backed the Unionist candidate, Major Charles McAndrew who won with 14,237 votes against 13,054 for Climie. In 1928 the vote was extended to women between the ages of 21 and 30—the so-called 'Flapper vote'.

The town was en fête on 12th May 1937 to celebrate the Coronation of King George VI. Originally it was his elder brother, Edward VIII, who should have been crowned that day, but he abdicated the previous December after a reign of eleven months. The Coronation went ahead as planned, only the principal performers were replaced. There was a big parade by Kilmarnock Burgh Band, Kilmarnock Pipe Band, the Police Pipe Band, the Territorials, the Town Council, the trades and youth organisations. In Howard Park, a tree was planted to mark the occasion, and joined one planted seventeen years earlier to celebrate peace after

Celebrating the Coronation of King George VI

the Great War. A grand ball was staged on the Friday evening preceding the Coronation and every child in the burgh received a souvenir cup and saucer and a bright, newly minted 1937 penny. How many of those were still unspent before the day was over? The Boy Scouts organised a system of relay runners bringing a torch from London which lit bonfires on hilltops across the country; Kilmarnock's bonfire was on Craigie Hill. Four of Kilmarnock's most prominent citizens were awarded Coronation medals. No one then realised that this would be the last occasion for national rejoicing for several years.

Postwar developments

Mention has been made of the disastrous flood of 1852 which hit the poorest families hardest. Further inundations occurred in 1888, 1904, 1911, 1932, 1953

and 1958; but undoubtedly the worst flooding took place in 1932. Prolonged heavy rain between 31st December 1931 and 3rd January 1932 caused both the Kilmarnock Water and the River Irvine to burst their banks, flooding streets in the congested south-western

Flooding in Willock Street, Riccarton, 1932

district of the town. Riccarton was also particularly hard hit on this occasion as a result of the Cessnock bursting its banks, surging through Riccarton Moss and dumping thousands of tons of sludge along the railway line between Riccarton and Hurlford. More than 150 families had to be evacuated in horse-drawn carts and sheep had to be rescued by small boats. Glenfield, Barr Thomson and other factories were badly flooded, while the power station was under 18 feet of water at one stage and electricity was cut off for 24 hours. Workers were given an extended New Year holiday in order to help clear up the mess left by the flood water. Like the flood of 1852, the flood of 1932 was blamed on the inadequacy of the channels, especially under the town bridges. In the ensuing months the river beds were extensively dredged and widened and the Council embarked on a crash programme of building or raising embankments along the River Irvine between Struthers Steps and the Victoria Bridge. The last severe flooding occurred on 6th September 1958 when parts of the town were under five feet of water. The only other disaster to strike the town in the 1950s was an explosion at the burgh power station in 1952, as a result of which five men lost their lives.

Kilmarnock made history in 1966 when James C.W. Nicol was appointed Town Manager. By now the town and its services had grown to such an extent that a more professional approach to the administration of local government was required. Mr Nicol continued in this capacity over the period of transition to the District Council and was awarded the OBE in 1979. He retired in 1983 but died in July 1986 at the relatively early age of 68.

By the 1960s the central part of Kilmarnock was almost entirely occupied by shops, offices, workshops, light industries and yards. Most of the slums had gone, but sub-standard housing still existed in Queen Street and Clark Street. Shortly before the Second World War the Ministry of Transport had started work on a by-pass west of Kilmarnock to divert the bulk of the Glasgow-Ayr traffic. Work came to a standstill during the war and when it was reconsidered afterwards it was found that new housing extended over the proposed area. Pending a decision on the routing of the main north-south road the Town Council took the initiative by demolishing the slums of the inner districts. The wholesale destruction of Fore, Princes and Waterloo Streets, the old Town Hall and such landmarks as Dick Brothers' garage, the Plaza cinema, King Street Church and the burgh police station was controversial at the time and has continued to be a contentious matter to this day; but in fairness to the planners, they were wrestling with a problem created by a town which had grown haphazardly over the centuries. A desperate situation called for a drastic remedy, but it was a matter for regret that so many places of historic interest, not to mention so much of the character of the old Kilmarnock, were lost in the process. The redevelopment of the inner town in the 1960s and early 1970s was accompanied by the construction of a dual-carriageway by-pass, carrying the A77 well to the east of the town. Kilmarnock now has its own miniature 'Spaghetti Junction' between Hurlford and Riccarton where the A77 crosses the A71.

Coat of arms of Burgh of Kilmarnock

From 1832 (when Kilmarnock became a parliamentary burgh) until 1975 the Town Council was headed by a provost; 33 gentlemen and, latterly, two ladies held this office as follows:

1833—1834	John Andrew	1910—1917	Matthew Smith
1834—1837	James Reed, MD	1917—1921	James Smith
1837—1840	Archibald Finnie	1921—1927	James B. Wilson
1840—1841	William Brown	1927—1931	David Jones
1841—1844	Matthew Strang	1931—1937	Henry Smith
1844—1847	John Brown	1937—1943	George H. Wilson
1847—1852	Robert Cumming	1943—1946	John H. Carnie
1852—1855	James Donald	1946—1950	Daniel Cairns
1855—1858	John Dickie	1950—1953	Alexander M. Clark, OBE
1858—1861	Archibald Finnie Jnr	1953—1956	William B. Gilmour
1861—1864	John Crooks	1956—1959	Daniel Cairns
1864—1874	John Dickie	1959—1962	Robert H. Banks
1874—1886	Peter Sturrock	1962—1965	Daniel B. Cunningham
1886—1895	Archibald McLelland	1965—1968	William Wallace
1895—1901	David Mackay	1968—1971	James Mackie
1901—1907	James Hood	1971—1974	Mrs Annie Mackie
1907—1910	Robert Gemmill	1974—1975	Mrs Maisie C. Garven

3 KILMARNOCK AND LOUDOUN DISTRICT

Arms of Kilmarnock and Loudoun District

In 1975 the local government of Scotland was revolutionised. The old counties were swept away and replaced by eleven regions. Only Orkney, Shetland and Fife retained their previous identities. The former counties of Lanark, Ayr, Renfrew and Dumbarton, with portions of Stirlingshire and Argyll, became Strathclyde Region—much more extensive than the Dark Age kingdom of that name. The region was divided into districts and Kilmarnock, as the leading town of north Ayrshire, found itself as the administrative centre of Kilmarnock and Loudoun District. Even before regionalisation, the Kilmarnock district was regarded as encompassing the parishes of Kilmarnock, Riccarton, Kilmaurs, Dunlop, Stewarton and Fenwick. In *The Third Statistical Account* (1951) this area amounted to some 62,000 acres, with a population of 60,800 (with 42,600 resident in the burgh of Kilmarnock itself). The new district, as its name implied, was not synonymous with the above area, including as it does Loudoun the parish of which Newmilns had been the chief town.

Thus the new district stretched eastwards up the Irvine Valley to take in the towns of Galston, Newmilns and Darvel. In the northeast the district boundary followed the line of the old Ayrshire-Lanarkshire border, attaining its most northerly point just south of the village of

Uplawmoor. On the north-west, however, the ancient bailiery of Cunninghame was divided between the new district of that name and Kilmarnock and Loudoun, the boundary running south-west along the Dusk Water to join the Garnock. The boundary then swung east to exclude the valley of the Annick Water, then west again to include Kilmaurs, Knockentiber, Crosshouse and Gatehead. On the southern flank it curved eastwards to take in the Irvine Valley, then north past Hart Hill and the headwaters of the Avon to Loudoun Hill. In 1975 Kilmarnock and Loudoun District had an estimated population of 84,000 (52,000 within the burgh of Kilmarnock), with an eventual target of 100,000. The 1981 Census, however, revealed that Kilmarnock had a population of 47,158 and the District as a whole had 81,743 inhabitants.

The new District had an area of 144 square miles and contained 29,839 houses with a rateable value of £282,170, the combined domestic and water rate being then set at 123p in the pound. Commercial and industrial property, however, boosted the rateable value of the District to £3,907,871. Land was made available for new development at Greenfield, averaging £10-12,000 an acre. At that time a typical semi-detached 3-4 apartment house could be purchased for about £12,000, while a detached luxury home cost in the region of £30,000.

Hurlford and Crookedholm, like Riccarton, are now virtually suburbs of Kilmarnock and have a combined population of about 4,200. This area to the east of the burgh developed rapidly in the nineteenth century, following the discovery of coal. Fireclay and ironstone were also worked extensively. Coal-mining is long a thing of the past and fireclay production ceased in the 1970s. No foundry-work and little in the

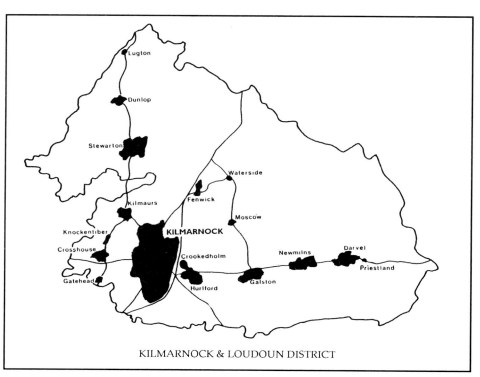

KILMARNOCK & LOUDOUN DISTRICT

37

way of metal industries remain and the bulk of the workforce now find employment in Kilmarnock. A poignant reminder of the heyday of the iron and steel industry of Hurlford is the ship's propeller erected at

Hurlford

the Cross in the lately redeveloped town centre.

Kilmaurs, two miles north of Kilmarnock, boasts a church dating from 1170 and received its charter as a burgh of barony in 1527. The village and its surrounding parish were long associated with the Glencairn family, but the last Earl sold the Kilmaurs estate to the Henrietta Scott, later Marchioness of Titchfield in 1786. The chief

Kilmaurs

industry in the nineteenth and early twentieth centuries was hosiery, but there were also coal mines in the neighbourhood. Kilmaurs had a population of 1,820 at the 1931 Census and it remained fairly static till the 1960s when the village expanded as a dormitory suburb of Kilmarnock, though many people now also commute to Glasgow. It now has a population of 2,764.

Crosshouse and Knockentiber, two miles west of Kilmarnock, have also developed in recent years as suburbs of the town, with populations of 2,500 and 400 respectively. Crosshouse grew rapidly in the nineteenth

Crosshouse

century following the discovery of coal in the area. In more recent years, however, it has expanded its housing as a community now mainly working in Kilmarnock itself, although a major development is the General Hospital, opened in 1982 and set in spacious grounds, which now serves the District and replaced the former Kilmarnock Infirmary. No fewer than 500 new houses were erected to accommodate hospital staff. A mile south of Crosshouse is the hamlet of Gatehead (population 300), lying athwart the road to Troon and still managing to retain its rural character.

Outside the Kilmarnock conurbation the district traditionally divided into two main parts, the textile towns of Stewarton, Galston, Newmilns and Darvel on the one hand, and the predominantly agricultural area. Stewarton, the second largest burgh in the District (population 6,425) is pleasantly situated in open countryside six miles north of Kilmarnock. The town motto 'Knit Weel' reflects Stewarton's long

Stewarton

connection with the wool trade and a major centre of bonnet manufacture for over four centuries. Blanket-making and the weaving of cotton and muslin were important industries in the eighteenth and nineteenth centuries, though they were largely superseded by knitwear and hosiery in more recent times. Its relative proximity to Glasgow has made it attractive as a dormitory town and many of the inhabitants now regularly commute into the city.

Galston, set in pleasantly wooded countryside

Galston

four miles up-river from Kilmarnock, is next in size, with a population of 5,407. Galston is steeped in history and has associations with Wallace and Bruce. After it received its charter in 1717 it developed rapidly as a centre of handloom-weaving and later the manufacture of gauze and lawn. From the beginning of the nineteenth century till 1933 it was a major coal-mining area, with no fewer than 15 collieries at one time. The textile industry which flourished till the 1960s has also shrunk, the last blanket mill closing recently; but the town has since diversified into meat processing and canning, mechanical and electrical engineering, road haulage and telecommunications.

Darvel

Darvel, most easterly of the textile towns, has a population of 3,514. Its situation in a broad, level part of the valley permitted planned development on the grid system in the mid-eighteenth century, although later the heights to the north of the town were also developed. Locally grown flax was the basis of the linen industry. It was replaced at the end of the eighteenth century by cotton handloom weaving, which was revolutionised in 1876 when Alexander Morton introduced power looms and the manufacture of lace. Inevitably this has shrunk in recent years, although to some extent it has been replaced by the manufacture of warp-knitted fabrics.

Newmilns (population 3,435) nestles in the narrowest part of the Irvine Valley. Despite its name,

Newmilns

it is actually the oldest burgh of the District, having received its charter a century before Kilmarnock. The people of Newmilns were staunchly Presbyterian and took a leading role in the wars of the Covenant. The handloom-weaving of figured muslin or leno in the eighteenth century gave way to machine-made textiles in the 1870s. Today mainly window furnishings are manufactured here using both cotton and man-made fibres. Newmilns is also an important centre of light engineering, producing water re-circulating machinery, heating and ventilating equipment and dairy engineering. The largest employer is Vesuvius UK who manufacture ceramics for use in the steel and

foundry industries.

Dunlop, 4km north of Stewarton, on the line of the Kilmarnock-Glasgow railway, is nowadays something

Dunlop

of a commuter town with a population of about 900. It was the centre of the dairy industry and long famous for its cheeses. Cheesemaking and bacon-curing were the main occupations from the sixteenth century onwards but nowadays it has added sawmilling, concrete fabrication and the production of animal feeding-stuffs. About 4km north of Dunlop lies Lugton, the most northerly village of the District, standing at the junction of the roads from Barrhead, Beith, Kilwinning, Irvine and Stewarton. Iron ore was mined in this vicinity at one time and a lime-works has been in operation since the 1940s.

North-east of Kilmarnock the main centre is Fenwick (population 980). Originally part of Kilmarnock parish, it was separated from it in 1641 and granted its own market charter in 1707. Fenwick really consists of two villages, the original settlement of Laigh Fenwick retaining its historic character and many of the old weavers' cottages. High Fenwick developed mainly in the nineteenth century and is now the main centre of

Fenwick

population. The Fenwick people were resolute upholders of the Covenant in the seventeenth century. In 1761 the Fenwick Weavers' Society was formed for the purpose of providing its members with weaving reeds and oatmeal for domestic consumption; by buying in bulk the Society passed on the saving to its members and thus anticipated the Co-operative movement of Rochdale by more than 80 years. Today Fenwick is almost exclusively residential, an attractive commuter village serving both Kilmarnock and Glasgow with extensive high-quality private development in recent years.

Three miles (5km) east of Fenwick lies the hamlet of

Waterside and Moscow

Waterside on the A719. South on the same road is Moscow on the Volga Burn. Despite fanciful attempts to find a connection between this hamlet and either Peter the Great or the Crimean War, it appears that the name is merely a corruption of the Anglo-Norman Moss-hall or Moss-haw, itself derived from a much more ancient Brittonic form. The deliberate change, in fact, dates from 1812 and Napoleon's retreat from the Russian capital. With a fine disregard for Russian geography, the inhabitants then named the stream passing through the village after the Volga. The hamlet never had a post office to give it an official identity in postmark form, but it had a telephone exchange and before the advent of all-number dialling it was possible to make a call to 'Moscow' from Kilmarnock for twopence.

When local government was re-organised in 1975 the parliamentary constituency remained unchanged. Continuity was maintained in the person of William Ross, Labour MP for Kilmarnock and District since 1946. A native of Ayr and educated at the Academy there and Glasgow University, he had been a schoolmaster before the Second World War in which he rose to the rank of major and was awarded the Military MBE in 1945. On Labour's return to power in 1964 he became Secretary of State for Scotland, a post which he held till 1970 and again from 1974 to 1976. He was thus deeply involved in the plans for the reforms in local administration which culminated in the emergence of the regional and district councils. When he retired from the Commons in 1979 he was elevated to the peerage and took as his title Lord Ross of Marnock, a fitting reference to the

constituency which he had served so well for 23 years. At the general election of 1979 he was succeeded by William McKelvey, a Dundonian who had previously been leader of the Labour group on Dundee District Council.

One of the last acts of the Town Council before demitting power was to confer the freedom of the burgh on three men who had done a great deal for the town: Lord Howard de Walden who had recently gifted Dean Castle and its contents to the town, Canon Matthew Littleton of St Joseph's and Willie Ross. The ceremony was performed by Provost Maisie Garven. Following the re-organization the title of provost was dropped, and William Aitken was referred to as Chairman during his term in office (1975-8). In 1978, however, Kilmarnock and Loudoun again had a lady as chief magistrate, when the local elections of that year resulted in Labour and Conservatives holding seven seats each and the Nationalists two. As Labour were not prepared to combine with SNP, this brought a Conservative-Nationalist coalition to power under the redoubtable Margaret Parker, during whose term the title of provost was revived. One of Provost Parker's first acts was to lead a delegation to Whitehall to argue the case for Kilmarnock, faced with the shrinkage or closure of its industries. Industrial decline was to be the keynote of the late 1970s and 1980s, and as nearby Irvine forged ahead as a New Town, attracting a wide range of new industries, Kilmarnock seemed doomed to decay. The story of how this process was arrested is told in Chapter 5. The electricity service which had been a burgh undertaking passed to the South of Scotland Electricity Board. The burgh's power station was closed and its giant cooling towers, so long a local landmark, were demolished in June 1976. In the same year, however, the Kilmarnock Centre and Burns Shopping Mall were opened near the Cross by Mrs Willie Ross (later Lady Ross of Marnock), giving a much-needed boost to the shopping facilities in the heart of the town.

As the legal and judicial centre of North Ayrshire, Kilmarnock got a new Sheriff Court more fitting to the task on 22nd December 1986. This impressive building contains five courtrooms, including provision for sittings of the High Court. Work on the construction by Melville,

Kilmarnock Sheriff Court

Square of Alès entrance to Burns Shopping Mall

as appropriate in the year of Kilmarnock's quatercentenary.

Since the revival of the title of provost in 1978 the office has been held by the following:

1978—1981	Mrs Margaret Parker
1981—1984	Andrew Nisbet
1984—1988	Tom Ferguson
1988—1992	James Mills

There was considerable anger and dismay in 1990, following the publication of *The Spread of Prosperity and the North-South Divide* in July of that year. This socio-economic survey of the United Kingdom was the work of academics from the universities of Wales and Newcastle. Out of 280 towns Kilmarnock was ranked 278th.

To be labelled as the third poorest town in the United Kingdom (only Greenock and Peterlee fared worse) was greeted with a sense of outrage, exacerbated by some dismissive articles in the Scottish national press whose journalists made fleeting visits to the town, noted the dereliction in Portland and John Finnie Streets, and scurried back whence they had come. They ignored the positive developments which have taken place in recent years. The survey relied on statistics which were out-of-date, notably an unemployment rate of 19.1 per cent in 1986, the blackest year in Kilmarnock's history, and ignoring the recovery of the late 1980s which reduced this level to 9.1 per cent by April 1990. This, of course, does not provide any grounds for complacency, but, as will be seen in subsequent chapters, Kilmarnock is working hard to attract new businesses and light industries to replace traditional sources of employment which had formerly dominated the area's economy.

and Dundonald Road, began in 1983 and eventually replaced the 134 year-old Court-house across the road. The old building, however, was refurbished and now houses the offices of the Procurator-Fiscal's department. A few months later the Galleon Centre opened in Titchfield Street (see Chapter 12). The Timmer Brig was demolished in 1991 but was replaced almost immediately by a new concrete and steel construction. In 1989 Balfour Beatty proposed a multi-million pound development for Portland Street and its environs which, it is hoped, will eventually transform the derelict area at the very centre of the town into a commercial and trading focus for Kilmarnock and a worthy expansion of the shops already in the Kilmarnock Centre. On a more symbolic note, plans were formulated for the restoration in 1992 of the Shaw statue to the Cross from which it had been banished in 1929. This was regarded

4 AGRICULTURE

The parish of Kilmarnock, after Fenwick was hived off in 1641, had an area of 8,340 acres, of which some 5,900 acres comprised the landward portion (that is to say, the countryside surrounding the burgh). The parish was about eight or nine miles in length and about four miles wide. The boundaries were precisely delineated in the 1870s as follows:

From the point where the Moorfield Burn falls into the River Irvine, a little below Cambuskeith Mill, up and along the river in an easterly direction, to the High Milton, including High Milton Mill and Armsheugh; then, north-east, as far as Sneddonhall (including the farms of Blackshill and High and Laigh Russia); then west along the Moscow road, with the estate of Darwhilling on the north; then to the farm of Watston and along the road to the junction with the Craufurdland road; following the latter, the south side of which lies in the parish, and along the bridge and through the gatehouse and across the Kilmarnock Water and through the lands of Dalmusternock to Craigspout; then north-west (including part of the farm of Meiklewood and traversing Fenwick Moor) to the farm of Redden; then south by Rowallan (including Rowallan Mill, Little Mosside, Meikle Mosside, Tannahill, Toponthank, Onthank and Little Onthank) to the Stewarton roadend on the Kilmaurs road; then still southwards along the road to the farm of Hillhead; then south-west (past Bonnieton farm) to the farm of Sprighill; then to the burn at Moorfield tilework; then along the course of the burn to Old Gatehead, across the Dundonald road at Thirdpart Kilns, to the point first described.

The terrain of the parish is generally flat, sloping gently southwards. Early writers praised the soil which was deep, strong and fertile, although giving way to moss and moor in the north-east. About 1763 the rent of the arable land was set at between 2s6d (12.5p) and 3s (15p) an acre. By 1790 the average had risen to 18s (90p) an acre, as a result of considerable improvements in land utilisation. The enclosure of the land began about 1765. Previously the land was unenclosed and at harvest time must have resembled the steppes of Russia—'a wild, dreary common' is how one writer described it, 'and nothing was to be seen, but here and there, a poor, bare and homely hut where the farmer and his family lodged.' Because of a shortage of stone, the parish was spared the riot of drystane-dykes which covered other counties, such as Lanarkshire and Dumfriesshire. Instead, the fields were enclosed by digging ditches and planting hawthorn bushes along their banks. This form of enclosure had the benefit of draining the land and helping to prevent soil erosion.

This process was achieved very gradually and had by no means been completed by the time of the first *Statistical Account* (1790) in which the Rev. John Robertson furnished a graphic description of the deleterious effects of the damp climate and the large amounts of surface water prevalent before the enclosure movement got under way. In summertime much of this surface water would have evaporated, but in the winter, when there was little heat from the sun, this water lay and stagnated on the surface of the ground, greatly injuring it and even destroying its vegetative

Reaping and traditional method of Hay-stacking

powers. 'The bad effects of this circumstance, however, are now not nearly so much, nor so generally felt as formerly,' wrote Mr Robertson. 'This, in a great measure, is owing to the numberless drains made by the ditches, which have been drawn, in all directions, for inclosing the grounds.'

In the old, pre-enclosure period, the cattle were allowed to wander about at will through all the neighbouring fields till the grass began to sprout in the spring. The beasts cropped what vegetation there was and did extensive damage to the waterlogged soil with their hooves. 'To such a degree was this mischief done,' says Robertson, 'that in many places it destroyed all prospect of any crop, worth the labour of the husbandman, for the ensuing year; and, in some instances, for many years to come.' Fortunately, that was now all in the past and Robertson was pleased to report that the scene was changed infinitely for the better. 'There is, at this time, scarcely a single farm, in all that wide-extended plain, that is not inclosed with ditch and hedge, and most of them with numbers of intermediate ones, to separate the fields from each other. By this means, the farmers have it in their power to confine the cattle, through the winter, to the fields where they can do least harm by poaching; the water is mostly drained from the surface; and the ground is, in some degree, sheltered by the hedges from the severity of the winter cold and storms. This, along with the other improvements made upon the soil, has rendered the grounds much more productive and fruitful than ever they were in any former period, probably three or four times at least.' As a result, sheep, formerly widespread, were virtually banished from the parish, though Robertson considered that some of the larger or tamer breeds might perhaps be tried to advantage.

The beasts which formerly roamed at will were black cattle, bred mainly for beef and hides. Kilmarnock parish did not, at this period, afford the lush pastures which encouraged the development of the famous brown and white dairy cows elsewhere in the county. Improving landlords and tenant farmers therefore concentrated on ameliorating the soil for arable purposes. As no marl (ideal for improving lime-deficient land) was discovered in the parish, the soil was manured with the dung collected from the town privies and the farm middens, mixed with coal ashes and lime. Quantities of cow-horn were imported from Ireland for the same purpose. Coal ashes did well enough for a year or two on a sandy soil, but were harmful in the heavy clays making up so much of the parish. Besides, ashes were only available from the town itself and their use was confined to farms close by. Some lime was worked in the higher parts of the parish but most of it had to be imported from much farther afield at considerable expense. Slaked lime and burnt shells were used, especially on ground which consisted of a very strong clay. Ideally lime was spread and left to lie for two winters and a summer before being ploughed in. Thereafter the land had to be limed and dunged in alternate years.

Every intelligent farmer, in this district, is now sensible, that a proper rotation of crops is of the utmost importance in husbandry; and that the ground, with the same manure, will continue in equal, or even in better heart, for at least double the time, under a rotation properly calculated for the soil, than what it will do under a constant succession of any one crop.

Robertson conceded that the same method would not suit all the different soils and that more attention ought to be paid to finding out exactly which crops did best and where.

Unfortunately the landowners of the parish had adopted a system of letting their land which effectively prevented their tenants from making much use of rotation.

In their leases, they bind the farmer to plow only three years, and then to keep the ground for six years in grass. The leases are in general for 19 years, so that a farmer has it only in his power, during that term to have two breaks of his farm, together with what he can plow in the last year of his lease. This plan is attended with great disadvantage to the proprietor, to the tenant, and to the public.

The result was that the land was exhausted long before the end of the lease. Even in those cases where the tenant succeeded in improving the land, he was held back and unable to reap the full benefit, otherwise he would have to give up the land to someone else or face a much higher rent. That this pattern did prevail is borne out by the steep rise in rents, not only in the enclosure period (1765-90) but in the ensuing years when the prolonged wars with France had a highly

Mortar and pestle for grinding flour

inflationary effect. By 1811, for example, the average rental had risen to £3 an acre - twenty times as much as it had been in 1763. William Aiton, writing about 1811, mentions the 73 acre farm of Silverwood which was rented for nineteen years prior to 1776 at £5 in cash and five bolls of meal per annum. By 1811, however, the annual rental had risen to £200.

The public also suffered as a result of the lease system, as more grain would undoubtedly have been raised had the farmer had the proper encouragement to exert himself in the latter part of his lease. Furthermore, the term of tillage was too short to allow any proper crop rotation. 'The ground is sown with oats when first broke up,' wrote Robertson, 'and everyone knows that the second year after breaking up affords the best crop of oats. These two years, therefore, the ground must be sown with the same species of grain, to enable the farmer to pay his rent.'

Apart from the ditches cut to enclose the fields, the land was eventually drained adequately after the introduction, in 1820, of tile drainage. This innovation was to the credit of the Duke of Portland. By 1839 over 800,000 tiles were being manufactured locally each year, and a further half million tiles were annually imported from the Moorfield tileworks just outside the parish boundary. Within twenty years about a third of the parish had been criss-crossed with a network of tile drainage, and as a result the annual rental had risen by about £500. What were previously the worst and most unproductive fields now yielded the best crops. The drains were placed about eighteen feet (6m) apart at a depth of eighteen inches. Where the bottom of the drain was soft or the land steep, soles were put under the tiles to prevent them from sinking or losing their regularity. When the field was 250-300 yards long, a main drain was drawn through the middle, and another ran at right angles across the foot of the field to collect the water from the furrow drains. These main drains were about two feet deep, considerably wider than the common drains, and the tiles always rested on flat soles.

Although the Duke of Portland took the lead in this matter, he was not the only landowner to pursue a policy of drainage. In the latter case, however, the landlords often sold the tiles to their tenants and left them to bear the costs of laying them. In many cases the farmers did not think it proper to lay out such a sum on land which might soon pass into the hands of another. In other cases, the farmer might have been willing to drain the land but lacked the necessary capital, upwards of £500 being required in 1840 to drain a farm of 100 acres.

By 1840 leases were generally for eighteen years, but in the intervening period since 1790 rents tended to be governed by the prevailing price of grain on the open market, so short leases were preferred by the landlords who could then derive benefit from the rise in the price of agricultural produce. By 1840, however, prices were much steadier than they had been in the war years and leases were tending to become longer, with 24 years not uncommon. This was seen as advantageous to both parties, the tenant having more scope for improvements. Instead of impoverishing the land by taking as much out, and putting as little in as possible, it was to the tenant's own profit to sustain the quality of the soil. The landlord, on the other hand, had the value of his property maintained, if not increased. This provided an incentive for further improvement and in the course of the nineteenth century the yield per acre steadily rose.

McKay, writing in 1879, commented that
Not a few fields that, in our own remembrance, were overspread with broom, whins, thistles, or rushes, and consequently of little value, are now in a high state of cultivation, and yield abundant crops. The wretched-looking farm-houses, too, of former years, have given place to others of a genteel, commodious,

Horse-drawn reaper

44

*and comfortable kind; and even the cottars'
dwellings, with their little gardens, have an air of
neatness and cleanliness, at once delightful to the eye
and creditable to the taste and industry of the
occupants.*

The living standards of the tenantry rose commensurately, 'so much so that many of them enjoy not only the necessaries, but the elegancies and luxuries of life'—in sharp contrast to the situation in 1778 when only two families in the country part of the parish could entertain their friends with a cup of tea.

In 1792 the Kilmarnock Farmers' Society was formed to encourage farmers to adopt the latest methods of animal husbandry and techniques of land improvement and crop rotation. This was part of a nationwide movement, but the Rev. Andrew Hamilton, writing in 1839, felt that no part of the country had benefited as much as Kilmarnock in this respect. 'While the stock is changing, the farmers are not remaining unchanged,' he wrote.

*A considerable difference exists between their
condition at present and their state fifty years ago.
Their manner of living is now more assimilated to
that of the landlord. Their knowledge advances with
that of general society, and, in the march of
improvement, they are seen working their farms to
the best advantage. In general, they are better able to
pay their rents than they were forty years ago.*

He went on to cite the superior manner of feeding dairy cattle which had greatly added to the returns yielded by it. Interestingly, in view of the situation prevalent in 1790, Kilmarnock parish now had 800 dairy cows, as well as 260 agricultural horses, 260 white-faced sheep and about 300 black-faced sheep. There was now no mention of the black cattle bred solely for their meat and hides.

The rotation of crops was now practised generally and along more scientific lines than before. After four years' pasture, the land was top-dressed and a crop of oats raised. Then manure was applied with a green crop such as potatoes, beans or turnips, followed by wheat or barley, and lastly hay and clover. In some parts a four-yearly cycle of oats, potatoes or turnips, wheat and clover was pursued, though this was condemned as likely to exhaust the soil no matter how well it was manured. Hamilton advocated prizes for the best pasture or the best oats (i.e. the first crop after pasture) as an inducement to tenants to let their fields lie fallow a year or two longer as the best method of enriching the soil. The farms in the parish ranged from 50 to 200 acres and there was some controversy over what was the optimum size. Various arguments were put forward in favour of small farms of 50 or 60 acres, while others argued the case for amalgamating them into much larger units. Hamilton, however, felt that there should always be room for farmers of all skills and levels of energy and thought that things were best left as they were.

The first *Statistical Account* complained of the indifference or neglect of the landlords regarding the buildings on their farms. Fifty years later, however, Hamilton felt that this complaint was no longer valid. Good, substantial farm-steadings were to be found everywhere, an improvement which increased the value of an estate in far greater proportion to the expense incurred. So, too, in the matter of the accommodation for the agricultural labourers. 'Cottages are universally neater than they used to be, and cottar vies with cottar in keeping his little house and garden in seemly order.'

The first *Statistical Account* was silent on the matter of farm implements. Half a century later, Andrew Hamilton stated that several kinds of plough had been introduced. That which was found most effective in the heavy soils of the parish was the iron plough invented by Wilkie of Uddingston. The same man had invented machines, such as the harrow, roller, cleaner and grubber for lifting turnips and potatoes and cleaning the ground. Semi-mechanical drills and hoes were also widely employed.

Farm carts were small and drawn by a single horse, reflecting the poor state of the rural roads in general and farm tracks in particular. Thrashing-mills were now widely used, every farm of any size possessing one. These were powered by horses and Hamilton felt that steam-power would be much more efficient. Grinding mills had sprung up along the banks of the Kilmarnock Water and River Irvine. The Milton, New and Cambuskethan mills ground flour, while the Crooksmills and Rowallan mills concentrated mainly on oats. A sixth mill, known as St Marnock's, had lately been erected in the town itself. A steady supply of water was guaranteed by the extensive reservoirs formed of the Kilmarnock Water in the high lands of the adjoining parish of Fenwick. In 1839 these six mills were producing 36,000 bushels of wheat and 120,000 bushels of oats. The actual production of oats

Stooking

in the parish amounted to only 46,000 bushels and of wheat only 7,500 bushels; but a considerable quantity of raw grain was imported from Ireland. Bean meal was also produced, but the amount was not sufficient to warrant listing in the *Statistical Account*. The flour and meal thus produced was conveyed to Glasgow and Paisley where it found a ready market.

In 1790 the raw produce of the land had not been worth itemising, so small was the area under cultivation and so inferior the yield. Half a century later, however, Andrew Hamilton could publish a detailed table

Blackface lamb

showing that 3,000 acres were under arable cultivation, producing oats, barley, wheat, beans, potatoes, turnips and rye-grass with an annual value of £16,810.

Dairy-farming in 1790 was conducted on such a small scale as to be not worthy of mention at all. Such milk cows and pigs as were kept were solely for the consumption of the farmer and his family and there was little, if any, surplus produce to go to market. The miracle of tile-drainage changed all that and in the 1830s Kilmarnock parish was transformed into some of the best pasturage to be found in the county. The extent under pasture was not stated in the *Statistical Account* but it must have been considerable, to judge by the amount of dairy produce it yielded. This included 600 sheep, 400 pigs, 400 young cattle and 20 young horses. There were 143 dairy cows in milk for an average of 105 days, producing about three and a half gallons of milk daily in that period, making a total of 52,500 gallons of milk which was sold fresh or sour at fivepence halfpenny a gallon. This was by no means the total milk yield, for an unspecified but very considerable surplus was converted into 192,000 lbs of cheese, yielding an income of £4,500 a year—as much as all other dairy and cattle produce put together. In the second half of the nineteenth century Kilmarnock cheeses attained a national reputation and an annual Cheese Fair drew buyers from every part of the country.

The pattern of land-holding in 1946 had not changed much over the past century. No fewer than 45 farms were of 50 acres or less. Out of 107 farms in the parish,

only about 20 were owner-occupied and the rest were occupied by tenants of large estates. Until the 1970s the chief landowner was Lord Howard de Walden. Though only occasionally resident in the parish, this family were considerable benefactors to the area. They gave

Ayrshire cow

to the town Kilmarnock House for use as an industrial school, and the land now forming Howard Park (1894), followed by Dean Park (1907) and the Scott Ellis playing field (1939). The eighth Lord Howard de Walden restored the ruined castle which, with its contents, including valuable collections of medieval armour and musical instruments, was gifted to Kilmarnock by the ninth Baron in 1974. Today the castle and its beautiful grounds serve the community as the Dean Castle Country Park.

When Archibald McKay published his history of Kilmarnock the other principal landowners were the Earl of Loudoun, John White of Grougar, Reginald Craufurd of Craufurdland, William Dunlop of Annanhill and Miss Parker of Assloss. At one time the Rowallan estate had been in the hand of the Mure family, one of whom, Elizabeth Mure had married King Robert II in the fourteenth century. The family name died out in the seventeenth century and the estate passed into the hands of the Earls of Loudoun. In the late nineteenth century it came into the possession of Thomas Corbet, MP who took the title of Baron Rowallan when he was elevated to the peerage in 1911. Rowallan Castle, in the northwest of the parish, was the seat of the second Baron Rowallan, Chief Scout of the British Commonwealth and Empire from 1945 until 1959.

By the middle of the present century Kilmarnock was still essentially a dairying parish, although many of the farms in the southern part of the district had almost half their acreage under arable cultivation. Improved methods of farming and the scientific breeding of better strains of cereals and root vegetables produced infinitely higher yields than could have been dreamed of in 1840. The area under pasture was slightly greater than in 1840, largely as a result of improving marginal land that had previously been unfit for use; but the parish now supported a much larger stock of beasts. Statistics available in 1946 and quoted by Dr John Strawhorn in *The Third Statistical Account* (1951) show that the number of cattle had risen from 1,280 in 1819 to over 4,000; sheep from 350 to 870, but pigs, at 260, were much the same as in 1819 and appreciably less than in 1839. While 840 of the 1,280 cattle listed in 1819 were dairy animals, practically all were of this type in 1946. The milk was sent to the Rowallan Creamery on the Glasgow road or to Waterside Creamery in Fenwick parish.

Agriculture today is in the main a modern efficient industry employing the latest technology and a high level of mechanisation. The trend away from the land which started in the 17th century continues today with a decrease in the agricultural work force. Despite this trend, which was most marked in the 1960s but though continuing, has tapered off, there are still more people deriving a living from the land than from any single manufacturing industry in Scotland.

Since the middle of the present century the most marked changes in cropping and stocking have reflected the increasing involvement (or interference) of governments and more recently of EEC directives from Brussels obliging farmers to increase farm acreages, reduce milk production or move into beef cattle as current economic circumstances dictated. Some changes reflect technical and scientific advances with higher yield crop strains or the occasional introduction of new crops such as the bright yellow fields of oil seed rape.

Ayrshire's famous native brown and white cow has also been replaced over a number of years by the black and white Friesian as the main dairy breed. Ayrshires now account for less than a third of the total of dairy cows, along with Ayrshire/Friesian crosses. The popularity of the Dutch Friesian is on account of its higher milk yield together with good beef calves. Nevertheless the harder Ayrshire still remains popular on rougher grazing to which the Friesian is not so suited.

Typical Ayrshire Farm

5 INDUSTRY

The location of Kilmarnock at the confluence of two rivers and athwart major road and rail routes encouraged a diversity of industries. These were also governed to some degree by the ready availability of raw materials, first wool and hides and later coal and iron, in the neighbourhood. Like everywhere else, Kilmarnock and Loudoun District has endured the decline and even the loss of many of its traditional industries, but with resilience and enterprise it has now diversified into an even wider range of trades and occupations.

Textiles

For centuries Ayrshire was a pastoral area noted for the high quality of its wool. By the sixteenth century, Kilmarnock was a centre of the woollen trade. Significantly there is no mention in the burgh records of the export of raw wool, but as early as 1603 there is a reference to the manufacture of 'hose or stockings'. Kilmarnock rose to importance in the seventeenth century by its production of striped woollen Kilmarnock cowls and broad blue bonnets. The blue and white cowls were used as nightcaps and were principally exported to Holland where they found especial favour with Dutch seamen.

By 1646, if not earlier, the Corporation of Bonnetmakers was in existence and there is a record of a court held by this body in the presence of Lord Boyd on 21st December 1647 when about thirty bonnetmakers 'compeared' and complained of various abuses which had crept into the craft. One of the important decisions taken at this meeting was to prevent servants (i.e. employees) taking up work at their own hand until they had produced a trial piece of the required standard. By 1684 weaving was so well established in Kilmarnock that a Weavers' Charter was granted to regulate the industry. A court of 25th August 1722 contains an interesting reference to what may have been an early attempt to form a trade union.

> *To prevent cabbawling [intriguing or plotting together] in the fields or elsewhere by the servants, there shall not be found above three together in one place, either to work or to play lawfully, without special leave asked and had from their masters at any time, under a penalty of Six Shillings Scots, to be detained of the first end of their week's wages; but if allowed by their masters they are to be exempted from the same fyne.*

The master bonnetmakers exercised a strict control over their employees, as shown by another ordinance of the period. If any servant was absent all night from his master's house 'without ane Lawful Errand' and failed to state in what house he had been entertained, he was liable also to pay a fine of six shillings Scots (sixpence sterling), or to be imprisoned for 24 hours, on a complaint being made by the master to the magistrates.

The wool produced up to about 1800 was hard, coarse and wiry, and smeared with a mixture of tar and butter to reduce the incidence of disease-carrying vermin. This unguent had to be removed by boiling the fleece in a copper vat and skimming off the oily tar from the surface of the liquor. When the Wool Sorting Station was established at Kilmarnock in 1729 under its Superintendent and Stampmaster, Andrew Boyd, copper boilers were installed for this purpose. The wools were much darker in colour than they are now, and as dyestuffs were expensive, not very fast, and limited to those obtained from vegetable extracts, most of the cloth was left undyed. This was the hodden grey worn by the majority of the people. Only prosperous burgesses wore dyed woollen cloth, while the nobility favoured imported 'fine stuffs', woven in England from Spanish merino wool.

The production of hosiery and bonnets was carried on as a cottage industry. Knitting stockings was regarded as women's work, but a skilled knitter could produce three large stockings a day. By 1790 this generated an annual revenue of £600, whereas bonnets yielded only £506 in the same period. By contrast, milled caps and mitts earned £1,200. Primitive machinery, powered by water-mill, had been introduced a few years earlier.

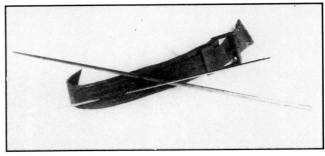

Hand-knitting bonnet needles and belt

Handloom weaving to satisfy local requirements would also have existed as a traditional craft from the earliest times, but as an organised industry it dated from 1684, the year in which the weavers received their charter of incorporation. Their output consisted largely of coarse blue serge which was bought up by three or four agents who exported it in large quantities to Holland. By 1790, however, the production of serges, mancoes and saddlers cloth amounted to no more than £611.

The more traditional knitted and woven goods were, to a large extent, overtaken by coarse fabrics, carpets, duffles, blankets and plaids, the manufacture of which was introduced about 1728 by Maria Gardiner, step-aunt of the last Earl of Kilmarnock. On her own initiative she brought spinners and weavers of carpets to Kilmarnock from Dalkeith, then renowned for its woollen products. Under Miss Gardiner's encouragement and enterprise the woollen or carpet trade grew dramatically in the space of a few years. In

1743 a society was formed for establishing a woollen factory. The Town Council provided land at the Greenhead (later Green Street) at low cost and the use of the freestone quarries for building materials. Subsequently the society was given a piece of land for a waulk-mill. The 'society' appears to have been a joint-stock company, for in 1749 the Earl of Glencairn and his eldest son Lord Kilmaurs became partners in the firm. In 1765 Richard Oswald of Auchincruive was enrolled as a director. At that time the company's stock in trade amounted to £6,150. In 1778 this woollen manufacture was taken over by the firm of Wilson, Gregory and Company. The *Glasgow Mercury* carried a brief report on 24th December that year, stating that the firm produced the following articles: 'Blankets of all sizes, in the English and Scotch manner, Dutch and Canada Blankets, Plush, Damask, and all kinds of Scotch Carpets, Narrow Tweeled Cloths of different colours, Horse and Collar cloths fit for saddlers.' The business grew steadily and in the course of the nineteenth century became Gregory, Thomson and Company.

The weaving of silk was introduced in 1770 and grew rapidly. A petition from the magistrates to the Lords of Council and Session in 1776 mentions silk manufacture as then being in a flourishing condition. Loch's *Essays on the Trades and Fisheries of Scotland* (1777) stated that there were 240 silk-looms in Kilmarnock by that date. Strangely, no mention of silk appears in the detailed list of products in the first *Statistical Account* and it may be that competition from France destroyed this particular branch of the textile industry.

In 1777 there were 66 looms employed in the weaving of carpets, 40 in the weaving of linen, 30 for blankets, 30 for serges and shalloons, 20 for duffles and six frames for making stockings. The blankets were made by Robert Thomson and Company from locally procured wool and were said to be equal in every respect to the best produced in England.

About 1770 calico-printing was introduced at Greenholm by John Macfee. By 1790 this was producing

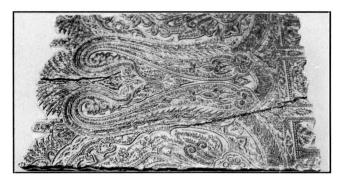
Design block for printing calico shawls

£6,500 per annum. In 1824 William Hall, 'an ingenious and enterprising calico-printer', introduced the manufacture of worsted printed shawls and had his premises at the Greenholm printfield. This enterprise was adopted at a time when muslin weaving was in a very depressed state. Within a very short time it grew enormously. In the space of twelve months (May 1830 to 1st June 1831) no fewer than 1,128,814 shawls were manufactured, the value of which was estimated at about £200,000. A decade later the value of this trade had risen to £230,000. The manufacture of worsted shawls gave employment to 1,200 weavers and about 200 calico-printers.

Messrs T. and J. Ferguson established a factory in 1854 for the weaving of cotton cloth using steam power. The works, situated on the Kilmarnock Water at the foot of West Netherton Street, were considerably expanded in the 1870s and within a decade had upward of 1,100 looms, giving employment to 600 workers, mainly women. Smaller cotton mills were operated in

Matthew Fowlds, Fenwick weaver

Carpet weaving

the latter part of the nineteenth century by A. and W. Douglas (Victoria Mills), James Wylie (Elmslie Mills), Hannah, Gibson and Brown (Mill Road), Laughland, Roxburgh & Co. (Townholm) and John Carnie (West Netherton Street).

In the late eighteenth century carpet-weaving was the mainstay of Kilmarnock's economy. In 1790 this produced a revenue of £21,400, the largest single source of the burgh's wealth and about a quarter of the total revenue from industry. Fifty years later it had been overshadowed by the worsted industry, but the yield had risen to £150,000 and carpet-weaving gave

Jacquard hand loom weaving

employment to about 1,200 persons. In addition to the more traditional Scottish carpets and rugs, the factories produced carpets of Brussels, Venetian and Turkish patterns. The quality of these carpets was said to be second to none, and in 1831 the Commissioners and Trustees for Manufactures in Scotland awarded Gregory, Thomson a prize of £150, with an additional premium of £30, for four carpets of Turkey fabric. These were the first of their type to be made in Scotland and the judges were particularly impressed by their high quality.

A century later Kilmarnock could still boast a score of textile factories. The number of employees was still around the same figure as in 1840, some 3,500 in all, but the pattern of working had changed beyond recognition. The credit for revolutionising the textile industry goes largely to one man, Thomas Morton. Born at Mauchline in 1783, he was brought to Kilmarnock three years later by his father who was a brickmaker. Even as a child, Thomas showed an inventive turn of mind, making baskets and hot air balloons, and at the age of fifteen he was apprenticed to Bryce Blair, turner and wheelwright. On completion of his apprenticeship he set up business on his own account and invented an ingenious lathe operated by wind-power. He was fascinated by scientific instruments of all kinds and eventually built his own telescope. His observatory in Morton Place became one of the major landmarks of the town. The more humdrum daily business included the repair of handlooms and Thomas soon realised that these were not as efficient as they might be. He gave a lot of thought to improving them but without success at first. Early in the 1800s he was asked by the proprietor of Fairlie House, Dundonald to repair a barrel organ. It occurred to him that the mechanism of this organ might be adapted to the loom but the solution to the problem eluded him for some time. Then one night the answer came to him in a dream. He awoke with the concept so clear in his mind that he grabbed a pencil and sketched the idea on the wallpaper before it slipped from his mind. Soon afterwards he built a barrel loom or carpet machine which was an immediate success as it required less labour and operated much faster than the traditional loom. Fearing that rival manufacturers would steal or adapt his idea (in the days before patent rights were secure), he negotiated with the Kilmarnock weavers to buy only from him, and in return he undertook not to sell barrel looms outside the burgh. This gave Morton a virtual monopoly of loom production and forced his competitors out of business, or at least to diversify into other areas. In 1808 the Board of Trade recognised Morton's achievement by awarding him a prize of £20.

Soon afterwards, however, Jacquard looms came into the country. These looms, controlled by punched cards, had a considerable impact on weaving of all kinds, from silk ribbons to carpets. Morton was quick to see the advantages of the punched card system and soon adapted it to his own looms. Later he invented a machine for weaving three-ply carpets which gave Kilmarnock the lead in this field. By 1825 the number of carpet weavers in the burgh had risen to 800 and the number rose by 50 per cent in the ensuing decade alone. This revolution was not achieved without social upheaval of far-reaching consequences. Textile workers were unused to automatic machinery, and many who had been accustomed to labour in their own homes refused employment in the new mills, owing to their dislike of the factory system and the long hours of toil which it entailed. Mercifully, Kilmarnock was spared the rioting and bloodshed of the Luddites or machine-wreckers which marred industrial relations in the textile districts of England between 1811 and 1816. In Kilmarnock Thomas Morton's achievements were recognised by a testimonial banquet in 1826, at which he was presented with a massive silver bowl. In 1835 he was elected to the Royal Scottish Society of Arts. On

Morton's Tower

the Valley could boast 250 lace curtain looms, employing up to 8,000 hands. By the start of the present century Alexander Morton and Co. Ltd had developed into one of Britain's largest manufacturers of soft furnishings including; lace, madras, chenille, taffetas, dresses and shirtings. The company also produced carpets in Carlisle and hand-tufted carpets in Donegal and Galway. In the years after the Second World War the company suffered several severe setbacks and eventually went into liquidation before reforming as Alexander Morton (Darvel) Ltd. in 1990.

Of Alexander's sons, James (1867-1943) left the district early to manage a family factory in Carlisle, but he later invented synthetic dyestuffs which earned him a knighthood. Gavin Morton (1867-1954), a nephew of Alexander, worked in the family business. In 1908 he invented a carpet power loom and as Alexander Morton and Company were unable to develop it he left the firm and joined forces with William Blackwood at Burnside in Kilmarnock.

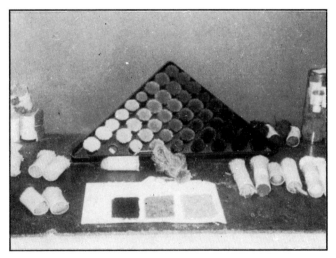

Yarn dyeing colour control

his death in 1862 his observatory and its contents were bequeathed to the town. For many years Morton's tower, popularly known as Killie's Castle (after its tenant, James Kilmurray, an amateur astronomer and weather prophet) was one of the town's best-loved landmarks. Sadly, it was demolished in 1958 to make way for new housing.

Thomas was not related, as far as can be ascertained, with another family called Morton which also had a tremendous impact on the development of various branches of the textile industry. Alexander Morton was born of good Covenanting stock in Darvel in 1844, the son of a handloom weaver. His father died when he was seven but when he was twelve he learned the craft from his mother and by the age of sixteen had scraped together enough money to buy his own loom. At nineteen he was married and eventually had nine children. When he was not operating his loom he was growing vegetables to feed his large family, but his nickname of Pansy San came from his skill in growing pansies which won many prizes in the local flower shows. The death of his wife's brother, who acted as agent for Glasgow middlemen, forced Alexander to take on the work of selling cloth on his own account. This led him into the business of selling, first to the 'manufacturers' (in reality middle-men) and later direct to the retailers. Eventually he was selling the cloth of the local weavers as far afield as Bath, Bristol and London. With the development of power lace-weaving looms in England Morton realized that the handloom weaving of the Irvine Valley would be hard hit. He formed the family firm of Alexander Morton & Company in 1874 and raised the initial deposit of £100 to secure delivery of a lace machine. After many setbacks the machine, initially driven by water-power and then by steam, started production in February 1876. From then on there was no looking back. Other firms soon followed suit and by the turn of the century

The Blackwood family had been bonnetmakers from 1625 till the 1750s, then cotton-spinners, worsted spinners, wool-spinners and in 1847 James Blackwood and his father set up as carpet manufacturers in Townhead mill. In 1860 James took his brother Robert into the business, the new company being Blackwood Brothers and Co. On the other hand, Hugh Wilson began in 1820 as a carpet manufacturer, later turning to worsted spinning and becoming a carpet yarn spinning company by the end of the century. The company remained in the hands of the same family for over 150 years. Incidentally Wilson's wife and Johnnie Walker's daughter-in-law were sisters. Wilson had a thriving export trade in ingrain carpets to the USA, wrapping a bottle of Walker's best whisky inside each carpet as a present to the buyer. Thus the demand for Wilson's carpets rose and Americans acquired a taste for Johnnie Walker!

Hugh Wilson's second son John set up business at

Burnside Works in the 1850s weaving Scotch carpets on hand looms. He sold his business in 1879 to James and Robert Blackwood but the brothers dissolved their partnership in 1882. James carried on at Townhead as Blackwood Brothers & Company, specializing in the production of high-quality woollen yarns for the carpet industry. In 1960 the dye-house of Blackwood Brothers moved from the High Street to more spacious premises on Western Road. The company became part of the Dawson Group in 1968 and six years later transferred its entire operations to purpose-built premises on Western Road. Since then the firm has expanded not only in Kilmarnock but in new factories at Kilwinning and Cumnock which today employ over 750 people. Today Blackwood Brothers are recognized worldwide as a market leader in fine carpet yarns and won the Queen's Award in 1983 and 1988. BMK are one of their biggest customers, and today yarn produced by Blackwood Brothers is to be found in carpets on the floors of Marks and Spencer's stores and in the lounges aboard the *QE2*.

Robert Blackwood carried on carpet-making at Burnside, trading as R. Blackwood & Sons. In 1908 Robert's son William took Gavin Morton into partnership, in a new company called Blackwood, Morton and Sons Ltd. With its famous logo, BMK has since become synonymous with quality carpets the world over. By 1950 about half of the textile workers in Kilmarnock were employed by this firm alone. In the late 1920s BMK moved to larger premises built on the latest and most scientific principles. The multi-storey, plate glass building became a symbol of Kilmarnock's industrial might. Between 1929 and the outbreak of the Second World War the company's output rose tenfold, and at the peak of production in the immediate postwar period was turning out 5,000 carpets, 12,000 rugs and 20,000 yards of piece goods every week. Continually adapting its products to accommodate changing tastes and fashions, BMK diversified into tufted carpets in 1966, opening its Thistletex works the following year. A slump in demand in the early 1980s forced the company to cut back its workforce, and drove it into receivership; but it was then bought by John Logue who turned the company round. In more recent years it has enjoyed a renewal of prosperity, securing in 1986-7 a number of highly prestigious overseas contracts in the Gulf states, the USA and Korea. Against stiff foreign competition, for example, BMK won the contract to re-carpet the Las Vegas Hilton, proving that BMK's international status is as high as ever. Today BMK carpets may be found in the world's most prestigious hotels, including the Mayfair (London), the Mandarin Hotel (Hong Kong), the Royal York (Toronto), the Intercontinental (Frankfurt), the Barclay (New York) and Scotland's own Gleneagles and Turnberry. Superlative design combined with hard-wearing characteristics have made BMK carpeting especially popular in the great ships of the present day, from P & O's luxury cruise liner *Royal Princess* to Finland's MS *Svea*. Distinctively designed carpets range from those in the Dome, Birmingham, the Hexagon, Reading and Glasgow's magnificent Royal Concert Hall. From the great mosque of Johore to the Emir's Palace in Abu Dhabi BMK carpets are to be found wherever sumptuous quality is prized regardless of cost.

Carpet picking

The General Strike of 1926 was followed by a recession which gradually deepened into the great Depression that dominated the 1930s. In 1933 a difference in policy led to the cautious Gavin Morton becoming sole partner in BMK. William Blackwood (who had urged for a programme of expansion) left the firm and purchased the hosiery company of Douglas Reyburn. He acquired premises in Mill Street, Riverside and started up as a yarn manufacturer, buying in loose wool, dyeing, spinning and finishing the yarn to sell direct to the trade. In the late 1940s the company was taken over by the Stoddard Group of Elderslie. Since then Douglas Reyburn has continued to operate independently, but are the main supplier of yarn to Stoddard who, in turn, are Reyburn's biggest customer. In 1979 Templeton of Glasgow were bought by the Guthrie Group but business continued to slump and in the early 1980s the company was acquired by Stoddard which subsequently traded as Stoddard Templeton. The spinning and dyeing operations of this group were transferred from Glasgow to Kilmarnock and Douglas Reyburn consequently expanded production considerably. At the same time increased mechanization meant that greater output could be achieved with less manpower. In the 1970s 450 people produced 30 tonnes of yarn a week; a decade later the workforce was reduced by two thirds, yet new machinery and more efficient working practices had increased output by 30 per cent.

Douglas Reyburn import wool from all over the world to mix with British wool in order to achieve the texture and colours demanded by their customers. The wool, after being spun into yarn, can either be dyed in bulk to give a uniform shade of yarn for use in producing Wilton (plain) carpets or hank-dyed where smaller quantities are dyed different colours to produce yarn as used for an Axminster (patterned) carpet. Today the bulk of the firm's output goes to Stoddard at Elderslie and Lyle in Cumbernauld, but the company also supplies yarn to other carpet manufacturers all over the world. In the late 1980s new machines, capable of

two and a half times the output for the same manning levels, were introduced. Today Douglas Reyburn boast the most advanced and sophisticated plant and machinery of its kind anywhere in the world with even more sophisticated, electronically controlled machinery now being installed in order to speed up the complex carding, spinning, twisting, reeling, dyeing and winding processes. At the end of the 1980s Stoddard took over the Sekers Group, manufacturers of upholstery and curtains. Today Douglas Reyburn is part of Stoddard Sekers PLC, and has recently negotiated a five-year contract to supply Louis De Poortere, the second largest carpet manufacturer in Europe and ranking ninth in the world. In 1987-91 the company spent over £5,000,000 in capital investment to gear up production to meet the demands of the twenty-first century.

Over the years, the fortunes of the various branches of textile working have waxed and waned. By the 1880s calico, once so important, had dwindled, whereas the manufacture of wincey, a cloth with a cotton or linen warp and a wool weft, very popular at the time in shirts and nighties, was then predominant. Production of knitwear with power looms began about this period and within fifty years a dozen factories were employing some 700 hands. Most of these concerns were quite small, only four of them with more than 50 employees.

Manufacture of the traditional blue 'Kilmarnock bunnet' evolved into the production of tam o' shanters and glengarry bonnets worn by the Scottish regiments. This eventually died out in Kilmarnock but is still carried on in Stewarton by Robert Mackie & Co. (Knitwear) Ltd., who also produce a wide range of traditional and fashion garments and scarves.

Stewarton bonnets

One of Kilmarnock's most prosperous companies owed its origins to an eccentric German professor of anthropology. Dr Gustav Jaeger of Stuttgart Royal Polytechnic had been a semi-invalid most of his life, suffering from chronic chills, piles and obesity. He conceived a phobia about cotton, linen and silk, but preached with messianic fervour the gospel of wool. As an animal fibre, wool alone was compatible with human health and well-being. Jaeger cured himself by

Jaeger Fashion garments

wearing wool and from this he evolved a health system, then a book, and finally a business to sell all things necessary for the woollen lifestyle. He created and then fulfilled the demand. Jaeger's all-wool regime came at the right time; the late-Victorian obsession with health culminated in the International Health Exhibition in London at which Jaeger's rational dress became all the rage. Edwin Chadwick the social reformer, Oscar Wilde and George Bernard Shaw became ardent disciples. Later Nansen, Scott and other polar explorers were to sing the praises of Jaeger woollen long-johns. Dr Jaeger's Sanitary Woollen System Limited may have started out as a faddist operation, but it was to develop into Jaeger's, the world leader in woollen fashions in the 1920s and 1930s; and as woollens and tweeds became elevated to the realms of high fashion the company never looked back. At the present time Jaeger Tailoring leads the field in knitwear production, and employs 442 people in its factory in Bonnyton Industrial Estate.

Unlike the mill towns farther up the valley, Kilmarnock produced little lace, although one firm Flemings Laces Ltd produced lace furnishings from 1881 onwards and later diversified into warp knitting and also hand-printing on a wide range of fabrics. Now, with the weaving and knitting divisions well established four generations on from the founding of the firm, further diversification has recently taken place with the introduction of fibreglass fabric production for the aerospace and automotive industries. This fabric is made by weaving, knitting or needle-felting as special requirements demand. Another speciality of the firm is the manufacture of fish nets for fish farming cages.

Leather Goods

From the earliest times a lucrative sideline of the raising and slaughtering of cattle was the tanning of hides and curing of leather. In the list of products given in the first *Statistical Account* tanned cow, calf and seal skins ranked third, with a net annual value of £9,000. Dressed sheep and lamb skins were listed separately and added a further £6,500 a year. On the other hand, the manufacture of boots and shoes, totalling £21,216, was only slightly less than the carpet business as the

principal moneyspinner, while the manufacture of leather gloves added £3,500. Thus leather, skins and hides, together with finished articles, produced no less a sum than £40,216—almost half the total for *all* industry in the burgh. This was a labour-intensive industry and although no figures are recorded for those employed in the tanneries the numbers must have been relatively small when compared with those working in textiles. The first *Statistical Account*, however, mentioned that the burgh had 56 master shoemakers who employed 408 men.

Fifty years later the manufacture of footwear was still very considerable. About 2,400 pairs of shoes were made each week, and three fourths of them were exported. The annual value of this trade was estimated at £50,000, a substantial increase on the figure quoted for 1790 and the £32,000 estimated in 1831. By 1839 the number of sheep and lamb skins dressed annually had risen to 140,000. There were, at that period, three tanworks, in which the trades of tanning and currying were carried on extensively, producing leather worth £45,000. By 1870 this business had contracted to some extent, although it was still carried on by William Muir and Sons at Ladeside.

Saxone Factory

The man who really put Kilmarnock on the world shoemaking map was George Clark, born at Hamilton in 1757. He served his apprenticeship as a 'souter' before enlisting in the Army. During the American War George served in the Dragoons but took his discharge in 1783. He settled in Kilmarnock and resumed his old trade. In due course his sons Thomas and James joined the family business which prospered to such an extent that by 1831 they were putting out cut uppers for stitching and partial finishing by home-workers, thus founding the tradition of skilled shoemaking which survives in Kilmarnock to this day. In 1840, a happy accident dramatically changed the nature and scope of the business. The second generation of Clarks were on excellent terms with Johnnie Walker the whisky-blender and when the latter found that a ship, loaded with whisky for export to Rio de Janeiro, had some spare cargo space he suggested to James Clark that he put a consignment of boots and shoes in the hold, for sale 'on spec' at Rio. The Brazilians loved the Clark shoes so much that soon James could scarcely cope with the demand, so his nephews George and James (sons of Thomas) were packed off to Rio to establish a retail outlet on the spot. Over the ensuing 60 years the Brazilian end of the operation prospered to such an extent that a network of over 40 shops had been established all over that vast country. From the Amazon to the Rio Grande do Sul Brazilians were shod with Kilmarnock boots. When the Brazilian government tried to stamp out this trade by imposing a crippling import duty Clark's promptly set up a factory which today, as Companha Calcado Clark of Sao Paulo, is the largest shoe manufacturer in Latin America.

The Kilmarnock factory however had to find an alternative market for its produce. In 1903 Clark's had formed an association with Frank and George Abbott of England and in 1908 the two companies merged to form the Saxone Shoe Company. An apocryphal tale has it that the name arose after Kilmarnock thrashed a rival football team 6-1. When one of the firm's directors heard the score he exclaimed 'Sax-one? That's it!' A more plausible explanation is that the firm wished to use the term Saxon which sounded rugged, but was unable to patent it because it was in common use. They got round the problem by tacking an 'e' on to the end. About the same time the firm dreamed up the brand name Sorosis for ladies' footwear, but this name was dropped some years later when it was pointed out that it sounded like the nasty skin ailment psoriasis.

At that time other firms measured the length of the foot, but Saxone introduced the innovation of breadth fitting which soon gave the company the edge over its competitors. Saxone opened retail shops all over the country, supplied by factories in Titchfield Street and Mill Street (Gleneagles) which concentrated on men's and women's footwear respectively. A third factory in West Netherton Street concentrated on repairs. In 1956 in an attempt to protect their position in the market Saxone amalgamated with Lilley & Skinner, who tended to concentrate on ladies footwear, and formed Saxone, Lilley & Skinner (Holdings) Ltd. a trading group with 470 retail outlets.

In 1962 Saxone, Lilley and Skinner acquired from Wolverine of America the UK franchise for Hush Puppies. Jack Abbott, Chairman of Saxone, was convinced of the marketability of these strange new pigskin casual shoes and in the face of stiff opposition decided to go into full production. There followed an unprecedented advertising and sales campaign which resulted in production being extended beyond the two Kilmarnock factories and in shoes needing to be bought in from America to keep up with demand. At the end of 1962 Saxone, Lilley & Skinner became a Division of the British Shoe Corporation, (BSC).

The Gleneagles factory which opened in 1949 has altered very little structurally despite dramatic changes in production methods, a fine testament to practical design. The Titchfield Street factory however was demolished and the site eventually cleared to make

Clicker cutting leather uppers

Saxone's Gleneagles Factory

General view of clicking department

way for the Galleon Leisure Centre. Incidentally, the Cordwainer Lounge is named in allusion to the shoe factory which originally occupied the site.

In 1988 Sear's, the holding company of BSC, decided that the corporation should concentrate on sales and marketing, so the manufacturing facility at Kilmarnock was sold to Burlington International. Burlington had exclusive rights to manufacture products with the names Saxone or Hush Puppies in the UK and sell them at home and overseas. In its heyday Saxone of Kilmarnock had around 2,000 employees and in its provision of sports, leisure and recreational facilities (notably the Clark Memorial Halls and a ten-acre sports ground) it made a major contribution to the amenities of the town.

During the trade recession the group went into receivership. The local factory was acquired from the receivers and from 13th April 1992 recommenced trading as the Kilmarnock Shoe Company Ltd. This company continues to manufacture Hush Puppies at the Gleneagles factory in Mill Street where the 270 employees produce 14,000 pairs of shoes a week. From its origin in Kilmarnock Saxone has become a household name for quality footwear all over the world.

Whisky, Beer, Mineral Waters and Jam

Nowadays Kilmarnock is synonymous with whisky worldwide, thanks to Johnnie Walker. Spirits do not figure at all in the list of products given in the first *Statistical Account*. At that time the favourite tipple was brandy (much of it smuggled from France via the Isle of Man and the south Ayrshire coast) and whisky was not highly regarded at all. In the second *Statistical Account* the trade in 'grocery goods, victuals and liquors' was dismissed in a single line, with the revealing comment that, in 1839, it probably amounted to at least £16,000. It is ironic, therefore, that the product which, more than any other, has put Kilmarnock on the world map, was not mentioned in either of these accounts. William Wallace and Company, distillers' agents and blenders of Highland whiskies, claimed to have been established as far back as 1760 and in their advertising in the 1890s mentioned their century and a quarter's experience in this field. This firm had their offices in Portland Street, but their bonded premises were in Titchfield Street and were erected in the late 1870s. Their blend was named The Real Mackay—not, as has been suggested, in tribute to Provost David Mackay who was latterly the company's principal, but purely because this expression signified the genuine article. A similar misconception has been perpetrated recently by the proprietors of Cutty Sark whisky, their slogan 'The real McCoy' being allegedly derived from a bootlegger named Captain McCoy who successfully ran the Customs blockade and smuggled this brand into the United States during the Prohibition era. Neither story stands up to examination; for the phrase 'the real Mackay' arose from the celebrated and long drawn-out lawsuit of the seventeenth century between rival contenders for chiefship of the clan, and had

'The Real Mackay' whisky jars

passed into common parlance long before William Wallace and Company was founded.

Andrew Thomson was another whisky blender, with premises in King Street. For his brand name he chose, appropriately 'Auld Killie' and following the unveiling of the Burns memorial in the Kay Park in 1879 he promptly registered a vignette of this as his trademark.

In 1820 John Walker set up in business as an Italian warehouseman and wine merchant. Even as late as 1880 Archibald McKay only commented in passing about the spacious building then recently erected (1879) on Strand Street 'belonging to Messrs John Walker & Son, wine merchants, comprising an Excise Duty Free Warehouse, or Bonded Store, and Bottling Warehouse, in which are conducted a large export and home trade in spirits, &c.' The company had moved from its original location near the town centre into premises in Croft Street in 1873, and from there expanded into

. . . . still going strong

neighbouring Strand Street when the bonded warehouse was extended and a bottling plant installed.

Originally whisky was sold as single malts or grain whisky, each recognisable by its distinctive flavour and quality. In the early nineteenth century, however, there developed the practice of blending different whiskies in order to produce a brand of standard flavour. Such blends contained Highland and Lowland malts, a small quantity of Islay and the remainder patent still spirit. This enabled the blenders to purvey a mild-flavoured spirit more cheaply than the single malts. Johnnie Walker based his phenomenal success on this formula, bringing together malts from distilleries all over Scotland and blending them at Kilmarnock to produce this famous brand. Eventually the firm became the sole proprietor of the Cardow (Cardhu) distillery in

Strathspey and Talisker, the only distillery in Skye, but also imported whisky from many other distilleries. Cardhu is sold in its own right in many world markets as a prestigious twelve-year-old single malt. Talisker, of course, produces a highly distinctive whisky which is also sold under its own name.

From the 1840s John Walker recognized the need to export. A London office was opened in 1880 and a decade later an office was established in Sydney. In the space of a century and a half the company has built up a worldwide distribution network which now extends to more than 200 countries. In fact, while most companies boast of the countries to which they export their products, John Walker can claim that there are only three countries in the world where their whisky is not sold. The secret of the phenomenal popularity of Johnnie Walker is superlative quality of course, but also a stroke of genius. In 1908 Alexander Walker, grandson of the founder, came up with the idea of Johnnie Walker, the Regency dandy in top hat and tail-coat with cane and quizzing glass, which was designed by Tom Browne; while Lord Stevenson, later joint managing director, coined the slogan 'Born 1820—still going strong'. The design and the slogan were both patented in 1910. Alexander Walker also changed the company's Kilmarnock Whisky brand and introduced both the now-famous square bottle and the red and black labels which were set aslant. These distinctive innovations, together with a renowned consistency of quality in the blends, ensured Johnnie Walker's international identity. Today the position of Johnnie Walker is unique. Of all the Scotch whiskies (and there are more than 2,000 different brands) one in every five

Strand Street bonded warehouse

will be Johnnie Walker. Red Label, with a 15 per cent share of bottled exports, is by far the largest selling whisky in the world. In the de luxe whisky market, the world's leader is Black Label 12, with a 5 per cent share of the total bottled exports. In 1991 the firm launched its ultra-luxury brand Johnnie Walker Premier,

Whisky cask storage

'Squaring the Johnnie Walker bottle,' a Heath Robinson Cartoon

containing whiskies that have been matured for up to 30 years. John Walker and Sons have received the Queen's Award to Industry for Export Achievement in 1966, 1967, 1970, 1972, 1976 and 1980.

By the 1930s the premises in Croft and Strand Streets were no longer adequate and a larger site, north of the railway station, was acquired. The Second World War intervened and it was not until 1950 that the company was able to move to its present location in Hill Street, completed in 1956. The company later became part of the Distillers Company which, in turn, was taken over by the Guinness group in April 1986, but the Johnnie Walker black and red label whiskies continue to be brand leaders worldwide. In April 1987 Guinness announced a £3.75 million investment programme over the three-year period 1988-90. The

firm currently fills about three million bottles a week and ranks as Kilmarnock's largest employer. With annual sales in excess of £200,000,000, much of this from exports, Johnnie Walker also plays a major role in ensuring Scotland's prosperity. It is arguable that, more than any other company, John Walker has been responsible for Kilmarnock's long-term prosperity and enabled the town to weather the economic upheavals in the wake of retrenchment in textiles and heavy industry.

Beer was brewed in Kilmarnock on a commercial basis at the Richardland Brewery erected in the early years of the nineteenth century on the west bank of the River Irvine at the end of East Netherton Street. It continued until the early twentieth century. At one time there were three small companies producing mineral waters. The oldest of these was Rankin and Borland, a firm of manufacturing chemists established in 1798 which diversified into aerated soft drinks about 1850.

Kilmarnock was also, in the nineteenth and early twentieth centuries, a notable centre of jam-making. Messrs Gilmour and Smith's Glencairn preserve works occupied a large site between Netherton Street and West Shaw Street and produced a wide range of jams, jellies and marmalades. Like Andrew Thomson, this firm appropriated the Burns monument for its

trademark and as a brand name.

Engineering

According to Archibald McKay, the industrial life of Kilmarnock began in 1780 with the erection of a forge on the northern extremity of the Townholm. The first *Statistical Account* (1790) was silent on the matter but the second *Account* was little better, engineering being dismissed in the phrase 'there are extensive manufacturers of machinery', so too much should not be read into this neglect on the part of the reverend compilers. On the map of 1819 the Townholm Foundry is clearly marked. By 1846 it was being run by Archibald Finnie and Company which later had their registered offices in John Finnie Street. Archibald Finnie was prominent in the town's affairs and served on the Council for many years, becoming provost in 1879 in nice time to preside over the unveiling of the Burns statue in the Kay Park. At the other end of the town was the Holm Foundry of Rodgers and Blair, established in Low Glencairn Street about 1840. Several other small foundries and engineering workshops existed in the same neighbourhood during the first half of the nineteenth century. Farther north, George Caldwell had an engineering shop in the Townholm, first mentioned in the Kilmarnock directory in 1840. It was later taken over by Grant, Ritchie & Co. One of the engineers employed by this firm was James Barr who transferred his services to the Kennedy Water Meter Syndicate in 1854 when this firm set up business on its original site on land almost immediately opposite Caldwell's premises.

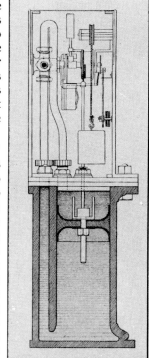

Original drawing of Kennedy positive water meter

Thomas 'Tobermory' Kennedy moved from his native Argyll in 1824 to Kilmarnock where he set up as a watchmaker and jeweller. A crack shot, he later turned to gunmaking and was secretary of the Kilmarnock Rifle Club. In later years he held the appointment as Gunmaker to the Prince Consort, having produced an improvement in rifle construction which was brought to Prince Albert's attention. He was a devout man who taught a Sunday School class and was at one time a leading adherent of the High Church. In 1843, however, when the Church of Scotland split on the issue of patronage, Kennedy and his friends Alexander Bruce and John Cameron left and joined the Free Church (later the United Presbyterian Church) in King

Street. On a Sunday School outing he and his pupils came across a pillar fountain from which water was spouting uncontrolled. 'Damned waste!' was his trenchant comment, and it is believed that his interest in water control was roused by this incident.

Kennedy concentrated his mind on the possibilities of designing a registering water meter, but (like Thomas Morton over the barrel loom) he had a seemingly insoluble problem. In this case it was how to make an accurately

Grandfather clock made by John Cameron, Kilmarnock

registering index. Instead of dreaming up the solution he turned to his co-religionist and fellow clockmaker, John Cameron. Cameron pondered the matter one morning during the Sabbath service and while the Rev. John Symington was preaching the sermon the idea gradually formed in Cameron's head. He began sketching the diagrams for the registering index on the fly-leaf of his Bible and, realising that he had got the answer he was seeking, he suddenly leapt to his feet, ejaculating 'By God! I've got it now!' and like a man possessed he walked out of the church to translate his inspiration more clearly on paper. Kennedy joined forces with Cameron and Sandy Bruce to form the Patent Water Meter Syndicate in 1852. Suitable premises

were found at the Townholm and the company went into production in 1854. The meter, used extensively by water companies, was an instant success and within a few years the company needed larger premises. A site was procured between Low Glencairn Street and the River Irvine. A few yards to the north, the Glenfield Iron Company was founded in 1865 and carried on an extensive business as iron founders and hydraulic engineers. It was logical and inevitable that the two companies, engaged in complementary lines of business, should merge.

Thus, in 1899, the firm of Glenfield and Kennedy came into being and eventually their workshops extended across the river to some further 26 acres,

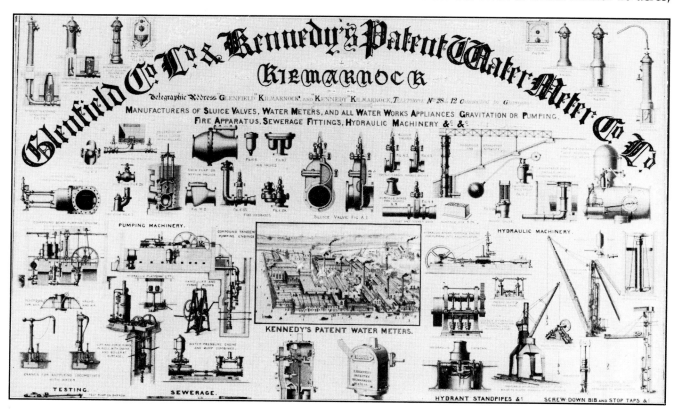

employing 2,400 workers. Glenfield and Kennedy have constructed everything from four-inch water meters to fourteen-foot balanced disc valves for dams and hydro-electric projects—every kind of machinery, in fact, connected to the control and measurement of fluids. They constructed river barrages in Africa and India as well as hydro-electric plants all over Scotland and in their hey-day were the largest firm of hydraulic engineers in the British Commonwealth. In the mid 60s the company was forced into retrenchment. It survived receivership in the late 70s but its premises in Glencairn Street were vacated and demolished, to make way for the Glencairn Industrial Estate, and part of the works also had to be relinquished. Later it survived two American takeovers but, now leaner and healthier, is once more in the forefront of valve technology, trading as Biwater Valves Ltd. Late in 1991 the company secured a contract to supply £700,000 worth of medium-range gate valves to Hong Kong, and a £291,000 order for tanker valve parts. The company, which now has around 230 employees, recently embarked on a £2,650,000 investment programme at their Queen's Drive factory, upgrading their advanced computer systems, valve-testing facilities and fusion bonding paint plant. This includes a million pounds allocated for new product design and a quarter of a million on improving the appearance of the plant's buildings. Some of the old buildings are now being refurbished and brought back into use. Enterprise Ayrshire is contributing to the environmental improvements, and the enhancement of the factory will significantly

Biwater sluice valves

improve one of the main approach routes to the town centre. In a way this ambitious programme and Enterprise Ayrshire's participation in it symbolize the new, more positive attitudes, evidence of Kilmarnock's industrial resurgence to meet the needs of the next century.

Glenfield & Kennedy's Kilmarnock works, 1960

Locomotive makers plate

Steam traction engine pulling loco in North Hamilton Street, 1903.

Andrew Barclay was one of the mechanics whose business as a loom maker and repairer was hard hit by Thomas Morton's monopoly. Forced to turn to other kinds of work he concentrated on steam engines and in 1840 Andrew Barclay and Son formed the Riverbank Engine Works at the southern end of Low Glencairn Street on the banks of the River Irvine. Barclay therefore got in on the ground floor of the great railway boom of the 1840s, building locomotives which were used not only on the mushrooming network of Scotland but were exported to every part of the globe. The secret of Barclay's success lay in flexibility and adaptability, producing locomotives to suit very unusual local conditions. The classic example was the firebox specially designed to burn palm kernels, fitted to a locomotive supplied to Indonesia in 1962 and still going strong. Barclay's coal-, oil- and wood-burning locos are to be found in remote and exotic locations to this day, from the high mountain passes of the Andes to the canefields of Queensland and Fiji. Later reconstituted as Andrew

Scottish Railway, the repair workshops were transferred to Barassie near Troon and the construction of locomotives and waggons at Kilmarnock was abandoned, a severe blow to the town during a period of postwar depression. Subsequently, Andrew Barclay and Company took over the old GSWR site and, at a time when there was little demand for new locomotives, diversified into stationary engines, boilers and pumping machinery.

In 1938 Barclay's sought finance from the Nuffield Trust, which had been set up following the long depression to help companies in designated development areas. The trust agreed to a loan of £35,000 to provide for the re-equipping and expansion of the works. The modern machine tools installed proved their worth throughout the forthcoming war during which Barclay's produced parts for Churchill and Valentine tanks, smoke mortar mountings, special presses for gun recoil gear and winches for barrage balloons in addition to their more usual work.

After the war Barclay's found itself in a very strong position. With modern machine tools and a full works order book Barclay's could choose the work best suited to their production facilities. In the 1950s the firm

Locomotive 'Five Islands' in yard at West Langland Street, 1897.

Barclay and Company, the firm established the very extensive Caledonian Foundry and Engineering Works.

In due course other loco works were established in and around Kilmarnock. The Glasgow and South Western Railway established extensive locomotive and waggon building works and repair shops at Bonnyton in 1859. At the height of activity the GSWR works employed up to 1,200 men. In 1921, however, when the company was absorbed into the London, Midland and

Andrew Barclay steam loco built 1913,
photographed in India in 1978

employed up to 500 workers and underwent a change of emphasis in production. At the start of the 50s Barclay's were producing mainly steam locomotives but by the end of the decade diesels were the norm.

Towards the end of the 60s, largely due to a contraction of the market, locomotive orders were becoming harder to obtain. It became obvious the company would have to further diversify. In August 1972, Andrew Barclay Sons & Co. Ltd., became a member of the Hunslet Group of Companies. Following the take-over Barclay's work load increased greatly and by the end of 1974 the Titchfield Foundry was working to capacity - sub contract, general engineering and fabrication work also increased and in addition to locomotives and winding engine braking equipment they also produced sack sewing machines and paper baling machines to name but two new products.

A downturn in business at the beginning of the 1980s led to a restructuring of the company which led to a new management team. On 5th January 1983 the firm diversified into the production of shipbuilding and heavy plate-working machine tools through the acquisition of Hugh Smith & Co. Established in 1875 this firm produced machine tools which can be found in shipyards all over the world. A new company, Hugh Smith (Engineering) Ltd., was registered (wholly owned by Andrew Barclay Sons & Co. Ltd.,) and the work transferred from Glasgow to Kilmarnock along with many of the highly specialised work force.

Telfos Holdings plc took over Barclay's holding company in September 1987, and in January 1989 a corporate decision resulted in the change of the companies name to Hunslet-Barclay, Ltd. Today Hunslet-Barclay is Scotland's only railway manufacturing business and has benefited greatly from the additional resources placed at its disposal by the parent company. As well as building locomotives Barclay's have in recent years won major contracts to refurbish railcars for British Rail and have diversified into the provision of locomotives, trained drivers and maintenance contracts. Recent major contracts to supply braking equipment and convert existing rolling stock have helped secure the future for Hunslet-Barclay, Ltd., and should ensure the continued association of the name Barclay with heavy engineering into the 21st century.

In the nineteenth century there were also important engineering concerns located in the vicinity of North Hamilton Street, principally involved in the manufacture of mining and pumping engines. The Vulcan Foundry and Engineering Works of Messrs Thomas McCulloch and Sons and the Britannia Engine Works of Allan Andrews and Company, the Portland Forge and the Titchfield Foundry were all on a compact site between the railway line and West Langlands Street. The Britannia Works were taken over in 1885 by Dick, Kerr and Company who specialised in the construction of tramways and light railway systems for collieries. South of Finnie's works (later renamed the Kilmarnock Foundry), was the Kilmarnock Forge and the Townholm Engine Works of Messrs Grant, Ritchie and Company, founded in 1859. McKerrow's factory in Beansburn produced agricultural machinery used in farms all over the British Isles and even farther afield.

The engineering industry of Kilmarnock has fluctuated over the years. Several engineering works, including the Britannia Works and Grant Ritchie, were forced out of business during the great depression of the 1930s. After the Second World War, however, a concentrated effort was made to attract new industry to the area and an industrial estate was created at Moorfield on the western outskirts of the town. This became the location of a subsidiary of Serck Radiators Ltd, making tractor radiators, and, in 1949, Massey Harris, a Canadian company specialising in the manufacture of tractors and combine harvesters. At the height of operations this firm (later known as Massey Ferguson) employed about 800 workers. Demand dropped sharply in the late 1970s and, after thirty years in Kilmarnock, Massey Ferguson closed down operations in February 1980 with the loss of 1,500

Hunslet Barclay Class 143 Units in service

Massey Harris MH744 Tractor made in Kilmarnock

jobs. The company then transferred its European operations to Marquette in France. As a sop to the town, however, Massey Ferguson founded Moorfield Manufacturing which created 200 new jobs. This venture provided facilities for a whole range of industrial machinery which had not been previously available anywhere in Scotland. The closure of Massey Ferguson came at a bad time for Kilmarnock as Monsanto Nylons in Cunninghame District had shut down the previous year and as a result many workers from Kilmarnock became unemployed. Sad to relate, Moorfield Manufacturing became a victim of the 1991 recession and went into liquidation on 29th October that year.

they produce metal bearings for the automotive industry. The workforce, numbering more than 1,000 at its height, acted through works committees and councils in determining factory conditions. Many of the welfare services, such as life assurance and non-contributory sickness benefits, which are now more or less taken for granted, were provided to the Glacier workforce from the outset. This firm was hard hit at the outset of the recession of 1990 and was forced to make a number of redundancies.

Also located in Riccarton is Barr, Thomson and Company, established by James Barr in West Netherton Street, Kilmarnock in 1884. On Barr's death in 1897 his trustees brought in Robert Thomson to manage the business. A limited company was then formed under the chairmanship of John Barr and thus Barr Thomson came into being. In 1900 the company moved to a larger site in Riccarton and employed 300 men in the production of cast iron and pressed steel components for pressure vessels and pipe bends. The dies for these processes were manufactured nearby at the Holm Foundry. The company weathered the recession of the Twenties, but was hard hit by the Depression which began in 1931. As if these difficulties were not enough, Barr Thomson were inundated by the floods at the end of 1932. Somehow the firm managed to overcome these problems, trade picked up in 1935 and the need for war production provided an added stimulus. In 1942 the company began manufacturing fabricated valves for the Admiralty. The development of welded fittings during the war also stood the firm in good stead in the postwar era when it was well placed to cope with

Glacier Metal Co. Ltd. No.3 Factory, Kilmarnock

In 1942 an English light engineering firm called Glacier Metal moved from Wembley because of air raids, and established temporary factories in Ayr and Kilmarnock. After the war, with generous assistance from the Board of Trade, the firm remained in Kilmarnock and in 1947 moved to a new location in Riccarton, on the site of the former Kirkstyle Pit, where

Glacier Metal Co. tool room

Hydrostatic testing at Barr Thomson Ltd.

the boom in the North Sea oil industry. In the 1950s the company had a workforce of 250. In 1965 Barr Thomson was acquired by Bonney Forge International, a subsidiary of Gulf & Western Industries of America. Ayrshire operations were rationalised by the development of the Bonney Forge facilities in Irvine. When these closed in 1983, Barr Thomson was sold to M & M Industries who acquired the exclusive licence to manufacture proprietory Bonney Forge 'Olet' pipe fittings in addition to the Barr Thomson heavy forging operations. Today Barr Thomson has 80 employees and manufacture a wide range of pipeline flanges and forgings for the oil, gas and petro-chemical industry.

Mining

Early records and contemporary accounts yield little about the coal industry, although by the early eighteenth century coal was being worked by hand in the vicinity of Dean Castle. The Rev. John Robertson (1790) stated, 'Coal, so necessary in almost every branch of manufacture, is found close to it in vast abundance, and may be had easier and cheaper than in any other town in the neighbourhood.' He elaborated on this elsewhere in his account:

There is an extensive and profitable coal work in the parish, about half a mile to the south west of the town. The mines are rich and abundant, affording coal of different qualities, some fit for export, and some for home consumption. The species that is raised for exportation is known in this country by the name of Blind-coal. It is of a fine quality, and much esteemed.

Kirkstyle Pit, Kilmarnock

In 1789 3,289 tons of coal had been exported at 9s a ton, yielding a revenue of £1,390 1s 6d. This immense quantity was carried overland to Irvine and thence exported to various parts of Ireland and the west Highlands. The coal burned locally was called seeing-coal, because it produced a flame bright enough to provide some illumination. Some 52,143 loads were sold annually at sevenpence a load, producing a revenue of £1,520 18s 3d. Thus coal of both kinds produced a yield of almost £3,000 per annum. Coalmining and its transportation to the coast gave employment to about 120 people.

Tantalisingly, Archibald McKay tells us little of mid-nineteenth century development in the industry, confining his remarks to observing that the prosperity of Kilmarnock was promoted by the numerous coal-works in the neighbourhood. 'So extensive, indeed, is

'The Collier' from *Etchings of Workers or Waning Crafts* by Robert Bryden

the coal trade now carried on, that clusters of miners' cottages, like so many little hamlets, appear in all directions round the town.' Characteristically he then devoted seventeen lines to the two churches erected for the benefit of the miners in Crookedholm and the 'munificent liberality' of John Galloway of Barleith and Dollars Collieries in providing a Working Man's Institute (*sic*) for the working-classes of Hurlford and neighbourhood, and the similar edifice erected by Mr Galloway in New Street, Riccarton.

We believe both of these Institutes are largely taken advantage of by the classes for whose benefit they were built; while their erection evinces on Mr Galloway's part a praiseworthy desire to improve the intellectual and moral condition of the industrial classes.

This epitomises so well the patronising attitudes of the high Victorian period, attitudes that survived in many quarters as late as the Second World War.

In a footnote, however, McKay expressed the belief that one of the first coal-works in the locality was near Dean Castle, an inference from a minute in the Town's Books dated 15th June 1736: 'The town gives £30 sterling to aid the coal-work at Dean, on the same terms as the other subscribers, in consideration that it will be of great benefit to the town.' Given the nature of the coal deposits in the parish, however, it is likely that outcrops would have been worked centuries earlier. There is also a record, cited by Dr John Strawhorn in his history of Irvine, of 20 tons of coal being shipped from that port in 1542, which points to coal being worked in the area, not just for domestic consumption, but for export, as early as the sixteenth century at least. There is also a record of mining being actively conducted in the barony of Caprington, two miles south-west of Kilmarnock, in 1665.

Miner's helmet with acetylene lamp and Davy lamp

Industrial archaeology has only received the attention it deserves in fairly recent years. Previously evidence of old mineworkings was regarded as a curiosity of no more than passing interest. Following the flood of 1852 the shaft of an old coal pit was discovered in the bed of the Kilmarnock Water at the back of the Townholm Foundry. The shaft was of circular form and lined with masonry. A footnote in McKay adds,

Considerable surprise was created by its appearance in such a situation, where no work of the kind could be wrought with safety. There is an old tradition, however, which the discovery seems to confirm, that the water at one time ran in a different direction, namely, to the east of the Foundry; and the probability is, that the pit would be sunk at that period.

McKay adds that some time in the middle of the eighteenth century, while eight or nine men were employed in a pit at Townholm in the same locality, water burst suddenly upon them from an 'old waste', and only one miner escaped with his life. During excavations in March 1863 an old mine-working was discovered at Townholm and in this were found several skeletons and antique picks and shovels, thus confirming the story of the mining disaster of a century previously.

Kilmarnock, in fact, stands on the Barren Red Coal Measures which had seams up to 40 feet (12m) thick. The strata are folded and formed a basin with its deepest part near the site of the old power station. North and south of this basin numerous seams came to the surface and provided the farming community with easy access to coal which they simply hewed out of the ground. Coal was worked on a desultory basis to provide domestic fuel until the late eighteenth century but with the advent of the Industrial Revolution it assumed commercial importance. The Caprington pits were the first to be worked on a large scale, followed, at the beginning of the nineteenth century, by pits at Kirkstyle (Riccarton), the Nursery and Wellington Pits (Crookedholm) and, to the north-west of Kilmarnock, the Annanhill and Grange Pits, the Bonnyton Pit and the Hillhead Pit. The proximity of coal from the Wellington Pit encouraged the development of the ironworks at Hurlford, exploiting the ironstone deposits of the locality; and indirectly stimulated the growth of iron smelting at the many foundries in and around Kilmarnock in the same period.

The easiest parts of the coalfield were soon worked out, leaving awkward and faulty seams interrupted by whinstone dykes which the early miners, with their primitive resources, ignored. When more modern techniques were applied these workings proved to be not worth exploiting, especially as, by that time, the town itself had expanded considerably in all directions, making large-scale mining impracticable. Water passing from the shallower workings to the lower levels proved an enormous problem, and entailed considerable expense in pumping. This, as much as the encroachment of the built-up areas, led to local mining being abandoned in the 1930s. The extraction of coal over a period of 150 years, however, left a honeycomb of shafts and passages under the town which inevitably filled with water. Strawhorn (1951) commented that 'a considerable part of Kilmarnock is now, as it were, floating on water. This water has its outlets to the surface and is under a constant pressure which if disturbed might cause much damage to surface property.' In 1950 the National Coal Board began prospecting for coal at the Mount, which led to hopes that mining would be revived in the vicinity of Kilmarnock; but this did not lead to any tangible results.

Pottery and brickworks

From the original name Clay Mugs given to Grange Street, it is believed that this was the site of a pottery in the seventeenth and eighteenth centuries producing

Kay Park lion

domestic hollow-wares. An extensive belt of fireclay from Saltcoats to Hurlford runs across the north and west of Kilmarnock and this was inevitably worked as an adjunct to the coalmining in the area, providing the bricks for the colliery workings and miners' rows. In addition, however, the introduction in 1820 of tile drainage as a means of

Kilmarnock personalised pottery

improving the land led to the development of tileworks by the Duke of Portland within the parish and this was yielding upwards of 800,000 tiles a year by 1840. A further half million tiles were produced at Moorfield in the immediate vicinity of the town. Somewhat later, a large brickworks was established at Hillhead north of Kilmarnock and provided the bricks and tiles used in the rapid development of the town in the late nineteenth and early twentieth centuries.

A. & J. Craig operated this works as well as others including one at the Dean, adjacent to Dean Quarry. In addition to bricks, tiles and drain pipes they produced a wide range of special products including chimney pots, glazed bricks, and human and animal figures. Several lions made by them can still be seen in Kilmarnock, for example in the Kay Park, and at Dean Castle. They also made the white glazed bricks used for the 'chinae buildings' in North Hamilton Street. A

Craig's works at Dean Quarry, 1859

tileworks was established at Gargieston west of the town on the Troon road and continued to produce agricultural drainage tiles. From the late-nineteenth century till the 1970s the Southhook Pottery in Bonnyton employed up to 500 workers in the production of tiles, bricks, hollow wares and architectural faience or majolica. A speciality of this company was glazed white bricks used extensively in public lavatories. At one time Messrs Shanks of Barrhead had a factory at Longpark north of the town where about 300 employees produced wash-basins, toilet bowls, bathroom fittings and other sanitary wares, but this closed some years ago.

Dairy Products

As the centre of an agricultural district, Kilmarnock has long been renowned for its dairy products and until the 20th century the largest annual cheese show in Scotland was held here. In April 1888 John Wallace Ltd was founded at Rowallan Creamery in

Rowallan Creamery from the air

Research laboratory at Rowallan Creamery

Glasgow Road, now the oldest margarine factory in Britain to stand on its original site. Prior to 1923 Rowallan also dealt with the full range of dairy products, but as a result of the great increase in demand for margarine during the First World War the company decided to concentrate on the production of this substitute for butter. In 1953 Rowallan amalgamated with a Glasgow shortening manufacturer and the product range was increased. A national salesforce was set up and distribution extended nationwide. After de-control in 1954 there were rapid developments in flavour and texture, leading in the 1960s to the launch of soft margarine in tubs.

In 1961 Rowallan was taken over by Associated British Foods which had been founded in 1935 by Garfield Weston. ABF had by that time become the largest baker in the world, and one of the largest grocers in the UK; under its aegis Rowallan expanded rapidly, handling the production of all fats and margarines for the group. Since the launch of Banquet Margarine in the early 1970s Rowallan's growth in the domestic market has been impressive; by the end of the 70s Rowallan had become established as one of the principal suppliers of own-label margarines for supermarket chains. The health boom of the 1980s, highlighting the dangers of cholesterol in animal fats, led to the launch of Sunflower Margarine in 1982. Healthy living and changes in diet also resulted in a dramatic upsurge in the sales of low fat spreads. In this field Rowallan are one of the market leaders. In November 1990 Rowallan took over Anglia's bakery fats operation and moved all production to Kilmarnock. Rowallan's range has now been augmented by Hedlex and Marmex shortenings, Sweetex high-ratio shortening, Suncup cake and short pastry margarines (complementing Rowallan's existing Kingcup and Queencup range) and Crisbak pastry margarine.

In 1991 the research bakery and laboratory were both re-furbished and re-equipped to ensure that Rowallan will keep in the fore-front of future developments in this industry.

Paper and Print

Coarse-paper manufacturing was at one time an important industry in Galston, but the bulk of the paper used in printing was imported from other parts of Scotland, notably Glasgow and the Edinburgh area. The first wooden printing press was imported into Kilmarnock in the mid-eighteenth century by a Mr McArthur and was allegedly the first in the county. About 1780 he was succeeded by John Wilson whose lasting fame is almost entirely due to his production of the first edition of the poems of Robert Burns in 1786, discussed more fully in Chapter 11. Wilson was a native of the town and had his bookshop in one of the buildings which stood where Portland Street opened into the Cross. The printing works occupied the attics of the tenement on the left of the Star Inn Close as entered from Waterloo Street. Wilson removed to Ayr in 1803 where he launched the *Ayr Advertiser*, the first newspaper in the county, and it was not till 1831 that printing was revived in the burgh. James Paterson launched the *Kilmarnock Chronicle* in January that year and though this newspaper was short-lived its legacy was the iron Columbian printing press which eventually passed into the hands of the Smith Brothers. This firm, founded in 1819, began life as a manufacturer of blocks

for the calico-printing trade, and in the twentieth century was Kilmarnock's leading printer of quality, and early in the field of colour printing. In 1974 the company became part of the MacFarlane Group (Clansman) PLC and in 1991 the Kilmarnock plant became the print manufacturing headquarters of the Group, other subsidiary companies being then transferred to Kilmarnock. After a settling in period it was decided to close down the litho printing division of the company and concentrate on producing printed self-adhesive labels. Today the company trades as N.S. MacFarlane & Co. Ltd.

John Ritchie, a devout member of the Christian Brethren, founded his business in 1880. He started by printing and publishing religious tracts and booklets. The business grew to include books and magazines,

One of John Ritchie's ranges of Christian literature

and the name of Ritchie became synonymous with sound Christian literature around the world. Although John Ritchie Ltd are no longer printers, they are a major publisher and distributor of Christian books, magazines and tracts, operating out of their premises in Beansburn.

A son of John Ritchie, also called John, broke away from the family business and started his own company called Ritchie's Paper Products. This firm grew to be a major supplier of packaging and was acquired in 1952 by the Saxone Shoe Company who were one their major customers. This firm was taken over successively by the British Shoe Corporation and then Sears Group plc before becoming (in May 1987) the subject of a management buy-out. Ritchie UK has operated as an

Premises which formerly housed 'The Kilmarnock Standard' printing works

Ritchie (UK) Ltd

independent company ever since, specialising in business forms and technical publications.

The *Kilmarnock Standard* was founded by Thomas Stevenson in 1863 and did all kinds of printing work besides newspapers. A Columbian hand-press was acquired and installed in a room-and-kitchen at the corner of Portland and Cheapside Streets. At first only two of the four pages of each issue were actually printed there, the other two coming from Glasgow. Within ten weeks, however, circulation had risen to 2,000 copies and it became necessary to acquire a larger and faster press. This, too, was hand-operated but several years

Architectural feature of Kilmarnock Standard building

later a new press powered by steam was installed by Hugh Dunn and Hugh Smellie, young engineers who later rose to eminence with Caprington and Auchlochan Collieries and the Glasgow and South Western Railway Company respectively. By 1865 the printing works moved to larger premises in Croft Street, but in 1891 a building specially designed for the purpose was erected on a triangular site on Grange Place. It is believed that this was the first custom-built printing works ever erected in Scotland. The red sandstone building, with its sculpted heads of Johan Gutenberg and William Caxton on the façade, is one of the prominent landmarks of Kilmarnock to this day. Under the ownership of Messrs Dunlop and Drennan, this printing works expanded into all forms of jobbing work as well as book and magazine production. Hand typesetting gave way to linotype, monotype and intertype machines in the 1890s. In 1912 a

Goss rotary press, one of the first to be used in provincial printing, was installed, along with a stereotyping plant for making illustration blocks. This replaced the traditional method of line illustration using wooden blocks engraved by hand. In 1931 the company joined forces with others to form Scottish Provincial Associated Newspapers. After the Second World War, however, it was acquired by George Outram of Glasgow and eventually became part of the Scottish and Universal Newspapers Group which transferred printing operations to their new premises on Irvine Southmoor.

The other principal publisher in Kilmarnock and Loudoun District is Alloway Publishing. Alloway, the publishing imprint of Walker & Connell Ltd, colour and commercial printers of Darvel, is now known world-wide in connection with the definitive editions of the Works and Letters of Robert Burns and many other titles associated with Scotland's National Bard, as well as a general range of mainly Scottish books.

Industrial Regeneration

The loss or shrinkage in the traditional industries of Kilmarnock and district, so much of a problem in recent years, is no new phenomenon. Kilmarnock was hit hard by the Depression of the 1930s and made a determined effort to counterbalance this. In 1934 the Town Council, in co-operation with the local industries, organised the 'Come to Kilmarnock' campaign, the highlight of which was a week-long programme of exhibitions, open-days and other events designed to show the world the range of products manufactured in the town. A Fair of Industry was

A collection of Burns titles by Alloway Publishing

organised in the Grand Hall and opened by Sir Alexander Walker of the whisky firm. There was even a Pageant of Ayrshire, with a re-enactment of Covenanting times. Even the Brownies and the Life Boys were pressed into service to make this procession as spectacular as possible. A cricket match, open-air concert, alfresco dancing, school sports, needlework exhibition and sculpture exhibition were among the varied events designed to tempt would-be industrialists and buyers to the town. It is difficult to say how effective this programme was, but within a year or two business began to pick up anyway, and as the Second World War approached Kilmarnock again enjoyed an industrial boom and full employment.

The loss of Monsanto Nylons and Massey Ferguson in 1979-80 and severe cutbacks in other industrial concerns hit Kilmarnock hard. Even John Walker, the one company which was 'still going strong', was forced to introduce a three-day week in April 1983. Mercifully this was of short duration and full-time working resumed six weeks later. Nevertheless, it was a dire warning that a more positive approach was needed to halt further decline, a position underlined in June that year when Moorfield Manufacturing made 81 employees (40 per cent of the workforce) redundant. In that year, therefore, Kilmarnock Venture was established by local and national authorities acting in partnership with the business community with the aim of creating 1,000 new jobs over a three-year period. By the time the project was completed in 1986 it had achieved its aims, by helping new firms to get started as well as assisting existing companies to expand. Its staff were then enrolled in the next stage of revitalising the local economy, in the Kilmarnock Venture Enterprise Trust. The Business Development Unit succeeded in helping to establish some 200 new companies within Kilmarnock and Loudoun District. The Unit recognised the need for low-cost premises for starter-firms and renovated derelict buildings in the inner-urban area. Typical of this was the Netherton Business Centre created in a dilapidated building which had once been a part of Saxone's old Netherton factory, and offering accommodation to twelve new companies and in the process providing 100 new jobs. Strathclyde Regional Council created an industrial estate at Bentinck Street, while the Scottish Development Agency developed the Glencairn Industrial Estate on the site of the old Glenfield offices, offering a full range of units from 1,000 to 10,000 square feet. Elsewhere in the District the SDA built a small development at Barrmill Road in Galston and units in Darvel, both of which will help local firms to expand and prosper.

The Kilmarnock Venture Enterprise Trust also compiled its Industrial Index which revealed that about 180 firms were operating within the town itself in 1988. Some 45 of these companies operated in the nine small industrial estates which have been established on the periphery of the town by Kilmarnock and Loudoun District Council acting in co-operation with bodies such as Strathclyde Regional Council and the former Scottish Development Agency. British Coal did its bit to create jobs to replace those lost in the run-down of the mining industry. To this end British Coal Enterprise was set up and by 1986 had created 1,850 new jobs, helping many ex-miner to re-train or set up their own businesses. Many of the new firms of the late 1980s and early 1990s are carrying on in the traditional branches of textiles or engineering; but others are exploring new fields, Proven Engineering of Moorfield, for example, specialises in micro-computer applications, robotics and wind turbines, while Detection Instruments of Bonnyton produce fire and gas detection and protection systems for marine and off-shore use, and Ayrshire Vending Services provided both the equipment and the ingredients for automatic snacks, from coffee and soup to full canteen facilities. Of the 45 firms located in the industrial estates, 23 had up to ten employees, nine up to 25, four up to 50, six up to 100 and two up to 150.

Outside the burgh, but located within Kilmarnock and Loudoun District, there have been some encouraging developments. The largest employer in Newmilns is Vesuvius UK (originally Vesuvius Crucible Company, now a member of the Cookson Group of companies) which makes specialised ceramics for the steel industry and crucibles for foundry applications. The conferment of the Queen's Award to Industry twice to Vesuvius UK indicates the high quality of workmanship to be found in Newmilns. The textile firm of Haddow, Aird and Crerar, Ltd. illustrates the vicissitudes of modern industry. It, too, won the Queen's Award, before going into receivership in 1990, though happily it has now been revived by new owners.

This account of the industry of Kilmarnock and District began with reference to the export, three centuries ago, of cowls, bonnets and serge to Holland where they found particular favour with the Dutch seamen. The wheel came full circle in April 1983 when the Loudoun Valley Manufacturing Company inaugurated its textile factory in Darvel. Today they are one of the largest producers of Arab head-dress and yashmaks, exported by the million to every part of the Moslem world.

Formed in 1991, Enterprise Ayrshire is a local enterprise company providing a comprehensive range of economic development assistance to local industry and commerce.

6 TRADE AND COMMERCE

At the time of the third *Statistical Account* in 1951, Kilmarnock provided employment for about 20,000. Engineering with 4,000 topped the list, followed by textiles (3,500) and other manufacturing industries, such as leather goods, footwear and ceramics, 3,500. About 1,500 were employed in building and allied trades and, somewhat surprisingly, a similar number found work in various branches of transport, dealt with in Chapter 9. The 1950 directory showed that in the town there were 12 builders, 21 contractors, 21 joiners, 21 electricians, 22 plumbers and slaters, 15 painters, 6 plasterers and 7 architects. Businesses in this category employed about 1,500 in all. Even in 1952, however, Kilmarnock had an unemployment rate of 3.6 per cent, compared with the national average of 1.6 per cent. By 1977 it had risen to 9 per cent and was at around the same level in 1991, slightly above the national average; but in the intervening years it had fluctuated on a number of occasions and peaked at 19 per cent in 1987. Over the past two decades the trend has been away from the traditional manufacturing industries, but by and large the service occupations have remained remarkably buoyant.

Shops

In 1950 over 3,000 were employed in a wide variety of shops and distributive trades. As a market town serving a wide agricultural community, Kilmarnock traditionally flourished as the place where people from the surrounding countryside would have come to buy clothing and footwear, furniture and furnishings, farming implements, saddlery and luxury goods of all kinds. They would also visit the pubs and alehouses, take in whatever forms of entertainment were currently on offer and, in turn, would trade their own surplus produce on market days and at the great annual fairs. An engraving of the 1820s has survived which shows some of the shop fronts of that period in King Street. Interestingly, the print shows the Wallace Tavern operated by William Stevenson—one of more than a hundred licensed premises in the town. Next door stood the imposing three-storey premises of Hugh Craig, a prosperous shopkeeper who espoused the cause of parliamentary reform. When the Reform Bill was being debated in 1832 he was one of the principal speakers at the public meetings. Later he went further and took up the cause of Chartism, being elected by his fellow townsmen as their representative to the great National Convention of 1838 which met, like a people's parliament, in London and later in Birmingham. The aims of the Chartists were moderate by present-day standards and all their aims, such as adult suffrage and a secret ballot, have long since been realised; but at the time the government viewed the movement as dangerous and revolutionary. Next to Craig's premises was the grocery shop of John Walker, the whisky blender who, more than anyone else, put Kilmarnock on the world map.

As well as shops with fixed premises, a great deal of the distribution of goods, especially the basic essentials, was conducted by street traders, either operating from the various market stances in and around the Cross or perambulating the streets with horse- or hand-drawn carts. Farmers used small carts with twin barrels known as luggies from which they dispensed sweet or sour milk into pint or half-pint stoups. This system continued well into the present century, in some cases as late as the Second World War, although pasteurisation and mechanisation, bottling and motor transport transformed milk distribution from the 1930s onward. Gradually the farmers moved from direct to indirect distribution, supplying their milk to creameries and dairies which bottled and sold

Sandbed Street in the 1820's, showing the original premises of John Walker (far right).

David Lauder, Ironmongers, Portland Street

healthful beverage of ale or porter, introduced in its stead.

By 1837 the number of licensed premises had risen to about 150, provoking the Rev. Andrew Hamilton to bemoan the fact that 'the evidences of intemperance are here, as elsewhere, in our day unhappily but too manifest.' He did point out, however, that there were 'few public-houses of the more degraded sort, common in larger towns, and the police are extremely vigilant in preventing them from making any undue encroachments upon the Lord's Day.'

On the subject of shops of all descriptions other than licensed premises, the first and second *Statistical Accounts* were mute. Fortunately, various trade directories exist from 1840 onwards which provide a detailed picture of the retail business of the town over the past 150 years.

By the 1950s Kilmarnock boasted almost 1,000 shops, employing about 3,000 men and women. About half of these shops were located continuously along Portland and King Streets, with many of the newer shops extending southwards along Titchfield Street. Many of them were old-established family firms which had been in existence since the late eighteenth or early nineteenth centuries; while others were branches of large nationwide multiple firms. Parallel with the main shopping thoroughfare (which also bore the greater part of the Glasgow-Ayr traffic), was the quieter, broader and generally more sedate John Finnie Street where some of the better quality shops were located. At the other extreme, there was, even then, a far greater number of corner shops—grocers, green-grocers, butchers, bakers, confectioners, newsagents and tobacconists—than there are today.

it to the retail outlets or to the customers. Street trading continued to be an important aspect which, in the prewar period, led to the development of 'The Barras' in the Strand area. When the old bus station in Portland Street was demolished in 1979 the vacant lot was utilised as a street market which continues to operate under the supervision of the District Council.

The first *Statistical Account* (1790) was silent on the matter of shops, with the curious exception of those purveying strong drink. In view of the fact that the compilers were 'men of the cloth' this is hardly surprising. The Rev. James Mackinlay gave the number of inns and alehouses in the town as 50, exclusive of spirit shops (licensed grocers).

These must have a pernicious effect upon the morals of the people; for in proportion as the number of houses of this nature is multiplied, the temptation to intemperance, and the ease and secrecy with which it may be indulged are evidently increased.

What, one wonders, would the good minister make of today's proliferation of wine stores and off-licences and the sale of beers, wines and spirits in supermarkets? He did add, however, that

In justice to the inhabitants of Kilmarnock, it must be observed, notwithstanding the great number of houses of this description, yet that in general they are as sober and industrious as the people of any town of its size in Scotland. Nay, to their praise, it must likewise be observed that the ruinous practice of dram-drinking has of late been, in a great measure, laid aside, and the more salutary and

G. McMurray & Sons Ltd., Portland Street

The Co-operative Movement

Mention has already been made of the pioneering efforts of Fenwick in the development of the co-operative movement. Following the lead of the Rochdale pioneers of 1844, a small group of Kilmarnock workers met at Craufurdland Bridge in August 1860 and resolved to establish the Kilmarnock Equitable Co-operative Society. This combined the qualities of thrift and self-help with the solidarity of the working classes. In an age when there were no welfare services, some form of mutual co-operation was vital.

Original premises of K.E.C.S. in Princes Street, window marked X.

In the early nineteenth century the only thing people could fall back on was their local friendly society. This system developed in the late eighteenth century, although a few societies were much older and one (the Incorporation of Carters in Leith) dated from 1555. They were given some form of regulation by the Friendly Societies' Act of 1793 'for enabling the industrious poor to provide support for themselves in sickness and old age'. By 1839 there were 37 friendly societies in Kilmarnock, several of very recent formation, while others had been in existence for more than twenty years. There were even friendly societies exclusive to females, notably the Kilmarnock Female Benevolent Society which was founded about 1810 to provide for female servants who had become infirm, or who were worn out by age and labour.

The same spirit of self-reliance inspired the Co-operative movement, raising thousands of the 'industrious poor' above the poverty level at which they had struggled all their lives. By combining to purchase goods in bulk the society was able to pass on the saving to its members not only in prices appreciably lower than those of ordinary traders, but also in the form of a dividend, hence the vulgarism 'The mair ye eat, the bigger the divvie'. Even with lower prices and the dividend to customers, the Co-op made a profit which was ploughed back into all kinds of services, ranging from reading rooms, libraries and recreational facilities to housing loans, school and university bursaries and, of course, financial help for those in need. More than anything else, the Co-op destroyed the patronising attitude of the upper classes for it proved that working men and women were just as capable of managing their own business as anyone.

In his preface to *Fifty Years of Co-operation in Kilmarnock* (1910) James Deans took immense pride in the achievement of the Society:

Success forms conclusive proof that the wage-earning classes are not an inferior species of the race but are the equal of any other section of society in their ability to organise, to legislate, and to administer. It would not be easy to name another movement or institution which has done more to make it possible for a working man to brave the blows of circumstance and grapple with his evil star.

The Kilmarnock Equitable Co-operative Society began with thirteen members and a capital of £1 3s 6d. Two evenings a week the premises in Princes Street were open for members to purchase tea, sugar and tobacco. Within a year the Society had to move to larger premises in Cheapside Street. Membership had now risen to 80 and a profit of almost £25 had been made on a turnover of £231. Further progress and expansion necessitated yet another move, in 1863, to more commodious premises in Waterloo Street.

The high hopes of the Co-operative movement were expressed at that time; it would

emancipate labour, abolish strikes, solve the problem of how we, the toilers of this country, may justly profit by our own skill and industry. It aims at elevating men morally, socially, physically, and politically by freeing us from the poverty and wretchedness which chain millions to an animal existence.

The directors closed their third annual statement with a call to the people of Kilmarnock to join the Co-op and 'rejoice together in the dawn of a brighter day for the sons of labour.' This emotive appeal stirred the working classes in a district renowned for its sturdy independence of thought, borne of the Covenant in religion and radicalism in politics. Interestingly, the directors exhorted their own employees to give all their time to the Society, to balance their accounts, to report receipt of inferior goods and not to lounge about! There was, indeed, an almost evangelical fervour about the Co-op in this early period.

Within a decade it had grown so large that it had to open two branches. The library was greatly expanded, a loan society formed, and grocery, drapery and footwear departments were flourishing. In 1879 the Society inaugurated fine new premises in John Finnie Street, hitherto the exclusive preserve of the shops patronised by the well-to-do of Kilmarnock and the surrounding district. This building, on the corner of John Dickie Street, cost £4,164, a considerable sum for the period; but only ten years later it was substantially augmented, the extension costing £18,000. Thirty years after the modest beginning, the Society had thirteen branches throughout the district covering all aspects of retail trade. The membership stood at

2,185 and sales were almost £63,000 a year. At the turn of the century the Co-op moved into luxury goods, opening a jewellery and furniture store. A building department with a loan capital of £10,000 was formed to assist members to buy their own homes. An education committee organised leisure and recreational facilities of all kinds, outings, cookery demonstrations, flower shows and social events. By the time of its jubilee in 1910 the Society had a membership of 7,890 and sales of almost a quarter of a million pounds. Changing patterns of consumption led to the closure of the Co-op premises in Portland and Titchfield Streets. The Co-op premises in Portland Street, the largest building in that street, was subsequently gutted by fire, and contributed to the sad air of neglect in that part of the town. Today the Kilmarnock Society is part of Ayrshire Regional Co-operative Society.

Modern Shopping Facilities

Supermarkets and self-service stores began to make their appearance in the 1960s. This process was greatly accelerated by the inner-town re-development of the 1970s and the creation of pedestrianised areas around the Cross, in King and Portland Streets and the Foregate, with the Kilmarnock Centre and Burns Mall (opened

The Foregate

by Mrs Willie Ross in 1976) as their focal point. By the time this shopping development was completed in 1979 it had cost over £9 millions. The shopping mall occupies a site which at one time included John Wilson's printing shop, a fact acknowledged by a plaque erected on the main concourse. Here, under one roof, may be found many of the town's leading shops, with ready access to the Western SMT bus station and taxi ranks as well as spacious parking facilities nearby. In 1987 Balfour Beatty announced plans to redevelop the upper part of Portland Street and Croft Street as a multi-million pound covered shopping precinct, but four years later no start on this project had been made and the area at the heart of the town remains in a semi-derelict condition. Unfortunately, because of its close proximity to both bus and railway stations, this tends to be the first view of Kilmarnock for some visitors.

Service Industries and Miscellaneous Occupations

In 1950 about 3,000 people were employed in other occupations. The major employers in this field were the electricity works (200), the Ayrshire Laundry (170) and the gasworks (100). The Town Council and its various services employed several hundreds alone, and since the creation of the District and Regional Councils in 1975 this has expanded considerably. Transport, health services, the Post Office, education, entertainment and sports facilities, all of which employ a growing number, are discussed in later chapters. 150 years ago there were relatively few functions of central government which extended to a local level; between them the Post Office, the Stamp Office and the Excise would have given employment in Kilmarnock to no more than a handful of people. Today Kilmarnock has agencies and offices of the Departments of Employment, Health and Social Security, and the Inland Revenue, all of which add substantially to the white-collar workforce.

Banking

It is a reflection of the rapid growth of Kilmarnock in the eighteenth century that in 1770 the town was still not considered important enough for the up-and-coming Ayr Bank of Douglas, Heron and Company to open a branch there. The Ayr Bank was, in fact, the first bank in Scotland to establish branches outside its main centre of operations and in a short space of time had seven branches as far afield as Dumfries and Edinburgh. When the Ayr Bank crashed in 1772 it ruined many of the landowners and businessmen in the south-west of Scotland and precipitated a depression in trade and industry. Such was the resilience of the Scottish economy, however, that recovery came fairly soon afterwards. The Bank of Scotland learned one important lesson from the episode and began opening branches (at Dumfries and Kelso) in 1774. Six years later it had added another four branches, at Ayr, Inverness, Stirling and Kilmarnock.

The Kilmarnock branch of the Bank of Scotland

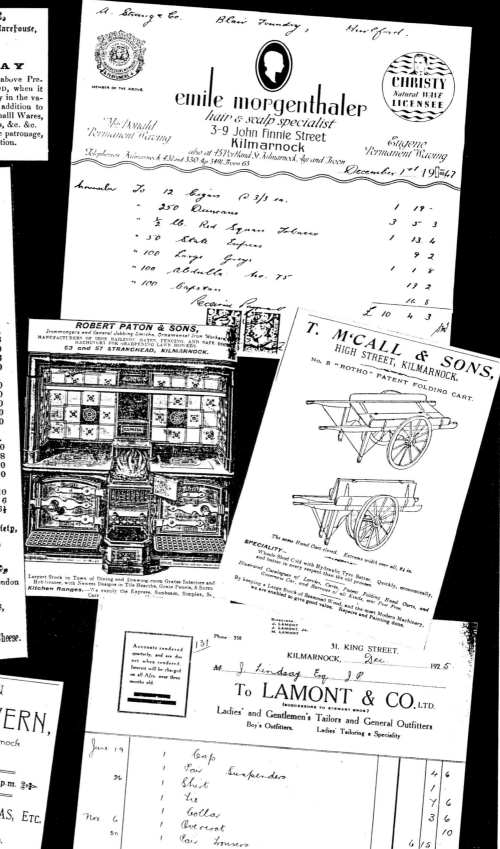
75

Premises now occupied by the Bank of Scotland, Bank Street

was sited in Low Church Lane in the oldest part of the town. Early in the nineteenth century this area was redeveloped and became Bank Street, leading to Bank Place, with pleasing Regency buildings on all sides. By the middle of the century the Bank of Scotland had been joined by branches of six other leading banks, namely the Union Bank, the Commercial Bank, the Royal Bank, the National Bank, the Clydesdale Bank and the British Linen Bank.

The Union Bank branch was, in fact, the lineal descendant of Kilmarnock's very own bank. In 1802 five local businessmen combined to form the Kilmarnock Banking Company with its premises in Bank Street. This consortium was headed by Major William Parker of Assloss and his brother Hugh who

The Commercial Bank building, King Street, now demolished

had previously acted as unofficial banker to many of the businesses in the town. William Parker seems to have taken risks that did not pay off and eventually got into difficulties which compelled him to part with the Barleith portion of his estates to settle his debts. By 1810 Kilmarnock was one of eight Scottish burghs to boast its own bank serving both the agricultural and the growing mercantile communities of the district. The bank occupied a modest building in a row running east and west at the north wall of the Laigh Kirk.

After the Napoleonic Wars, however, these burgh banks declined in number and importance, their activities being encroached upon by the national and joint-stock banks, and many of them failed when they were hit by local crises. The Kilmarnock Bank did not fail, but was taken over by an Ayr rival, Hunter's Bank (founded in 1773, the year following the crash of the original Ayr Bank). In turn, Hunter's Bank was bought in 1843 by the Glasgow Union Bank which changed its name that year to the Union Bank of Scotland. In 1955

Clydesdale Bank branch at Portland Street,
East George Street corner, now demolished

the Union Bank merged with the Bank of Scotland. The early banks in Kilmarnock were unpretentious in appearance, but in the mid-nineteenth century the Union Bank in Bank Street and the Royal and British Linen Banks in Portland Street erected large imposing buildings which, according to McKay, were 'truly ornamental to the town in an architectural point of view.'

The original Royal Bank, erected in 1855, was replaced by an attractive building in 1939. With its distinctive copper dome overlooking the Cross, this

The Royal Bank of Scotland

offices above-mentioned, each bank maintains a branch in Glencairn Square or Low Glencairn Street to serve the southern parts of the town.

Scotland pioneered savings banks, the first in the world being established at Ruthwell near Dumfries in 1810. Eleven years later a savings bank was opened in Kilmarnock. The account of this bank given in the second *Statistical Account* (1839) is not without interest:

> *The depositors are chiefly labourers, operatives and maid-servants. At the commencement of the institution, many of these classes did not well understand its nature; and some of them even suspected that the Government had some design on their purses. But explanations by the clergymen, and the publication of the annual reports, have completely removed their suspicions. They now appreciate its merits, and avail themselves of the opportunity thus offered to them, to deposit their savings where they are perfectly secure, and constantly increasing by the accumulation of interest.*

This bank would receive sums from a shilling to £10, but when the latter amount was reached, the depositor had to withdraw it and place the money with one or other of the national banks. In its first sixteen years in operation the savings bank had attracted 3,156 depositors, many of whom had subsequently graduated to one of the major banks. On 31st May 1837 the savings bank had 955 accounts in progress. This worthy institution eventually became part of the Trustee Savings Bank which today has its offices at 53 John Finnie Street, with branches in Darvel and Newmilns.

Kilmarnock's Post Office savings bank, opened in 1862, was one of the first in the United Kingdom. Today the facilities of the National Savings Bank are available from the head post office in John Finnie street as well as the sub post offices in Kilmarnock and the other towns and villages of the District.

has been for more than half a century one of the town's principal landmarks. Since the redevelopment of the Cross in the 1970s and the pedestrianisation of Portland Street and the Foregate, the Royal Bank has taken on an even more impressive appearance, enhanced by the planting of trees around it. It has been overshadowed to some extent by the splendidly ultra-modern Royal Bank building, opened in 1975 on John Finnie Street, taking the place of two earlier buildings which had, in a previous incarnation, been the branches of the National and Commercial Banks which merged in 1958 and were then absorbed by the Royal Bank ten years later. Not to be outdone, the Clydesdale Bank now occupies an excitingly avant-garde building at the top of the Foregate, an interesting feature being the cylindrical, columnar staircase detached from the main building. In 1951, before the wave of bank mergers and takeovers, Kilmarnock had eleven banks. Today, of the three note-issuing banks, the Bank of Scotland and the Clydesdale Bank each have two branches in Kilmarnock and the Royal Bank has three. In addition to the main

Hotels

In 1900 there were seven hotels in Kilmarnock; by 1939 the number had fallen to only three. When the Jubilee Burns Conference was held in Kilmarnock in 1935 the event had to be shared with Ayr mainly because Kilmarnock lacked sufficient accommodation to cope with the number of delegates. The town's premier hotel was the George, erected in the early years of the nineteenth century on a triangular site at the corner of West George and Portland Street, near where the roads from Kilmaurs and Glasgow converged. It started life as a coaching inn, but rapidly developed and by the 1840s was providing not only comfortable accommodation to the traveller and visiting businessmen but was becoming an important social hub. It boasted a large hall which was often used for public meetings and even church services. It was here that the Kilmarnock Burns Club met from 1841 onwards and the world-wide Burns Federation was inaugurated in 1885. It provided more sumptuous facilities than the Town House and consequently was used for civic banquets. It was here that Ensign Ewart

Clydesdale Bank, Foregate

Former George Hotel photographed about 1890.

Hotel; in this guise it continued till 1879. The Royal Hotel was originally located at 98 King Street and flourished till 1869. A decade later another hotel of the same name was opened at 13 Duke Street in succession to the Commercial Hotel and continued until 1915. From the 1920s, apart from the Ossington, Kilmarnock was served by the Broomhill and Foxbar hotels in London Road and Carrick Court in Hill Street, but the last named no longer exists. In 1975, however, the Swallow Hotel group opened the luxury 45-bed Howard Park Hotel on Glasgow Road on the northern outskirts of the town. It is Kilmarnock's only major hotel and has a staff of 60, with a restaurant seating 90 and a number of function and meeting rooms. In 1988 it was substantially upgraded by Interscot at a cost in excess of £100,000. According to a report in the *Kilmarnock Standard* in March 1978 this hotel was erected 'near the site of the medieval church of Kilmaurs parish'. This may have had some bearing on the curious occurrence that month when unearthly screams were allegedly heard coming from room 312 which was empty at the time. In actual fact, however, the site of the medieval church was the same as the location of the present Kilmaurs church, and therefore the ghostly screams—if such they were—must have some other explanation.

was wined and dined when he was made a freeman, and later Andrew Carnegie and Andrew Fisher were similarly honoured. The hotel closed in 1920 and a portion of it, including its hall, was then converted into the George Cinema which later became the Hippodrome night-club. The building still stands but in later incarnations has served as shops, offices and estate agent's premises.

A few yards west, at the corner of John Finnie and George Streets, stood the Ossington Hotel which started life as a temperance lodging-house. A hotel sign still appears on the balcony of the upper floor, although nowadays the building has been converted into apartments and business premises. The Commercial Inn originated as a tavern where commercial travellers (or travelling sales representatives as they would now be termed) could put up for the night while visiting their business contacts. It stood in Croft Street and appears in various editions of the Kilmarnock directory till 1868. Thereafter it was upgraded and acquired the name of the Commercial

The Howard Park Hotel

7 RELIGION

If the traditional interpretation of the town name is correct, then it would be true to say that Kilmarnock owes its very origin to the development of Christianity in the district. Whether Marnock or Ernin lived or died in the area will never be known, nor does it actually matter. What does matter is that a church has probably existed above the bend of the Kilmarnock Water for over a thousand years.

In medieval times the church of Kilmarnock belonged to the monks of Kilwinning who enjoyed the tithes and revenues of the church and appointed a curate to serve the parish. From a Latin document of November 1547 it appears that under Catholicism the parishioners enjoyed a measure of democracy and the privilege of electing their priest, though the fact that the young man then elected, Alexander Boyd, was the son of Robert, Master of Boyd (and thus grandson of the then Lord Boyd) may mean that the election was little more than a rubber-stamping exercise, and that real power, then as later, rested with the temporal lord of the district.

The Reformation

By the time of the Reformation in 1560 the monks had a revenue from Kilmarnock amounting to 347 bolls 2 firlots and 1 peck of meal and 21 bolls 2 firlots and 1 peck of bere (barley). A boll was a measure about 140lbs (63.5kg), while the firlot and peck were a quarter and an eighth of a boll respective. In addition to this payment in kind they had £33 6s 8d in cash, being the rent of a part of the tithes, which were leased for payment of that sum yearly. The lands which belonged to the Church passed into lay hands at the Reformation. In 1619 Archbishop Spottiswoode, Commendator of Kilwinning, transferred the patronage of the Church, together with the tithes, to Robert Lord Boyd as proprietor of the lordship of Kilmarnock, and the latter obtained a charter from King James VI to this effect in August that year. The patronage (i.e. the right to present the minister to the parish) continued in the Boyd family till 1746 when it passed to the Earls of Glencairn and from them, about 1790, it was purchased by Henrietta Scott, later Duchess of Portland. This right of patronage, vested in the local laird, continued till 1874 and was the cause of the Disruption of 1843 when a third of the ministers and their congregations seceded to form the Free Church.

In Kilmarnock, the transition from Catholicism to the Reformed Church seems to have been smoothly achieved. It would be misleading to suppose that there was a revolution which overnight swept away the old order, and many of the bishops, abbots and priests of the old faith continued in their livings for many years after 1560. After the death of John Knox in 1572 the new Church moved to the left, with the appointment of Andrew Melville in his place. Melville was what would today be described as a hard-liner, recently arrived from Geneva with an implacable hatred of ecclesiastical tyranny and determined to institute the Presbyterian system, which had evolved under Calvin and Beza at Geneva. At that time Scotland had no clear-cut clerical organisation, but this was crystallised in the *Second Book of Discipline* (1577). This laid down a system of ordained ministers, pastors or bishops, these terms being regarded as synonymous (but later open to different interpretation), doctors (teachers in schools and universities), elders (laymen who wielded considerable spiritual powers as well as being responsible for congregational discipline) and deacons (responsible for matters of church property). The adoption of the Presbyterian system in Scotland created a division between it and England where the established church was hierarchical, with the reigning monarch as titular head, and an elaborate system of archbishops, bishops, deans, canons and clergy which virtually excluded laymen from the decision-making and general administration. As the years passed, this division became greater.

Soon after the Reformation the parishes of Kilmarnock (then including Fenwick), Riccarton and Loudoun were briefly amalgamated. The first Reformed minister of whom we have record was Robert Wilkie, appointed in 1574 at an annual stipend of £133 6s 8d Scots. He was assisted by James Hall as 'reidare' (reader) at Loudoun (Newmilns), with a salary of £20 Scots. Wilkie was one of the leading lights of the Reformation, frequently mentioned in the Acts of the Secret Council (1587) and the Convention of the Kirk (1592) as one of those specially instructed to watch and report the activities of 'all Papists, Jesuites and reseatters of them within thair bounds, and all uther weightie enormities that sall fall out and com to thair knawlage.' Early in the seventeenth century the minister of Kilmarnock was Hew Fullarton, succeeded by Michael Wallace who held office till 1640. From then till 1670 the chief minister of the district was Matthew Mowat, one of the influential figures of Presbyterianism in the neighbourhood. He took part in the celebration of the Lord's Supper on Mauchline Muir in June 1648 when the Covenanters were attacked by troops under the command of the Earls of Callander and Middleton. In June 1644 a church was established at Fenwick, then known as 'the New Kirk of Killmarnok'. The Rev. William Guthrie was ordained to this new parish on 7th November that year. Despite the separation of Fenwick to form a distinct parish, the remaining parish of Kilmarnock had, by the middle of the seventeenth century, grown to the extent that it was too much work for one man. In 1648 an assistant was appointed to help Mr Mowat. James Rowat was thereupon appointed 'conjunct' or 'colleague' with Mowat. No other second minister is recorded till the appointment of the Rev. William Wright in 1700, when the Kirk Session, the Town Council and the heritors made unusual exertions to secure a stipend for the second charge.

Fenwick Church c1890

The Wars of the Covenant

In 1603 King James VI of Scotland became King James I of England and immediately began the attempt to assimilate the Scottish church to that of England. He set up plenary courts in 1609 with powers to effect this, and in 1612 the act which had established Presbyterianism was rescinded and Episcopacy became the legal church system of Scotland. The introduction of bishops to Scotland at this time had little effect on the people as the forms of worship were not altered. Trouble started in 1633 when Charles I belatedly came up to Scotland to be crowned, eight years after ascending the throne, and brought with him Archbishop Laud, hell-bent on imposing the English system of worship. A book of regulations was published in 1636 setting out the English forms of worship and ignoring elders and kirk sessions. Laud's liturgy was introduced in St. Giles, Edinburgh in July 1637, provoking Jenny Geddes to hurl her stool at the celebrant for preaching Mass at her lug. This tumult triggered off the nationwide defiance which began as petitions against the new regulations and culminated in the National Covenant, signed in Greyfriars Kirkyard on 28th February 1638. The Covenant was seen as a revolt against legal authority and its supporters, the Covenanters, were regarded eventually as rebels.

The Scottish parliament accepted the Covenant in 1639 and even Charles I was forced to back down, but his actions came too late, for by that time he was embroiled with the English parliament. In the ensuing Civil War the Scots allied themselves with the English Puritans and out of this came the Solemn League and Covenant of 1643. Scottish churchmen attended the Westminster Assembly which evolved a form of worship (1645) that was so austere that no forms of prayer were allowed to be used.

On this basis the Covenanting army commanded by General Leslie took an active part in the Civil War which resulted in the surrender of Charles I in 1646. On his refusal to accept the Solemn League and Covenant the Scots handed him over to the English. Later Charles agreed to establish Presbyterianism in England and the Covenanting Army now took the field on his behalf, but was defeated by Cromwell at Preston in 1648. After Charles I was executed in January 1649 the Scots transferred their allegiance to his son, Charles II on condition that he subscribe to the Covenant. Cromwell defeated the Scots again, at Dunbar in 1651 and Charles fled into exile in Holland.

Following the Restoration of the monarchy in 1660 Charles II broke his promise and the legislation of the previous twenty years was swept away. By the Rescissory Act of 1661 Episcopacy was restored in Scotland. Even more galling was the insistence that ministers who had been appointed since 1642 (when patronage had been abolished) now had to obtain retrospective permission from the lay patrons of their parishes. This regulation was enforced in such a high-handed manner that in the south-west of Scotland alone over 300 ministers left their manses rather than comply. Their places were filled with untrained, inexperienced or incompetent men, and as a result the congregations deserted the churches, preferring to worship in conventicles or hill meetings where the outed ministers conducted the services. The government reacted savagely and imposed harsh measures and penalties against those who attended the conventicles or refused to give information against those who did. Large forces of ill-disciplined dragoons and troopers were quartered on the districts believed to be disaffected. This military violence, together with judicial severity, the subsequent imprisonment, torture, confiscation, expatriation and even murder of the adherents of the Covenant makes gloomy reading.

The people of Kilmarnock were steadfast adherents of the Covenant and consequently paid a heavy price. In 1666 the heads of John Ross of Mauchline and John Shields of Nether Pollok, who had been executed at Edinburgh for adherence to the Covenant, were sent to Kilmarnock to be displayed publicly on spikes. This was intended as a deterrent to the populace. A stone in the Laigh Kirk burying ground marks the spot where these gruesome relics were eventually interred. Goaded by persecution, the people rose in rebellion but were defeated at Pentland on the outskirts of Edinburgh in 1667 by General Tam Dalziel who, for some time, made Kilmarnock his headquarters while 'pacifying' Ayrshire. Dalziel extorted 50,000 merks from the inhabitants and incarcerated many of the town's leading citizens in the dreadful dungeon known as the Thieves'

Hole. When one of the inmates took ill he was only released on condition that his body, dead or alive, would be returned. He died shortly afterwards but his grieving relatives were compelled to carry his corpse back to the jail where it lay exposed to the public gaze in the street. A man named Finlay, from an adjacent parish, was brought in for questioning one day and on failing to give the General the information he sought, Dalziel ordered him to be shot on the spot. Afterwards Finlay's body was stripped of all clothing and left naked in the street as a public spectacle.

Although Lady Boyd is said to have been sympathetic to the persecuted Presbyterians the attitude of her husband is not recorded; but from the fact that Dean Castle was garrisoned by Dalziel's troopers it can only be assumed that he acquiesced in these and other foul deeds. In truth, there was little or nothing which he could have done to prevent these atrocities. At least one poor woman was immured in the Castle dungeon merely because she failed to see where a fugitive had gone; she perished in the dungeon from disease and starvation.

In 1678 Charles II decided to terrorise the Lowlands on a grand scale and to this end he unleashed on the south-west a vast rabble of Highland freebooters. The Highland Host roamed at will, raping, assaulting, murdering and pillaging with impunity. Many of these ruffians were forcibly quartered on the citizens of Kilmarnock for weeks on end and stripped them of their victuals and valuables. A Mr Dickie, who was compelled to provide free quarters to nine Highlanders for six weeks, was finally robbed of all his possessions and suffered two broken ribs when he tried to protest. Even worse, his poor wife, then heavily pregnant, was stabbed in the side and died soon afterwards. When the parish minister, Alexander Wedderburn, one of the few 'indulged' clergymen of the county, tried to restrain these brigands from ransacking the town during divine worship, he was struck on the head by musket blows from which he succumbed soon afterwards. The total damage sustained during this Highland incursion was estimated afterwards at £14,431.

Brutalised by these and similar actions the Covenanters once more resorted to arms. When dragoons attempted to break up conventicles they were driven off by well-armed men and in 1679 the Covenanters went on the offensive. Archbishop Sharp was murdered near St Andrews in May and on 1st June the Covenanters of the Irvine Valley met the King's forces commanded by John Graham of Claverhouse at Drumclog near Loudoun Hill. The Covenanters were, for the most part, on foot, but their impetuous charge routed the King's cavalry and Claverhouse narrowly escaped with his life. The spectacular success of this engagement encouraged a general insurrection and the Covenanters marched northward with the intention of occupying Glasgow, but three weeks later, at Bothwell Brig, they were decisively defeated by the Royalist army. The prisoners after the battle were taken to Edinburgh and lodged in the concentration camp set up in Greyfriars Kirkyard, scene of the signing of the Covenant forty years earlier. Twelve hundred men and women were concentrated here without shelter or adequate food for three months while their fate was being determined. In the end most of the survivors were released, but 257 were sentenced to be transported to penal servitude in the American plantations, including six men of Kilmarnock. They boarded a prison ship at Leith on 27th November, but on 10th December the ship foundered on rocks in the Pentland Firth during a severe storm and about 200 prisoners drowned. The only man from Kilmarnock to survive this ordeal was Patrick Watt who clung to some floating timbers and managed to escape. A stone in the Laigh Kirk yard pays tribute to Thomas Finlay, John Cuthbertson, William Brown, Robert and James Anderson who drowned on that occasion, and also John Finlay who was executed at the Grassmarket, Edinburgh on 15th December 1682.

New measures, including the infamous Test Act, were passed in 1681 to suppress dissent. Those who absented themselves from church were subject to heavy fines and imprisonment and many took to the moors and hills rather than submit. There they were hunted down like animals and shot by the troopers. James Robertson, a hawker from Stonehouse, was arrested at Kilmarnock in 1682 on suspicion that he had nailed a protest against the Test on the door of his parish church. Although there was absolutely no evidence against him he was taken to Edinburgh, tortured, tried and convicted. Ironically, Robertson had been arrested

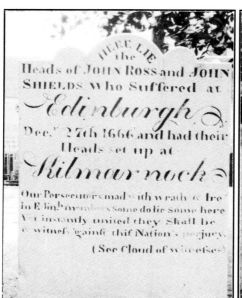

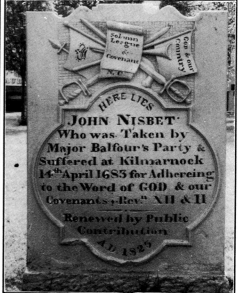

when he obtained permission to visit an old friend of his named John Finlay who at that time was being held prisoner by Major White, commander of the military garrison in Kilmarnock. What crimes were alleged against John Finlay of Muirside were not specified but he, too, was taken to Edinburgh and eventually sentenced to death. On the scaffold in the Grassmarket Finlay singled out John Boyd, baron bailie of Kilmarnock

> for his bloody courses in many things, and especially in his uplifting the cess and bloody fines, and in oppressing the poor in their consciences, and laying on of dragoons upon them most cruelly, which he did upon me four times; I wish God may forgive him for what he has done in that matter.

During the so-called Killing Times (1679-89), when the haphazard brutality of the military increased in ferocity, Captain John Inglis commanded the garrison at Dean Castle responsible for many of the outrages in the kirkyard, but his remains were interred in Greyfriars.

Patrick Inglis, son of Captain John Inglis, led a party of troopers which disturbed a band of Covenanters at the farm of Little Blackwood in May 1685. James White was shot dead on the spot, two others managed to escape through a hole in the thatch, but the other seven, including the farmer, James Paton, were seized and bound. Before departing, however, the troopers severed White's head and played a game of football with it. One of the prisoners, an old man named Findlay, was severely wounded in the fray and later, because he was hampering the progress of the party towards Newmilns, was shot at the roadside. Next day Captain Inglis ordered that the six surviving prisoners be summarily executed, but saner counsels prevailed, and he despatched his son Patrick to Edinburgh to get confirmation of his order. While the matter was delayed, friends of the captives mounted

Laigh Kirk

locality. In the local demonology he ranks on a par with the hated Grierson of Lag who persecuted the Galloway Covenanters, and even with 'Bloody Clavers' himself. On the other side, this grim period produced martyrs for the cause and heroes whose exploits are remembered to this day. In April 1683 John Nisbet of Loudoun, a fugitive since the Battle of Bothwell Brig, was apprehended by troopers under the command of Major Balfour and taken to Kilmarnock where he was publicly hanged at the Cross in order that the inhabitants might be cowed into submission by the fearful spectacle. He was interred in the Laigh Kirkyard and a handsome tombstone erected by public subscription in 1823. The leader of the Covenanters of this district was Captain John Paton of Meadowhead in Fenwick parish who eluded the government troops till the spring of 1684 when he was captured at Floak in Mearns parish and taken to Kilmarnock for interrogation. Subsequently he was taken to Edinburgh where he was executed on 9th May. A fine memorial to Paton stands in Fenwick

an attack on the Tower House in Newmilns where they were being held, killed two of the soldiers, broke down the door and liberated the prisoners. One of the assailants named John Law was killed in this daring assault. Captain Inglis and his troopers searched the countryside for the escapees but in vain; in revenge they shot two innocent bystanders instead.

A monument to James White was later erected at Fenwick, his native parish, and bore six lines of doggerel that vividly conveyed the brutality of the incident:

> This martyr was by Peter (sic) Inglis shot,
> By birth a tiger rather than a Scot;
> Who, that his monstrous extract might be seen,
> Cut off his head, then kick'd it o'er the green;
> Thus was the head which was to wear the crown,
> A football made by a profane dragoon.

The legacy of a quarter of a century of tyranny and oppression reverberated throughout the south-west of Scotland for more than two centuries and finds expression, to some extent, in the Orange movement right down to the present time. So embittered and fanatical did a section of the Covenanters, especially the Cameronians or followers of Richard Cameron, become that they refused to recognise the ecclesiastical settlement of the Glorious Revolution of 1689 which re-established the Presbyterian form of church government but did not renew the Covenant. Though narrow and doctrinaire in the maintenance of their religious convictions, they deserve credit for defending civil liberty throughout those years of arbitrary and despotic government.

Two Churches

Until 1731 there was only one church in Kilmarnock, but in order to accommodate the rapidly expanding population a second church was erected at the head of Soulis Street. This was classed as a chapel of ease, or overflow church, and named the High Church from its geographical location, in contrast to the original church which came to be known as the Low Church or Laigh Kirk. This meant the appointment of two ministers to the parish but in order to maintain impartiality it was decided that the incumbents should preach turn about in the new church. This system continued until 1764 when separate ministers were assigned to each church. The High Church cost £850 to build, not counting the steeple which was not added till 1740. The High Church presents severely simple lines externally, the square appearance being relieved only by the 80-foot steeple. Internally, however, it was beautified by a tastefully ornamented ceiling and two rows of massive pillars supporting the roof. In 1811 the Court of Teinds elevated this chapel of ease to the status of a separate parish church and assigned a portion of the parish of

The Old High Kirk

Kilmarnock to it. It has accommodation for 952.

The first permanent minister of the High Church was the Rev. James Oliphant (1735-1818) who was translated to Dumbarton in 1774 and succeeded at Kilmarnock by the Rev. John Russell, ordained in May that year. A native of Moray, he had been a schoolmaster in Cromarty before entering the Church. He ministered

at Kilmarnock till 1800 when he accepted a call to Stirling. This unbending advocate of Auld Licht principles and a powerful preacher in the hellfire and damnation tradition was satirised by Burns as Black Russell in 'The Holy Fair' and wordy Russell in 'The Twa Herds' which publicised his unseemly quarrel with the Rev. Alexander Moodie of Riccarton. In 'The Ordination' he was held up as an opponent of the more liberal New Lichts. As Rumble John he was lampooned in 'The Kirk's Alarm'.

McKay paints an unflattering portrait of him:
His appearance completely harmonized with his severity of manner; for he was uncouth and robust in person, remarkably dark-complexioned, and stern and gloomy in countenance. On Sabbaths, during the intervals of Divine service, he would frequently go through the streets, and even to the outskirts of the town, with a large walking-stick in his hand, watching for disorderly boys and other stragglers; and such as he discovered, he would visit on the following morning, and severely rebuke for their ungodliness.

The Sunday School movement, begun at Gloucester by Robert Raikes in 1780, spread to Kilmarnock about 1798, and it was Russell who instituted the first of its kind in the town.

In 'The Ordination' Burns cryptically refers to 'Curst commonsense, the imp of hell, cam in wi Maggie Lauder'. She was the wife of the Rev. William Lindsay, inducted at the Laigh Kirk in 1764. Due to the death of the Rev. Robert Hall in June 1762, the second charge in the Low Church fell vacant. It is not known whether the congregation had their eye on someone for the job, but the Earl of Glencairn, as patron of the living, decided to appoint Mr Lindsay, then minister of Cumbrae. Lindsay was a liberal in religious matters, but his New Licht principles were not in accordance with the feelings that then prevailed in the burgh. Rumours that the appointment had been fixed, however, circulated wildly and fuelled the antagonism which this appointment aroused.

On 23rd September 1762 the Kirk Session appointed a committee under the Rev. James Leslie, minister of the first charge, to meet with the Town Council and draw up a petition to the Earl of Glencairn in order that a number of young ministers be interviewed for the position. Glencairn ignored this petition and went ahead; the Session were informed of the Earl's decision by the Presbytery of Irvine on 24th November. The Session met on 23rd December and 'unanimously declared their disapprobation both of the manner of the Presentation and acceptance.' They appointed yet another committee to draw up their objections. A document formally laid before the Presbytery which, though sympathetic to the objectors, was powerless to revoke the appointment.

On 3rd February 1763 a committee of the Presbytery met at Kilmarnock and signed the call, effectively inviting Mr Lindsay to take up the appointment. The call was signed by Charles Dalrymple of Orangefield (on behalf of the Earl of Glencairn), William Paterson, writer in Kilmarnock and other heritors, but not by any members of the Kirk Session. The Presbytery delayed judgment till the middle of March when they decided that they could not sustain the call. Glencairn's faction then appealed to the Synod of Ayr and when that body upheld the judgment of the Presbytery the matter went to the General Assembly at Edinburgh. Meanwhile the Earl tried to compromise by saying that if the Session would accept the Rev. William Auld of Mauchline he would give him the presentation. The parishioners unanimously favoured Mr Auld and delegates from the Kirk Session and the Town Council then hastened to Mauchline to get Mr Auld to accept, but he refused.

The General Assembly took its own course and, without a vote, revoked the decisions of the Synod and Presbytery, ordering the latter to proceed without delay with the matter of Mr Lindsay's transfer. Thursday 12th July was eventually fixed as the date for his admission. Ten days before the final decision of the Assembly, the minister of the first charge had died, so Kilmarnock was now in a state of ecclesiastical anarchy. The Town Council were violently opposed to Lindsay and it was at this time that they altered the constitution of their own chapel of ease (the High Church) to prevent Lindsay from setting foot within it. With amazing alacrity they appointed a minister of their own, the Rev. James Oliphant, to fill the High Church pulpit.

Now that Mr Lindsay was actually to be installed, a great popular discontent gathered momentum and as the date of the induction drew nearer the dissatisfaction got louder. At length the day dawned and, by all accounts, Kilmarnock was the scene of tumult and disorder, the like of which was never seen before or afterwards. Workers downed tools and mobs assembled in the narrow streets. As the hour of the induction approached the crowds thronged the lanes around the church, determined to prevent the ceremony from taking place. When the intrepid Earl and the clerical dignitaries assembled for the occasion tried to make their way towards the church they were subjected to a storm of execration and pelted with mud, dead cats, garbage and excrement. Incredibly, they managed to gain the interior of the church. The precentor, William Steven, had his wig torn from his head. The wig of one of the magistrates was tossed into the air, amid the cheers of the mob. The Earl of Glencairn was struck on the face by a dead cat and Mr Halket, the minister of Fenwick, rushed from the church, mounted his horse, and fled the scene in the utmost consternation.

As it happened, an English commercial traveller was leaving the town at the same time to go to Glasgow. He asked the way, which was then somewhat difficult to find, and was told by bystanders 'Keep after that man for the first four miles, and you cannot go wrong'. The minister, finding a horseman hard on his heels, thought it was an outraged Calvinist and spurred his horse harder than ever. The Englishman, put his horse to speed too, and so the mad dash became something

of a race. At last the poor clergyman turned down a side road and called out to the farmer to bring out his people and save his life. The commercial traveller followed him up the farm track and into the yard when, instead of mortal combat on theological grounds, the unfortunate confusion was soon explained. The whole party enjoyed the joke so much that the farmer insisted on keeping the Englishman as his guest for the night.

The induction service broke up in disarray and the Earl and his entourage retreated to a nearby house. The induction was later held at the safe distance of the Presbytery house in Irvine. The bailies (still virtually servants of the baronial superior) issued a proclamation by tuck of drum, offering a reward of £10 sterling for the apprehension of the ringleaders. Ten men were subsequently arrested and indicted. When they came to trial at the autumn court in Ayr seven of them were acquitted, but Alexander Thomson, William Wyllie and James Crawford were found guilty and sentenced to a month's imprisonment, whipped through the streets of Ayr and cautioned to keep the peace for a twelvemonth.

Lindsay did not enjoy his new charge for long, for he died in 1774 and was succeeded by the Rev. John Mutrie. Soon after Mutrie's death in June 1785 he was followed by the Rev. James Mackinlay, DD whose ordination was the subject of Burns's satirical poem of that name. Born at Douglas in 1756, he was ordained in 1782 and through the influence of Sir William Cunningham, in whose family he had been tutor, he obtained the presentation to the Laigh Kirk from the Earl of Glencairn. The fourteenth Earl would have preferred to appoint a moderate but, mindful of the problems faced by his father over the Lindsay affair, he opted for Mackinlay, a prominent Auld Licht. Unlike Russell, however, Mackinlay was an elegant preacher. 'The sweetness and compass of his voice imparted a charm to all his sentiments,' said McKay and his skills were recognised by Glasgow University which conferred on him a doctorate.

The Rev. John Robertson, (1733-98) was ordained in 1765 and for many years was minister of the first charge. As previously mentioned, Mackinlay and Robertson between them compiled the account of Kilmarnock parish published in the first *Statistical Account*. Robertson was a moderate, and he, too, was mentioned by Burns in 'The Ordination': 'Now Robertson harangue nae mair, But steek your gab for ever.' The tragic incident in the Laigh Kirk on 18th October 1801, which led to the rebuilding of the church the following year, has already been mentioned.

Dissent and Disruption

The attitude of the General Assembly to the Lindsay affair was coloured by the great debate then going on between the Popular party or Auld Lichts which desired greater strictness in discipline, and the Moderates or New Lichts who argued that patronage had made the Church the dignified and powerful institution it had become. The struggle between the Auld Lichts and New Lichts was to weaken Church unity throughout the eighteenth century and drag on into the nineteenth century. Apart from purely doctrinal points the Scottish Church showed a distressing tendency to schism, often on organisational matters which strike us nowadays as trivial in the extreme. The Church was like an amoeba, splitting and re-splitting and thereby multiplying numerous sects whose shades of Presbyterianism were often, to the outsider at least, difficult to distinguish. Few causes of disruption, however, were as trivial as that which divided the Lifters and the Anti-Lifters in Kilmaurs, the bone of contention being the precise moment in the Communion service at which the minister was expected to lift up the bread. A sect of Cameronians in Crookedholm split in 1826 over whether, in psalmody, the line should be read before being sung, or that the congregation should at once join in praise.

The question of patronage caused the first great rift in the Church. The election of ministers by their congregations was one of the concessions hard won by the Covenanters at the Revolution of 1689, but it was severely damaged by an Act of 1712 which restored lay patronage by the lairds. In 1732 the General Assembly itself abolished the last remnant of popular election by declaring that in those cases where lay patrons neglected or declined to exercise their rights, the minister was to

Martyrs U.F. Church

be chosen, not by the congregation, but by the elders and h e r i t o r s (landowners of the parish). This decision was taken by the Assembly d e s p i t e overwhelming opposition from the i n d i v i d u a l Presbyteries, and led to a protest movement led by the Rev. Ebenezer Erskine of Stirling. He was joined by others who formed an Associate Presbytery in 1733, disowning the authority of the Assembly. By 1745 it had 45 congregations and formed the Associate Synod. Two years later this breakaway movement itself split into Burghers and Anti-Burghers (over the religious oath taken by burgesses in Edinburgh, Glasgow and Perth). Both sects grew rapidly and amalgamated in 1820 to form the United Secession Church. In 1847 it joined forces with the Relief churches to form the United Presbyterian Church and, in 1900, it joined with the mainstream of the Free Church to form the United Free Church.

The Burghers, Anti-Burghers and others standing apart from the Church of Scotland were generally known as ranters, dissenters or seceders and maintained their own meeting-houses and chapels. In 1772 the first dissenting chapel was erected by the Burghers in Kilmarnock at the Gallowsknowe. This was a very plain, unpretentious building, and was eventually demolished in 1861. Two years earlier, however, the congregation had moved to a more commodious and elegant building in Portland Road. This congregation had split in 1818 and the seceders joined the Auld Lichts but held on to the Gallowsknowe church, thus forcing the main congregation to decamp to a temporary place of worship in East George Street. A disagreeable lawsuit then ensued as the two groups tussled for possession of the Gallowsknowe church. The matter was finally resolved by mutual consent and the Auld Licht party then relinquished the Gallowsknowe church and built their own place of worship in Wellington Street, later known as the Free Henderson Church. This body rejoined the Church of Scotland in 1839, but left again four years later at the Disruption.

Meanwhile, the Anti-Burghers established a meeting-house in 1775 and this later came to be known as the Clerk's Lane Church. This church was rebuilt on a larger scale in 1807 and eventually contained 1,000 sittings. Its original occupants were a branch of a dissenting congregation formed in 1740 by Mr Smeaton of Kilmaurs, the first of the Associate Synod groups established in Ayrshire. This sect had as their minister the redoubtable James Robertson, one of the great preachers of the eighteenth century whose fame extended far and wide, second only to the great Dr Mackinlay as the most popular preacher in Kilmarnock. When Mackinlay was absent from the town many of his congregation had no compunction about attending Robertson's services, a matter which he regarded with good-natured sarcasm. One Sabbath, when their own favourite preacher was absent, Mackinlay's follower's made a rush into Mr Robertson's chapel just as he had concluded the prayer. The rustling which their entrance occasioned attracted his attention; and, in his usual laconic manner, he said, 'Sit roun', sit roun' my friens, and gie the fleein army room; for their wee bit idol, ye ken, is no at hame the day.' Robertson was also a powerful tent-preacher and pamphleteer, and in the latter context is best remembered for his broadside denouncing the errors and heresies of Dr William McGill expressed in his essay *The Death of Jesus Christ* (1786). This heretical publication (as many reckoned it) created considerable controversy and gave rise to Burns's poem 'The Kirk's Alarm' in which he satirised the worthy doctor's opponents.

This congregation split in 1841 following the publication by its then minister, the Rev. James Morison, of a pamphlet entitled *What must I do to be saved?*. Morison's theological

Communion Token

views were at odds with those of many of his congregation as well as his fellow clerics. He was eventually tried for heresy by the Secession Synod and excommunicated from that body. The bulk of his congregation remained loyal to him and they remained in possession of the church which continued as the Clerk's Lane Free Christian Church affiliated with the Scottish Unitarian Association. The followers of Dr Morison withdrew and held their services for a time in the hall of the George Hotel and later in the Academy, pending the erection of a church in Princes Street. The Rev. David Jamieson was appointed to this charge in 1842. The following year Morison and his adherents joined forces with some other churches to form the Evangelical Union, whereas the original Secession congregation eventually joined the United Presbyterians. The followers of Dr Morison eventually formed the Evangelical Union Church in Winton Place, with a membership of about 400 (1950).

> Mackinlay adds the interesting observation that *notwithstanding so many divisions, the people in general, of all denominations, live together in the best habits of friendship, as Christians ought to do; and that ecclesiastical rancour has fortunately given place to the milder dispositions of forbearance, benevolence and charity.*

Another dissenting congregation of Kilmarnock was that which broke away from the parish church of

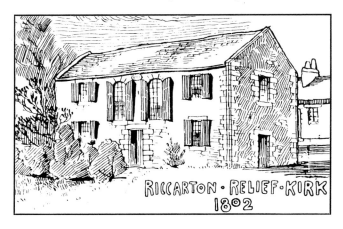

RICCARTON · RELIEF · KIRK 1802

Riccarton in 1799 as a result of the patron refusing to grant them a choice of minister. Immediately afterwards they connected themselves with the Relief Presbytery of Glasgow and until better accommodation could be procured they met for divine worship in a barn in Riccarton. In 1802 they erected their own meeting-house in the village, the Rev. Daniel Macnaught being inducted at that time. In 1811 the Rev. James Kirkwood was appointed. His ability as a preacher attracted a large following, including many people from Kilmarnock. Eventually the Kilmarnock adherents outnumbered the Riccarton members so it was decided in 1814 to move to a new site. A church was then erected in King Street and replaced by a much larger building on the same site in 1832. This congregation

entered the United Presbyterian Church in 1847 along with the main body of seceders. Architecturally eclectic in style, the King Street Church presented a most impressive appearance, topped by a steeple 120 feet high. The four-dial clock, by Breckenridge and Son of Kilmarnock, was visible from most parts of the town, while its bell, the largest and loudest in the district, could be heard everywhere. This imposing landmark was demolished in 1966 to make way for a new shopping development.

King Street Church

Despite the counter-attraction of all those dissenting sects, the Church of Scotland itself began expanding in the 1830s to cope with the increasing population of the town. In 1836 an ecclesiastical survey was made of the parish and, although it was imperfectly completed, it yielded some interesting statistics. There were about 15,200 people in Kilmarnock parish and of these 8,957 belonged to the established Church, 6,119 belonged to the other denominations, and a mere 174 did not belong to any church. A lay missionary had been appointed in 1834 to work among the poor in the slum district of the south-west. It was felt that the adherents of the established Church had suffered the most, from the purely material viewpoint, since, while the population had risen dramatically, no new place of

St Marnock's Church

West High Church interior

worship connected with the Church of Scotland had been erected for more than a century.

The established Church was not slow in remedying this defect. St Marnock's Church, in the street of the same name, was designed by James Ingram and opened late in 1836. It was the largest church in the town and had sittings for 1,730. Because of a shortage of funds, however, it could not afford a minister of its own and was supplied, turn about, by ministers from the parish church until the Disruption of 1843 when it was closed. It remained in limbo for fifteen years, but was then re-opened and a new congregation formed. In January 1859 the Rev. Charles Stewart was appointed and under his energetic efforts it was raised to the status of a separate parish church in 1862. St Andrew's Church at the foot of East Netherton Street was built in 1841 at a cost of £1,700. Soon after its completion the Rev. Neil Brodie was ordained minister, but he left, with the greater part of the congregation, at the Disruption of 1843. From then till 1848 it was only intermittently in use, but late in that year the Rev. Daniel Macfie was appointed.

In the 1830s the influence of dissent, combined with a rapidly rising religious fervour, gave to the established Church a sense of divine mission which, it was felt, should be carried out without the obstruction of any worldly authority. This notion focused on the age-old problem of patronage and gave rise to a ten-year conflict which began when the Assembly passed the Veto Act. This declared that no minister should be imposed on a congregation contrary to the will of the people. A simple majority of heads of families could veto the appointment made by the parish patron. The legality of this Act was soon tested in the civil courts and the Court of Session rejected it in 1838. This was

upheld by the House of Lords in 1839. The Church of Scotland then tried to resolve the matter by protracted negotiation with the government. The Home Secretary gave a negative answer in January 1843 and a final appeal to Parliament in March 1843 was rejected. The matter was hotly debated at the General Assembly in May. A substantial body, led by James Chalmers, took the view that the decision of the courts and Parliament made it impossible to hold a free assembly of the Church by law established, and therefore they had no alternative but to withdraw. Chalmers and his followers walked out of the Assembly on 18th May and immediately formed the Assembly of the Free Church, with Chalmers as Moderator. Some 451 ministers out of a total of 1,203 left the Church of Scotland, followed by a majority of their congregations. This number later increased and by 1847 there were 700 Free Church congregations with their own churches.

In Kilmarnock, the Free St Andrew's Church under Neil Brodie was erected in Fowlds Street in 1844 at a cost of £1,200. The Rev. Thomas Main of the High Church (inducted in 1839) also walked out at the Disruption and the Free High Church in Portland Street was built within the year at a cost of £3,000. In

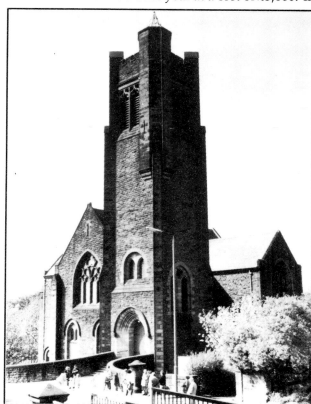

Henderson Church

St Andrew's North Church, 1943

1876 there was a secession from this church to form the Grange Church, and four years later a secession from St Marnock's formed St John's Free Church. The Original Burgher Associate Synod congregation of the Henderson Church in Wellington Street (1818), on the other hand, allied itself in 1839 with the Church of Scotland, but at the Disruption the Rev. Peter Campbell and his congregation joined the Free Church. Campbell was succeeded as pastor in 1851 by the Rev. David Landsborough, remembered today as the author of an interesting book entitled *Contributions to Local History* published about 1879. Landsborough was one of the more kenspeckle characters of Kilmarnock in the second half of the nineteenth century, so much so that most people referred to his church as Landsborough's Kirk, and were not aware of the fact that it was the Henderson Church, until it moved to its present location on London Road.

The various Presbyterian churches gradually amalgamated. Following discussions in 1896 the Free Church and United Presbyterian Church amalgamated in 1900 to form the United Free Church. The six Free and four U.P. churches in Kilmarnock joined forces in that year. In 1929 they joined the five congregations of the established Church in the reformed Church of Scotland. The fifteen congregations maintained their identities and had a total membership of 13,000; five of these churches had over 1,000 communicants apiece. After 1929 the voice of dissent was maintained by a small group adhering to the United Original Secession Church, which died out in 1947. Inevitably, of course, not everyone was happy about the union of the churches. Those who wished to have nothing to do with an established Church in any shape or form came together as the United Free Church congregation which eventually had its own church in the Longpark housing estate, served by Kilmarnock's first woman minister. In 1896 the Evangelical Union united with the Congregational Union of Scotland and the Winton Place congregation followed suit, but in the ensuing decade it gradually withered away and passed out of existence in 1907. In the postwar period the shift of population to the newer suburbs has led to the erection of new churches in Onthank and Shortlees. Howard St Andrew's Church in the modern idiom was erected on Portland Road just west of John Finnie Street in the 1970s to accommodate parishioners in the Bonnyton, Grange and Gargieston districts.

The Catholic Church

In the seventh century wandering Irish priests set up the chapel in honour of St Marnock which gave Kilmarnock its name and brought Christianity to the district.

In the years after the Reformation of 1560 the Catholic faith was outlawed and Kilmarnock grew into a thriving Presbyterian town. There were virtually no survivors of the old religion.

Occasionally groups of Irish Catholic reapers would pass through the district or a visiting priest would be in the neighbourhood but the second coming of the Irish to Scotland, when it came, was not caused by missionary zeal this time but by the need to find work.

Around the end of the eighteenth century Scotland had become a land of opportunity to the Irish. New methods of making goods created a huge demand for labour so that Irish newspapers were full of advertisements for jobs and the new Belfast to Glasgow steamers were full of hungry workmen risking all they had in a cheap passage to Scotland. This time, unlike the reapers, there would be no returning: their aim was permanent employment in the new mills, the new factories, in the new coalpits, in the building of the railways and roads.

By 1840 the Irish had poured into Scotland: Glasgow had 45,000, Paisley had 5,000 while Kilmarnock had nearly 2,000.

The Kilmarnock district was only twenty miles from Glasgow, twelve from Ayr, and six from Irvine, all walkable distances, and to the tramping Irish, headed inland from the ports, arriving in Kilmarnock was almost inevitable.

The incomers were dreadfully poor, living almost at starvation level and seeming to be a burden on the land. So, in 1835, the government made an official enquiry into 'the state of the Irish in Scotland'. Witnesses in this enquiry stated:

The thriving town of Kilmarnock attracted many Irish immigrants from the 98 Rising. They were employed in labouring and muslin-weaving, as surfacemen in the Duke of Portland's colliery near the town, in the building trade, as stonebreakers and in drainage work. Generally the Irish labourers do all the drudgery of the place. As in the other towns of Ayrshire those of the immigrants who were unfitted for strenuous open-air work found employment as shoemakers and tailors. Others who had acquired a little capital set up as brokers so that with one exception all the second-hand dealers in Kilmarnock were Irish.

It was the obvious duty of the Catholic bishops to provide a priest and a chapel as soon as possible. But there were hundreds of places with the same desperate need and this meant that Kilmarnock had to wait its turn as the few priests who were available had to be placed where they could serve as wide an area as possible. In 1882 Fr. William Thomson was transferred to Ayr where for many years the people had been 'miserably in want of a clergyman.' The main stations of Fr. Thomson's mission were at Girvan, Irvine and Kilmarnock.

For more than twenty years Fr. Thomson was the only parish priest in Ayrshire until in 1846 Fr. Thomas Wallace, a Limerick man, ordained in Maynooth and serving in the parish of St Andrew's Glasgow was sent to Kilmarnock to open up a new mission. Prospects of success were far from bright: no money, no owned property and for the time being his Masses were said in hired halls - the George Hotel hall and the Crown Hotel hall in Cheapside, now both long demolished.

Money must have come to Fr. Wallace from somewhere for very soon the purchase was effected of a piece of ground on Kilmaurs Brae (now Hill Street) behind a villa with the comforting name of Mount

Nazareth House

Pleasant and inside two years he had built a new chapel capable of seating more than 750 people.

He had built St Joseph's and a fine church it was. The building was in the Gothic style with a Gothic window and an imposing belfry. Inside, two rows of iron pillars divided the body of the church into a nave and two aisles, while above the 'lobby' was a gallery holding a small but powerful organ.

Behind the altar a concealed passageway linked the two vestries. The side altars must have come later as there is no mention of them in the original description of the church. A commodious presbytery adjoined the chapel.

St Joseph's was opened by Bishop Murdoch on Sunday, June 13th, 1847, when it was estimated that the Catholic population of Kilmarnock was 3,000, with 1,700 living in the town or close to it and the others in the out-stations.

Fr. Wallace died on April 9th, 1863. The next two parish priests of Kilmarnock were destined to become bishops. John McLachlan who came from St. Andrews in Glasgow to succeed Fr. Wallace was a Glasgow man of Highland stock. He came to Kilmarnock in 1854 and went to Paisley in 1866. When all the Scottish dioceses were restored in 1878 he became the first bishop of Galloway. His successor in Kilmarnock, Fr. George John Smith, stayed only a few short years before he went to Rothesay and from there eventually to be Bishop of Argyll in 1893.

In the course of time 'stations' in the surrounding areas took leave of Kilmarnock as their mother church and became established congregations with resident priests—Irvine in 1864, St Paul's, Hurlford in 1883 and St Sophia's, Galston in 1886.

Greenbank Villa was purchased in 1893 and became the new presbytery. A new entrance-way to the church was cut, giving us the modern lay-out of St Joseph's.

A Convent of the Poor Sisters of Nazareth was established in Kilmarnock in the late nineteenth century, and opened the Nazareth Home for Orphans and Old Folk in 1890.

By the turn of the century Kilmarnock had grown to be by far the biggest congregation in Galloway.

Immune to the schisms and divisions which rent the Protestant Churches, the Catholic Church in Kilmarnock went on from strength to strength and by the end of World War II with a steady rise in the parochial population it had reached 6,000 members and there was clearly a need for new churches in the housing-schemes at Onthank and Shortlees, although for a time nothing could be done because of the shortages caused by the war.

However, despite setbacks the first of the housing-scheme churches was opened in Shortlees in 1953. The new church, St Michael the Archangel, because of restrictions was simply a plain red brick building with accommodation for 500 people.

By comparison, in more affluent times Bishop McGee laid the foundation stone of the church of Our Lady of Mount Carmel in December 1961. This elegant third church costing over £100,000 to construct has many striking architectural features such as the magnificent window above the main entrance, a splendid example of modern adaptation of the old craft of glass mosaic; filling the centre of the window is the imposing twice life-size crucifix. Other features are

St Ninian's Church

St Matthew's Church

a font fashioned from a single piece of Sicilian marble, the octagonal baptistry using the same mosaic glass as the main window, and the oak baldachino on its four 'legs'.

The Catholic church in Kilmarnock has come a long way since the poverty-stricken days of Fr. Wallace and Mass in a hired hall.

Other Denominations

Holy Trinity Episcopal Church, (popularly if erroneously known as the English Church) situated at the corner of Dundonald and Portland Roads, was erected in 1857 at a cost of about £1,400. Built in the Early English or Pointed style to the design of James Wallace of Kilmarnock, it has a nave with an organ-gallery, a chancel and a vestry. The chancel, which was highly regarded from the outset, was lit

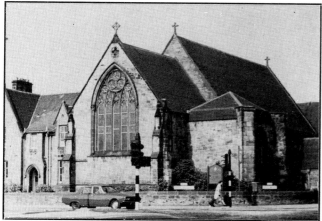

Holy Trinity Church

by a large Gothic window of stained glass, erected to the memory of Patrick Boyle of Shewalton. The first pastor of the Episcopal flock was the Rev. R. Wildbore who died in 1852 some years before the church was built, but he was commemorated by an inscription on the memorial font. The erection of the church was, in fact, largely due to the energies of the Rev. Edward James Jonas, appointed in 1855. The chancel and organ-chamber were added in 1865 and decorated with a beautiful mosaic pavement. In 1950 it was estimated to have about 800 members and adherents.

A Baptist Church was erected at the top of Fowlds Street in 1869 and opened in September 1870. The foundation stone was laid by Thomas Coats of Ferguslie, one of the famous textile family. The Grange Free Church in Woodstock Street arose from a secession from the Free Church in Portland Street. The breakaway congregation met at first in October 1876 in the hall of the George Hotel and continued to worship there till 15th July 1877 when they moved to their own hall. Alongside, the new church was then in course of erection. The Rev. James McCulloch was appointed minister and held services in the hall until the church itself was completed in August 1879. The layout of this church was unusual for the period in having the pews

radiating from a central point where the pulpit stood. This church had accommodation for 860 and was distinguished by a spire 160 feet tall. The Early English building, to the design of Robert Ingram, was of red sandstone from the Ballochmyle quarries and cost over £8,000 in all.

The religious zeal for which Kilmarnock had long been noted continued beyond the end of the nineteenth century. Entirely new bodies which had no previous connection with the various Presbyterian churches also sprang up in the latter part of the nineteenth century, filling a need for a more evangelical approach. The Christian Brethren began proselytising in Kilmarnock about 1870 and eventually had four assemblies in the burgh. This movement, laying stress on personal conversion, had two assemblies of the Open Brethren, with about 400 members between them, while the other assemblies belonged to the Exclusive Brethren and the Needed Truth respectively.

Other sects and religious persuasions represented in Kilmarnock included the Christadelphians (dating from 1883), the Spiritualists, the Christian Scientists, the Salvation Army, the Society of Friends (Quakers), the Apostolic Church, the Jehovah's Witnesses, and several independent missions: the Railway Mission in Bonnyton, the Cross Mission (occupying the old Original Secession Church) and the Ayrshire Christian Union. Compared with the single church in 1731 there were, in 1950, no fewer than 19 separate sects and denominations represented by 32 assemblies. At the present time there are 35 churches in Kilmarnock and Loudoun district.

Although actual church attendance has declined considerably from its zenith of a century ago, the churches continue to play an active part in the religious and social life of the community. Women's guilds (begun in the Church of Scotland in 1887), Sunday schools and Bible classes, youth clubs and fellowships provide a valuable adjunct to the more traditional role of the churches. In 1950 ten churches had youth clubs and eight had Girls' Associations. There were two groups of the Girls' Guildry, two church companies of Boy Scouts and three of Girl Guides as well as junior branches of Toc H and the YMCA.

8 EDUCATION IN KILMARNOCK

In 1633 the Scottish Parliament passed an Act for the establishment of a school in every parish 'upon a sum to be stented upon every plough or husband land according to the worth'. This was reinforced by a more comprehensive Act in 1696. That a school existed in Kilmarnock long before it became obligatory by Act of Parliament is borne out by a reference in early records to 'John Andersoune, scholemaster of Kilmarnock' who died in 1629. The Town records also mention the appointment on 2nd December 1647 of 'Thomas Mure, Doctor of the School'. At that period 'doctor' was a courtesy title given to schoolmasters. Subsequently James Alexander, David Airth and James Osburne held office in Kilmarnock, the last named later becoming parish minister (1688-96).

The earliest reference to the school itself occurs in an undated document formerly in the Boyd charter chest, and concerns a grant by James Lord Boyd

for keeping ane schoole within the parocheine of the Old Kirk of Kilmarnock, and for provisioune of ane constant rent and stipend for holding ane scholemaister in the said parocheine of the Old Kirk of Kilmarnock, quho may also serve as musician in the said Old Kirk in all tyme coming.

The reference to the Old Kirk dates the document to some time after the separation of Fenwick (the New Kirk) in 1642. From a Kirk Session minute of 14th December 1676 the quarterly payments from the 'schoolers' (scholars) amounted to 23s 4d for Latin and 16s 8d for Scots, the two languages whose reading and writing were then taught. This alludes to the fact that the schoolmaster was paid in two forms, by a small regular stipend augmented by small sums paid quarterly by the pupils or rather their parents. When Osburne demitted office in 1677 he estimated the balance owing to him as 'six pounds starling money'— the first reference to sterling in the burgh records.

On 10th May 1677 Robert Young was appointed 'maister of the grammar-school' with a stipend of 160 merks, plus scholars' fees. It appears that the school had been allowed to languish for some time previously. A minute of the Kirk Session dated 24th May enjoined the various elders to survey their respective districts and produce a list of boys fit for the school. Pupils whose parents were too poor to pay the modest fees were to be maintained by the Session. Finally, the Session 'appoynts that non be put to inferior schools who are fitt for the publick school'. This seems to imply that, in addition to the parish school, there were various small, private schools of an inferior quality. This was by no means an unknown phenomenon. Till the late nineteenth century private schools varying in size and quality flourished in every town conducted by freelance or itinerant schoolmasters. Readers will doubtless recall the *ad hoc* arrangement by which young John Murdoch taught the sons of William Burnes and other small farmers at Alloway (1765-7).

The next schoolmaster was Matthew Cunningham who seems to have taught under Episcopal auspices and combined his academic duties with the post of parish registrar. He was apparently dismissed at the Revolution in 1689, but the restored Kirk Session (Presbyterian) had considerable difficulty in getting the parochial registers out of his hands. It is not surprising that education in Kilmarnock was severely disrupted in the latter part of the Killing Times and the Revolutionary period. There are several intimations in the records of the time that 'the Doctor of the School is not sufficientlie provided' and the Kirk Session had to make advances for the support of the school 'till they should be riplie advised about a settled sallarie.' This was a nationwide problem which the Act of 1696 eventually sorted out.

The first permanent teacher after the Revolution was John Sprott, appointed in 1690. From the Kirk Treasurer's books we learn that Mr Sprott's salary, for the period from Lammas to Martinmas 1693 was a mere £5 Scots (five shillings sterling or 25p in our modern currency). The Session records make no mention of the school-house itself or where it was located, but it seems to have been a very humble structure. An entry of 1693 mentions a payment of 6s Scots (sixpence sterling) to a thatcher to cover the roof of the school with turf. On 29th January 1694 the school was fitted with glazed windows, James Cathcart being paid £3 18s Scots for this purpose. The payment worked out at sixpence sterling per foot of glass. Sprott was poorly paid and soon gave up the job, to be followed in quick succession by James Menteith and Robert Murdoch. By that time the 1696 Act, which made the provision of schools the responsibility of the heritors (landowners) of each parish, was in operation. This improved the situation for Murdoch lasted five years. Shortly before the end of the century he was followed by John Thomson from Prestonpans. These early schoolmasters acted also as session clerk and keeper of the parish registers.

The next incumbent was Robert Montgomerie, appointed in 1704. For some unspecified reason he was suspended in 1709 and not restored to office till 1716. During the interval his duties were performed by John Adam and Thomas Breckenridge. Montgomerie thereafter held the post for twenty years and was succeeded by James Smith in 1736. During Montgomerie's tenure, the parish school was made a collegiate charge, i.e. the teaching duties were divided between two masters operating in separate buildings known as the parish school and the burgh school. Montgomerie continued in the parochial or grammar-school and confined his activities to the teaching of Latin and Greek. The teacher at the burgh school concentrated on English reading and writing, and arithmetic. The parish school was supported by the landward heritors, and the burgh school from the town's funds. This arrangement came into force in 1727, the Session voting to give £40 Scots per annum for the encouragement of an English school, augmenting the £20 Scots provided for this purpose by the Town Council. The Presbytery refused to support this move, and in November 1728 the Session were forced to discontinue their payments. The burgh schoolmaster had to struggle on with a reduced salary till 1736 when it was doubled to £40 Scots (£3 6s 8d sterling), but over the ensuing seventy years it gradually increased to £15 sterling.

Stray minutes of the Town Council provide us with glimpses of the state of education in Kilmarnock in the eighteenth century. In 1748, for example, James Smith, the parish schoolmaster, complained that his burgh counterpart, William Dun was 'assuming to teach Latin, and thereby encroaching on Mr Smith's privileges'. The English teacher's position itself was later undermined by private enterprise. A minute of 1766 complained that 'several strangers have of late set up English schools to the prejudice of the public teacher' and a committee was appointed to inspect these private institutions. If their teachers were found to be not properly qualified the committee was empowered to close them down.

John Graham, who was master of the grammar school from 1763 till 1779, later published his memoirs and gave an interesting account of the school in that period. By that time the school enjoyed a considerable reputation far beyond the confines of the parish and the sons of the nobility and even boarders from families of distinction in the American colonies attended it. Much of the success of the school was due to the qualities and teaching calibre of Graham himself. Originally intended for the Church, he was forced to terminate his studies at the University of Glasgow on the death of his father. Later he was employed as tutor to one of the noble families in the south-west of Scotland and returned to the University with the son of the family and eventually graduated alongside him. During this second stint at the University he was employed as assistant to Dr Moor (formerly tutor to the family of Lord Kilmarnock and then professor of Greek). This may have been the connection which led to his appointment as parish schoolmaster of Kilmarnock in 1763. He married the daughter of a Douglas farmer and it was she who looked after the boarders so capably that this side of the school was greatly expanded.

All would have been well had Graham been content to remain in Kilmarnock. Unfortunately he came under the spell of a confidence trickster named Hunter who persuaded him to leave Scotland and establish a boarding-school in London. So extensive were his library, furniture and personal possessions at the time he left Kilmarnock that the sale lasted an entire week and netted him a considerable sum. He hired a coach to transport himself, his wife and eight children, together with a maid-servant, to London—a very expensive undertaking in those days. He established his school at St Pancras Wells north of the City. The enterprise was under-capitalised and soon over-extended. In desperation Graham turned to forgery and conspired

with an engraver then in the Fleet Prison to manufacture a plate for forging Bank of England notes. The engraver pocketed Graham's money, engraved the plate and promptly informed the proper authorities. Graham was arrested and brought to trial in October 1781. As none of the notes had been issued he escaped the scaffold but was sentenced to six months' imprisonment. Far from deterring him, this spell in gaol spurred him on to defraud the Bank by converting £15 notes into £50 notes, by erasing the last letters of the word 'Fifteen'. Mrs Graham had the task of passing the fake notes. Inevitably the fraud caught up with the Grahams and they were apprehended at Southampton. At their trial each blamed the other but both were found guilty. Mrs Graham was recommended to mercy and drew a stiff prison sentence, but her luckless husband was hanged at Tyburn on 15th October 1782.

Graham's successor at Kilmarnock was John Duncan, afterwards minister of Ardrossan. He was the first of the parish schoolmasters officially designated as rector of the Grammar School. The first *Statistical Account* (1790) noted that the parish school had fallen into disrepute some years previously, 'but from the attention and ability of the present teacher, is increasing in numbers and celebrity'. In 1797 William Thomson took up the position and raised the standards of teaching to new levels. During his tenure, no other teacher in Ayrshire sent to the University so many well-qualified youths. In 1790 the burgh school was said to have always been well attended and for many years had upwards of 100 pupils. At the beginning of the nineteenth century the burgh school was in the hands of Andrew Henderson who had a large establishment of boarders. He died in 1805 and was succeeded by a Mr Morton, but when he left to take up an appointment at Dunbar two years later, William Henderson, son of Andrew, got the job.

The first Academy

In the second half of the eighteenth century the parish school occupied a house at the corner of Green Street next to the Corn Exchange. It was erected about 1752 and was a single-storey building. It may have been the successor to an ancient school located in a narrow lane named College Wynd near the Laigh Kirk whose yard was used by the schoolboys as a playground. The College Wynd school was burned down about the middle of the eighteenth century. The location of the burgh school is not known but it was probably adjacent to the parish school for the convenience of the scholars who were taught different subjects in each institution. At any rate the two schools co-existed until 1807 when it was decided new accommodation was necessary. A site was chosen within a stone's throw of the parish school.

The new building which first bore the name of Kilmarnock Academy was of two storeys, containing four classrooms, and with its playground occupied most of the triangular space bounded by Green Street, London Road and the Kilmarnock Water.

Half the cost of building this new school was defrayed by the landward heritors and the rest from burgh funds and private subscriptions. William Thomson became rector of the Academy, while William Henderson was elected teacher of English and William Jamieson appointed to the commercial department. Henderson resigned in 1813 and opened his own school in King Street. One suspects that he felt restricted in the Academy, for in a short time he had 700 pupils in his own school—no mean feat at a time when the population of the entire parish was little more than 12,000. It is recorded that he taught from six in the morning till late at night on weekdays, but on Saturdays he was devoted to field sports. His place at the Academy was then filled by the Rev. William Thomson, son of the rector and afterwards minister of Old Monkland parish (1820). Until 1830 there were only three masters in the Academy, but in that year James Connell joined the staff as a teacher of geography and maths. This appointment was short-lived as no funds were forthcoming for an additional salary and Connell soon left for a post in Irvine. From 1834 till his death in 1846 he taught in Glasgow High School and his scholastic abilities, notably his achievements as a naturalist, were recognised by the degree of LL.D. It may be added, in passing, that the high ratio of pupils to staff in these early schools only became possible because of the system of relying heavily on the older scholars to assist in the teaching of the younger pupils. This operated unofficially for many years, but was given formal sanction in 1846 when the government introduced the pupil-teacher system, providing small emoluments to these scholars who were, in effect, apprentices.

By 1839 there were three schools in the landward part of the parish. Two of these were branches of the parish school, one at Rowallan and the other at Grougar. Each had a house for the school and the teacher, a small garden and half a chalder of victual. The half chalder was paid voluntarily by the heritors to the teacher at Rowallan,

because he has not yet been appointed according to the terms of the schoolmasters' act; but the payment to the teacher in Grougar is now regularly assessed

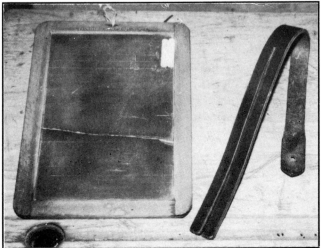

School slate and belt or tawse

for, as he was lately chosen in the manner prescribed by law.

This statement in the second *Statistical Account* alluded to an Act of that year which introduced the principle of State aid to schools, though it did not wholly eliminate the traditional parish system. At that time the *Account* noted that there were in the burgh itself no fewer than twenty schools, employing 28 teachers, both male and female. The Academy had 300 pupils, its rector enjoying the maximum salary (unspecified) with a garden and a house sufficiently large to accommodate several boarders (whose lodging was a perquisite of the rector's wife). The second and third masters had salaries of £15 a year without house or garden. The management of the Academy was then vested in a board of directors, five being chosen annually from the heritors, five chosen by the Town Council, and the three clergymen of the established Church. In addition, all subscribers of £20 and upwards were entitled to a directorship, while five were chosen from among the subscribers of £5-£20. As the Merchants' Society subscribed £50, its preses was also, *ex officio* a director. These directors fixed the rate of school fees and selected teachers to fill vacancies as they occurred, but no mention is made of any powers to visit the school and examine pupils.

Early nineteenth century schools

For many years the Act of 1696 was the sole statute governing the organisation and conduct of schools in Scotland. Across the river the parish school of Riccarton was located in a side street east of the toll, and though it was a modest one-teacher establishment it, too, rejoiced in the name of the Academy. Though it has long since disappeared its memory has been perpetuated in the name of Academy Street and the Academy Playing Fields at Jeffrey Street. In 1803 an Act was passed strengthening the connection between parish schools and the established Church, but also made better provision for teachers' salaries. The Act of 1839, introducing a system of State aid and inspection in England and Wales, was subsequently made applicable to Scotland as well. At that time upwards of 2,000 pupils in Kilmarnock parish attended schools outside the parochial system. Two of the schools in the town were erected for the reception of the children of the poor, whose education would otherwise have been neglected, and were supported by voluntary subscriptions among the inhabitants generally. The first of these was the Female Industrial School in West Netherton Street, maintained by the ladies of the town. In 1839 this school accommodated 25 girls who were taught English reading (but not writing), needlework and the knitting of stockings. As the name of the school suggests, it was not entirely altruistic, educating girls just sufficiently to make them competent domestic servants.

The other free school, maintained by the gentlemen of the burgh, existed in Dundonald Road and was divided into a day school and an evening class. Into the day school orphans and neglected boys and girls were admitted indiscriminately so long as they were at least five and a half years old. In this school reading and writing were taught free of charge and the average number of the scholars was 190. In the evening class some 90 boys and girls of more mature years, engaged in work during the daytime, were given the chance to catch up with their education. One teacher catered to both day and evening classes and must certainly have earned his salary of £50 a year!

The second *Statistical Account* gave no details of the private schools which provided education of varying quality to upwards of 1,700 children. Most of these were single-teacher establishments with an average roll of 100 pupils, so the calibre of the tuition must have been fairly rudimentary. The number of young people in 1839 who could not read or write was said to be 'very inconsiderable'. The Rev. Andrew Hamilton of the High Church wrote: 'The natives of Kilmarnock, in general, are fully alive to the benefits of education, and covet them above all things for their children. They struggle hard to render them scholars, and if possible great scholars.'

There were exceptions, however. 'These are not numerous,' he continued, 'and occur chiefly among those who are natives of Ireland, or who have become poor and indifferent about the education of their children, from the frequent use of ardent spirits.' To lump the children of the Irish immigrants with that small section of the population which had gone to wrack and ruin as a result of drunkenness probably reflects the prejudice of the worthy minister who wrote these words rather than the true state of affairs. The chief obstacle to gaining education for their children was the innate fear of the Irish incomers against the subtle (or not so subtle) conversion to Protestantism to which these children might be subjected.

A potent factor in holding back the children of the 'industrious poor' was cited by the Rev. Andrew Hamilton.

> *The greatest enemy to education in this and other commercial towns, is a disposition on the part of poor parents to avail themselves of the fruits of their children's industry. They can often procure employment for them in some of the factories, when, for the small sum of 2s or 3s per week, they are daily confined ten or twelve hours.*

All too often children, sometimes as young as six or seven, were employed in dangerous and menial tasks in the textile mills and even the coalmines.

The education of the children of the Irish immigrants was principally carried out by the Catholic Church. Prior to the opening of St Joseph's Church in 1847, Kilmarnock had been established as one of the main 'stations' to be covered by Fr. William Thomson, the priest based in Ayr. As a designated station Kilmarnock was a central point at which Fr. Thomson would say Mass on pre-arranged Sundays and attend to the spiritual needs of those who attended. The hired hall was also used as a Sunday School to ensure 'children instruction in their religion and enough secular education to keep them away from Non-Catholic schools where Protestant catechisms were compulsory'. Shortly after the opening of the church the first Roman Catholic school, located in a rented flat, was started in George Street Lane. The teacher, William Lennox, had fewer than forty pupils but for Fr. Wallace, the incumbent priest, it was a beginning.

In 1865 St Joseph's, the school, moved to a newly built single-storey building which faced on to College Wynd. By the end of the decade the school roll was 170 and the staff consisted of a schoolmistress and four pupil teachers.

Subsequent increases in the school roll, and possible loss of school grant due to overcrowding, were countered by dividing the school into two and adding two new classrooms through the purchase and conversion of a house on land beside the school. It is strange that McKay and other nineteenth century historians have omitted to mention the founding of St Joseph's School.

Frequent mention is made in the records of the eighteenth and nineteenth centuries to the establishment or improvement of schools as a result of voluntary subscriptions. Prior to 1872 the provision of education for the poor, who could not afford the modest fees charged by the Academy and the various private schools, depended almost entirely on charity. The largest single act of munificence, however, came from Sir Alexander Kay, a local boy who made good in the Glasgow world of insurance. Following his death in January 1866 he left £10,000 to purchase and lay out the park which ever since has borne his name; and a further £6,000 for erecting and endowing two schools for the benefit of children belonging to the humbler classes, giving them 'a plain, practical and useful education' (to quote from Kay's will). The bequest

Painting of Kay School, Bentinck Street, 1860

stipulated that the education was to be comparable with that given in the best parochial schools 'but not to include what is usually called a classical education.' The two schools were erected in 1869, in Bentinck

Street and Wellington Street, under the headship of Peter Anderson and James Stevenson respectively.

The Education Act (1872)

In 1861 an Act relaxed, but did not sever, the ties which bound the parish school to the Church. In 1870 an Education Act was passed for England and Wales which brought in sweeping changes. A separate Act was passed for Scotland two years later. This established elective school boards and vested on them the existing parish and burgh schools. This Act made the school boards responsible for the supply of school accommodation and introduced compulsory attendance for children between the ages of five and twelve. Funding would come from central government based upon the number of children receiving elementary education. Results were to be measured by inspection from a new body of H.M.I. The school-leaving age was subsequently raised to fourteen in 1901.

The first election of the Kilmarnock School Board took place in March 1873 with Provost John Dickie as chairman. One of the first acts of the Board was to take a census of children of school age in the burgh. A distinction was made between those attending and not attending a school, in order to determine what additional provision would need to be made. The Academy was no longer adequate so plans for a new one were immediately put in hand. The foundation stone was laid on 20th November 1875 and the school was opened the following year on a one-acre site at the junction of North Hamilton and Woodstock Streets. The handsome building was erected by Andrew Calderwood at a cost of £4,500 to an Elizabethan or Tudor design by William Railton. Considerable difficulty was experienced by the School Board in framing a constitution for the Academy which enabled it to be classed as an elementary school within the meaning of the Act (and thus entitled to government

support), while retaining its character for providing education of the highest class. This object, however, was ultimately accomplished and the action of the Kilmarnock Board was subsequently imitated throughout the country. Hugh Dickie, formerly of Dumbarton Burgh Academy, was appointed rector and from the outset had a large staff of qualified teachers. The school roll of 426 pupils in 1876 rapidly increased to a peak of more than 700 from which it settled down to an average of around 650.

The new Academy took the cream of the schoolchildren of the burgh, but two other elementary schools were required to provide sufficient coverage, and both were opened within the same year. These were the High Street School (headmaster David Walker) and the Glencairn Street School (headmaster Thomas Scott), each accommodating some 400 pupils. The School Board also acquired the Female Industrial School and the Dundonald Road Free School. The latter, changed its name to Kilmarnock Grammar and, under the headmastership of John Lindsay, was rapidly enlarged and offered facilities not far short of the

Old Kilmarnock Academy, 1875

Academy itself. The Female Industrial School was renamed West Netherton School and, under George Smith (late of the old Academy), expanded to cover the full range of elementary subjects.

The genesis of technical education in Kilmarnock began in 1865 with classes taught in a room adjoining the Kilmarnock Library in the Corn Exchange Buildings. This school followed the curriculum set down by the Department of Science and Art at South Kensington, an outcome of the Great Exhibition of 1851. This was taken a stage further in 1878 with the erection of the School of Science and Art in Woodstock Street. William Railton, architect of the new Academy and a member of the committee for the establishment of the Science School, was again employed to produce suitable designs. The cost of the building was about £1,550, of which the Department of Science and Art provided £420, and the rest was raised by voluntary subscription. The style of this building was described as 'Tudor Gothic', with pointed windows in the upper storey and a square tower over the entrance at one corner. F.M. Black was in charge of this school from its earliest days in the Corn Exchange till he was promoted to Perth School of Art in 1877. The new School of Science and Art had two teachers from the outset, A.B. Miller and W.H. McHowl. Between them, they coped with 170 pupils in both day and evening classes. The school accommodated science laboratories for the Academy as well as metal working and engineering facilities and eventually became Kilmarnock Technical College at the turn of the century.

The passage of the 1872 Act led to a drop in the number of private schools, but some of the larger and older-established schools continued. Among these was the Holm School in East Shaw Street which had been founded in 1798 by the feuar of that district. This school taught reading, writing, grammar, arithmetic and book-keeping. Langlands Street School was founded by James Rose in 1845 and likewise concentrated on the three Rs. Several private girls' schools flourished in the latter half of the nineteenth century, namely the Union Street School under Miss Stephen, Miss Grant's School in London Road and the young ladies' establishment conducted by the Misses Henderson in Dundonald Road.

Twentieth century developments

In the 1890s plans were drawn up for the erection of a much larger Academy on a new site between Braeside Street and Elmbank Avenue. The architect was Mr. R.S. Ingram and the building was to incorporate a gymnasium, swimming bath, workshop and playground. Due to overcrowding at the 'Old Academy' the transfer to the 'New Academy' was made in 1898 before the completion of the building work. The school was opened by Sir Robert Murdoch Smith, a former pupil of the Academy, when it had been located in Green Street, and a celebrated archaeologist who had been responsible for arranging telegraphic communication between Persia and India.

Kilmarnock Academy

After the transfer the old building became Hamilton Street Primary School.

More than any other rector it is Dr Hugh Dickie, rector from 1876-1904, who established Kilmarnock Academy's reputation as one 'of the best known and best reputed provincial schools in Scotland.' Sir Alexander Fleming was only one of many distinguished names to have studied under Dr Dickie's rectorship.

In 1910 the Technical Building was added and Dr Clark, took great pleasure in being known as Rector of Kilmarnock Academy and Director of the Technical School. He was also the last rector to be responsible for evening as well as day classes. Kilmarnock Academy was to remain until 1946 the only school in Kilmarnock able to furnish students with university entrance level qualifications.

Technical School

Additional powers were conferred on the school boards by the Education (Scotland) Act of 1908, including the provision of school meals and the means of conveyance, or travelling expenses, to enable children from remote areas to attend their nearest school. Both of these provisions were to prove an immediate boon to the poorer children of Kilmarnock on the one hand, and to children in remote farming communities in the landward part of the parish on the other. Children neglected by reason of ill health or poverty of the parents, could now be supplied with food, clothing and medical attention, thereby anticipating the sweeping provisions of the Welfare State embodied in the National Insurance Act of 1911. The most important, long-term provision of the 1908 Education Act, however, was to enable (though not to compel) school boards to make provision for continuation classes up to the age of seventeen. It laid upon school boards the duty of making suitable provision for such classes in the crafts and industries practised in the district. In Kilmarnock additional facilities were provided in engineering and textile technology. Greater attention was also given to what was then termed 'higher class public' (i.e. secondary) education. Secondary schools were now defined as those providing a five-year course, whereas intermediate schools were defined as those limiting this to three years after elementary education had been completed. Later this part of the programme was largely superseded by a three years' advanced course at primary schools for pupils between the ages of twelve and fifteen. The 1908 Act introduced the qualifying examination, taken at the age of eleven or twelve, to determine whether a child should follow the advanced primary, intermediate or secondary courses.

Ten years later, the Act of 1918 reorganised the system of education and swept away the school boards which could no longer meet the costs involved in maintaining schools in their area. Inflation, the need to replace school buildings and movement of the population due to industrial development created financial problems for the school boards, as they were responsible for such small areas.

An ad hoc committee called the Ayrshire Education Authority came into being in 1919. 'Specially selected by public vote' the A.E.A. received over half of their financing from the Scottish Education Department the rest being raised from a local education rate. The A.E.A. was responsible for the finance and general administration of education in the county with School Management Committee's being set up to take care of local administration. The abolition of double rating and the apathy of voters towards the A.E.A. elections led to the formation of the County Council Education Committee in 1930 and the abolition of the Ayrshire Education Authority ad hoc Committee. The 1918 Act resulted in a large increase in expenditure, at both local and national levels, and many hitherto voluntary or private schools were taken over by the local authorities. The Act contemplated the raising of the school age to fifteen, but this was not legislated for until the Act of 1944 and not actually implemented until 1948. The Act of 1918 also served to put the education of children attending St. Joseph's on an even footing with those attending state owned schools. The Education Authority, rather than the church now being resposible for the provision of adequate buildings and resources.

St Joseph's transferred from College Wynd to Elmbank Avenue in 1903. The new school consisted of 7 classrooms which had been built as wings onto an existing two storey building which was used by the Catholic Young Mens' Society. This move had been forced on Father Woods under threat of losing the educational grant due to overcrowding at College Wynd. The cost of the new school was £7,420 which

had to be met by the church. Money was raised to pay for the school by selling the property in College Wynd and from donations. However by 1909 the debt still stood at £3,329. In contrast to this, following the 1918 Act, the school which had grown to 715 pupils by 1925 had a new building added at the expense of the Education Authority. This new building came into operation on the 12th of November 1926 with an extension being added in 1931.

By 1944 St Joseph's High School as it was now known had 300 secondary and nearly 800 primary pupils taught by a staff of 35 under the headship of Charles Mackay. Pupils who wished to study beyond third year however had to travel to either St Aloysius' or St Mungo's in Glasgow, St. Michael's in Irvine or transfer to Kilmarnock Academy. James Breen took over the running of the school in 1945 and identified his main task as building the secondary department to university entrance level. This he managed to do although, throughout his tenure, the girls still transferred to St Michael's after third year. Mr Breen was also responsible for the introduction of school uniform and the school badge during his ten years at St Joseph's.

Redevelopment of the inner town area and the general movement of population to the more spacious suburbs affected the pattern of schools in Kilmarnock in the first half of this century and this was accelerated by the 1944 Education Act. Of the schools established in the nineteenth and early twentieth centuries, the Grammar School (500 pupils), Loanhead (600), Bentinck Street (600) and High Street (400), together with the former Riccarton parish school (120) continued as primary schools into the postwar period. Others were closed as the population in their district dwindled or moved away.

Two schools were designated as junior secondaries with facilities to take their pupils on to the new school-leaving age of fifteen; these were Glencairn and Grange Schools, with 500 and 200 pupils, of post qualifying age, respectively.

Rev. James Hamilton

The James Hamilton Central School formerly established near the London Road in 1933 with only junior secondary departments, and took pupils from twelve to fifteen from various schools in the district after completing the primary course. The school, named in honour of the Rev. James Hamilton who had been Chairman of the Ayrshire Education Committee for many years, opened under the rectorship of Mr. George Hope, with

500 pupils and a staff of 21. Over the years the schools role changed and this is reflected in its progressive name changes to, James Hamilton Junior Secondary, James Hamilton High School and with the advent of comprehensive education the change to its current name, James Hamilton Academy.

In 1951 a junior secondary school was opened, in the new housing scheme of Shortlees but in contrast to the James Hamilton's progression the advent of the comprehensive system resulted in Shortlees being changed to a primary school.

The dramatic expansion of the town and its population from the 1950s onwards led to the need for additional primary schools in the surrounding housing estates. Non-denominational primary schools were opened at Bellfield, Gargieston, Annanhill, Silverwood and Onthank, while the original Riccarton school was replaced by a new school at Kirkstyle.

roll of around 800. The school roll was to increase to just under 1,100 pupils by 1965. However, with the opening of Mount Caramel Primary, Onthank in 1965 and St. Matthew's Primary, New Farm Loch in 1973 the school roll reduced to a more practical number.

St Columba's was to see the return of secondary education, if only briefly, in session 1973-4. Although plans for an extension at St Joseph's had been mooted as long ago as the 1960s the only concession which had been made to the increasing school roll had been the addition of hutted classrooms. By 1971 the school roll was 850 and rising, this in a school originally designed to house 650. Building work commenced in 1972 on an extension but work did not go well and by the start of session 1973/74 the extension was still not in use. The first year had to be taught at St Columba's with teachers shuttling back and forth by taxi to take their classes. The extension work was not completed until 1975 but the main teaching block was ready for

The original "James Hamilton", now Kilmarnock Training Workshop

Catholic education took a major step forward in 1956, with the opening of the new secondary school at Grassyards Road. The school had been occupied in 1955 under the headship of Mr E. Keating, before construction was complete and although only 560 pupils were housed in a school with a capacity for 650 initially conditions were cramped giving 'the impression in the early days that the school had almost as many work-men as it had pupils,' according to Mr Keating.

The school was located in open country side surrounded by pasture land which was later to become the New Farm Loch housing estate.

The new St Joseph's High School was fully a co-educational secondary school and offered courses up to university entrance level. The primary department which stayed behind in Elmbank Avenue changed its name to St Columba's and continued under the Headmastership of John P. McCready with a school

occupation by Easter 1974 thus allowing St Joseph's to be housed on one site again.

The current head teacher of St Joseph's is Ian McEwan, appointed April 1986, who presides over a current school roll of 580 drawn in the main from St Columba's, Mount Carmel and St Matthew's primary schools in Kilmarnock as well as St Paul's in Hurlford and St Sophia's in Galston.

The exigencies of the expanding population in the 60s and the dilapidated condition of Grange School led the Education Committee to authorise the construction of what we now know as Grange Academy. The Grange School had originally been built in 1875 as 'The Academy' before changing its name to Hamilton Street Primary School in 1898 when the new Academy building was opened and later to 'Grange School' in order to avoid confusion' with the James Hamilton Central School which opened in 1933.

On the 28th August 1967, Grange High School, under the headmastership of Mr Blackwood moved into the newly erected buildings in Beech Avenue. The opening school roll of 775 pupils consisted of 403 primary and 372 secondary pupils, however by the time comprehensive education was introduced, in session 69/70 the school roll had risen to 1,113 of which 648 were in the secondary department.

The 1972/73 session was an important one for 'The Grange' with the introduction of SCE Higher Grade Courses meaning pupils would no longer need to transfer to Kilmarnock Academy to gain University entrance qualifications. The opening of Annanhill Primary in 1973 and the consequent transfer of the primary department turned Grange into a purely secondary school with a roll of 889.

By the mid 1970s the number of students was growing beyond the capacity of the school. In order to cope with the projected increase in the school roll over the coming years extra blocks were built to the rear of the school in 1978.

The present rector H.G. Millar was appointed in 1981 and has seen the school roll rise to its highest ever level, in session 1983/84, of 1,314 pupils. In the current session 1991/92 there are just over 1,000 students, mainly drawn from the associated primaries of Annanhill, Gargieston, Hillhead, Onthank and Crosshouse. The site of the original Grange School, in Woodstock Street, was redeveloped as a special school in the 1980s.

The 'Jimmie', as it is affectionately known locally, moved to its current location in Sutherland Drive, New Farm Loch in 1976, although it was not officially opened until September 1977. Under its present Headmaster Bill McGregor the school roll consists of 479 students including 24 adults. The associated primaries are New Farm Loch, Silverwood and Crookedholm although a substantial number of pupils have come from other primary schools in Kilmarnock. Although currently working well under its capacity of 1,280 students the James Hamilton Academy has an excellent academic record added to which it is the only Academy in Kilmarnock designed to cater for the needs of disabled students, ramps and special toilets being unique features of the school. At the present time re-allocation of the primary school population is being looked at as one way to increase the school roll.

The Kilmarnock Academy playing fields, located between Queen's Drive and the River Irvine, were opened on the 24th September 1928 at which time A.R. Cumming was rector of the school. Mr Cummings successor Robert MacIntyre presided from 1938 till 1964 during which time the Academy became a purely secondary school. The new main building and games complex were opened in 1968 a year ahead of the first comprehensive intake of pupils. Following the introduction of the comprehensive system the Academy's roll reached its highest ever total of 1,960 pupils in session 1976/77. Christmas 1977 saw the retiral of James Hislop from the rector's position which he had held since 1964.

The current rector Frank Donnelly was appointed

in January 1978, and presides over a school roll currently standing at 1,218 pupils who have come mainly from the associated primary schools of Shortlees, Bellfield, Kirkstyle, Kilmaurs, Fenwick, Crossroads, Loanhead and Symington.

Since 1975 the responsibility for education has rested with Strathclyde Regional Council, through its sub-regional office at Ayr. This body now administers six comprehensive schools in the district (the four academies in Kilmarnock plus academies at Galston and Stewarton) and 25 primary schools. Another postwar trend has been the increased attention focused on pre-school education and today the District boasts seven nursery schools, four in Kilmarnock and one each in Darvel, Galston and Kilmaurs.

Before the Second World War Park School was established as a special school for 100 physically and mentally handicapped children. Nowadays the trend is to educate the handicapped in smaller units and Kilmarnock and District has three such facilities now looking after some 60 pupils. West Park School, which was previously located in Kilmaurs but is now in Crosshouse, caters for the educational needs of children whose hearing is impaired.

Further Education

Like Kilmarnock Academy, the Technical College outgrew its original building and in the mid-1950s technical education and vocational courses were also provided in the building which had previously been Glencairn School. In 1955 students were transferred to a Further Education Centre accommodated in a building in Soulis Street which had previously been a model lodging house. In 1966 an entirely new Technical College was opened in Holehouse Road. Today, known simply as Kilmarnock College, it has 3,000 students on full-time, block and day-release courses, covering a wide range of subjects from catering and hairdressing to engineering and electronics. In addition, a very comprehensive range of evening classes and further education courses are now available to students of all ages (including retired people) through the network of primary and secondary schools, where everything, from yoga to shorthand, from guitar tuition to stained glassmaking, is on offer.

At one time Kilmarnock was also the location of the West of Scotland Agricultural College. The Scottish Dairy Institute was founded in 1889 by the combination of the dairy associations in the south and west of Scotland. One of the Institute's first acts was to fit up part of the steading at Holmes Farm on the southwestern outskirts of the town as a dairy school, the costs being entirely defrayed by Lady Ossington. For ten years the Institute contributed towards its maintenance. In 1899 the dairy school was incorporated with the newly formed Agricultural College, but within four years demand for tuition far outstripped the capacity of the College, so that it became necessary to plan an entirely new suite of buildings. Plans for the College buildings were drawn up and the cost of erection was estimated at £5,500, the money being raised partly from government grants and partly from funds made available by the Highland and Agricultural Society, the county councils and the leading landowners of the southwest. The new College opened in 1904 and continued to serve agricultural students from all over the southwest of Scotland until 1937 when it moved to more spacious premises at Auchencruive. The buildings were then taken over by the local authority and converted for use as a maternity hospital.

Youth Educational Services

The range of activities available to young people should not be overlooked. The Kilmarnock and District Council of Youth was established just after the Second World War and each youth club and organisation in the area sent two delegates to what was then described as a 'youth parliament'. To direct the 60-odd youth clubs and other young people's organisations the Education Committee formed a District Youth Panel with a full-time Youth Organiser. In the third *Statistical Account* (1950) the youth organisations in the burgh consisted of twenty mixed clubs, including six open clubs, three junior branches of works' clubs, seven youth clubs attached to Church of Scotland congregations, one for Roman Catholics and two sponsored by the Salvation Army and one by the Co-operative Society. There were eighteen other organisations for boys only—five Boys Brigade companies and six Boy Scout troops, each with its affiliated organisations (Lifeboys and Cubs); pre-service organisations comprising the Air Training Corps, Sea Cadets and Army Cadet Force, and a Combined Cadet Force contingent at Kilmarnock Academy; youth branches of the YMCA, Toc H and the Adult School club. There were twenty girls' organisations, consisting of six Girl Guide units, two Girls' Guildry companies, a Red Cross detachment, the Girls' Training Corps, eight Girls' Associations and one church Girls' Club. Today the activities of the youth clubs and young people's community services are co-ordinated by the Community Education Office at The Gateway in Kilmarnock.

Aerial view of St Joseph's Academy, 1980

9 TRANSPORT AND COMMUNICATIONS

The trade and industry of Kilmarnock developed to some extent on account of the town's excellent transport and communications systems. Conversely, the want of good communications till the late eighteenth century undoubtedly hindered the development of the town. No wheeled vehicles of any kind were used in Kilmarnock until 1718, according to the Town records. Aiton stated that carts were not introduced till 1726 when they were used to cart stone from the quarries to the site of the bridge then being built over the river between Kilmarnock and Riccarton. In the matter of roads, Scotland was very backward. The only reasonably good roads by the middle of the eighteenth century were those which ran from Edinburgh south to Berwick and west to Glasgow. Elsewhere military roads were constructed from 1724 onwards by General Wade for the more efficient policing of the Highlands in the aftermath of the first Jacobite Rebellion, but in the Lowlands pack-horses continued as the main method of communication. A stage-coach was inaugurated thrice weekly between Edinburgh and Glasgow in 1749 but discontinued shortly afterwards through lack of demand.

Roads

Rough tracks connecting Kilmarnock with Glasgow, Irvine, Ayr and other towns developed over the course of many centuries, but until the second half of the eighteenth century they were impassable to wheeled vehicles. The road from Kilmarnock to Irvine via Dreghorn and Annick was built, or rebuilt in 1695. Certainly long before that date the trade from Kilmarnock along that route was very considerable. As far back as 1658 Irvine took unsuccessful legal action against Kilmarnock for infringing its rights as a royal burgh. In a report of 1692 to the Convention of Royal Burghs, Irvine complained of seven burghs of barony in Cunninghame 'which are very prejudiciall to them in point of trade, and serve the most pairt of the countrey with goods by retaill and that ther houses are better and more of them than many royal burghs, particularly Kilmarnock.' In 1700 the ancient antagonists,

Ayr and Irvine, actually joined forces to protest that 'the trade of Kilmarnock in import and export to France, Holland, Norway, Virginia and Ireland and other forraigne parts has been above half of the trade of both of the Burghs of Ayr and Irvine'. Dr Strawhorn, in his history of Irvine (1985), points out that Irvine benefited from its new and continuing function as a port for Kilmarnock.

The rough roads which ran from Kilmarnock to Irvine and Ayr bore an astonishing amount of goods. In 1789 some 3,289 tons of coal were exported from Kilmarnock to Irvine and thence exported to various ports in Ireland. By that time, however, there had been a considerable improvement in the Kilmarnock-Irvine road. This was achieved as a result of the Ayrshire Turnpike Acts of 1767 and 1774. These made provision for 22 roads, six of which ran through Kilmarnock. They were constructed and maintained by turnpike trusts which derived their curious name from the spiked barriers thrown across the roads to prevent the free passage of vehicles. These barriers were erected at toll-gates whose keepers were responsible for exacting tolls or charges from road-users, the money being used to defray the costs of the roads and provide funds for their extension, although much of the labour was provided free by the inhabitants who were liable for a certain number of days' service on road-works. Those unwilling or unable to perform these duties could opt out by paying sums of money for substitute workers.

According to Wood's map (1819) toll-gates were erected just north of Shilling Hill (near the present railway station) on the road to Paisley, on the Glasgow road north of Gillsburn, on the Mauchline road at Braehead road-end, and at the junction of the Irvine and Bullet roads on Grange Street. The 1832 map shows that the toll-gate on the Paisley road was by that time moved farther north to Strandhead. This map omits any reference to the toll on the road to Mauchline; on the other hand, it now shows Riccarton Toll just south of the bridge from Kilmarnock, on the road

The toll-house at Riccarton, part of the turnpike road system

leading to Ayr. Conflicting accounts regarding the state of these toll roads suggest that they varied considerably in quality in different parts, as well as at different times of year. Though tolerably good in a dry summer, they were well-nigh impassable in winter, while heavy rains in the spring and autumn turned their deeply rutted surfaces into quagmires. There were numerous complaints by the mercantile classes against the inefficiency and incompetence of the turnpike trustees. The turnpike roads were completely ignored in the account of Kilmarnock given in the first *Statistical Account* and dismissed in the second by a single sentence: 'There are two or three turnpike roads which intersect the landward parish in different directions, of no great extent, but which are all kept in good repair.'

The minor roads in the parish were of two kinds; both acted as feeders for the turnpikes. The various landowners built roads on their estates, for their own and their tenants' benefit, while the Town Council were responsible for the roads and streets within the burgh boundaries through which the thoroughfares connecting with the turnpikes ran. The Rev. Andrew Hamilton (1839) commented that

The roads in the parish are commodious, and kept in excellent repair, and there have been many improvements, especially of late, effected upon them, which render them equal probably to any in Great Britain.

However, he was less complimentary in respect to the burgh streets.

The old streets of the town are narrow and inconvenient, but all the modern thoroughfares are spacious and handsome. No town possesses more ample means of communication with the surrounding country. The intercourse with Glasgow, in particular, is very frequent, and the rapidly increasing number of carriers is a sure indication that trading is on the increase.

He also noted that there were at that time five bridges over the Kilmarnock Water within the burgh, all in excellent repair, and two over the River Irvine between Kilmarnock and Riccarton, in the same condition.

Communication with the outside world improved immeasurably in the 1780s. In 1784 the Post Office began operating mail-coaches on the London-Bath road. These vehicles were a vast improvement on the stage-coaches then widely used and greatly accelerated the transmission of the mails between these two cities. As the mail-coaches also carried passengers they soon posed a serious threat to the stage lines who made strenuous efforts to improve their own services. Thus the public in general benefited from this postal enterprise. A mail-coach from London to Edinburgh via the Great North Road was instituted in the summer of 1786 and mail for Glasgow and the south-west of Scotland was thence transported on horseback. On 7th

'Kilmarnock Cross' Oil painting by David O. Hill

July 1788 the mail-coach service from London to Glasgow direct was inaugurated. In 1787 the Post Office began operating a feeder service between Glasgow and Ayr which meant that the burgh could now send and receive letters each day. McKay, however, was in error in supposing that this service was the mail-coach between Glasgow and Carlisle; for that did not materialise till a year later and never passed through Kilmarnock. Moreover, the 'Camperdown' coach which he mentions in this connection, was not actually instituted till 1798, the year after Admiral Duncan's famous naval victory of that name.

On Saturday 3rd March 1827 the district was hit by a snowstorm of unparalleled ferocity and extent. In

floundering about for six hours, came again in their wanderings upon the coach, which they at first mistook for a house, and were taken in greatly exhausted; and there till next day did those eight remain in great distress, and half suffocated by the snow drifting over them to the depth of four or five feet. The third passenger, Mr John Brown, shoemaker, Kilmarnock, was not, however, even so fortunate. He missed both his way and his fellow-travellers, and sank beneath the shelter of the shapeless drift. His body was found on Monday, and brought to Kilmarnock in the evening.

By 1839 the chief turnpike road was that which ran from Glasgow to Portpatrick via Kilmarnock and thus bore a great deal of the overland trade of Scotland with

A convoy of Glasgow & South Western Railway Co. horse-drawn wagons in John Finnie Street

several parts of the town snow lay up to twenty feet deep and some of the roads in the surrounding countryside were so completely buried that only the tops of the hedges gave any clue as to their whereabouts. The *Ayr Advertiser* reported the storm and mentioned:

The Ayr Telegraph for Glasgow, which left Kilmarnock with six horses, came to an anchor between the two Fenwicks; that for Ayr lies at the foot of Drumboy Hill. The Regulator is somewhere about Logan's Well; the Kilmarnock coach, the Britannia, near the Mearns; and the English coach, about Mauchline. The Telegraph coach from Glasgow seems to have encountered the greatest difficulties. On her being stopped at Drumboy Hill, the guard joined the five inside passengers in the coach, whilst the driver and three outsiders resolved to proceed to King's Well, about a mile and a half distant, to procure assistance; and the driver accordingly, after many deviations, reached the inn with some of the horses. Such was the war of the elements, that no aid could be given at this time, and the six people remained in the coach. About midnight two of the outside passengers, after

Ireland. This road actually ran through the burgh for a distance of a mile and a quarter (2km), and through the parish from north to south a distance of about four miles. By that time there were four coaches plying daily between Kilmarnock and Glasgow, one between Kilmarnock, Irvine and Ardrossan, and one between Kilmarnock and Edinburgh, via Loudoun and Strathaven.

By the Roads and Bridges Act of 1878 road tolls were abolished. Responsibility for roads in the parish but outwith the burgh passed eventually to Ayr County Council, established in 1889. The Local Government Act of 1894 abolished the old parochial boards and instituted parish councils. The General Police and Improvement Act of 1862 provided for greater efficiency in the construction and maintenance of roads within the burgh. Great improvements were made in the turnpike roads in the early years of the nineteenth century under the influence of Thomas Telford and John Loudoun McAdam. It is worth noting that McAdam began his great career in civil engineering in the 1780s when he was a turnpike trustee in Ayr and also applied a more scientific approach to road-building, beginning with his own estate at Sauchrie. These experiments, conducted at his own expense, met with considerable opposition locally before his ideas were accepted. McAdam's ideas were not widely adopted till 1827, following his appointment as General Surveyor of Roads, but thereafter 'macadamising' (the use of broken stone for road metalling) and 'tarmac' perpetuated his memory. By the time of his death in 1836 the turnpikes had attained their widest extension, with over 1,100 systems nationwide. The advent of the railways, however, spelled disaster and many roads fell into disrepair during a long period when they were neglected by the parochial authorities.

After half a century in the doldrums, road building and maintenance gradually recovered and by the end of the nineteenth century the roads in the Kilmarnock district were mostly metalled. The main roads had been constructed in the turnpike era wide enough for the passage of two coaches each drawn by four horses. This continued to govern the width of roads till after the First World War, but by that time the growing use of motor traffic demanded a crash programme of road-widening and the improvement of cambers and drainage. Many of the unemployed ex-servicemen returning from the War found work on these road schemes which helped to alleviate distress. That this was a national problem was recognised in 1919 by the establishment of the Ministry of Transport which co-ordinated and supervised the work of the local authorities and allocated funds for road-building as well as the widening of streets in towns. Ten years later parish councils were abolished by the Local Government (Scotland) Act of 1929 which regraded Ayr and Kilmarnock as large burghs and downgraded Irvine (a royal burgh) and fourteen other towns to the status of small burghs, with commensurately reduced powers. While Kilmarnock continued to be responsible for roads within its boundaries the County Council was now given greater authority over the roads in the landward areas of the district.

From 1920 onwards, however, the volume of traffic using the roads invariably increased faster than road improvements could cope. Until the Second World War the network of main roads, secondary roads and country lanes remained virtually the same as it had been a century earlier, but clearly something drastic was required to relieve the town of the bulk of the through Glasgow-Ayr traffic. Just before the outbreak of War the Ministry of Transport began the construction of the by-pass to divert the Glasgow-Ayr traffic. Work on this by-pass was scheduled for completion in 1942, but ground to a halt during the War and was never completed, due to the expansion of the town's new housing schemes in Hillhead and Bonnyton; but today its legacy is Western Road (B7064) which leaves the Glasgow Road at a roundabout near Wardneuk and then runs in a south-westerly direction to peter out on Munro Avenue in Bonnyton where it meets the Irvine Road (A71). Even this important east-west road suffered from the abandonment of the original scheme for it has a slightly dog-legged appearance where it

crosses Loanfoot and Munro Avenues. Western Road is traversed farther north by a roundabout which permits the smooth flow of traffic from the Kilmaurs Road into Hill Street and thence into the town centre.

Although Western Road provided a ring-road for traffic to and from Irvine it did not solve the age-old problem of the Glasgow-Ayr traffic which continued to be funnelled through the town centre. The Cross was the worst bottleneck in the traffic and from the 1950s onwards various attempts to tinker with the problem resulted first in a roundabout and then (in 1966) a one-way system. In the 1970s the problem of traffic congestion was eased by the drastic re-development of the town centre which ripped the heart out of the old town. This resulted in an improved inner road system running south from the Glasgow Road / Western Road interchange along the B 7038 to Beansburn, Dean Street and Wellington Street, then by Union Street into Green and Sturrock Streets and doubling back along Fowlds Street to head south again along Titchfield Street. This inner system, permitting cross-town traffic at West George Street, London Road and Old Mill Road, now has enough problems just coping with the local traffic. In the late 1970s, however, the north-south through traffic was finally removed by the creation of the Kilmarnock By-pass (A 77 trunk road). A roundabout at the northern end gives access to Glasgow Road and thence Western Road, while an interchange system just south of the River Irvine provides access to the A 71 (Riccarton-Edinburgh road), the A 76 (Dumfries road) and Queen's Drive which leads to Welbeck Street and thence into the town centre.

Canals and Rivers

'The chief disadvantage under which the place labours,' wrote the Rev. James Mackinlay in 1790, 'is its inland situation, being about six or seven miles distant from the sea. This occasions a considerable expence in the land carriage of raw materials, as well as in their exportation, when manufactured.' John Goldie (1717-1809), who earned immortality from the verse epistle addressed to him by Robert Burns and beginning 'O Gowdie, terror o the whigs', was something of a Renaissance man whose restless mind roamed over a wide range of topics, from religion to mining speculation. In 1780 this miller turned cabinetmaker and wine merchant, published a best-seller on various moral and religious topics, popularly known as Goudie's Bible. Six years later, however, he turned his attention to the problem of improving the town's communications. He looked west to Troon which had one of the best deep-water harbours on the south-west coast and reasoned that a canal from Troon could be cut in order to link Kilmarnock with the sea. He even went to the trouble and expense of having the proposed route surveyed, from below Troon Point, via Loans and Dundonald, and then from Caprington up the River Irvine to the bridge at the south end of Glencairn Street. The idea was enthusiastically taken up in some quarters, and Mackinlay mentioned it in his parish account:

This undertaking would no doubt be attended with great expence; but as, from all accounts, it is practicable, (the lands through which it would run having no great ascent), if accomplished, it would certainly render Kilmarnock the most eligible and flourishing manufacturing town in the west of Scotland... Perhaps the canal, instead of stopping at Kilmarnock, ought to be extended to Glasgow, which is only 21 miles farther.

This encouraged the Town Council to apply to Parliament for the necessary Act in 1796, but the scheme foundered when the costs involved were made known.

For a town situated at the confluence of two rivers, Kilmarnock has made surprisingly little use of either as a waterway, but for a few years in the early 1930s there was a modest waterborne service on the River Irvine, operated by Jack Robertson of New Mill Road who offered small boats for hire. This was a purely recreational facility with its boathouse and dock on the river opposite the foot of Samson Avenue. From skiffs and sculls, Mr Robertson progressed to a motor launch, the *Nancy Stair* which took excursionists on a cruise down the river as far as the Glenfield works. This pleasure boat, however, was withdrawn from service some time before the outbreak of the Second World War.

Railways

Although Goldie's canal scheme was doomed to failure it quite literally paved the way for one of the first railroads in Scotland. This railroad received its Act of Parliament in 1808 and was laid out between Kilmarnock and Troon in 1811-12 at a cost of £50,000. The railroad had its eastern terminus on St Marnock Street near Kilmarnock House and ran in a generally south-westerly direction to Gatehead (2.75 miles), Drybridge (5 miles) and Barassie (8.5 miles) to Troon, a total length of nine and a half miles (15km). The practicability and usefulness of this line were governed primarily by the very gradual ascent from sea level at

Troon to a mere 80 feet at Kilmarnock. An ancient-looking tower near Caprington was, in fact, a signal box on this line, while Laigh Milton Viaduct was the oldest railway viaduct in Scotland. The line was a double track, constructed with flat iron rails resting on blocks of durable stone. The wagons were hauled by horses and the carriage of freight was charged at the rate of twopence (less than one new penny) per ton per mile. It was so successful that the Earl of Eglinton tried to get in on the act and proposed a branch line to Irvine, but the proprietors of the line did not find the proposition attractive enough.

In 1816, the Duke of Portland, who used the line to transport coal from his mines to his port at Troon, introduced a steam locomotive. The *Duke* was constructed by George Stephenson's brother Robert and re-assembled at Kilmarnock. As a result of its defective construction and ill adaptation to flat rails it could only haul ten tons at a top speed of 5mph, and as soon as it got to the first gradient at Gargieston it began to slip back on the flat rails. The experiment was deemed a costly failure and no attempt was made to repeat it for twenty years. During this period the horse railroad continued to give good service and transported over 200,000 tons of coal to Troon. A claim has been made that, at this early date, the horse railway carried passengers as well as freight, and if this were true it would make it the first passenger rail service in Scotland. Horsedrawn tramways or wagonways had, of course, existed in various parts of the country, notably the Clyde Valley, the Tyne and South Wales since the sixteenth century, and as far back as February 1804 Richard Trevithick successfully hauled a train of five wagons, containing ten tons of iron ore and seventy men, at Pen-y-Darran near Merthyr Tydfil. John Blenkinsop (1811) and William Hedley (1813) both built steam locomotives before George Stephenson built his first locomotive in 1814. Certainly the horse railroad carried passengers at a later period. Describing the advantages of this mode of transport (1839), the Rev. Andrew Hamilton wrote, 'The farmer gets lime cheaply conveyed to his farm, the landlord's property is increased in value by the facility of communications with the market-town, and the public have a ready means of transport to convenient watering-places.' Incidentally, the development of Troon as a fashionable seaside resort dated from this period.

George Stephenson's Stockton and Darlington Railway, opened in September 1825, was the world's first public passenger-carrying railway, but significantly the passenger coaches were drawn by horses till 1833. Four years later the Kilmarnock and Troon Rail Road received its Act of Parliament, enabling it

Scotland's first railway bridge at Laigh Milton Mill

Kilmarnock Railway Station

and the valley north of Braehead, to Hurlford where it curved south towards Auchinleck (opened on 9th August 1848) and continued on eventually to Dumfries. This line, terminating at Carlisle, was completed on 28th October 1850 when the last stretch, linking New Cumnock to Closeburn, was opened. On the very same day the Glasgow, Dumfries and Carlisle Railway Company joined forces with the Glasgow, Paisley, Kilmarnock and Ayr Railway to become the Glasgow and South Western Railway. The more direct route from Glasgow, via Nitshill, Barrhead, Caldwell, Lugton, Dunlop, Stewarton and Kilmaurs, was not opened until 1873.

In 1844 the old mineral railroad to Troon was upgraded and converted to steam working. A branch line diverged from the main route just north of Forge Street and curved southwards to link up with the original track south-west of Grange. The original railroad into Kilmarnock was subsequently converted to steam working but the track, which ran parallel to Dundonald Road and terminated near the corner of that road and Portland Road, was confined to freight traffic until it was discontinued at the turn of the century. Little vestige of this old track, Kilmarnock's first railway, now exists. It ran from the present railway line at a point just north of Rowanhill Place, skirted Rugby Park and crossed South Hamilton Street just south of the bowling green, then Seaford Street near the corner with Ellis Street.

While the Duke of Portland was planning to link Kilmarnock and Troon, the Earl of Eglinton had an even more ambitious scheme to link Ardrossan and Glasgow by canal along the Garnock Valley. This

to convert the track for steam locomotion. Locomotive engines had made enormous progress in two decades and already several lines operated from Glasgow and Edinburgh to the iron and coal towns of the central belt. The Kilmarnock-Troon railway had not managed to take the matter further by the time the Rev. Andrew Hamilton wrote his account for the second *Statistical Account* in 1839.

Since then [1816], no attempt has been made to introduce steam power. As it will in a few years very possibly become a branch of the western railway, several changes may take place in its construction, and it is not unlikely that the only propelling power used will be steam.

Hamilton lamented that Kilmarnock was unlikely to participate in the advantages of an immediate communication with the Glasgow and Ayrshire Railway—the 'western railway' mentioned earlier. 'It was the wish of the directors of the railway to have brought it through a place so important, but the difficulty of finding a practicable level prevented so desirable an object.' In the ensuing years, however, this problem was overcome and the railway from Glasgow was completed as far as Kilmarnock in 1843. This line took a rather roundabout route via Paisley, Johnstone, Kilbarchan, Glengarnock, Dalry, Montgreenan, Cunninghamehead and Crosshouse before curving to approach Kilmarnock from the north-west and terminating on Shilling Hill. The railway station was later considerably enlarged and its elaborate battlemented façade was erected in 1877. The line was driven eastward, via a viaduct, across the old town centre

Standard 0-4-0 sadde tank locomotive built by Andrew Barclay Sons & Co.

project was never completed, though the section from Glasgow (Port Eglinton) to Paisley (Canal Street) came into operation, and it was eventually overtaken by the rise of the railways. A railway followed the line of the proposed canal and linked Glasgow, Paisley, Dalry, Kilwinning, Irvine and Ayr. As already mentioned, a branch line south of Dalry was pushed forward to Kilmarnock, via Montgreenan, Cunninghamehead and Crosshouse. Another line was constructed in 1848 from Kilmarnock to Irvine by the Glasgow and South Western Railway, but only after its rival, the Caledonian Railway threatened to get there first. This line ran due east via Dreghorn and linked up with the Dalry line at Crosshouse. The railway network reached its zenith at the turn of the century. A loop from the Troon line ran in a broad eastward curve south of Kilmarnock to bypass the town and link up with the line to Dumfries at Hurlford. This line ran south of Gargieston and along the south bank of the River Irvine, crossing Riccarton near Willock Street and running north of Kirkstyle. Another loop eventually linked this line with the main railway, crossing London Road to join the main line near the bridge crossing MacPhail Drive and following the curve of Culzean Crescent. From 1881 a line from Hurlford, operated by the Lanarkshire and Ayrshire Railway (a subsidiary of the Caledonian Railway), ran eastwards up the Irvine Valley, with stations at Galston, Newmilns, Darvel and Loudounhill and thence via Strathaven to link up in 1905 with the lines through Lanarkshire.

In 1922 the Glasgow and South Western Railway became part of the London, Midland and Scottish Railway which, in 1948, became part of British Rail (Scottish Division). The route through Kilmarnock terminated at Glasgow St Enoch and London St Pancras. The railway network survived more or less intact until 1960 when, as a result of the Beeching Report, the Irvine Valley line was closed. Four years later the line to Irvine and Ardrossan was discontinued and even the main north-south line was subject to severe retrenchment. In the 1980s it was converted to single-track working, although it remains dual-track within the old burgh boundaries. There is now a frequent commuter service to Glasgow, via Kilmaurs, Stewarton and Dunlop, and less frequent services to Ayr and Dumfries.

Tramways

Wagonways and mineral railways such as the Duke of Portland's Kilmarnock-Troon Rail Road originally had wooden rails but from the early eighteenth century onwards they were capped with iron to make them more durable. Solid rails of cast iron with flanges, or ledged on their inner side to keep the wheel on the track, were first produced by the Coalbrookdale Iron Company of Shropshire in 1767. These flanges were known as trammels because they 'trammelled' or confined the wheel to the rail. Lines bearing these flanged rails therefore came to be called trammelroads, later shortened to tramroads or tramways. In July 1803

Tram route from Hurlford ending at the Cross.

the Surrey Iron Railway from Wandsworth to Croydon was opened to the public. This, the world's first commuter train, was hauled by horses. Horsedrawn trams and streetcars eventually became a familiar sight in many towns and cities on both sides of the Atlantic. Later street railways and tramways preferred wrought iron rails with a deep groove into which the flanged wheel could fit securely. Steam locomotion was never popular for this purpose as it required heavier rails and tracks and the pollution of the atmosphere was a major hazard. Horse traction remained the preferred medium till the 1880s when cable cars (still used in San Francisco) were briefly in fashion. Within a decade, however, electric traction solved the problem.

Kilmarnock Town Council applied to Parliament and received an enabling Act in 1903 to establish an electricity generating station to provide street lighting and traction for a tramway system. Overhead power cables were erected in October that year and on 10th December the eighth Lord Howard de Walden drove the first tram from Beansburn to Riccarton. A second line ran from the Cross eastwards to terminate at Hurlford. Apart from the section from the railway station south to the Greenholm car sheds, the line was single-track but passing places were provided by loops at half-mile intervals.

The original eleven single-deck, open-topped cars were augmented in 1905 by two more of the same pattern. Fares were modest and ranged from 1d to 3d for adults, with half fares for children between three and fourteen years of age. Children under three were carried free of charge. A special tariff 'for labouring classes' permitted 'bona-fide Workers of these Classes' to obtain two-journey, four-journey and six-journey tickets at reduced rates. The catch was that these workmen's tickets could not be used after 6.30pm on weekdays or 2pm on Saturdays. Originally this could be circumvented by producing an overtime permit from one's employer, but this concession was cancelled in 1923.

While the electricity undertaking was a great success and even exported surplus power to Irvine from 1914 onwards, the trams themselves lost money. The situation was exacerbated during the First World War when replacement parts were almost impossible to obtain, and breakdowns in the ageing equipment were becoming more and more frequent. By this time the trams were facing competition from private enterprise in the form of various bus operators. The trams suffered the major drawback of being inflexible, so that when one broke down on the single track others following behind or coming in the opposite direction were held up. In 1924 the Council tried to recover lost business by itself installing four Thornycrofts and four Albions on the burgh bus routes but this only accelerated the decline in the popularity of the trams. The General Strike of 1926 finally put them off the road, and when normal working was resumed after the strike the trams were permanently retired from service on 15th December that year. The tracks were promptly lifted and the overhead wires dismantled, although the massive iron brackets can still be seen on some buildings, notably above Ladbroke's in Portland Street. Two trams were sold to Ayr Corporation but the rest ended up as huts and outbuildings on farms and small-holdings.

Bus Services

At the turn of the century Sam Cowan operated a horse-bus from the George Hotel to Riccarton Toll, an hourly service with a maximum fare of a penny. There was also a Fenwick bus which ran from the Sun Inn in Green Street, but this was only a weekly service on Fridays for the benefit of farming folk coming to market. In 1913 Robert Johnstone of Fenwick organised the first service by motor-bus in the district. His sixteen-seater wagonettes operated between Kilmarnock and Fenwick, but in 1914 he began a route from Kilmarnock to Irvine and the town councils of both burghs provided him with stances or bus-stops at a very nominal sum. This service was a success, despite wartime shortages, and in 1919 was joined by rival services which eventually ran to Ardrossan and Ayr and even as far as Glasgow. The 1920s was an era of cut-throat competition in which the safety of passengers and pedestrians was sometimes put at risk and many services were ephemeral, operated by one-man outfits. As previously mentioned, the Corporation itself entered the fray, with four Albions and four (later eight) Thornycrofts which superseded the tramcars from 1926 onwards. The buses were faster, more flexible and much more economic to run than the trams. Overshadowing the small operators, however, was the giant Scottish General Transport Company which established its headquarters in Portland Street in 1925. Here a large (for the period) and well-appointed bus station was erected, complete with passenger waiting rooms and facilities for the repair and maintenance of the growing fleet of buses, which included the Corporation buses, sold to the company on 31st December 1931. In 1932 this company merged with Scottish Motor Traction and Kilmarnock became the nerve centre of what has since become Western SMT. Faced with competition from this large organisation no fewer than 21 smaller companies combined to form the Ayrshire Bus Owners (A1 Services) Limited to offer an alternative service on the lucrative Kilmarnock-Irvine-Ardrossan routes; and

Western SMT bus station, Portland Street

about the same time other firms joined forces to become the AA Motor Services Limited, mainly covering the routes along the Clyde coast.

Western SMT (now the Western Scottish Bus Group) and A1 continue to serve the community to this day, operating local routes in and around the town as well as long-distance routes. While A1 concentrate on the routes to Irvine and the coast, SMT provide a service linking Kilmarnock with Glasgow and Dumfries and all points in between. The old bus station was demolished in the 1970s when the inner town area was redeveloped, but was replaced by a splendid new structure in the Foregate north of the Burns Precinct with which it is linked. This facility, with its spacious forecourt, is infinitely safer than the old transport station where buses, emerging straight on to Portland Street, were often a hazard to other road users.

Posts and Telegraphs

When the General Letter Office was established in 1661, following the Restoration, Kilmarnock was one of the few towns in Scotland to be granted a post office. This was not because the town itself was then a place of importance, but because it lay on the direct route from Edinburgh to Portpatrick and thence to Ireland. At that time, and for almost a century thereafter, the mails came and went once a week and were conveyed by foot-messengers between Glasgow and Ayr. By comparison, Irvine, though a royal burgh and a place of much greater commercial importance, did not get a post office till 1689. In the early eighteenth century the service was improved to three times a week and accelerated by the use of mounted post-boys (who could, in fact, be quite old men). Originally the cost of a single-sheet letter from Kilmarnock to Edinburgh, Glasgow or Ayr was two shillings Scots (2d). By 1790, however, the cost of a letter to or from Glasgow had risen to 3d and to Edinburgh the charge was 4d. Rates rose sharply during the Napoleonic Wars and by 1814 even the cheapest letter cost 7d. Kilmarnock enjoyed the benefit of a mail-coach service from 1787 onwards, but in 1813 the Post Office introduced an additional halfpenny charge on all letters conveyed in Scotland at some point of their journey by a vehicle having more than two wheels. The purpose of this tax (which never applied to mail conveyed within England, Wales and Ireland) was to raise money to pay the charges imposed by the turnpike trusts. In effect, however, the Post Office got around this iniquitous levy by drastically curtailing the number of mail-coach services and substituting two-wheeled gigs or reverting to foot and horse posts wherever practical. This ridiculous situation continued until December 1839 when the additional halfpenny tax was abolished. By that time the cost of sending a letter from Kilmarnock to London had risen to 1s3d—a day's pay for the average mill-worker or coal-miner—but when Rowland Hill's uniform postage was introduced the charge was reduced to 4d and then, on 5th January 1840, to 1d per half ounce, regardless of the number of sheets (or envelope) or the distance

involved. Uniform penny postage was a tremendous boon which not only stimulated trade and commerce but gave even ordinary individuals an incentive to communicate with friends and relatives more frequently than before.

In 1790 the revenue of the postal service in Kilmarnock yielded about £400 a year. In the same period the excises on ale, spirits, candles and other dutiable articles produced an income of £1,700 per annum. 'Both these branches of revenue are rapidly increasing, with the trade and population of the place,' wrote Dr Mackinlay. He also stated baldly, 'There is a post-office in the town, for this, and for the neighbouring parishes.'

The location of the original post office is not known, but as it would have been situated in the house of the postmaster it tended to move around the town every

Andrew Fisher and a Barclay locomotive,
on stamps of Austrailia (1972) and Jersey (1985)

few years. One of the last of the traditional postmasters was David Rankin, a prominent businessman who played a notable part in the celebrations marking the centenary of Robert Burns in 1859 and who later served as captain of the Fifth Company of Ayrshire Artillery, from its inception in May 1860. He was appointed in 1843 in succession to his father William Rankin, a solicitor who had operated the post office since 1803. Between them, the Rankins served the Post Office for almost seventy years. William Rankin originally had his post office at the foot of the Foregate near the Cross, but in 1834 he moved to more commodious premises at the corner of King Street and Market Lane. In 1840 the office moved to the corner of King Street and Queen Street, but following David Rankin's retirement in 1872 it was relocated by his successor farther along Queen Street.

With the absorption of the telegraph business in 1870 and a dramatic growth in business in the ensuing decade, the Post Office decided that the time had come to establish a Crown post office on a permanent site, and select a postmaster from among its professional staff. A site was purchased on John Finnie Street and a handsome red sandstone building was erected in 1878. William K. Bryson, previously overseer at Inverness, was appointed postmaster in 1879 and continued till 1886 when he was promoted to postmaster of Perth. During his term of office the parcel post was inaugurated (August 1883) and postal orders were introduced (1885); both led to a tremendous growth in mail order business. His successor, John Ballantyne, came from Glasgow where he had been superintendent of the sorting office and this pattern of appointments has continued ever since. The head post office was enlarged and renovated in 1907 and has been substantially extended on several occasions since then.

Mackinlay was correct in stating that the Kilmarnock post office served the entire district. Galston got a post office in November 1824 and Fenwick in May 1837, but Darvel had no post office till 30th July 1852 and Newmilns was without postal facilities till 1st June 1872. Other post offices in the surrounding countryside were established at Waterside (1852-1916), Crosshouse (April 1883) and Gatehead (April 1937). A sub office under Irvine was opened at Drybridge on 1st October 1914 but was transferred to the control of Kilmarnock in 1932 and closed on 12th January 1974.

Within the burgh of Kilmarnock as eventually constituted, the first sub post office was a receiving house established in Riccarton on 4th April 1844. For many years it functioned as an independent rural sub office, gaining the status of a money order office in July 1891. It was converted to a town sub office of Kilmarnock on 1st May 1900 and closed on 31st May 1985, a casualty of the redevelopment on the line of the new road south.

The oldest sub office in the town is now that located in Titchfield Street which first opened for business on 1st October 1886 and was a money order office from the outset. A sub office with money order facilities was established in Wellington Street on 20th November 1886 and continued till 26th November 1971. On 1st April 1893 two new money order offices were opened, in Glencairn Square and in North Hamilton Street. Both closed in the early 1970s due to redevelopment and the redistribution of population in the town. A town sub office opened in Welbeck Street on 29th July 1896 and was raised to money order status a year later. It closed on 28th February 1943. A sub office opened in Duke Street on 18th June 1900 but due to redevelopment closed on 30th September 1967, being then superseded by the post office in Waterloo Street. The expansion of the town was reflected in the offices opened in the course of this century. A sub office opened at Beansburn on 1st April 1909 and was granted money order facilities from the outset, but these were withdrawn at the end of 1915. This office closed on 31st May 1985. The sub office in Bonnyton opened on 1st March 1933 and that in Knockinlaw was established on 1st February 1941. In the postwar period sub offices were opened at Shortlees (12th November 1951), Onthank (23rd October 1955), Whatriggs Road (1st July 1958) and Samson Avenue (1st June 1961). The last named was very short-lived, closing down on 31st May 1962 after exactly twelve months in existence. More recently, sub offices were opened at MacPhail Drive (8th January 1970) and New Farm Loch, Lindsay Drive (8th April 1974).

In the re-organisation of postal services in recent years Kilmarnock has assumed responsibility for a wide area which now stretches from Arran to the head of the Irvine Valley. A measure of the town's postal

importance was the introduction of mechanised stamping as long ago as 1912. At one time the towns and villages of the surrounding district postmarked their own mail but over the past twenty years this has gradually been concentrated on Kilmarnock. Kilwinning (March 1970), Cumnock and Mauchline (10th October 1971), Irvine (February 1979), Ardrossan, Stevenston and Saltcoats (1st June 1980), Millport (June 1982) and Brodick (October 1983) are all places which formerly had their own cancelling machines but surrendered this function to Kilmarnock on the dates specified. The smaller towns as far afield as Darvel and Stewarton formerly handstamped their mail but this, too, now goes to Kilmarnock for machine cancellation.

The Post Office Savings Bank (now the National Savings Bank) was inaugurated in 1861 but it was some time before the main post offices were equipped to handle this business, and Kilmarnock was authorised to deal in savings from 17th February 1862. Many of the minor sub offices which did not have money order status were permitted to sell and encash postal orders from 1885 onwards, a considerable boon in agricultural communities where many farmworkers (especially from Ireland) were thus enabled to send remittances back to their families. This facility, coming hard on the heels of the parcel post (inaugurated in August 1883) greatly stimulated the growth of the mail order business which likewise tended to benefit rural areas in particular. In 1869 the telegraph services, previously in the hands of the railway companies and private firms, were nationalised and handed over to the Post Office to operate. An electric telegraph attached to the railway station had operated at Kilmarnock since 1855, but it became a Post Office concern from 1st January 1870, when the telegraphic code KK was adopted. Riccarton got telegraphic facilities on 10th November 1891 with the code RCN. The only other telegraph offices in the district were at Newmilns with the code NHT (11th November 1876) and Crosshouse with the code CXQ (21st May 1892). Telegraphic facilities were withdrawn in 1982. The National Telephone Company connected Kilmarnock in 1881, the first subscriber in the burgh being Messrs John Walker. The service was nationalised in 1912 and likewise delegated to the Post Office until the establishment of British Telecom ten years ago.

The Local Media

Although Kilmarnock had a printing-press as far back as 1780, the town did not have the benefit of any newspapers or periodicals until the early nineteenth century. In August 1817, however, two periodicals appeared, each, in the fashion of the period, having *two* titles. These were the *Ayrshire Miscellany* or *Kilmarnock Literary Expositor* and the *Coila Repository* or *Kilmarnock Monthly Magazine*. The latter lasted only a year, but the former, being a more 'down market' publication, flourished. It was published weekly at twopence and was read in every town and village in Ayrshire. It combined the functions of a newspaper with that of a literary journal and purveyor of popular knowledge and survived till May 1822, a comparatively long life for the period. Soon after it commenced, there was a third periodical, entitled the *Literary Gleaner* or *Kilmarnock Mirror* but it, too, lasted only a few months. The proprietor, editor and chief reporter of the *Miscellany* was James Thomson (1775-1832), Captain in the Kilmarnock Sharpshooters since 1804. Previously he had worked for a year on the *Scottish Review*; been intended for the ministry of the Secession Church; was a partner in the family tanning business and an officer of the Argyll Militia. To crown his manifold achievements, he was also a poet of no mean talent, as will be found in the next chapter.

In January 1831 the first newspaper in the burgh began under the name of the *Kilmarnock Chronicle*; but though it was a lively paper advocating popular principles it met with scant success and after struggling to boost its circulation it came to an end in January 1832. Its founder, James Paterson, was not the man to let the matter go so lightly, and four months later he re-launched the paper, but the second attempt was no more successful than the first and the paper finally packed up the following winter. It was Paterson who introduced the first iron printing press, a Columbian which later passed into the hands of Smith Brothers. In February 1833 another paper was started and printed at the same press, under the title of the *Ayrshire Reformer and Kilmarnock Gazette*. Its proprietor and editor was Dr John Taylor of Ayr, a man of great talent and boundless energy; nevertheless even he was unable to cultivate in the people of Kilmarnock a taste for newspapers, for it, too, ceased after a short time.

It was a case of 'third time lucky' for yet another newspaper was launched on 7th February 1834. This

time, the *Kilmarnock Journal* caught on with the reading public and enjoyed the relatively long life of 23 years. To judge from Paterson's *Autobiographical Reminiscences* the reason for the failures of his paper was lack of a sound business footing rather than any want of public support. Consequently, the *Journal* was started as a joint-stock company for the promotion of Reform principles. Like the Vicar of Bray, however, it learned to trim its political sails and later became moderately Conservative before espousing the Liberal cause. It was singularly fortunate in its first editor, John Donald Carrick, a literary figure in his own right, who

contributed many fine articles to the paper. Among the later editors was James Paterson, founder of the first newspaper. In July 1855 it was considerably enlarged and otherwise improved but in so doing incurred such a loss that it folded on 8th May 1857.

Until July 1838 the *Journal* was the sole newspaper in Kilmarnock; but as it was then going through its Conservative phase the radicals of the town were anxious to have a forum for their political views and consequently launched the *Ayrshire Examiner*. It was ably edited by John R. Robertson but, like its predecessors in support of popular politics, it sickened for want of encouragement and came to an end in November 1839. James Mathie, a bookseller in the town, launched the *Kilmarnock Herald* on 20th September 1844 and ran it till 19th May 1848. Its first editor, Alexander Russell, had previously worked on the *Scotsman* and for a time this Liberal paper flourished before inevitably succumbing. In January 1854 another Liberal organ was launched, by the bookseller James Millar, under the title of the *Kilmarnock Chronicle*. It began modestly as a weekly, but in June 1855 it became a thrice weekly paper. However, this increase in output was its undoing for after only 27 numbers in this format it ceased publication. During its early months it was edited by J.C. Paterson who had been the last proprietor of the ill-fated *Journal*. James McKie, a

bookseller and noted Burnsian, started the *Kilmarnock Weekly Post* in November 1856 and under his editorship it ran till October 1865. The *Kilmarnock Advertiser and Ayrshire Review* started on 22nd August 1868 and collapsed on 12th December of the same year. It was edited, printed and published by Hugh Henry.

Eight newspapers in 37 years was an unenviable record; it seems astonishing that there was never any shortage of able men ready and willing to come forward and gamble their money on what, to all appearances, was the riskiest of ventures. Even a reasonably well-established paper like the *Journal* could run into terminal problems when it tried to effect improvements. For seven years McKie's *Weekly Post* was the sole newspaper in the burgh, but in June 1863 Thomas Stevenson founded the *Kilmarnock Standard* and, against all the odds, it not only flourished but survives to the present day. By the time of its centenary it was selling 25,000 copies and was widely read throughout the county, with over 1,200 copies each week being sent overseas to Killie expatriates everywhere. For over a century the *Kilmarnock Standard* remained in local ownership, but in 1971 it was taken over by Scottish and Universal Newspapers Limited

and re-launched as a tabloid. In 1978 production was transferred to SUN's new premises at South Newmoor, Irvine. By contrast, the *Kilmarnock Herald*, re-launched in 1880 as a Conservative paper, and its stablemate the *Ayrshire Gazette* never rose above a combined circulation of 10,000. The publishers of these papers launched a third title in 1945, a weekly catering to weekend sport and Labour Party views. The *South Western Courier*, however, never exceeded sales of 1,000 a week. All three ceased publication in 1955, when they were being edited by Richard Aitken and owned by Willie Mitchell.

Over the years, the *Standard* has lived up to its name, setting very high standards in local journalism which continue to this day. A number of journalists and authors of national or international repute were associated with the paper. In the first category may be mentioned Hugh Taylor, later a sports writer with the Glasgow *Daily Record* and then the *Daily Mirror* in London. He was also the author of *Go Fame*, the history of Kilmarnock Football Club. Hugh Cochrane of the *Glasgow Herald* and Hugh McIlvanney of *The Observer* also got their start with the *Standard*, under the editorship of Willie Scott. Tom Lyon (1943-63) a veteran of the First World War, himself published *In Kilt and Khaki* (1915) and *More Adventures in Kilt and Khaki* (1917). John Malkin, a journalist on the *Standard* from 1942 till 1977 when he became Public Relations Office to the District Council, has written poetry and children's stories. He is also the author of several books, including biographies of Sir Alexander Fleming, Robert Colquhoun and Andrew Fisher, and his widely acclaimed *Pictorial History of Kilmarnock* (1989).

George Dunlop (1862-1909) was born in the Gas Brae and educated at the Academy where he became a pupil teacher. He did not find teaching very congenial, however, and soon switched to printing. He entered Brown's printing-shop in King Street and later worked for James McKie in a similar capacity. He also acted as Kilmarnock correspondent for the *Ayr Advertiser* and this experience led him into journalism. When Thomas Stevenson started the *Standard* Dunlop soon joined the staff and when Stevenson died George took over the operation, eventually in partnership with William Drennan. From a tiny four-page news-sheet Dunlop developed the *Standard* into a broadsheet of many pages. He was a prolific writer, contributing many feature articles as well as leading columns. He was official shorthand reporter at the Sheriff Court for many years, and also found the time to contribute articles to other papers and magazines.

On his death in 1909 he was succeeded as editor and proprietor of the *Standard* by his son George Brown Dunlop who, in 1938, married Annie Isabella Cameron. Born at Strathaven in 1897, Miss Cameron was educated at Glasgow High School for Girls and graduated from Glasgow University with first class honours in history. This was followed by a Ph.D. from Edinburgh (1922) and a D.Litt. from St Andrew's (1934). A Carnegie scholarship took her to Rome in 1930 where she worked on the archives of the Vatican. A staunch Presbyterian, she was on speaking terms with three Popes and in 1972 Pope Paul VI conferred on her the papal decoration Bene Merenti, a rare honour for a non-Catholic. After her marriage, Dr Dunlop contributed a weekly column to the *Standard* under the title of 'Ayrshire Notes' but later, as her travels widened, this became 'Leaves from a Historian's Notebook'. After her husband's death in 1950 she continued to write, and produced a number of learned works on aspects of medieval Scottish history. She was also Vice-President of the Ayrshire Archaeological and Natural History Society and, in 1951, was the first lady to become an Honorary President of the Burns Federation.

10 LITERATURE AND THE ARTS

In the worlds of poetry, literature and bibliography Kilmarnock immediately brings to mind the first edition of the works of Robert Burns, often referred to as the Kilmarnock Edition, or even the Kilmarnock Poems. Burns was neither native to, nor resident in, the burgh or parish; yet, as we shall see in the next chapter, Kilmarnock exerted a powerful influence on the budding poet. Over the past four centuries, however, Kilmarnock has produced an impressive number of literary figures of its own.

Sir William Mure

Pride of place must go to Sir William Mure, born at Rowallan Castle about 1594. An uncle on his mother's side was Alexander Montgomerie (c1550-c1610), a prolific poet now best remembered for his 'Cherry and the Slae', first published in 1597 and undergoing many editions down to the present. Sir William inherited something of his uncle's poetic talents and, while still a boy composed many poems, one of which was published in the *Muse's Welcome*, an anthology compiled to celebrate the visit of King James VI and I to Scotland in 1617. Mure's poetry had a strongly mystical and religious flavour with political overtones; his published pieces include 'The True Crucifixe for True Catholics' (1629) and 'The Cry of Blood and of a Broken Covenant' (1650). His poems, distinguished by their delicacy of conception and execution, have been compared favourably to those of his illustrious contemporary, Drummond of Hawthornden. Though rather a bookish man, Mure also played a notable part in the religious and civil conflicts of the mid-seventeenth century. He was a member of the Scottish Parliament which met at Edinburgh in 1643 to ratify the Solemn League and Covenant and the following year he served in the army of Oliver Cromwell, being wounded at the Battle of Marston Moor and later taking part in the Roundheads' siege of Newcastle. During the Commonwealth he retired to his ancestral estate and carried out many improvements, including the extensive planting of

THE

HISTORIE AND DESCENT

OF THE

HOUSE OF ROWALLANE.

BY

SIR WILLIAM MURE, KNIGHT,

OF ROWALLAN.

WRITTEN IN, OR PRIOR TO

1657.

trees, many of which are still standing. He died at Rowallan in 1657 and was succeeded as baronet by his son of the same name.

He is best remembered, however, for a work which was never published, but which exists in manuscript form in the library of Glasgow University. This was his metrical version of the Psalms which seems to have enjoyed a high contemporary reputation. When Principal Baillie served as one of the Scottish commissioners to the Westminster Assembly of Divines in 1643 for the purpose of selecting a standard version of the Psalms he spoke of Sir William's in one of his letters: 'I wish I had Rowallan's *Psalter* here, for I like it better than any I have yet seen'. The committee appointed to revise the edition of Francis Rous, later Provost of Eton College, was instructed 'to avail themselves of the help of Rowallan's'. This edition, first used publicly at Glasgow in May 1650, is employed in the Presbyterian churches of the world to this day.

Contemporaries of Burns

Among the more prolific Kilmarnock writers of the late eighteenth century was John Goldie, previously mentioned on account of his proposals to construct the Kilmarnock-Troon canal. All his life he took an intense interest in religion and religious controversy and was an active participant in the protracted arguments

John Goldie

between the Auld and New Lichts. In 1780 he had printed at Glasgow a collection entitled *Essays on various important Subjects, Moral and Divine, being an attempt to distinguish True from False Religion*. A second edition appeared in 1785 with an even lengthier title, *Essays on various Subjects, Moral and Divine, in one volume by John Goldie; to which is added, the Gospel recovered from a Captive State, in five volumes, by a Gentle Christian*. Fortunately this extremely popular work was usually known to its readers more simply as 'Goudie's Bible'. Inevitably, this book was not without its critics and satirists and even Burns was moved to poke some gentle fun at the author in his verse epistle which began:

O Goudie, terror o the Whigs,
Dread o black coats and rev'rend wigs,
Soor Bigotry, on her last legs,
   Girnin, looks back,
Wishin the ten Egyptian plagues,
   Wad seize you quick.

In his *Contemporaries of Burns* (1840) James Paterson

recounts an anecdote concerning Goldie who happened to go into a bookshop in Ayr one day and bumped into a clergyman of his acquaintance on his way out. 'What have *you* been doing here?' jocularly enquired Goldie. 'Just buying a few ballads,' retorted the minister, 'to make psalms to your bible!'

In addition to the *Essays* Goldie was the author of a volume entitled *Conclusive Evidences against Atheism* which was actually printed at Kilmarnock, in 1808. Goldie also had in preparation a book entitled *A Reform of the present System of Astronomy* but he died in 1809 before the project could be completed. He was then in his 92nd year. Posterity has not served Goldie too kindly and later critics were to say that 'as literary productions, his writings are rather defective', though McKay conceded that in some instances they exhibited Goldie's reasoning faculties in a favourable light.

Gavin Turnbull was born in the Borders but at an early age he was brought to Kilmarnock by his father, a dyer who, though rather an eccentric character, had the good sense to bestow on his son the rudiments of a classical education with a view to qualifying him for some respectable profession; but some family tragedy blighted this ambition and marred Gavin's prospects. In adulthood he lived in the greatest poverty. McKay, in his book *Burns and his Kilmarnock Friends* (1874), provides an interesting description of Turnbull's humble domicile.

> He resided alone in a small garret in Soulis Street.
> The bed on which he lay was entirely composed of
> straw, and had only an old patched coverlet, which he
> drew over him during the night. He had no chair or
> stool. A cold stone placed by the fire served as a
> substitute; and the sill of a small window at one end
> of the room was all he had for a table from which to
> take his food, or on which to write his verses. In
> short, the bed alluded to, an old tin kettle (his only
> cooking utensil) and one spoon, comprised the whole
> of his household property—the lid of the kettle on
> every occasion making up for the want of a bowl or
> plate!

Turnbull's works were printed at Glasgow in 1788 under the title of *Poetical Essays*. Although they were favourably noticed by Campbell in his *History of Poetry in Scotland* it seems doubtful whether they received a similar welcome from the general public. Coming only two years after the publication of Burns's poems, poor Turnbull's work was all but totally eclipsed. In point of fact they were but pale imitations of Gray and Shenstone, writers whom Burns himself consciously emulated in his 'English' poems, but without Burns's spark of genius and originality. The failure of his *Poetical Essays* goaded Turnbull into leaving Kilmarnock. For a time he led a nomadic existence and went on the stage, eventually marrying an actress. While following this profession Turnbull came to the Theatre Royal in Dumfries (1793) and renewed an old acquaintance with Burns who refers to him and his poetry in one of his letters to George Thomson: 'The following is by an old acquaintance of mine, and I think

it has merit... Possibly, as he is an old friend of mine, I may be prejudiced in his favour, but I like some of his pieces very much.' Perhaps Burns gave him the encouragement he needed, for the following year there appeared a second volume, entitled *Poems, by Gavin Turnbull, Comedian*. Turnbull also enjoyed the friendship of Alexander Wilson, the poet and ornithologist of Paisley, and like him, he subsequently emigrated to the United States. What became of Turnbull after that is not known.

Jean Glover was the daughter of a weaver named James Glover, and was born at Townhead on 31st October 1758. The education she received was in keeping with the humble circumstances of her parents, who instilled into her youthful mind the principles of morality and religion. Respecting her history, little is known, but she deserves immortality on account of her song 'O'er the muir amang the heather'.

Another kenspeckle character was the balladeer named Hunter (his Christian name is not given) who earned his niche in Kilmarnock's poetic hall of fame on account of a long 'scoffing ballad' composed in 1764 on the occasion of the violent induction of the Rev. William Lindsay. Though not on the same poetic level as Burns, this ballad has the merit of providing a graphic eye-witness account of the event, and its rollicking verses mention no fewer than eleven of the participants in that extraordinary business. Hunter was the author of a number of other coarse, satirical ballads. One of these, entitled 'The Yill-wife's Lamentation' was the means of frustrating a scheme which the brewers' wives had formed for raising the price of ale. Hunter was a native of Kilmarnock and served in the Army during the American Revolutionary War for which he received a pension of sixpence a day. McKay, as a teenager, could remember seeing this worthy about 1820, a couple of years before he died at a very advanced age.

> He was rather below the ordinary size, wore tied hair,
> was dark complexioned, and, to use a homely phrase,
> very spare made. Indeed, he was latterly so reduced
> in body, that he himself waggishly remarked one day
> to a neighbour, that his friends would be able to carry
> him to the grave in a pocket-napkin!

James Thomson, the proprietor and editor of the *Ayrshire Miscellany*, was born at Kilmarnock on 9th May 1775, the son of a tanner. He received a liberal education and was intended for the ministry. Indeed, he went so far as to become a licentiate of the Secession Church, but owing to poor health and, more probably, pressure from his father to return to the family business, he abandoned his plans and went into partnership in the tannery. When the Napoleonic Wars were at their height Thomson was appointed to the command of the Kilmarnock Sharpshooters and was so devoted to his military duties that he neglected the family business, as a result of which he fell out with his brother and father. 'His patriotic enthusiasm involved him in pecuniary embarrassment,' says McKay quaintly, 'and called forth the censure of his more immediate friends.' As a result the tanning business was dissolved and the tanyard and stock were soon afterwards disposed of. Thomson then went to Edinburgh where he was employed by the *Scottish Review*, but the call of fife and drum was too much for him. He obtained a commission in the Argyll Militia and served in Ireland for some time, but was invalided out and then returned to Kilmarnock.

He eked out a precarious living in some humble capacity, but consoled himself in poetic composition. This led to the publication of a slim volume which 'procured him the esteem of several philanthropic gentlemen' and presumably put some cash in his pocket. This encouraged him to launch the *Miscellany*, many of whose contributions flowed from his own nimble pen. His prose style was lively and taut, for the period, and it is a matter for regret that this venture was so short-lived. In 1824 he published a second volume of poetry under the title of *The Ayrshire Melodist, or Select Poetical Effusions*. He also had ambitious plans for a volume of Paraphrases, and from the few pieces he issued as samples of his work in rendering the Psalms in a more modern guise it is evident that 'in his hand the sacred lyre was not degraded'. Ill health, however, struck him down and for fifteen years he was too incapacitated to do any work. He died on 23rd July 1832 in his 57th year.

Contemporary with Thomson were John Burtt and John Kennedy, both of them remembered today as among the Kilmarnock reformers or martyrs commemorated on the monument in the Kay Park. Both men, however, pursued literary careers which deserve consideration here. Burtt was born at Knockmarloch in Riccarton parish about 1790. At the age of five or six he moved with his grandfather into Kilmarnock where he received his education and was taught the weaver's craft. From a very early age he had a thirst for knowledge and, like many another weaver, by diligent application to books and by private study he acquired a considerable understanding of French and Latin as well as English literature. He might have succeeded eventually in attaining a respectable situation in society, but for the bad luck to be visiting Greenock one day in 1807 when the press-gang was about its lawful business of rounding up able-bodied young men. A gentle soul who recoiled from all that was cruel and oppressive, he was confined aboard one of His Majesty's warships and subjected to the full rigours of naval discipline. Five years elapsed before he secured his release and returned to Kilmarnock where he resumed his work as a weaver and picked up his studies where he had left off. Later he opened one of the many private or 'venture' schools in the burgh and was pretty successful. In 1816 his little volume, entitled *Horae Poeticae* (poetic hours) was published. Despite the title, this book contained an equal mixture of poems and prose pieces, 'an exalted tone of morality, feeling and intellect pervading its pages', and bearing 'the impress of a truly-cultivated mind'. Burtt was also the author of several lyrical productions which appeared in the provincial magazines and newspapers of his time, the best-known being his poem entitled 'O'er the

mist-shrouded Cliffs' which was so sublime that some editors mistook it for a work of Burns. Later the same year he removed to Paisley where he was embroiled in radical politics. When his liberty was threatened he fled in the summer of 1817 to the United States where, about two years later, he published another volume entitled *Transient Murmurs of a Solitary Lyre: consisting of Poems and Songs in English and Scotch*. As in his previous publication, the lyrical pieces were prefaced by prose comments which added considerably to the value of the work. In America Burtt prospered by dint of sheer hard work and application. He acted as schoolmaster for a time but afterwards studied at Princeton College and was later ordained minister of a Presbyterian congregation at Salem, Massachusetts. In 1831 he moved to Philadelphia where he edited a newspaper called the *Presbyterian*. In 1833 he went to Cincinnati where he combined his clerical duties with the editorship of *The Standard* and was appointed professor of ecclesiastical history in the Theological Seminary of that city in August 1835. In his declining years he was pastor of a Presbyterian church at Blackwoodton near Philadelphia.

John Kennedy was born at Kilmarnock in 1789, bred to the loom and acquired a love of learning and a superiority of intellect. Anxious to get away from the weaver's trade and improve himself, he enlisted in the Royal Ayrshire Militia in 1807, but this proved to be a bad career move. The harsh discipline, with its constant floggings and other brutal punishments, left an indelible mark on him. When he gained his discharge in 1815 at the end of the Napoleonic Wars he was inspired to compose a paean. Like Burtt, he returned to Kilmarnock and devoted himself to the cultivation of his mind. He was on intimate terms with Burtt, a like-minded individual, and when the latter went to Paisley it was Kennedy who took over his private school. It fell to Kennedy to play a prominent role in the Reform agitation which gripped the burgh at the end of 1816 and, intermittently surged during the next four years. Significantly, the theme of his passionate address at the Dean Park demonstration of 7th December 1816 was military flogging and the miseries and degradation to which soldiers were subjected.

The story of Kennedy's subsequent political career has already been recounted, but in spite of the harassment, persecution and imprisonment to which he was subjected he found the time to produce three volumes of poetry under the generic title of *Fancy's Tour with the Genius of Cruelty, and other Poems*. He is best remembered for his novel entitled *Geordie Chalmers, or the Law in Glenbuckie*, published posthumously in 1833.

Mid-nineteenth Century Writers

Another of Burns's contemporaries was the Rev. Dr James Mackinlay. Three years older than the poet, he outlived him by 45 years. Inducted at Kilmarnock in 1785 on the death of the Rev. John Mutrie, he continued in that charge till 1841. Six years previously, on his

Rev. James Mackinlay

golden jubilee, a banquet chaired by Provost Reed was held in his honour. After his death a substantial volume of his sermons was published, with a memoir by his son, the Rev. James Mackinlay of Glasgow. It is difficult, at this remove in time, to appreciate the popularity and tremendous impact which volumes of this sort enjoyed with the public at large, but its appearance, in 1842, coincided with the upsurge of piety and religious fervour which marked the Victorian era as a whole. Mackinlay's *Sermons* were by no means the only volume of this type to lay claim to a Kilmarnock origin. A near contemporary of Mackinlay was the Rev. Adam Brown of the Reformed Presbyterian Church who died in 1838 in the 36th year of his ministry. The following year a volume of his discourses was published, with a well-written memoir by his successor, the Rev. Peter Macindoe, DD. Dr Macindoe was a prolific writer in his own right and published a number of important literary and religious treatises, but the most important of these was *A Treatise on the Application of Scriptural Principles to Civil Governments*, a work which was replete with liberal sentiments and sound argument. Macindoe, a native of Lanarkshire, ministered at Kilmarnock till shortly before his death, at Troon, on 2nd September 1850 at the relatively early age of 56.

Not all of the reverend authors chose religious subjects. The Rev. Edward James Jonas of Holy Trinity Episcopal Church (1855-61) was the author of *Recollections of Syria and Palestine*. The Rev. David Landsborough, inducted at the Henderson Church in July 1851, is remembered for his highly informative *Contributions to Local History*, published at Kilmarnock about 1879.

Among secular writers of this period Archibald McKay was pre-eminent. His father, Alexander McKay, was a native of Kildonan, Sutherland who came to Kilmarnock with the Sutherland Fencibles in 1793 and married a local girl, Janet McGill, the following year in Glasgow. Later they returned to Kilmarnock and settled in the Tanyard House in the High Street where Archibald was born in 1801. He was apprenticed to a weaver, but left to learn the trade of bookbinding and afterwards set up in business as a bookseller and stationer in King Street. He founded a circulating library and from an early age wrote poetry. He made his first contribution to the *Kilmarnock Miscellany* when he was sixteen. In 1828 he published his poetic masterpiece, *Drouthy Tam*. Later publications included *Ingleside Lilts*. *Recreations of Leisure Hours* appeared in 1844 and contained essays on a wide range of topics, including a perceptive piece on the moral character of Burns. McKay's *History of Kilmarnock* made its debut in 1848 and over the ensuing three decades underwent three further editions (1858, 1864 and 1880). The additions, revisions and other textual changes between

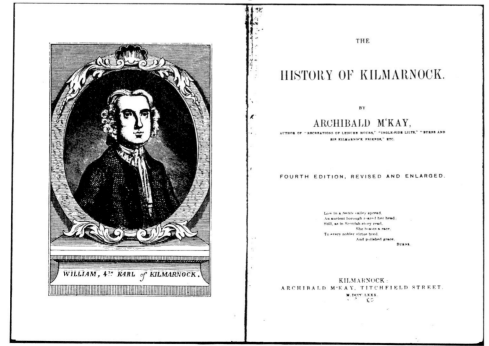

Title page of McKay's *History of Kilmarnock* published 1880

the editions of 1848 and 1880 reveal the extent to which the town had grown in that momentous period. A fifth edition was produced posthumously by Dr William Findlay in 1909. Like many men of his time, McKay was also a noted Burns scholar and in 1874 published a useful work entitled *Burns and his Kilmarnock Friends*. He died at his cottage in Titchfield Street on 14th April 1883, in his 82nd year. McKay's reviser, Dr Findlay, was born in the High Street in January 1846 and educated at Osborne's school and the Academy. Later he studied medicine at Glasgow University before returning to Kilmarnock. He published *In My City Garden* (1895), *Ayrshire Idylls* (1896) and combined his medical knowledge with a love of the national bard in *Robert Burns and the Medical Profession* (1898). He also wrote poetry under the pen name of George Umber and in 1902 published his collected works under the title of *Carmina Medici*.

Less comprehensive than McKay's *History*, but much more entertaining, is James Paterson's *Autobiographical Reminiscences* (1871). Spanning some fifty years, it covered many of the topics to be found in McKay's book, but racy accounts of local elections vividly brought to life many of the figures who were mere names in McKay's much more staid account. Paterson was particularly interesting for his inside accounts of the problems and vicissitudes of printing and newspaper publishing. His *magnum opus*, however, was his two-volume *History of the County of Ayr* which he published between 1847 and 1852 and contains a great deal of material which has never been surpassed. In his autobiography Paterson mentions a Kilmarnock poet named David Wood who approached him one day to print his poems. When Paterson asked him for his manuscript Wood countered, 'Whit's that? D'ye mean writing? If so, I have none. It's all here,' and he tapped his head. 'But,' remonstrated Paterson, 'the compositor can't set the types from your head.' In the end Roxburgh Clerk was summoned to take down the text from Wood's dictation and in a fortnight the manuscript was ready for the press. Wood was the only author Paterson ever met who carried the entire text of a book in his head. His book made 200 pages and 1,000 copies were produced, to retail at 5s each. 'But the soul of poetry was not in him,' concluded Paterson. In the same *genre* was Henry Shields (c1814-1900), a native of Ireland who kept a shop in High Street. One of the 'characters' of Kilmarnock, he closely resembled, in spirit and bathetic doggerel, the more celebrated William McGonagall. His *Poems and Songs* were published by J. Aitken about 1890.

John Ramsay, born at Kilmarnock in 1802, served his apprenticeship as a carpet-weaver and pursued this trade throughout his working life; but in his spare time he turned to poetry. One of his earliest effusions was a little poem entitled 'Lines to Eliza' which was published in the *Edinburgh Literary Journal* accompanied by some encouraging comments by Henry Glassford Bell who then edited that periodical. Encouraged by the commendation of such a reputable critic, Ramsay continued to cultivate his poetic talent and in 1836

published his poems in collected form under the title of *Woodnotes of a Wanderer*. No fewer than seven editions, each of a thousand copies, were printed in the ensuing years. Ramsay stood out from many of the minor poets of the period in the boldness and versatility of his writings which could be poignant, satirical, humorous or forcible as the occasion demanded. He was what would now be termed an occasional poet, deriving much of his inspiration from contemporary scenes and events and his masterpiece was the long, rambling poem entitled 'Eglinton Park Meeting'. The rambling nature of the subject allowed him to indulge in various moods; while no small scope was afforded for satirical sallies, and for portraying the ludicrous, a style of writing in which he was usually successful. There is also a dash of pawky satire in the more homely 'Sports of Fastern's E'en' and several of the more prominent worthies who used to frequent the race-ground were delineated with considerable perception and ability.

Marion Paul Aird was born in Glasgow of Ayrshire parents, but her family moved to Kilmarnock when she was a baby. As a girl, she showed a talent for drawing and it was quite by chance that she stumbled into poetry, having been asked by a friend to try her hand at some verses on a certain subject. She was amazed to find that she had a facility for rhyme and this awakened her finer sensibilities. The first of her poems to appear in print was published anonymously in the *Journal* in the summer of 1838, but her identity was revealed at a banquet in honour of Dr John Bowring, MP at the end of that year. Some verses of hers were recited on that occasion and she was honoured by a poetical reply from the worthy doctor soon afterwards. Her collected poems appeared in 1846 under the title of *Home of the Heart and other Poems*. The eponymous poem, with which the volume opened, contains several beautiful passages couched in simple language. Several of the other pieces, though not marked with the masterly touches of genius, were nicely delineated and 'evidently the conceptions of a mind alive to all that is beautiful, tender and virtuous'. In 1853 Miss Aird brought out a second volume consisting of both poems and prose pieces, with the title of *Heart Histories* and met with considerable success. A third volume entitled *Sun and Shade* appeared in 1868.

Undoubtedly Kilmarnock's most famous poet was Alexander Smith, born on 31st December 1829 in a little thatched cottage at the foot of Douglas Street. His father, a native of Old Rome, was then a pattern-drawer in one of the calico printfields. When Alexander was three or four, however, the family moved to Paisley where he received a rudimentary education. Later he returned to Kilmarnock and went to work as a putter-on in a printwork belonging to Bailie William Geddes. Subsequently he returned to Paisley for some time before settling in Glasgow where he began the study of the classics, but through lack of money he abandoned this course to enter a linen factory as a pattern designer. He found a poetic outlet from the daily routine, having begun writing verse when he was sixteen or seventeen years old. Although he had been an ardent admirer of the beauties of nature from early boyhood he showed no interest in poetry till his mid teens; but, as a family friend later wrote, his poetic genius 'seems to have burst into summer all at once'. His earliest pieces were published in the *Glasgow Citizen*. Before he was twenty he had written the greater part of 'Life Drama', a work of considerable length and abounding in beautiful and striking passages. This long poem first appeared in *The Critic* in 1852 and made a tremendous impact in literary circles at the time. Soon afterwards it was published in separate form and attained sales of 10,000 in Britain and 30,000 overseas.

His reputation established virtually overnight, Smith applied for the post of Secretary to the University of Edinburgh and was selected, despite stiff competition from many other distinguished applicants. He conducted his duties in a very able manner right up to the time of his premature death on 5th January 1867. Smith rapidly became the leading exponent of the Spasmodic School and, with P.J. Bailey and Sydney Dobell, he was satirised by W.E. Aytoun (1854) in *Firmilian: A Spasmodic Tragedy*. In the same year Dobell came to Edinburgh and an acquaintanceship at once sprang up between the two, which resulted in their collaboration in a book of *War Sonnets*, inspired by the Crimean War. Smith also issued a work in 1857 entitled *City Poems*, well received at the time for capturing the spirit and feeling of urban living. After *Edwin of Deira* a Northumbrian epic poem (1861), Smith turned his attention to prose and published a volume of essays under the title of *Dreamthorp* shortly before his tragic death. A year younger than Burns at his untimely death, Alexander Smith died before his work had fully matured and it is idle to speculate in what other directions or to what new heights his talents might have taken him. A memoir by P.P. Alexander was prefixed to a volume of his most recent essays published posthumously as *Last Leaves*.

Archibald Adamson is best remembered for *Rambles Round Kilmarnock* which first appeared in 1875 and ran to an expanded second edition in 1883. *Rambles through the Land of Burns* came out in 1879 and Adamson also contributed numerous poems and articles to the local press under the *nom de plume* of the Rambler. The Rev. Thomas Dunlop, born at Kilmarnock in 1839, later became minister of churches in Balfron, Edinburgh and Bootle. In 1897 he published *John Tamson's Bairns and Other Poems*. George Cunningham (alias Pate McPhun) was born at Inchgotrick in Riccarton parish on 13th June 1848, worked as a miner and later was employed by John Walker. A regular contributor of poems to the local newspaper, he published a separate volume, *Verse and Prose, Grave and Gay*, in 1903. Nine years later appeared *Verses, Maistly in the Doric*. Matthew Anderson, known locally as the Policeman Poet, was a native of Dalmellington but he spent 36 years in the Kilmarnock Constabulary and continued to live in the burgh for many years after retiring from the force in June 1923. He was a prolific writer whose works appeared in a number of volumes: *Poems and*

Songs (1891), *Poems of a Policeman* (1898), *Poems* (1912), *A Poetical Souvenir* (1921), *Poetical Works* (1928) and *John and Jean* (1945)—part 'hamely cracks' and part poetry.

Contemporary Writers

The most prominent Kilmarnockian of the present day is undoubtedly William McIlvanney, journalist, broadcaster, poet and novelist. Born in Kilmarnock in 1936 and educated at the Academy and the University

William McIlvanney

of Glasgow, he qualified as a teacher and was, until 1975, Assistant Rector of Greenwood Academy in Irvine. Turning to fiction in his spare time, he published *Remedy is None* (1966) which won the Geoffrey Faber Memorial Award the following year. This was followed with *A Gift from Nessus* (1968) which won the Scottish Arts Council Publication Award in 1969. *Docherty* (1975) was given the Whitbread Award for Fiction the same year. *Laidlaw* (1977) marked a new departure into the realms of detective fiction, and was followed by *The Papers of Tony Veitch* (1983) and *Strange Loyalties* (1991). In between, however, came *The Big Man*, recently made into a film starring Liam Neeson, a collection of short stories entitled *Walking Wounded* and a volume of poetry *These Words—Weddings and After* (1984). McIlvanney has been writing poetry since his teens and, in fact, had his first volume of poems published in 1970. His elder brother Hugh is now one of Fleet Street's leading sports journalists, having been for many years chief sports writer of *The Observer*.

Elspeth Davie was born in Kilmarnock but educated in Edinburgh where she now lives. After teaching art in the Borders, Aberdeen and Northern Ireland for several years she began writing. As well as several volumes of short stories she has published four novels, *Providings*, *Creating a Scene*, *Climbers on a Stair* and *Coming to Light*. Her achievement was recognized in 1978 by the award of the Katherine Mansfield Prize.

Henry Mair, born at Kilmarnock in 1945, works in an Irvine factory but has published two volumes of poetry: *I Rebel* (1970) and *Flowers of the Forest* (1979) as well as an autobiography *Alone I Rebel*. He has had the honour of having his poetry translated into Russian. Sam Gilliland of Springside published *Masquerade of the Pen* in 1979. George Ballance combines poetry with painting and held one-man exhibitions of 'Poetry Illustrated' at Ayr, Irvine and Edinburgh. The volume *From Tourism to Reality* (1976) was the outcome.

Galston-born Billy Kay was educated at Kilmarnock Academy and Edinburgh University. As a producer with the BBC, he created the acclaimed Odyssey series

Billy Kay

of documentaries, later as a freelance writer and broadcaster continuing this theme in a number of documentaries for BBC Scotland. He has written two plays for Radio and one for the stage, 'They Fairly Mak Ye Work,' which broke box office records at the Dundee Rep in 1986. A popular lecturer, he gives talks all over Scotland and in 1989 was invited to the University of Guelph, Ontario, while in 1987 the British Council sponsored his tour of the German Universities. His radio series 'The Scots Tongue' won an international award from the Australian Academy of Broadcasting Arts and Sciences.

Kirsty Wark, although born in Dumfries and a graduate of Edinburgh University, spent her formative

Kirsty Wark

years with her family in Kilmarnock. She joined the BBC in 1976 as a graduate researcher and one year later became a radio producer on Good Morning Scotland. In 1982 she joined BBC TV in Scotland as a director and laterly as daily editor of Reporting Scotland. But it is through her work in current affairs and political programmes such as 'Left, Right and Centre' and for the live-broadcast General Election programmes that she is best known and appreciated for her integrity and skill as a TV presenter and interviewer.

Artists

In the fine arts Kilmarnock has produced a number of painters who achieved great eminence. Foremost was James Tannock who was born in Grange Street in 1784 and evinced a talent for painting at a very early age. In 1803 he went to Edinburgh to study under Alexander Nasmyth, then one of Scotland's leading landscape artists, although best known today for his portraits of Burns, which later inspired Tannock to execute a considerable number of similar works. These Burns portraits were essentially Tannock's own interpretation of the famous Nasmyth bust, but as they were not painted from life it must be conceded that they are derivative, though very competently executed. Tannock had a studio in Paisley for about two years before prosecuting his art in Irvine, Greenock and Stirling. In 1810 he went to London and enrolled in the Royal Academy where he was a pupil of Benjamin West. At the same time he attended lectures in anatomy under Sir Charles Bell who introduced him to many distinguished patrons. Soon afterwards Tannock enrolled as a student at the British Gallery.

In this period he was intimate with such *literati* as the Irvine-born novelist John Galt and the historian George Chalmers whose portrait he painted. Sir James Shaw also patronised Tannock who, in 1817, executed the full-length portrait which was later presented to the Town Council. Several other works by James Tannock are preserved in the National Portrait Gallery in London and the Scottish National Portrait Gallery in Edinburgh. His original works, painted from life, are remarkable for their accurate delineation and feeling for the subjects. Benjamin West, on seeing one of Tannock's portraits, thus wrote of it: 'It is nature itself; it is the man sitting before you. He [Tannock] is a man of genius.' Although he settled in London, Tannock habitually visited his home town each year and it was there that he died on 6th May 1863. As an artist he was modest and unassuming, and as a man amiable and intelligent.

His younger brother William was also an artist of considerable skill, though perhaps not touched with that flash of genius that distinguished James's work at its best. William Tannock continued to reside in the burgh and had a picture gallery at his house in Grange Street where he conducted business as a dealer specialising in old masters of the Dutch and Flemish schools.

In 1831 a number of amateur artists in and around the town formed themselves into a society under the name of the Kilmarnock Drawing Academy, with the object of mutual instruction and improvement. They rented premises in Cheapside Street where they held art classes and occasional exhibitions. Although this enterprise foundered after a couple of years (the cholera epidemic of 1832 sounded its death-knell) it succeeded in heightening artistic awareness and gave encouragement to a small group of painters who later achieved some merit in this field. William Macready, a leading member of the society, subsequently became a teacher of drawing and many of his pencil sketches of animals and rustic scenes have survived, testifying to his skilled draughtsmanship. He died in October 1854 after a short illness, at the age of 46. James Douglas (1810-88) moved to Edinburgh where he made a living as a portrait painter. 'In imitating the old masters and retouching and repairing ancient pictures, he is said to be very successful,' commented McKay ingenuously. Later he moved to London and died at Croydon in March 1888. His portrait of Lord Melville hangs in

Archers' Hall. His son Edwin was born in Kilmarnock but raised in Edinburgh and by the age of seventeen had three paintings in the Royal Scottish Academy exhibition. The following year he exhibited a painting of Dean Park. He moved to Dorking in 1872 and worked there as a landscape artist and animal painter. Charles B. Millar was a founder of the Kilmarnock School of Science and Art in 1865, but two years later he studied at South Kensington where he gained his diploma in 1873. Five years later he returned to Kilmarnock as head of the Art department at the Academy and taught there till his death 36 years later. He exhibited at the Royal Scottish Academy and specialised in nature subjects.

The most successful of the Kilmarnock School was John Kelso Hunter familiarly known to art-lovers in the west of Scotland as the Kilmarnock Cobbler, from his having been trained in this craft in his early years, John K. Hunter had a long and, at times, very difficult struggle to become established. Once again we have a prime example of a man who succeeded in overcoming overwhelming odds through sheer dogged determination and single-mindedness. He toiled hard at his cobbler's last to support a wife and eight children, yet found the time to study art and was the most energetic of the Drawing Academy's founder-members. When it held its first exhibition, of the 45 paintings on display Hunter contributed more than a third, though he probably had less leisure time than any of the others. 'Visit the Academy during daylight,' reported the *Kilmarnock Chronicle*, 'and you will find the shoemaker a devoted student of Titian; and at night go to his dwelling, and you will find him the hard-working son of Crispin; instead of delineating with a pencil the divine features of the human face, he is beating out the soles of a pair of shoes with his hammer—labouring to support a wife and family.' Like his contemporaries, Hunter moved away from Kilmarnock in search of fame and fortune. In 1838 he settled in Glasgow where he enjoyed moderate success on both counts as a portrait painter, and died there on 3rd February 1873. He was a regular exhibitor at the Glasgow Institute of Fine Arts, while his self-portrait (1847) was exhibited at the Royal Academy.

William Fleming (1808-37) was a house and sign painter who never aspired to membership of the Drawing Academy; but although he was entirely self-taught he practised a wide range of the fine arts. Portraits, landscapes and genre subjects he produced with astonishing facility, but his speciality was likenesses of the public figures and local worthies which abounded in Kilmarnock at that time. His ability in capturing the whimsy and drollery of these eccentric characters was seen at its best in his portrait of Tam Reyburn which was subsequently reproduced in the *Illustrated London News* under the caption of 'The Ayrshire Hermit'. Many of these portraits of local worthies were executed clandestinely without their subjects' awareness (or permission!) and their skilful

rendition speaks volumes for Fleming's uncanny artistry and deft touch. Sadly, he succumbed to tuberculosis in his 30th year before his talent could be fully developed. An even younger artist, only 26 at the time of his death in November 1863, was James Reid who eventually settled in Edinburgh where he painted various canvases graphically representing domestic scenes from Scottish life.

In the second half of the nineteenth century worthy successors to the Tannock Brothers emerged in the Mackay Brothers. Alexander specialised in portraits while his younger brother James concentrated on landscapes and narrative paintings. Alexander's best-known work was his portrait of Sir Alexander Kay which at one time hung in the Burns Monument in the Kay Park. Another pair of brothers were William (1823-94) and James McDougall Hart (1828-1901). Though regarded as American artists (their family emigrated in 1834), William was born in Paisley and his younger brother was born in Kilmarnock. Both were landscape painters, though James also excelled at animal studies. John Curdie (1821-96) enjoyed a high reputation in the latter part of the century as a landscapist, inspired by the scenery and landmarks of Kilmarnock itself and the surrounding countryside. He was apprenticed to a house-painter and had a business in Nelson Street where he sold paints and artists' materials. A customer one day was Horatio McCulloch, one of the leading landscapists of the nineteenth century; he was most impressed by a painting hanging on the wall and when Curdie admitted that it was his and that he had never had a lesson in his life, McCulloch took him under his wing. The great artist actually stayed with Curdie for three months and later the two of them went on painting tours. Due to McCulloch's encouragement and tuition, Curdie later exhibited at the Royal Scottish Academy and the Glasgow Fine Arts exhibitions. He became the first president of the reformed Kilmarnock Arts Club and had a great influence on Michael Shaw and George Boyd. He executed a wide range of landscapes, noted for their clouds and sunset effects. His great masterpiece was 'The Meeting of the Lugar and Ayr'.

Michael Shaw, one of Curdie's pupils, was a coal-miner who later became landlord of the Bickering Bush pub in Riccarton. He gave up the pub in June 1900 to devote himself full-time to art, but died five years later. A critic of the period says that Shaw 'had a spark of genius enabling him to interpret nature'.

Stuart Park (1862-1933) was born in Kidderminster, Worcestershire on the 29th April 1862, his father originally hailed from Catrine and his mother from Craigie. It is interesting to note he was known within the family as James. His mother's maiden name was Stewart which he adopted as J. Stuart Park until 1890 when the J. was dropped. His talent for painting developed early and on completing his schooling he attended Glasgow School of Art.

By 1889 he was working with David Gauld and the Group of painters known as the 'Glasgow Boys'. This

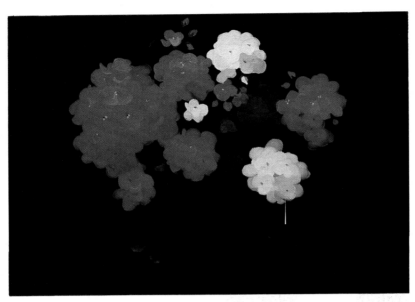

'Red and White Geraniums' by Stuart Park. Oil on Canvas

boyhood. He was a pillar of the Art Club and was always well represented in its annual exhibitions. He also participated in the Glasgow Fine Arts exhibitions and the Royal Scottish Academy, as well as at art shows in Liverpool, Birmingham, Manchester and London. He was a competent all-rounder, but eventually he concentrated on landscapes, many of his best works being inspired by the landmarks and scenery of Kilmarnock and district. He also travelled extensively, and this was reflected in his landscapes of Cornwall, Belgium, Holland and France. His art was still developing, with some interesting experiments in modernism, when he died suddenly of influenza at Deanbank Cottage where he lived with his mother.

Andrew Law (1873-1967) was born at Orr's Land, Crosshouse, in the very same cottage as Andrew Fisher the Australian statesman (see Chapter 16), but when he was quite small his family moved into Kilmarnock where he was educated at the Academy and the Art School. He attended Glasgow School of Art (1891-96) under the direction of Fra Newbery. He was awarded the Haldane Travelling Scholarship which took him to Paris to further his studies, later returning to Glasgow where he taught at the G.S.A. for twenty years, working on commissions and renting an attic studio in Renfrew

communal influence undoubtedly contributed to a number of exceptionally well executed flower paintings and portraits in that year, *Roses* (Glasgow Museums and Art Galleries) and *A Gypsy Maid* (Dundee City Art Galleries and Museum) among them. These works showed a lightness of tone and form with influences of fellow artist George Henry and looked forward to the work of Peploe and the Colourists. In time, his painting became minimal with simply formed flower petals placed to contrast on a dark background. He settled in Kilmarnock after his marriage making his home at 'Elmslie', London Road and he had exclusive use of an outbuilding at Bellfield House which he used as a studio with access to the greenhouses. This provided him with an abundant amount of subject material to work from. The flower paintings became extremely popular and he would hold annual exhibitions of his work at the McLellan Galleries, Glasgow. His paintings are represented in many civic collections including the Dick Institute, Kilmarnock; Paisley Art Galleries; Glasgow Art Galleries; Lillie Art Gallery, Milngavie; Dundee and Dumfries.

John Douglas (1865-1936) was born and brought up in Kilmarnock and after leaving the Academy he entered the firm of Douglas Reyburn. Subsequently he spent five years in America before giving up business and concentrating on art. He enrolled at the Glasgow School of Art and trained as a landscape painter. For many years he had a studio in King Street and worked in the impressionist style, strongly influenced by Whistler and delighting in sombre hues of grey and brown. Many of his paintings dwelt on local scenes painted in twilit shades. During the First World War he was employed by the government at Ayr and afterwards retired to Kirkmichael where he died in 1933.

Charles Aird (1883-1927) was a partner in the firm of James Aird and Sons, painters and decorators, but had an artistic talent which manifested itself in early

'Kilmarnock Cross' by Andrew Law. Oil on Canvas

Street, Glasgow which he continued to use until the early 1960s. He exhibited at the R.S.A., G.I. and the Paris Salon. In 1958, at the age of 85 Glasgow Art Club honoured him with a special exhibition of his work, his first ever one man exhibition. He was an excellent all-rounder, producing many landscapes, still life subjects and genre scenes, his technical mastery evident in such masterpieces as *'Fan-tail Pigeons'*, *'Alicia'* and *'Glasgow from Blythswood Square'*; but it is as a portraitist that he is best remembered and eleven of his portraits of provosts are preserved in the Dick Institute. During the Edwardian period when he was working in Kilmarnock, he met and married Elizabeth Wilson who worked as an assistant in Robertson's art supplies shop in King Street. They moved to Glasgow in 1912 where Law spent the rest of his life, though he often returned to his birthplace and in the early 1920s and 1930s he painted many town and landscape scenes in and around Kilmarnock at times with his friend Charles Aird. Many of his paintings of this period are now in the Dick Institute.

Robert Colquhoun (1914-1962) is perhaps one of the most renowned of 20th century Scottish painters and certainly the most internationally known of artists with Kilmarnock origins. Born on 20th December 1914 at Kirktonholm Place and educated at the Academy he was an excellent linguist and artist. He left school at fifteen to take up an engineering apprenticeship because

'Weeping Woman' by Robert Colquhoun.   Oil on Canvas 37 x 54cm.

his parents could not afford to keep him at school but James Lyle, the art teacher, persuaded them to let him continue his studies by securing financial assistance to make this possible including the help of Sir Alexander Walker of John Walker and Sons, Ltd., Kilmarnock. In 1933 he obtained a scholarship to Glasgow School of Art where he met fellow Ayrshireman Robert MacBryde, from Maybole, with whom he lived and worked over the ensuing thirty years. He studied under Hugh Adam Crawford and the young Ian Fleming and he owes much to their influence in these early years. From 1937-1939 scholarships from the School of Art enabled Colquhoun and MacBryde to travel to France and Italy and pen and ink drawings *Campidoglio, Toro* and *Fort St. Jean, Marseille* by Colquhoun in the Dick Institute date from this period. Invalided out of the army in 1941 with heart trouble Colquhoun settled in London with MacBryde in the hope of obtaining work as war artists. They mixed with the artistic set including John Minton and John Caxton and other English Neo-Romantics and Colquhoun experimented for a time with landscapes in this fashion. By 1943 the influence of Graham Sutherland, Braque and Picasso predominated and he soon moved towards the angular lines of Wyndham Lewis with whom he later became friends and that of the Polish painter Jankel Adler who moved into the same building as Colquhoun. Adler encouraged Colquhoun to concentrate on figurative painting and in 1943 Colquhoun had his first one-man show at the Lefevre Gallery, London to be followed by many others in the late 40s and early 50s. It was during this period he was given an official War Artist's Commission through the influence of Kenneth Clark. The peak of his painting powers came in 1944-46 with arguably some of Colquhoun's greatest figurative paintings being produced in this period *Woman with Leaping Cat* 1946, Tate Gallery and *Woman with a Birdcage* 1946, Bradford Art Gallery and Museum. In 1946 he began experimenting with monotypes and also visited Ireland. In 1949 he travelled to Italy. However by this time his work was considered passé and an exhibition of his Italian pictures at the Lefevre Gallery in late 1950 was a commercial flop. The two Roberts went on to design sets and costumes for the ballet *Donald of the Burthen's* produced at Covent Garden in 1951 and in 1953 Colquhoun produced designs for *King Lear* at Stratford. On both these occasions the work showed Colquhoun's strong Celtic origins.

In the same year he received a major commission from the Arts Council of Great Britain for a large canvas for their *Festival of Britain* exhibition. However his work deteriorated and after his 1958 Whitechapel retrospective he never seriously painted again but continued only to draw and produce monotypes, a perfectly executed example being the earlier *Man and Goat* 1948, Glasgow Museums and Art Galleries. In 1962 he was offered an exhibition at the Museum Street Gallery, London. A few days before the exhibition was due to open and while working late into the night to complete the work, Robert Colquhoun collapsed and died of a heart attack. MacBryde eventually moved to Dublin where he was killed in a road accident in 1966.

Colquhoun's achievements, after many years of neglect, are now clearly recognised. While accepting the serious decline in his way of life and artistic output towards the end of his life, he is now given credit for some of the most powerful images produced in Britain in the postwar years and examples of his work can now be found in most major city collections in Europe, America and Japan.

In the late 1960s local artist Davie Brown, then a student at Glasgow School of Art and on whom the painting of Colquhoun had made a profound impression, was one of the main champions in re-establishing local public awareness of Colquhoun's work. With the help of writer John Malkin they helped in the creation of the Colquhoun Memorial Award and the Memorial Gallery which existed for a time in Green Street, Kilmarnock. Retrospective exhibitions of Colquhoun's work, impressive in their range and quality, have been held at the Dick Institute in 1972, 1982 and 1990.

Eleanor Allen Robertson (née Moore) was born at Glenwhirry, Co. Antrim in 1885. The family moved to Scotland in 1888, first to Edinburgh and then to Newmilns in 1891. Her father Rev. Hamilton Moore was minister of Newmilns Parish Church. Educated at Kilmarnock Academy, in 1902 she attended Glasgow School of Art and under the directorship of Fra Newberry won several awards. In 1922 she married Kilmarnock born Dr Robert Cecil Robertson and for a while made their home at 'Morningside', Portland Road.

In 1924 Dr Robertson accepted an appointment as Public Health Officer with Shanghai Municipal Council and the family, including their two year old daughter Ailsa, travelled to China in 1925. They stayed there until British women and children were evacuated to Hong Kong in 1937 at the outbreak of the Sino-Japanese war. Throughout her stay in Shanghai Eleanor painted at every opportunity, producing sketches and, more particularly, watercolours of the people and their surroundings. She briefly returned to Kilmarnock in 1934 exhibiting with the Kilmarnock art dealer Ian McNicol. Two fine watercolour landscapes, now in the Dick Institute collection, date from this period. After the war she returned to Scotland and died in Edinburgh in 1955. In recent years her contribution to Scottish painting has received greater recognition with a retrospective exhibition of her work at the Dick Institute in 1981 and more recently her inclusion in Glasgow Museums' 1990 exhibition 'The Glasgow Girls' did much to increase her reputation.

It should be noted that Eleanor's husband, Robert C. Robertson was an accomplished painter in his own right. Eldest son of R.G. Robertson, house painters, the family owned an artist supplies shop in King Street. He produced a large number of oil paintings while working in the Far East. His dealer Ian McNicol would sell his work in both Kilmarnock and Glasgow. However many of Robert's works did not survive the journey back to Scotland after his death in Hong Kong in 1942. The painting tradition continues with their daughter Ailsa who graduated from Edinburgh College of Art. Married with a grown up family of her own she now lives in Helensburgh.

John Taylor was born in Darvel in 1936. He was educated at Kilmarnock Academy and graduated from Glasgow School of Art in 1959. He later completed a

'The Group' by John Taylor. 93 x 90cm screen print

Higher Diploma in Art at Birmingham Polytechnic. As founder member of the New Charing Cross Gallery, Glasgow in 1963 along with fellow artist Bet Low and the enthusiasm of Cyril Gerber he did much to prompt public awareness of contemporary Scottish art at the time. He has become a well established painter and screen printer with recent principal one-man shows at the Compass Gallery 1985 and 1987; Demarco Gallery and Glasgow Print Studio 1987 and 1991. His recent work shows strong images of human suffering, in particular the issue of the human costs of nuclear or conventional war. His work straddles the line between visual harmony while portraying an underlying sinister vision of carnage. These powerful works date from 1987 (*View from the Bunker*, Compass Gallery) and continue in his more recent work. John Taylor now lives in Glasgow and is currently working out of the Glasgow Print Studio. He has exhibited in mixed exhibitions in New York, Venice, Cracow, Heidelberg, Nuremberg and Kilmarnock's twin town Herstal. Taylor's work can be found in many public and private collections including The Scottish National Gallery of Modern Art, the Scottish Arts Council, Aberdeen, Glasgow and Birmingham City Art Galleries. There is also a number of works by the artist in the collection of the Dick Institute.

'The Asparagus Bundle' by Glen Scouller.   Oil on Canvas 30 x 40 ins.

Glen Scouller R.G.I. who lives in Newmilns, studied at the Glasgow School of Art (1968-73) where he later returned as lecturer and tutor, combining this with his work as a professional artist. He resigned his teaching post at the Glasgow School of Art in 1989 to devote all his energies to painting. In the same year he was made a Member of the Royal Glasgow Institute of Fine Arts. He has exhibited regularly and his work is to be found in many private and public collections. His most recent exhibition was held in 1992 in the Portland Gallery, London.

Malky McCormick, trained as a commercial artist and worked for STV in that capacity. He turned full-time professional in 1971 when he moved to live in Waterside where he has his studio. With his distinctive style and a wicked sense of humour he is now one of Scotland's best-known cartoonists. His work is greatly

'Kilmarnock Bunnet' by McCormick. Ink and guache

in demand both in Scotland and on the wider international market.

A much respected figure in Scottish art circles is Emilio Coia, LL.D, FRSE. A graduate of the Glasgow School of Art he worked for five years in Kilmarnock in charge of public relations work for the Saxone Shoe Company before finally moving to Glasgow as a full time freelance artist. His fame lies principally in his works as a caricaturist with a prolific output over the years, published widely, as well as his work as an art critic and broadcaster.

A new generation of professional artists is also emerging. Gino Ballantyne attended Kilmarnock College and graduated BA (Hons) in Fine Art at Glasgow School of Art. He specialises in painting and now lives in Buckinghamshire. Kilmarnock-born Alan Ramsay, educated at Kilmarnock Academy obtained his painting degree at Edinburgh and works out of a studio in Leith. He has had a number of group exhibitions including a shared exhibition in the Dick Institute in 1991 with another local artist Donald Peter Clark from Kilmaurs and also an Edinburgh College of Art graduate. Donald continues to live and work in Edinburgh.

Christine Borland from Darvel obtained her BA (Hons.) at Glasgow School of Art (1983-87) and later MA (Fine Arts) at the University of Ulster. She had her first solo exhibition in 1989 and since then has exhibited widely with two London gallery shows forthcoming in the current year.

In addition to full-time professional artists, the district has a great wealth of artistic talent. Among the many may be mentioned Georgie Young, Douglas Lennox, John Grant, Jim Wylie, Jim Clark, John Faulds, Fiona Thorburn, Alison Keith and Felicity Walker.

For the duration of 1992, the Dick Institute appointed Glasgow-born Alan Dunn as artist-in-residence. Selected to work with the collection from a fine art approach, Dunn's large two-dimensional work, much of which is displayed in public settings, takes on the particular visual quirks of the given place. Familiar sights such as the use of the squirrel image in Kilmarnock are addressed through a year-long sequence of works spanning exterior banners, backdrops and paintings.

Few artists connected with Kilmarnock have made their name in sculpture. James Thom (1802-50), the Tarbolton stonemason who gave the droll figures of Tam o' Shanter and Souter Johnny to the world, was apprenticed to a builder in Kilmarnock and it was here that his earliest essays in architectural sculpture were carved. The outstanding Kilmarnock sculptor, however, was David McGill. He was born at Maybole in March 1864 but when he was an infant his family moved to Crookedholm. He was educated at the Academy and the School of Art before moving to

London where he worked at the turn of the century. He exhibited regularly at the Royal Academy from 1889 onwards and at the Paris Exposition of 1900 he got an honourable mention. In 1904 he became a founder member of the Royal Society of British Sculptors and designed their medal. He worked mainly in bronze, his masterpiece being the colossal statue of Sir Wilfred Lawson on the Victoria Embankment (1909) together with the allegorical figures of Peace, Charity, Fortitude and Temperance around its base. Other works include 'Ingenue' (1908), 'Bather shivering on the Brink' (1908), 'Victor' (1911) and 'The Greek Herald' (1912). His figure entitled 'Renunciation' (1906) now stands in the entrance hall of the Dick Institute while his bas-relief of 'The Jolly Beggars' graces the pedestal of the Burns statue in Ayr. He was commissioned to do the sculpture for Kilmarnock's war memorial and 'Victor' which is the centrepiece was exhibited at the Royal Academy in 1923. He died at West Moors, Dorset in 1947.

At the present time David Howie, a graduate of St Joseph's Academy and the Duncan of Jordanstone College of Art, Dundee with a degree in fine art, works in the Sculptors in Greater Manchester Association. He was sculptor-in-residence at the Glasgow Garden Festival in 1988 and also exhibited in Kilmarnock the same year.

Another Kilmarnock artist whose work combines sculpture, painting, sound and vision in its make-up is Wendy Gunn. She was deeply involved in 1990 in Glasgow's European City of Culture celebrations and took part in an exhibition which toured seven European cities from Istanbul to Glasgow. She currently lectures at Strathclyde University on architecture.

Sculpture and ceramics are the speciality fields of Kilmarnock born, Rosann Cherubini. She completed her BA degree in ceramics at Glasgow School of Art in 1984, and was a scholarship student at the School of the Art Institute of Chicago and received her Master of Fine Arts degree there in 1989. In 1990 she was an artist-in-residence at the Musée Adzak in Paris, and in 1991 at the University of California. Rosann's work extends from sculptural ceramics to 'installations' in which mixed media and ceramic elements contribute. An exhibition which originated from the Dick Institute in 1991 is currently touring Scottish venues.

In 1992 Gourock based sculptor George Wylie was commissioned to produce 'The Kilmarnock Flyer' a sculpture in welded steel, depicting the age of steam with a stylised locomotive taking flight as it lifts itself into a new generation of rail travel. This humorous yet respectful affection for the age of steam reflects Kilmarnock's long association with locomotive building and serves as a reminder of the skills and traditions in locomotive engineering which continue today.

The Performing Arts

The most distinguished singer from the neighbourhood was John Templeton, born at Riccarton into a family remarkable for their vocal and instrumental talent. His eldest brother became a celebrated music teacher in Edinburgh and it was he who first perceived that John, then aged ten, possessed a voice of great sweetness and power. He ensured that his young brother received the proper training to develop his talent. John became choirmaster to one of Edinburgh's most fashionable churches and supported himself by giving singing lessons before going to London to study under the *maestri* of the period. He entered his professional career as a theatrical singer at Worthing and Brighton before securing an engagement at Drury Lane Theatre. Here he came to the favourable attention of Ellen Wood the actress (later better remembered as a novelist and authoress of *East Lynne*) and John Braham who were both performing there at the same time. The celebrated Tom Cooke, out of compliment to Templeton's extraordinary range, used to call him 'the tenor with the additional keys'. He took the leading roles at Drury Lane and Covent Garden opposite the great diva Madame Malibran for two seasons (1833-4). In 1836-7 he made his first extended tour of Scotland and Ireland where he met with unprecedented success. In 1842 he toured the Continent for the first time and enjoyed considerable acclaim in Paris. After a further season at Drury Lane (1843) he developed a one-man show, combining singing, elocution and lectures, which he subsequently took all over the United States.

James Anderson, the son of William Anderson, Session Clerk of Kilmarnock, was born at Townend in 1802 and became an accountant with the Union Bank. Later he set up in

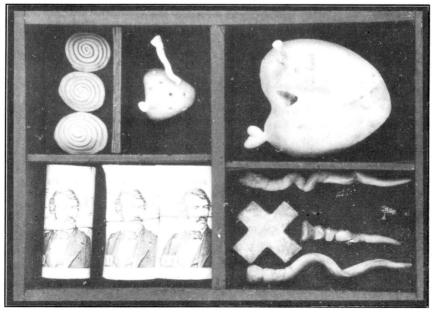

'Atheistic Anecdote' by Rosann Cherubini. Ceramic Sculpture

business on his own account and was eventually chairman of the Bellfield Trust. He was a very talented musician, and composed a number of hymn tunes, of which 'St Marnock's' is appropriately the best remembered today.

In his day and generation the name of Robert C. McCrone LRAM, FTCL was synonymous with music in the Kilmarnock area. Principal teacher of music at Kilmarnock Academy in the 1920s, 30s and early 40s he was one of a group of dedicated teachers of music who helped to establish music as a subject in the Higher Leaving Certificate. His school choirs were well-known for the beauty of their singing and were frequent prize-winners at the Ayrshire Music Festival. Organist and choirmaster for many years in Henderson Church, Kilmarnock in 1936, he formed the Henderson Choral Society which after the Second World War became the Kilmarnock Choral Union and still flourishes today.

He was also the Ayrshire organising secretary for Trinity College of Music, London and for his services to this College over many years he was awarded an Honorary Fellowship.

Over the years Kilmarnock has produced many bands and groups who would probably have performed locally, but only one group, the Anteeks, ever looked like making the big time. This six-man band formed in the early 1960s got as far as London where they were signed by one of the record companies and cut their first disc; but chart success never came their way and they seem to have faded into oblivion soon afterwards.

Music and drama were an integral part of family life in Kilmarnock to James Miller so, it would appear almost inevitable with a fine bass baritone voice that he should become a professional singer and actor. He was educated at Kilmarnock Academy and a graduate of the Royal Scottish Academy of Music and Drama (1967-71). Singing under the stage name of James Miller-Coburn, he has spent most of the last twenty years with Welsh National Opera. He was also on the London stage for a spell of four years in 'Brigadoon' and was for a time with the Madrigal Players, performing world-wide.

In the field of the performing arts one of the most remarkable and enduring successes of recent times has been that of Kilmarnock Concert Brass.

The driving force behind the success of the band is Andrew H. Keachie, DRSAM. He started playing cornet at the age of eight in the local Salvation Army junior band. Educated at Kilmarnock Academy and a graduate of the Royal Scottish Academy of Music, he is at present principal teacher of Instrumental Service for the Ayr Division of Strathclyde Region.

In 1970 he formed what was then called the Kilmarnock Youth Band. The band gave its first public performance in February 1971. In 1974 the band became Scottish Section 4 Champions, followed in 1975 by taking the top honour in Section 3, did the same in Section 2 the following year and crowned four magnificent years by being placed third in the Championship Section in 1977. In 1977-78 they became the Scottish Band of the Year, and in 1979 achieved the highest possible award in the Scottish brass band world in becoming the Champion Band of Scotland.

Since then the band has appeared on television on 'The Best of Brass' and 'Fanfare', has played in countless venues including the Royal Albert Hall, London, had a successful tour of West Germany in 1975, played by invitation at the SNO Prom Concert in the Kelvin Hall, was the first brass band to receive the Scotstar Award as the Scottish Band of the Year in 1983 and has competed successfully in virtually every competition open to it, gaining over fifty awards through the years. The band has also cut three long-playing records.

Although the band 'came of age' with its 21st Annual Concert in 1991, the accent is still on youth. The three-tiered organisation of the band into Kilmarnock Concert Brass 'A', 'B' and 'C' bands has ensured a continuity of talented musicians, many of whom have shown exceptional ability and have achieved distinction as soloists in their own right. The average age of the eighty or so band members is still around twenty.

A fitting climax to the activities of Kilmarnock Concert Brass to date came when, with the stirring performance of the band, complementing the massed voices drawn from all sections of the community, 'Songs of Praise' was televised from the Grand Hall on 23rd February 1992 as part of the Kilmarnock 400 celebrations.

Kilmarnock Concert Brass at a recording session in the Grand Hall

11 THE BURNS CONNECTION

Kilmarnock vies with Alloway and Dumfries, the places where he was born and died, as a mecca for devotees of Robert Burns, the national bard of Scotland and the poet of all humanity. Although he never resided within the burgh or parish, the poet had numerous connections with the district and both his poetry and his voluminous correspondence are peppered with allusions to Kilmarnock and its inhabitants. Quotations given in this chapter are taken from either the *Complete Works* (Alloway Publishing 1986) or the *Complete Letters* (Alloway Publishing 1987), denoted by CW or CL respectively and followed by the relevant page number.

Above all, Kilmarnock was the town where Burns first saw his works in 'guid black prent' and, always conscious of its role in launching Burns upon his literary career, the town has ever since been assiduous in promoting the 'immortal memory'. Its Burns club is not only among the oldest in existence but it was also,

Robert Burns' Oil painting by James Tannock, (see page 120)

by the second half of the nineteenth century, one of the most active, and took the lead in the formation of the Burns Federation which, to this day, has its global headquarters in Kilmarnock.

Early Associations

Years before the poet was born, his father, William

Burnes had come from the east of Scotland in search of employment and about 1750 had worked as a gardener at Fairlie House, Gatehead, two miles (4km) south-west of Kilmarnock, for two years before moving on to Alloway. The poet's aunt was Jean Broun who married James Allan, a carpenter on the Fairlie estate. The couple lived in an estate cottage at Old Rome Ford, on the east side of the Kilmarnock-Troon road by the River Irvine, and it was thither that Burns came in the spring of 1786 when Jean Armour's father James took out a warrant against him. A despairing letter from 'Old Rome Foord' (*sic*) dated 30th July 1786 to his bosom friend, John Richmond (CL 77-8) shows Burns in a very low state, despite the fact that his volume of poems was about to be published the following day: 'Would you believe it? Armour has got a warrant to throw me in jail till I find security for an enormous sum.—This they keep an entire secret, but I got it by a channel they little dream of; and I am wandering from one friend's house to another...' The ancient ford, a little upstream from the present-day bridge at Gatehead, can still be discerned, but the estate-workers' cottages where Burns found refuge from the vengeful Armour have long gone.

When William Burnes moved his family from Mount Oliphant in 1777 to Lochlie, the centre of their world shifted from Ayr to Mauchline, but Kilmarnock, only a few miles to the north, was now their nearest town. The same was true when Robert and Gilbert Burns took the lease of Mossgiel in 1784 after their father's death. While Mauchline provided the poet with social intercourse and was the nearest market, he would have been familiar with Kilmarnock during this period. In *The Ayrshire Hermit and Hurlford* (1875), M. Wilson averred that Burns was accustomed to visit the area to purchase coal from Norris Bank, a mine located south of the Cessnock Water but now long since vanished from the map. After the move to Mossgiel in 1784 Burns became an increasingly frequent visitor to Kilmarnock. Even then, his reputation as a forceful and witty personality ensured entry to Kilmarnock's social scene, and Burns became a habitué of the Bowling Green House, an inn on the east side of Portland Street opposite the north side of West George Street. The inn, in the 1780s, was situated at the foot of Back Street and was kept by Sandy Patrick whose house was a rendezvous for the merchants and shopkeepers and the few professional men of the town. They would meet for a social glass or two after a game of bowls. It was here that Burns is said to have met the seedsman Tam Samson (who was Patrick's father-in-law), his brother John and his nephew Charles, the vintner Robert Muir, the poet Gavin Turnbull, the physician William Moore or Mure, the brothers William and Hugh Parker, the businessman and Town Clerk William Paterson, the brewer Bailie Thomas Greenshield and the merchant William Brown among many others.

Several of these gentlemen were later immortalised in the poetic works of Burns. First and foremost was Thomas Samson (1722-95) who, as well as heading one of the town's oldest nursery gardens, was a noted sportsman Burns tells us, in a note on his elegy to Tam Samson (CW 240-1), that this worthy hunter on one occasion, when going on a shooting excursion, expressed a wish to die and be buried on the moors, and that the poet immediately took the hint. From other local sources we learn that, on this occasion, Samson was longer than usual in returning from the grouse moor. Burns was then in town and being in company with Charles Samson, Tam's nephew, the conversation turned to the shooting season. 'By the bye,' said Charles, 'have you heard anything of my uncle today?' 'Not a syllable,' replied Burns, 'but why that question?' 'He has been longer than his wont in returning from his sports,' answered Charles, 'and his wish about dying among the muirs has, perhaps, been realized.' 'I recollect the words of the game old cock,' said Burns, 'but I trust it will turn out otherwise.' The poet, however, became a little thoughtful and, taking a piece of paper from his pocket, wrote the first draft of the celebrated elegy and epitaph. In the course of the evening Tam returned safe and sound. A meeting of his friends then took place and Burns amused them by reciting his elegy. 'Na, na, Robin!' cried the subject of the poem, 'I'm no fond o that mournfu story. I wad rather ye wad tell the warld that I'm hale and hearty.' To gratify his friend, Burns retired for a short time to another room and wrote the *per contra*, with which he immediately returned and read to the assembled company:

> Go, Fame, and canter like a filly,
> Thro a' the streets and neuks o Killie;
> Tell every social, honest billie
>   To cease his grievin;
> For, yet unskaithed by Death's gleg gullie,
>   Tam Samson's livin.

Needless to say, the recital of this verse restored the old sportsman's customary good humour. Tam, in fact, lived till December 1795, nearly ten years after the composition of the famous elegy. His grave in the Laigh Kirkyard is marked by a handsome tombstone on which are engraved the epitaph with which the poem originally closed (CW 241):

> Tam Samson's weel-worn clay here lies,
>   Ye canting zealots, spare him:
> If honest worth in heaven rise,
>   Ye'll mend or ye win near him.

Interestingly, Tam Samson's grave lies alongside those of the Rev. Dr James Mackinlay and the Rev. John Robertson, both of whom were mentioned with Tam in the opening verse of the poem:

> Has auld Kilmarnock seen the Deil?
> Or great Mackinlay thrawn his heel?
> Or Robertson again grown weel,
>   To preach an read?
> 'Na, waur than a'!' cries ilka chiel,
>   'Tam Samson's dead!'

Tam Samson resided at Rosebank, Braehead where Burns was always welcomed with the utmost cordiality. The house was still standing in the 1960s but, despite a campaign to save it, it was then demolished. A plaque on the wall of the Academy playground marks the spot. At this house Burns frequently dined in company with a few choice friends who were drawn around him by his fascinating conversation. Among these may be mentioned John Laurie of Isles, or Old

Tam Samson

Laird Laurie as he was commonly known. Another individual who was seldom absent on these convivial occasions was Tam's nephew Charles, then a clerk employed by William Paterson.

The third stanza of 'Tam Samson's Elegy' alludes to 'The Brethren o the mystic level', the members of St John's Lodge, Kilwinning number 24 (now number 22), to which Tam and many other worthy citizens then belonged. The lodge held its meetings in the old Commercial Inn in Croft Street, demolished in the 1870s to make way for the premises of John Walker and Company, the whisky blenders. The minutes of the lodge of 26th October 1786 reveal that 'Robert Burns, poet in Mauchline, a member of St James, Tarbolton, was made an Honorary Member of this Lodge, [signed] Will Parker.' Major William Parker of Assloss, the Right Worshipful Master, was himself mentioned in the masonic song (CW 255) which Burns composed to celebrate his honorary admission: 'Ye sons of old Killie, assembled by Willie'.

Major Parker's brother Hugh, a prominent banker in Kilmarnock, was another of the poet's friends. In a letter to Muir (CL 89) Burns refers to him and his brother as Messrs W. & H. Parker, adding 'I hope Hughoc is going on and prospering with God and Miss McCauslin'. Hugh himself received a verse epistle (CW 322) which Burns wrote in mid-June 1788, shortly after his move to Dumfriesshire, when he was residing temporarily in a smoke-ridden hut near Isle Tower, waiting for his farmhouse at Ellisland to be built.

Robert Muir, only a few months older than Burns, was probably the closest of the poet's Kilmarnock friends. Gilbert Burns, in a letter to Dr James Currie, the poet's biographer, furnished an interesting description of the Kilmarnock wine-merchant who had his premises on the Foregate near the junction with Regent Street: 'He was one of those early friends that Robert's poetry procured him, and one who was dear to his heart.' That the death of Muir in his thirtieth year affected Burns very greatly may be determined from the curious 'conscience' letter which the poet wrote to Mrs Dunlop on 13th December 1789 (CL 181-2). This strange epistle, provoked by remorse and the recollection of 'Highland Mary' Campbell some three years after her death, was written while Burns was clearly suffering a severe bout of depression 'groaning under the miseries of a diseased nervous System'. In this melancholy frame of mind he looked forward to death and the after-life. 'There should I meet the friend, the disinterested friend of my early life; the man who rejoiced to see me, because he loved me & could serve me—Muir, thy weaknesses were the aberrations of Human-nature, but thy heart glowed with every thing generous, manly & noble; and if ever emanation from the All-Good Being animated a human form, it was thine!'

Muir gave proof of his staunch friendship by taking 72 copies (of a total printing of 612) of the Kilmarnock edition of the poems, and subscribed to 40 copies of the first Edinburgh edition. Originally he wished to take 60 copies, when he could ill afford it, and Burns, ashamed of the princely generosity of the man, insisted in reducing the number. Robert Muir was the recipient of seven letters from Burns, written over a two-year period (20th March 1786 to 7th March 1788). In this correspondence there are several references to the sales of Burns's poems, to which Muir had so nobly contributed. In the last letter Burns mentioned his next trip to Edinburgh, adding that he had meant to come by Kilmarnock, 'but there are several small sums owing me for my first Edition, about Galston and Newmills' which he hoped to recoup.

In the same letter Burns set forth what was probably his frankest statement concerning his religious beliefs. After quoting lines from 'The Grave' by Robert Blair, Burns continued:

If we lie down in the grave, the whole man a piece of broken machinery, to moulder with the clods of the valley,—be it so: at least there is an end of pain, care, woes and wants: if that part of us called Mind, does survive the apparent destruction of the man—away with old-wife prejudices and tales! Every age and every nation has had a different set of stories; and as the many are always weak, of consequence they have often, perhaps always been deceived: a man, conscious of having acted an honest part among his fellow creatures; even granting that he may have been the sport, at times, of passions and instincts; he

goes to a great unknown Being who could have no other end in giving him existence but to make him happy; who gave him those passions and instincts, and well knows their force. These my worthy friend, are my ideas; and I know they are not far different from yours.—It becomes a man of sense to think of himself; particularly in a case where all men are equally interested, and where indeed all men are equally in the dark.

Later Burns composed the epitaph for his friend, engraved on his tombstone (CW 322):

What man could esteem,
    or what woman could love,
Was he who lies under this sod;
    If such Thou refusest admission above,
Then whom wilt Thou favour, Good God?

The Kilmarnock Poems

John Goldie, who has already been described in the context of the proposed canal and as one of Kilmarnock's early literary figures, first met Burns at Mossgiel in 1785 when he happened to be in Mauchline on business, and later invited the poet to visit him at Kilmarnock. Thereafter Burns was a frequent caller at Goldie's premises near the Cross and it was here that he is said to have corrected the proofs of the sheets before his poems went to press. Goldie was one of those local businessmen who stood surety to the printer John Wilson for the production of the Kilmarnock edition.

John Wilson, born at Kilmarnock in the same year as Burns, took over the original McArthur wooden printing press in 1780. Most of the work done on this press was jobbing work, such as bills, tradesmen's cards and letterheads; but in 1785 Wilson brought out an edition of Milton's *Paradise Lost*. Wilson's printery was in the attic of the Star Close, a building which at that time belonged to James Robertson of Tankardha'. His sister, Mrs Bunten, used to recount how, when living in the close, she frequently saw Burns visiting the premises while his work was going through the press.

It is impossible to say with certainty when Burns first got the idea of publishing his poems. His poetic output increased dramatically in 1785, in the year following his father's death when inspiration seems to have gone hand in hand with a liberating influence. Though much of what he produced was not intended for general consumption (to judge from the significant omissions from the Kilmarnock edition) it is out of the question that he would have composed such an amazing quantity of poetry without at least giving some thought to the most logical means of attaining that fame which he craved. Despite Robert Fergusson, 'my elder brother in misfortune, By far my elder brother in the muse', there was at that time no fashion for vernacular poetry, and to embark on such a course was quite daring and original. It is worth noting that Gavin Turnbull, an exact contemporary of Burns, confined his effusions to pure English in the high-flown sentimental style pioneered by the English poet William Shenstone. By

The Kilmarnock Edition of Burns's Poems in its original binding

late 1785, however, Burns had already tested the market, by circulating many of his pieces in manuscript among his friends and acquaintances. An undated verse epistle addressed to James Smith of Mauchline around this time (CW 169-73) contains the earliest hint of his ambition to see his work published:

This while my notion's taen a sklent,
To try my fate in guid, black prent;

From this it may be inferred that the idea was in his mind some time before this epistle was composed. The most prolific period of Burns's short life was the nine months from July 1785 till the end of March 1786, and it was broken only by the crisis over Jean and the Armour family. In April he contemplated leaving the country but needed some ready cash to pay for his passage to Jamaica. It was then that the notion of publishing his poems surfaced again. In his long autobiographical letter to Dr John Moore, written more than a year later (2nd August 1787), Burns gave a somewhat fanciful account of the circumstances leading up to his decision to publish:

Before leaving my native country for ever, I resolved
to publish my Poems.—I weighed my productions as
impartially as in my power; I thought they had
merit; and 'twas a delicious idea that I would be
called a clever fellow, even though it should never
reach my ears a poor Negro-driver, or perhaps a
victim to that inhospitable clime gone to the world of
Spirits... I was pretty sure my Poems would meet
with some applause; but at the worst, the roar of the

Atlantic would deafen the voice of Censure, and the
novelty of west-Indian scenes make me forget
Neglect.

Unfortunately, he gave no clue to the precise steps which he then took to realise his ambition, but it seems obvious that he should approach the only printer in the county. John Wilson was the obvious choice. That Wilson approached the venture with caution may be seen in the need for Burns to obtain sureties against financial loss. But as Burns saw this project as a means of making money, he clearly had the confidence that Wilson lacked.

Successive letters in March 1786 were written to John Kennedy enclosing 'The Cotter's Saturday Night' and to Robert Muir enclosing 'Scotch Drink'. Then, on 3rd April, he wrote to Robert Aiken of Ayr, enclosing the lines which he had inscribed in a work by Hannah More when presenting this book to a young lady. Almost as an afterthought, however, he added the bald statement, 'My Proposals for publishing I am just going to send to the Press.' Clearly something of the sort must have been discussed with Aiken, and probably other friends, previously. The subscription blanks, which were printed by Wilson over the ensuing days, were delivered to Burns on the evening of 14th April; one of the first people to receive a copy was Gavin Hamilton to whom he wrote the following day (CL 65). '[I know that] you would wish to have it in your power to do me a service as *early* as any body, so I inclose you a sheet of them.'

The document which announced Burns's intention to the world was brief and to the point:

PROPOSALS
FOR PUBLISHING BY SUBSCRIPTION
SCOTCH POEMS,
BY ROBERT BURNS
The Work to be elegantly Printed,
in One Volume, Octavo.
Price Stitched *Three shillings*.
As the Author has not the most distant
Mercenary view in Publishing, as soon as
so many Subscribers appear
as will defray the *necessary* Expence,
the Work will be sent to the Press

Burns had 96 copies of this notice printed, 'a great deal more than I shall ever need,' as he told David McWhinnie on 17th April (CL 106). Only one example of this document has apparently survived and is now preserved in the Burns Museum at Alloway. This advertisement is doubly interesting. It shows that Burns originally intended to confine his book to poems in the vernacular. Characteristically, it also shows the poet's repugnance at being seen to make money from his poems. In view of the fact that he had finally been spurred into publication to raise the fare to Jamaica, his strident disclaimer has a rather hollow ring.

The sole surviving prospectus bears the signatures of sixteen subscribers, but four were subsequently crossed out, and opposite the name of a fifth, William Lorimer, the words 'sent per Charles Crichton' were crossed out and the entry endorsed 'The Blockhead refused it'. These subscriptions were collected by William Johnston who personally took three copies of the book. His initials appear in the margin opposite each name as the subscribers paid up. Finally there is a note on the right-hand side in the handwriting of Gilbert Burns 'W. Johnston paid me for 11 Copies'. This sheds an interesting light on the manner in which the production of the book was funded. McWhinnie, to whom Burns sent four subscription sheets, secured 20 orders. John Kennedy of Dumfries House near Cumnock got as many more, as did John Logan of Knockshinnoch. Gavin Hamilton (40), James Smith (41), Gilbert Burns (70), Robert Muir (72) and Robert Aiken (145) brought the total of subscriptions up to 428 which yielded an income of £64 4s—more than enough to defray the costs of the paper, ink and press-work which totalled £35 17s. Later, Burns claimed to have cleared £20 from the sale of his poems, but as all 612 copies were soon sold out, his profit was substantially more.

By 13th July sufficient subscriptions had been promised for John Wilson to commence the actual printing of the book, although the typesetting (using loose type) must have been going on apace. The book, running to 240 pages, was printed, collated and bound in blue paper wrappers, ready for distribution by the end of that month. Four weeks later Wilson had only

John Wilson, printer

thirteen copies left. Burns kept only three copies for his own use and the entire edition was sold out by September.

On 6th October Burns settled the account with Wilson in full and about two days later he wrote at great length to Robert Aiken (CL 92-4). Apart from containing the first inkling that Burns had been considering an Excise career, this letter is interesting for the light it sheds on the poet's subsequent dealings

with John Wilson. 'After I had paid him all demands, I made him the offer of the second edition, on the hazard of being paid out of the *first and readiest*, which he declines. By his account, the paper of a thousand copies would cost about twenty-seven pounds, and the printing about fifteen or sixteen; he offers to agree to this for the printing, if I will advance for the paper; but this, you know, is out of my power; so farewell hopes of a second edition 'till I grow richer! an epocha, which, I think, will arrive at the payment of the British national debt.'

In fairness to Wilson, however, he probably felt that the first edition of 612 copies was sufficient to cater to local demand and that consequently there would be little interest in a second edition. 'Neither author nor publisher having much faith in the marketability of a second printing, the two men brought their relations to a

Gravestone of John Wilson in Laigh Kirkyard

close, each having done more to make the other known to the world than he could well have dreamed,' concludes Professor Snyder (1932), and that is certainly true. Wilson's canniness, of course, later compelled Burns to seek a national, rather than a local, publisher for his second edition. Without that, he might have been another nine-days' wonder and Wilson himself would long have been forgotten.

As previously stated, Wilson and his brother moved to Ayr where they founded the *Ayr Advertiser* in 1803. John Wilson prospered in the county town and became a magistrate there. He died at Ayr in May 1821, but his body was brought back to his native town and interred in the burial ground attached to the Old High Church. Of the printery which first gave the works of Burns to the world nothing now remains, though a plaque in the Burns Precinct marks the spot. The wooden press went to Ayr with the Wilson Brothers and eventually passed into the hands of T.M. Gemmell who carried on the printing business. About 1858 the press, which had long been pensioned off, was cannibalised to produce an elaborate chair in preparation for the Burns Centenary celebrations the following January. A carved wooden bust of Burns was mounted at the top of the back, flanked by figures of Tam o' Shanter and Souter Johnny, while the Twa Dogs formed the arm-rests. A roundel carved in bas-relief was set in the top of the chair-back and featured the Burns Monument at Alloway and the auld Brig o Doon. This oaken extravaganza was placed in the County Buildings at the Centenary celebrations and a silver plate testifies to the fact that it was first occupied by Sir James Fergusson, Bart. It now reposes in the Birthplace Museum at Alloway. It is a matter for supreme regret that the printing press should have been subjected to such well-meaning but sadly misplaced Victorian ingenuity.

Allusions to Kilmarnock in Burns's poems

Although Burns had to look to Edinburgh to secure wider recognition for his works, he served Kilmarnock well. The word 'Kilmarnock' appears six times in his poems, and 'Killie' another five. In 'The Holy Fair' (CW 135) we have the image of the batch of wabster lads (weavers) 'Blackguardin frae Kilmarnock, For fun this day'. The references in 'Tam Samson's Elegy' have already been touched upon. The 'new song from an old story' which Burns sent to William Stewart under the title of 'Godly Girzie' (CW 409) mentions 'Kilmarnock gleam'd wi candle light' and the 'Cragie hills' (Craigie, south of the town). 'Killie' likewise appears in 'Tam Samson's Elegy' and also in the 'Masonic Song' previously mentioned. In 'The Inventory' (CW 195) Burns lists his rear left-hand plough-horse as 'a weel gaun fillie, That aft has borne me hame frae Killie'. In 'The Kirk's Alarm' (CW 360) the Rev. James Mackinlay of the Laigh Kirk is addressed: 'Simper James! Simper James, leave the fair Killie dames', and in that splendid song of illicit love with Jacobite overtones, 'Here's a Health in Water' (CW 590) we find a reprise of the 'nooks (or neuks) o Killie' which were previously featured in 'Tam Samson's Elegy'—a kindly reference to the narrow, crooked lanes and corners of the old town. The best references, however, occur in the long poem entitled 'The Ordination' (CW 192-3). As well as those memorable lines 'Kilmarnock wabsters, fidge an claw' and 'Now auld Kilmarnock, cock thy tail' we find references to two of the town's landmarks of the period in the opening stanza. The Laigh Kirk was, of course, the venue for the controversial induction of James Mackinlay (see Chapter 7). Later in the same verse occur the lines:

> Then aff to Begbie's in a raw,
>> An pour divine libations
>>> For joy this day.

In the manuscript original which he circulated privately to his friends under the *nom de plume* of Rob Rhymer, Burns had Crookes's, which was either the name of a hostelry long lost and forgotten or (less probably) a reference to the Crooks family which was prominent in the tannery business at the time. Begbie's in Market Street was just across the Water from the Laigh Kirk and the most convenient place for 'divine libations' after the service of ordination. The bridge across the Water was so narrow that churchgoers were compelled to walk in single file, hence the reference 'in a raw' (row). This pub later became the Angel Tavern, but has long since vanished. The same poem has a stanza satirising the Rev. John Robertson and ends with the lines:

> Or to the Netherton repair,

> An turn a carpet weaver,
>> Aff-hand this day.

This refers to the area south of the town which was then the carpet-manufacturing district.

As well as Mackinlay and Robertson, Kilmarnock ministers mentioned in Burns's works include the Rev. John Russell ('Black Jock'), the Rev. James Oliphant and Mackinlay's predecessor, the Rev. John Mutrie. Though not mentioned himself, the Rev. William Lindsay's own controversial ordination twenty years before Mackinlay was alluded to obliquely in the lines which mentioned his wife:

> Curst Common-sense, that imp o Hell,
>> Cam in wi Maggie Lauder;

'Bold Richardton' in 'The Vision (CW 117) refers to Sir Adam Wallace of Riccarton, a cousin of Sir William Wallace of Ellerslie, the Scottish patriot. Riccarton's minister, the Rev. Alexander Moodie, appears in a couple of poems. As 'Singet Sawnie' he was satirised in 'The Kirk's Alarm (CW 360) while under his own surname he appeared in 'The Holy Fair' (CW 136). The unseemly squabble between Moodie and the Rev. John Russell of the High Church, Kilmarnock over parish boundaries, however, inspired Burns's satirical lamentation, 'The Twa Herds: or, the Holy Tulzie' (CW 90). Both ministers were fundamentalists of the Auld Licht persuasion and, as such, legitimate targets for Burns's barbed wit. On one occasion, however, Burns had a set-to with Russell when they ran into each other in a barber's shop in Fore Street. Whether Russell knew the poet and meant to chastise him for his reputed heresy is not known; but they soon became engaged in a heated discussion respecting some particular point of faith and, according to an eye-witness, Burns, for all his ingenuity and argumentative powers, was so baffled by his opponent that he fell silent and left the shop in a hurried manner.

There was one other connection between Burns and the town. On 21st June 1784 the poet's brother Gilbert married Jean Breckenridge at Kilmarnock and he travelled north from Ellisland to attend the wedding. Jean was a member of a prominent family in the burgh and her father James was a prosperous merchant. She herself inherited a tenement property in the burgh, according to a sasine of April 1781.

Early Patrons

It should not be forgotten that Burns owed his early recognition in no small measure to a number of influential gentlemen who brought his work to the attention of the *literati* and also helped in various practical ways to secure the Edinburgh edition which launched him on the wider world. Chief among these was James Cunningham, fourteenth Earl of Glencairn (1749-91), principal landowner in, and lay patron of, Kilmarnock parish. According to Cromek (1808) it was Alexander Dalziel, Glencairn's factor, who introduced the Kilmarnock Poems to his lordship and later encouraged his master to persuade Burns to try for a second Edinburgh edition. Dalrymple of Orangefield, whose wife was Lady Glencairn's sister, gave Burns a letter of introduction to Glencairn when he went to Edinburgh in the autumn of 1786 and the Earl's warm interest undoubtedly helped the poet win entry to Edinburgh society. Burns himself was conscious of the immense debt he owed the Earl. When Glencairn died in 1791 Burns wrote to Dalziel (CL 506): 'God knows what I have suffered at the loss of my best Friend, my first my dearest Patron and Benefactor; the man to whom I owe all that I am and have!' Glencairn made a brief appearance in 'The Ordination' as 'Our patron, honest man! Glencairn' but was later the subject of two poems, 'Verses intended to be written below a Noble Earl's Picture' in January 1787 (CW 265-6), and 'Lament for James, Earl of Glencairn' (CW 423-5) composed soon after the Earl's tragic death. The loss that Burns felt was also expressed in the final stanza of his verse epistle to Robert Graham of Fintry (CW 432).

One of the purchasers of the Kilmarnock Poems was the Rev. Dr George Lawrie (1727-99), minister of Loudoun, the parish east of Kilmarnock which today forms the easterly portion of Kilmarnock and Loudoun District. Lawrie was so impressed that he sent a copy of the Poems to his friend Dr Blacklock and he responded so enthusiastically that Lawrie showed Blacklock's letter to Gavin Hamilton who, in turn, showed it to Burns at a crucial moment when he was on the point of departing for Greenock to take ship to Jamaica. This encouraging letter from Blacklock 'overthrew all my schemes by rousing my poetic ambition' as Burns subsequently recounted to Dr Moore.

Early Burns celebrations

Within a few years of Burns's death in 1796 friends and devotees of the bard were beginning to meet informally on the anniversaries of his birth and death to hold dinners in his honour. Friends in the vicinity of Ayr began meeting at the birthplace in Alloway as early as the summer of 1801. These annual birthday celebrations continued till 1819, but a Burns club on a formal basis did not commence at Alloway till 1908. Thus the honour of forming the first club fell to Renfrewshire, although the actual title has been hotly disputed by Greenock and Paisley for over a century. Greenock claims to have established a club in July 1801, but unfortunately the material evidence now extant does not bear this out conclusively, hence the rival claim of Paisley whose original club is well documented from its inception in 1805 till its demise in 1836. It was not revived until 1874 but has had a continuous history ever since. Kilmarnock claims the next most senior club whose members met for the first time on 29th January 1808 in the Angel Inn, formerly Begbie's tavern, under the genial chairmanship of D. Campbell of Skerrington. Throughout the entire period of its original existence, this club celebrated the bard's birthday four days late. The error was only realised in 1814, the last occasion on which the club was to meet until it was

revived in 1841, when the singer John Templeton was the principal guest of honour. It had a second period of life till 1849, was dormant again for some six years, and finally resuscitated by John McMillan in 1855, since when it has never looked back. Archibald McKay, the poet and historian, was then appointed club secretary and under his energetic tutelage the club was finally put on a sound footing.

From 1841 onwards the Burns Suppers of the reformed club were held in the banqueting hall of the George Hotel and it was here that the main centenary celebration took place on 25th January 1859. That Tuesday was treated informally as a public holiday, most of the shops and business premises being closed, to enable as many as possible to join in the trades' demonstration. Unfortunately the day was cold, wet and windy, and this put a damper on the occasion. Nevertheless, there was a good turn out of the towns' trades, the freemasons and the workers from the mills and factories, notably the men from Andrew Barclay's Caledonian Works, accompanied by a brass band. In the evening no fewer than fifteen public meetings and dinners were held throughout the town. James Tannock's bust portrait of Burns was unveiled in the Council Chambers as part of the centenary celebrations.

At the principal banquet, Provost Archibald Finnie was in the chair and among the chief participants was William Tannock the artist, who was responsible for the decorations in the hall. The dinner was an all-male affair, but it was followed by a ball at which 120 ladies and gentlemen were present.

Rival celebrations were held by the masons of St Andrew's Lodge which met in one of the lesser banqueting rooms of the George Hotel. A party of 40 gentlemen met in Miss Wylie's Commercial Hotel under the chairmanship of a Mr Malcolm, while about 120 men representing the United Literary Associations of Kilmarnock met in St John's Masonic Hall at the Sun Inn with James McKie in the chair. Even the Abstainers' Union got in on the act by holding a 'social tea' in Robertson's Coffee-house. Interestingly, this appears to have been the only Burns event (other than the ball) at which ladies were present. Several Burns Suppers were held by industrial concerns: 30 workmen at Bicket's, 40 engineers at Barclay's, an unspecified number at the brewery of George Paxton and Sons, and a similar gathering at George Roome's. About 30 men employed by the Glasgow and South Western Railway met at a supper in Mr Wales' Rainbow Tavern, the stationmaster, Mr McDonald acting as croupier. John Begg, son of the poet's sister Isabella, was then a railway employee in Kilmarnock and, by virtue of his descent, was the guest of honour. Upwards of 70 members of the Shoemakers met at the Victoria Inn, while operatives of the Bonnetmakers' Corporation partook of a very sumptuous dinner in the Angel.

The Burns Monument

Considering the worldwide celebrations marking

the centenary of Burns's birth it is surprising that only one memorial was erected in that momentous year, and that was only indirectly associated with the bard, being, in fact, an obelisk marking the last resting place of Burns's eldest sister Agnes who had died at Stephenstown, Ireland in 1834. Her remains were interred in the Presbyterian burial ground at Dundalk and it was here, in January 1859, that Irish admirers of the poet erected the monument which coupled the names of Agnes and Robert Burns. The craze for Burns statuary got under way in 1872, with a campaign in Glasgow which led eventually to the erection of a statue in George Square.

Kilmarnock was not slow to emulate Glasgow, the publisher and Burns collector James McKie leading the way. An appeal for subscriptions was launched at the Burns Club's annual dinner on 26th January 1877, when both Provost Sturrock and James McKie spoke effectively to the motion. McKie and Bailie John Baird were principally responsible for raising most of the £2,893 which was subscribed for the erection of the impressive monument that stands in the Kay Park to this day. This provided the opportunity for two ceremonies. According to the *Standard* 4,000 people took part in the procession which wound its way along Dundonald Road, St Marnock and King Streets to the Council Chambers to escort the provost, bailies and councillors to the Kay Park. Estimates of the number of people who actually gathered in the park itself ranged from 10,000 to 15,000.

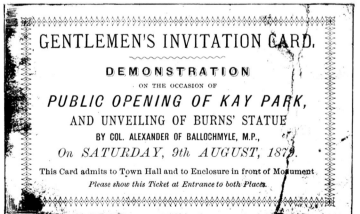

The monument itself, constructed of red sandstone by Andrew Calderwood from a design by James and Robert Ingram, was said at the time to be 'a noble erection in the Scottish Baronial style' but it can perhaps more accurately be described as an asymmetrical neo-Gothic extravaganza, a chaotically glorious mixter-maxter of every architectural conceit from the past 2,000 years, from the Egyptian capitals surmounting the Grecian columns to the splendid Romanesque arch framing the statue of Burns. Medieval corbels and stone bosses vie with Norman bowshot windows, the Renaissance frets and Baroque curlicues of the topmost

pinnacle and the rococo ornament of the lintels. It has many ecclesiastical features but its tower has embrasures and battlements for good measure. It represents Victorian taste at its most exuberantly pretentious but the result, on its commanding site overlooking the park and the town, has been to provide Kilmarnock with a readily recognisable landmark which immediately identifies it, much as the Eiffel Tower and the Opera House symbolise Paris and Sydney. It is a matter of record that comparatively few Scottish towns have a prominent feature of this sort which immediately identifies them.

The building was completed in time for a second mammoth ceremony, which took place on 9th August 1879. An even larger and more elaborate parade of the trades and masonic lodges proceeded over the same route as before, but more than 30,000 people now assembled in the Park. Provost Sturrock, in taking delivery of the deed of gift of the monument, said:

> *The Monument and Statue which it contains, with the grand demonstration you have seen today, speak more eloquently than words can do of the respect and admiration which is universally felt for the genius of the Bard; for there is no doubt that the great gathering, with which we are surrounded, is due almost entirely to the magic of his name.*

The statue itself, of Sicilian marble, is larger than life-size and was chiselled by William Grant Stevenson, noted for his colossal statuary of historic personalities. It has the merit of being one of the most faithful likenesses of Burns, thanks to the sculptor's painstaking study of the various authentic portraits (i.e. painted during the poet's lifetime) and also from his having used a cast of Burns's skull when modelling the head. Burns is shown in the act of composition, with a pencil poised in his right hand while the left grasps a notebook resting against a tree-stump. The unveiling ceremony was performed by Colonel Alexander of Ballochmyle, the MP for South Ayrshire, and a relative of 'the bonnie lass o Ballochmyle', Wilhelmina Alexander. The cost of the building was about £1,500, while the statue cost £800. The work of W.G. Stevenson was chosen as a result of a public competition in which his brother David was runner-up.

McKie's chief motive in promoting this monument was to provide a permanent repository for the Burnsiana, with more than 800 books, many manuscripts (including seventeen holograph poems and several letters) and numerous relics, which he had so assiduously collected over a period of many years. Until fairly recently the two-storey monument acted as a Burns museum and the McKie Collection, at that time the most comprehensive in the world, was available for inspection each day (except Sundays) from 10 am till dusk. One gem which eluded McKie, however, was an example of the Kilmarnock edition itself; but around the turn of the century this defect was remedied by Dr A.C. McLaren who generously donated a copy. This lacked the original blue paper wrapper, having been bound in full calf. In 1908 a fine copy in the original binding hit the headlines when it was purchased from

Mr Veitch of Paisley by W.H. Dunlop of Doonside on behalf of the Burns Cottage at Alloway. The sum paid on that occasion was £1,000, believed to be a record for that time.

In more recent times, the Monument has been perceived as something of a white elephant. Not for nothing did the late and much lamented J.F.T. 'Jock' Thomson, Secretary of the Burns Federation (1968-81), hold very firm views against perpetuating the memory of Burns by monuments. He felt strongly that the best method of promoting the 'immortal memory' of the bard was by charitable works, of which the National Memorial Homes and the Jean Armour Homes at Mauchline were the best examples. By 1958, on the eve of the celebrations marking the bicentenary of the poet's birth, the Monument was suffering sadly from neglect. J.W. Egerer, then working on his doctoral thesis on Burns bibliography, visited Kilmarnock that year and was shocked to find the Monument in such a lamentable condition. Even worse, the contents had deteriorated owing to exposure to sunlight and damp. When his complaint, communicated to Jock Thomson, hit the national headlines, Egerer added that he had been particularly shocked to find the walls covered in graffiti and a glass panel covering the portrait of Burns had been smeared in lipstick with the words 'I love Tommy Steele'. As if this vandalism was not bad enough, however, Egerer added his contempt for the local authorities who had seen fit to place in the museum a monkey band—totally out of keeping with these hallowed precincts. This turned out to be a coin-operated mechanical toy which had once belonged to a prominent local businessman. The official explanation for its presence was that it encouraged children to visit the Monument! Children's attraction or no, the monkey band was swiftly moved to a more suitable venue, the damaged books and manuscripts were removed for repair and conservation, the lipstick and graffiti were cleaned off and the Monument generally tidied up in time for the Bicentenary celebrations in January 1959.

After the acquisition of Dean Castle, the local authorities transferred the bulk of the relics thither for greater security. Thereafter, the Monument was allowed to lie fallow and was only opened up by special arrangement. In this respect it suffered the same fate as the Burns Monument in Edinburgh, both being relics of an era in which security had never been a problem. In December 1987 the Monument was severely damaged by vandals who demolished one of the pillars and toppled the Italianate balustrades flanking the staircases at the front. Provost Tom Ferguson fulminated publicly against 'Morons on motorcycles going in and tearing the place apart.' The District Council took immediate action by erecting a galvanised iron security fence at a cost of £8,500 but this corrugated palisade was widely regarded as aesthetic vandalism, utterly at variance with the eclectic architecture of the Monument it was supposed to protect. Subsequently a programme of refurbishment and renovation costing £380,000 was undertaken to save the Monument from destruction. Part of the problem is that the Monument stands in a park which is secluded by trees and therefore difficult to keep under constant surveillance. The fact that the building had been standing empty did not help the situation. This problem, it was hoped, would disappear when some full-time use could be found for the Monument to ensure its regular occupancy. Various solutions were mooted, including handing it over to the Burns Federation for their permanent headquarters, but its relative remoteness from the town centre has so far militated against this option.

The Burns Federation

The world-wide federation of Burns clubs was founded, not in Scotland, but on the banks of the River Thames in London. Nevertheless, Kilmarnock can lay fair claim to being the true birthplace of the movement. On 26th July 1884, Burnsians from all over the country congregated in the Embankment Gardens to see the Earl of Rosebery unveil the seated statue of Burns by Sir John Steell. Colin Rae-Brown, formerly of Greenock and the founder of the London Burns Club, had been the promoter and organiser of the Centenary celebrations of 1859. On this occasion he was

Star Inn Close (off Waterloo Street)
location of John Wilson's printing works

accompanied by Provost David Mackay and Captain David Sneddon of Kilmarnock. After the ceremony. Rae-Brown brought up the subject of the centenary of the Kilmarnock Poems, imminent in 1886, and it was then that Provost Mackay remarked that it would be a good idea to set going a federation of Burns clubs and societies throughout the world. Rae-Brown followed this up by convening a preliminary meeting at London in February 1885, a month before the unveiling of a bust of Burns in Westminster Abbey. At this meeting it was resolved that a Federation of the members of Burns clubs and societies throughout the world be formed, with the motto 'A man's a man for a' that'. The object of the Federation was 'to strengthen and consolidate the bond or union and fellowship presently existing amongst the members of Burns' clubs by their universal affiliation.' The resolution went on to decide the rules for membership, the fees and the election of an Executive Council.

It was also resolved that the headquarters of the Federation should be in Kilmarnock, on the grounds that this was the town in which the works of Burns had first been published. Doubtless the progenitors also had in mind the fact that the celebrations marking the centenary of the Kilmarnock edition would give the new organisation a good send-off. But it should also be noted that, from the outset, the members of the Kilmarnock Burns Club played a dominant role in the Federation, far beyond their numbers or importance. Unfortunately no list of those attending the February 1885 meeting in London has survived; but on 17th July that year seventeen gentlemen met in the George Hotel to inaugurate the Federation. The signatures of those present were headed by Colin Rae-Brown, but of the sixteen others, no fewer than fourteen were members of the Kilmarnock Burns Club.

In 1885 the principal office-bearers of the Federation were Provost Peter Sturrock (President), Captain Arthur Sturrock (Treasurer) and David Sneddon (Secretary). Adam Mackay, son of David, was for many years Auditor, and it was he who explained how the numbering of the clubs on the Federation roll was arranged. 'Colin Rae-Brown represented that as the idea of a Federation originated in London, the London Burns Club... should be No. 1 on the Roll. My father claimed that Kilmarnock Burns Club should have this distinction. Captain Sneddon, however, persuaded my father to let Mr Colin Rae-Brown have his wish. Captain Sneddon was called on to read the Roll of Clubs willing to join the Federation it was an agreeable surprise to the Kilmarnock Club member to find that Captain Sneddon had allocated No. 1 on the Roll to London Burns Club and No. 0 to Kilmarnock.' By the end of the year ten clubs, including two in England, had joined the Federation. A further 23 joined in the course of 1886, including six in England, two each in Australia and the United States, and one each in Ireland, Canada and New Zealand. The momentum slackened subsequently, with only four new affiliations in 1887 and one in 1888. No new members came in 1889 but two clubs joined in 1890.

The notion of the Federation at this early date was too abstract and vague to serve any real and tangible purpose. It is, perhaps, significant that the influential clubs in Dunfermline and Paisley, in Ayr and Dumfries, which regarded themselves as the old-established custodians of the Burns legacy and may have seen the Kilmarnock folk self-appointed to regiment the rest of the Burns world, held aloof. Alone of the earliest clubs, Greenock affiliated in 1886, but Paisley held out until 1891 and Dunfermline till 1896, while Dumfries did not deign to join until 1913 and Ayr until 1920.

It was a happy decision, in 1891, to give the movement a forum for the interchange of ideas and information. The *Burns Chronicle*, which first saw the light of day in January 1892, was edited by John Muir of Galston and printed by D. Brown and Company of King Street. Muir resigned when the inaugural number was unfairly criticised and the editorship was then taken up by Duncan McNaught who continued till 1924. This annual review of Burns-related activities was just what the movement needed to stimulate interest and in the run-up to the centenary of the bard's death in 1896 the Federation made dramatic progress.

In the early years the Burns Federation did not run to anything as grand as an Annual Conference; it got by with something much more modest known simply as the Annual Meeting. This was invariably held at the George Hotel and was attended by members of the Executive and representatives of the affiliated clubs. The first of these meetings to be recorded for posterity in the pages of the *Chronicle* took place on 19th September 1893. Delegates from the clubs in London, Glasgow, Dundee, Govan, Gourock and Kilmaurs were mentioned. Kilmarnock was not named, but as most of the Executive belonged to that club it seemed superfluous to mention it! After that, the Annual Federation Meeting as it was renamed was held in a different venue each year, beginning with Glasgow in 1894 and Dundee in 1895. It returned to Kilmarnock in 1896, 1900 and 1906, but almost three decades elapsed before it was next held in the burgh.

By 1935 the Annual Conference had grown from a single-day event to an entire weekend and the number of delegates and their spouses had increased to several hundreds. For this reason the Golden Jubilee Conference had to be divided between Kilmarnock and Ayr, lack of sufficient accommodation in the town being the principal reason. No further Conference was staged in Kilmarnock till 1986 when the town hosted the event unaided, to mark the bicentenary of the Kilmarnock Poems.

The day-to-day business of the Federation was conducted by the officials from their own premises. As late as 1968 the Secretary and Treasurer, Tom Dalgleish, dealt with the Federation's affairs from his place of business. In that year, however, Jock Thomson was appointed in his place and this marked the beginning of an era with a permanent secretariat based at the Dick Institute. Mrs Rita Turner, who had previously been in the employment of Mr Dalgleish, came to work at the

Institute for Mr Thomson who was then Burgh Librarian. This arrangement continued after the re-organisation of local government in 1975, when Mr Thomson became Manager of the Department of Cultural Services for Kilmarnock and Loudoun District Council, and following his untimely death in 1981 he was succeeded by William Anderson, the present Chief Librarian of the Dick Institute. Mrs Turner retired as Assistant Secretary in 1989 and was succeeded by Mrs Margaret Craig as the Federation's only full-time employee.

The early association of the Burns Federation with the burgh of Kilmarnock was singularly fortuitous for it gave this world-wide movement a secure base in a town where the spirit of Burns has always been strong. The Kilmarnock area has given the Federation seven of its presidents, whose tenure filled no less than 39 of the 106 years in which this body has been in existence. By contrast, the runner-up, Glasgow, has contributed eleven presidents who held office for a total of twenty years, while Irvine's four presidents served a total of four years. From time to time there have been proposals to move the Federation's headquarters to a more convenient centre of population, but such a move, which would require a change in the Federation's Constitution, has never been seriously entertained. Of the 1100 Burns clubs which have at one time or another been affiliated to the Federation, about a third are currently active; and with a membership spanning the globe it has made Burns synonymous with Kilmarnock the world o'er.

Later Burns celebrations

The slow start to the Burns Federation was all the more surprising in view of the fact that, barely a year after its foundation, it was to be heavily involved in the celebrations that marked the centenary of the publication of the Kilmarnock Edition. The celebrations, on 7th August 1886, took the form of a monster procession from Barbadoes Green in Dundonald Road to the Monument, where a music festival was staged and the editor of the Glasgow Herald, Dr J.H. Stoddart, delivered the oration, followed by a banquet at the Corn Exchange. Although the festival took place at a bad time—many of the townspeople were absent on the annual Fair holiday—the turnout was spectacular by any account and the pageantry laid on by the various companies and trade organisations, as well as the masonic lodges and Burns clubs, presented a very colourful sight as the procession headed for the Kay Park and smothered the statue of the poet in garlands of flowers.

Ten years later the commemoration of the centenary of Burns's death was a much more sombre occasion. At eight o' clock on the morning of Tuesday 21st July, before leaving by train to take part in the principal demonstration at Dumfries, the office-bearers of the Burns Club proceeded to the Kay Park and paid a graceful tribute to the memory of the poet by depositing a magnificent wreath of holly and daisies at the statue.

The morning was drizzly but this did not deter a goodly number of townspeople from assembling around the Monument to witness the ceremony. Three days later, two descendants of the poet visited Kilmarnock. Miss Annie B. Burns and Miss Margaret Burns Hutchinson, grand-daughter and great-grand-daughter of Burns respectively, spent some time viewing the places of interest in and around the town connected with their illustrious ancestor.

The Burns Temple Hoax

On Saturday 29th August 1903 Andrew Carnegie, the Dunfermline-born American steel magnate and philanthropist, came to Kilmarnock in answer to the combined invitation of the municipal authorities and the School Board. He received the freedom of the burgh, laid the foundation stone of the Loanhead School and was afterwards entertained to dinner. All went well till a delicate hint from the chairman informed Mr Carnegie that he would now have an opportunity to part with a modicum of his £60,000,000. 'You have spoiled my day,' was the unexpected reply of the millionaire, and the subsequent proceedings interested him no more. This brusque response affected some of the town wags to such an extent that they resolved to have revenge, and from this originated the great Burns Temple Hoax. The concocting of the plot, the composition of the epistle, and its reproduction on paper that gave a semblance of authority by using a typewriter in one of the public offices, were easily accomplished.

At the Council meeting of Wednesday 10th February 1904 Provost James Hood announced dramatically that Andrew Carnegie wished to spend £500,000 on the erection of a Burns Temple in the town. He read a letter which purported to come, on Carnegie's behalf, from Hew Morrison of the Edinburgh Public Library and the great man's Scottish agent. This letter read as follows:

I have just received word by this mail that Mr Carnegie, who was deeply impressed with the progressive tendencies of Kilmarnock during his recent visit, has had under consideration a project of more closely identifying the town with the name of our National Bard. He recognised Kilmarnock as the Mecca of Burns lore, where the peerless poems were first published to the world, and where all literature associated with his honourable name has been carfully compiled and widely disseminated. Mr Carnegie has therefore decided to erect at his own cost, within the town of Kilmarnock, a temple to the memory of our national pride, provided the Town Council will grant a free site. It is his intention to make the memorial a most elaborate one, the building to be constructed of granite, white marble, or some superior material, and to be of magnificent design, while the interior will contain statues of Burns contemporaries, and the principal characters of his creation, and under the dome a chaste figure of the immortal genius will stand. Artistic panels will embellish the walls, illustrative of scenes depicted in his poems, and the whole building will be lavishly treated at a cost not exceeding £500,000. While Mr Carnegie will retain in his own hands the plans and details of construction, he wishes the management of the temple to be vested in a committee of trustees, consisting of the Provost, Magistrates, and three of the people's representatives in the Town Council; the president, vice-president, secretary, and other three members of the Kilmarnock Burns Club; and the Editor of the Burns Chronicle. *In selecting a site, Mr Carnegie has confidence in the judgment of the Kilmarnock Town Council, but when in Kilmarnock he was impressed with a commanding position at the entrance of your Park, opposite to Tam Samson's house; imposing flights of steps could be led up to the structure and made add to the effect. Mr Carnegie will be glad to learn if the Kilmarnock Town Council are prepared to entertain the conditions of this gift, so that he can make the necessary arrangements for immediately proceeding therewith.*

OUR ARTIST SUGGESTS THE ABOVE DESIGN FOR THE CARNEGIE BURNS TEMPLE WHICH WAS TO BE ERECTED AT KILMARNOCK

THE KILMARNOCK HOAX.

This document was received with wild acclamation and an enthusiastic cheer for the millionaire philanthropist. At the same time, there was present a magistrate no less, who knew full well that the letter was bogus. There was a psychological moment for an honest confession, which would have received hilarious absolution, but the chief hoaxer remained silent, the far-reaching effects of the joke depriving him of his usual presence of mind.

The next morning Kilmarnock awoke to find itself famous. The news travelled like wildfire and made banner headlines in the national dailies. All too soon, however, a furious Dr Morrison contacted Provost Hood. He wrote immediately: 'I offer my sympathy in this wretched and silly hoax, which, I learned last night at 11.30, has been perpetrated upon you; a hoax which I think not only silly, but an insult to the people of the town over which you worthily preside. The writer must have had knowledge of Mr Carnegie's appreciation of Kilmarnock, but the rest of the letter was not characteristic of Mr Carnegie, Especially silly was the part regarding the structure of the temple and its composition. I at once repudiated the letter, and characterised it as an impudent and cruel hoax. I am very much distressed that such a trick should have been so far successful.'

This was meat and drink to the newspapers; the real temple might have merited a paragraph or two, but the spurious one was treated to columns in which each paper tried to outdo its rivals in facetiousness. By contrast the Kilmarnock and Ayrshire papers were filled with letters from angry readers threatening dire retribution to the hoaxers. The story ran and ran, and kept both local and national papers going for almost a year.

When the Council called a special meeting to devise a plan for getting to the bottom of the mystery opinion began to swing in the opposite direction, and the press lampooned the Council as a body singularly lacking in humour. The farther afield, the more this view tended to be held and for a time Kilmarnock was held in even greater ridicule from London to Boston. The affair was spun out with a plethora of jokes, cartoons and bad verse which must have had poor Burns positively birling in his Mausoleum. The Council would not be deflected, however, and set to with a will to unmask the culprit.

A determined search was made through the town and specimens of writing from every typewriter were compared with the hoax letter. Astonishingly the machine on which the letter had been typed was tracked down in the office of the Kilmarnock Constabulary. Sergeant Martin of the burgh police later admitted typing the letter, at the behest of a magistrate no less. In this manner Bailie William Munro was unmasked. Suitably abashed, Munro made a donation of £50 to the Kilmarnock Infirmary in reparation for his misdeed. Provost Hood hoped that that would be the end of the matter and attempted to hush up the affair; but the public would not be fobbed off and demanded to know the identity of the perpetrator. Bailie Munro was forced into the open; he apologised publicly and tendered his resignation from the Council.

For some time ex-Bailie Munro kept a low profile. Two months later, however, the *Standard* observed his prominent presence at a public lecture. The *Kilmarnock Herald* gave publicity to his charitable work, especially his labours as secretary to the Howard Park Old Men's Cabin and his contribution to the annual outing to Troon. Munro's rehabilitation had begun. By October he was offering himself as a candidate in the local elections scheduled for the following month. Personal conceit, arrogance and a fine contempt for the Town Council came across loud and clear in the speech he delivered in Riccarton Institute. He made a jibe at

> those who profess to uphold the dignity of our town, but who have yet to learn how to conduct themselves in dignity... I have never ceased to consider myself your representative... I don't claim to be above the average in wisdom, and would never think of advocating that the Council should be composed of twenty-five Bailie Munros. But I am sure you will agree with me that, if it were so constituted, more business would be transacted and there would be less nonsense than there has been these last number of years.

Munro topped the poll in the Fifth Ward and returned to his civic duties less than eight months after his disgrace. The *Herald* commented on his re-election: 'No-one can be blamed for the affair except the author. It is likely the perpetrator of the hoax never anticipated that his joke would go so far. It is all very well for a joker to get his wit out, but it is infamous that a town should be made the laughing stock of the world because of one fool's craving for fun.'

Burns in the present century

The celebrations of the poet's Ter-Jubilee (1909) and death anniversary (1946) were muted affairs, but Kilmarnock Burnsians were well represented at the main events held at Alloway and Dumfries respectively. The latter occasion, coming so soon after the Second World War, at a time of austerity, precluded a more

by the scale and magnitude of the International Burns Festival of 1955 which was hosted by Ayr and Kilmarnock and attracted visitors from all over the world, including the USSR, Canada, Rhodesia and India. This was a curtain-raiser for the celebrations marking the poet's bicentenary in 1959. Inevitably the main commemoration took place at Alloway, but the Burns Federation hosted a dinner in the Grand Hall, Kilmarnock on Saturday 24th January, attended by a galaxy of national celebrities as well as local worthies. The principal guests included the First Lord of the Admiralty, the Earl of Selkirk and his wife, Lord and Lady Mathers, Greta Lauder (niece of Sir Harry Lauder), Dr Tom Honeyman of the Glasgow Museums and Art Galleries, the provosts of Ayr and Dumfries as well as local civic dignitaries. Burnsians from as far afield as Australia were present on this occasion.

In more recent times there have been public events celebrating the re-dedication of the Monument (1978), the centenary of the Burns Federation (1985) and the bicentenary of the Kilmarnock Poems (1986). So successful was the event marking the centenary of the laying of the foundation stone at the Monument (30th July 1978) that this subsequently became an annual event. Known as Kilmarnock and Loudoun Burns Day, it has been the opportunity for a glorious open-air concert as well as many supporting events and now draws numerous visitors to the town. It should also be noted that no fewer than nineteen Burns clubs in Kilmarnock were affiliated to the Burns Federation at one time or another. Many of them have died out or disjoined, but for every active Burns club meeting regularly throughout the year there are probably dozens of Burns Suppers held by women's guilds, rotary clubs and other organisations. The spirit of the bard flourishes as strongly as ever, and for this Kilmarnock, through its Burns clubs and the Federation, must take a large amount of credit.

lavish celebration. There was a pessimistic feeling that, perhaps, the Burns movement was moribund, attracting only those who were well on in years and not appealing to the young. Any doubts on this score were dispelled

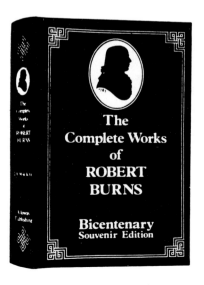

Bicentenary edition of *Complete Works of Robert Burns*

12 SPORTS

Archibald McKay quoted an anonymous writer as commenting that Kilmarnock in olden times abounded in strong and valiant men, and went on to cite a number of centenarians. 'Perhaps it was mainly to out-door recreations and athletic sports and games, which were then common, that the men of Cunninghame were indebted for that robustness of constitution,' he concluded. Games and pastimes of one sort or another must always have existed, but a documentary record of them goes back no further than the early eighteenth century. Today, few towns of its size have such an abundance and variety of sporting amenities as Kilmarnock offers both for participants and for spectators.

Bowling

Although predated by bowling greens at Glasgow Candleriggs (1695) and Haddington (1709) Kilmarnock Bowling Club have long subscribed to the claim made for them by Hawkes and Lindley in their *Encyclopaedia of Bowls* that they are "the oldest continuous club in Scotland," founded in 1740 and continuing without interruption up to the present day. The Town Council voted the sum of £5 to a Mr Paterson for the laying of a bowling-green and the purchase of bowls. McKay states that bowling was introduced as a more agreeable diversion than shooting, but other sources say that it was cock-fighting which the Council wished to replace.

Original site of Kilmarnock Bowling Green

The original bowling-green was on ground near where the George Hotel was later erected, on the north side of what is now West George Street near the railway station. Mention has already been made of the Bowling-green House, a pub kept by Tam Samson's son-in-law, Sandy Patrick, where Burns and his cronies habitually met. The bowling-green moved in 1790 to a more commodious site nearby and then in 1867 transferred to its present location adjoining the approach to the Kay Park, off London Road. The Kilmarnock Bowling Club was a private club, whose facilities were available only to gentlemen holding its £2 shares. Oddly enough, the Club did not purchase its grounds and clubhouse until May 1905. In 1938 the latter was considerably extended and renovated at a cost of £2,200. At that period the Club had a tennis section but subsequently this was let go—an unfortunate decision as this would have provided the Club with a useful diversification in later years, when stiff competition was offered in the form of indoor carpet bowls. A liquor licence was not obtained till 1975 but catastrophe struck on 16th October that year when the clubhouse was destroyed by fire. An entirely new clubhouse was opened on 3rd June 1979 by Bernard Scott of Strathclyde Regional Council.

Opening of new clubhouse, June 1979

A second private club, the Portland, was opened on 10th July 1860. Among its founder members were the postmaster, David Rankin, Provost Archibald Finnie, two past provosts (Robert Cumming and John Dickie) and one future provost (Peter Sturrock). The green, on the west side of South Hamilton Street, was the largest in the town at the time.

These two clubs catered to the wealthier, leisured classes of the burgh, but in the second half of the nineteenth century the notion that workingmen should also have recreational facilities gradually developed. It was left to the workers themselves to take the initiative, and thus it was that the Workingmen's Bowling Green was opened at Townholm by Provost Dickie in July 1870. Although intended for the 'mechanics and operatives' of the burgh, it was founded on exactly the same principles as the middle-class clubs, its 60 members holding £1 shares and paying annual subscriptions of 7s6d. Contrast the humble origins of the Townholm Club with the situation in 1989 when Provost Jim Mills inaugurated the new clubhouse. This was erected at a cost of £80,000 but was actually worth a great deal more, as much of the materials and labour were contributed free of charge or at cost price. It is interesting to note that YTS trainees also helped in its construction. With its spacious main lounge, well-equipped games room, quiet lounge and bar facilities, it is the last word in luxury.

A second workingmen's club was founded at West Netherton a year later, and opened by Provost Dickie on 21st July 1871. It adjoins West Netherton Street and provided fine views overlooking Barbadoes Green and the Lady's Walk on the far bank of Kilmarnock Water. This club was funded by its members who subscribed for 100 ten-shilling shares.

The Springhill Bowling Club, opened on 5th June 1897, was a fine example of late nineteenth century 'do-it-yourself'. Bailie William Gibson, David Orr and a band of stalwarts themselves cleared a piece of waste ground at the foot of Fullarton Street. Turf from Irvine Flats was the gift of the Earl of Eglinton and the whole project masterminded by Andrew McCulloch.

By 1908 Glasgow had no fewer than ten municipal bowling-greens which were free to the inhabitants. In Kilmarnock, even the so-called workingmen's clubs were, in fact, private clubs. In that year, therefore, the Town Council first considered following Glasgow's example, but the project was abandoned when it was ascertained that a green in the Howard Park would cost about £400. The matter was raised from time to time thereafter, but shelved because of the First World War. By the time the Council got around to taking a positive decision on this matter costs had escalated. When the Howard Park bowling-green was opened on 4th May 1923 the cost had risen to over £2,000. With bowling clubs in Riccarton and Kilmaurs (the latter dating from 1868) the town and surrounding district boasted no fewer than eight bowling facilities. Since then greens have also been established in Bellfield and Bonnyton.

Cricket

On 18th March 1852 James Henderson, James Thomson, Alexander Urie and James S. Wilson met in the Commercial Inn and formed the Kilmarnock Winton Cricket Club, in honour of the Earl of Eglinton and Winton, one of the great all-round sportsmen of his day. Within a few weeks they had recruited eleven others and thus had the nucleus of a cricket team. A bat, stumps and three balls were procured, and the use of a field at Holmes Farm obtained free of charge from Mr Guthrie. This proved to be too remote from the town, and the following season the Club negotiated for the use of a part of Barbadoes Green (now the Howard Park). This proved abortive, and the infant club had a hard struggle to keep going; but in 1855 'two rigs of Barbadoes Green' were rented to the Club by William Smith at £6 per annum. This ground was far from ideal, for it was on a slight incline. In the early years the standard of cricket was quite low, the only competition being provided within the Club or from scratch teams in the surrounding villages. Real competition, from the Glasgow clubs, was precluded on the ground of distance. In the 1860s, however, the Club obtained a pitch at the foot of St Andrews Street and from then on the sport took off. In the latter part of the nineteenth

century Kilmarnock had no fewer than ten cricket clubs; including the Winton, the Shaw, Stewart, Portland Thistle, Newfield, Struthers, Burnbrae, Shewalton and Elmbank which all sprang up in this period, while the surrounding district had clubs in Troon, Irvine, Hurlford, Perceton, Crookedholm, Cumnock, Glengarnock, Kilwinning and Muirkirk, not to mention several teams in Ayr. The image of cricket is of a rather leisurely, always gentlemanly, game; so it comes as something of a shock to learn that, more than a century ago, one match between Hurlford and Portland was thus reported: 'the play on both sides was good but the conduct of the spectators was anything but gentlemanly'; or that when Stewart played Cumnock, the latter team walked off the field when Stewart refused to accept the ball Cumnock were using.

In 1870 Kilmarnock CC was arranging its first fixtures outside the district, with Clydesdale and Greenock, and although Kilmarnock lost both matches, the team acquitted itself well. The Earl of Eglinton's XI contained a hard core of English professionals, and matches against this formidable side gave Kilmarnock its first taste of real competition. In the 1870s the Club began to acquire a wider reputation, though one early writer attributed this, rather grudgingly, to the possession of a good pitch. In 1876 the Club rented a new site from a builder named Auld, at £45 per annum. Holm Quarry was a mile from the Cross, to the west of the main Kilmarnock-Ayr road, and the Club spent quite a lot of money on laying out the pitch and erecting a pavilion. Part of the costs were offset by staging athletic sports on the grounds. During the winter months the ground was sub-let to rugby and hockey teams, and even cattle were grazed on the land, in a bid to work off the deficit incurred at the outset. In the seasons of 1885 and 1886 Kilmarnock beat Uddingston, Kelburne, the West of Scotland, Glasgow University and Dumfries, but subsequent seasons were less successful. In 1898 Kilmarnock CC finally managed to defeat the Eglinton XI.

Just when the Club were looking forward to celebrating their half-century, they received a bombshell in 1902 from the Council which took over the grounds for the erection of a new gasworks. The media of the period were less than sympathetic. One paper speculated whether 'the flannelled fools... will require to betake themselves to the rearing of canaries, the beating of the big drum in the local band, or some other similar institution to which the Common Good is such a liberal contributor.' There ensued a wrangle with the Council over compensation, the Club seeking £712 and the Council offering a derisory £200. The matter then went to arbitration, as a result of which the Club were awarded £548 15s, plus legal costs.

With this money the Club acquired its ground at Kirkstyle on the south bank of the River Irvine, east of Riccarton. The new pitch was laid out under the supervision of A.E. Street, a Surrey professional then playing with Lord Eglinton's team. The task of clearing

Kilmarnock Cricket Club's first pavilion at Kirkstyle, 1904

the ground near the Kirkstyle coal pit was immense, and it was not until 25th June 1904 that the pitch was ready for its first match, between Kilmarnock and Ayr. The Western Union had been in existence since the turn of the century, but it was not until 1907 that Kilmarnock joined. Membership of this body, enlarged and renamed as the Western Union, put the Kilmarnock cricketers on their mettle. Aesthetically, the Kirkstyle ground left much to be desired, with its view of the Glenfield works, the railway line and the coal pit's slag heaps. The clubhouse was derisively known as the Hen-house because of its cramped changing facilities. Later, however, a tea hut was erected by Kilmarnock Harriers (who used the ground in the winter months) and this amenity was greatly appreciated. The First World War hit the Club hard, several promising players being killed and others maimed in that conflict. When play was resumed in 1919 the Club was sadly depleted and it had quite a struggle to keep going. In the severe flooding of January 1932, however, the Club suffered its worst setback, when 2,000 tons of peat moss and silt were deposited on the pitch as a result of the Cessnock overflowing. All of this debris had to be removed in barrows and a temporary railway was even laid so that the silt could be removed more easily. In 1936 the Club beat Glasgow University at the West of Scotland ground in Hamilton Crescent, Partick, to win the Rowan Charity Cup, the Club's first major trophy.

The Second World War disrupted progress, but not to the same extent as in 1914-18. Even when the war was at it height, the Club was able to develop a new ground at Kirkstyle, inaugurated in September 1944. The momentum sustained during the war was helped, to some extent, by the Club's junior section, started in 1933, which was a valuable training ground for the First and Second XI. One of its inaugural players was James Aitchison who graduated to the adult teams in 1937 and was the Club's star performer over the next three decades. As the compiler of the Club's centenary handbook, he modestly played down his own role, but Nisbet Gallagher, writing in the sequel 25 years later, maintained that Jim Aitchison was 'arguably the best batsman Scotland has ever produced'. During a career from 1937 to 1967 Aitchison scored 31,051 runs at an average of 45.7, hitting 61 centuries and 230 fifties. Between 1946 and 1963 he played for Scotland 69 times. The highlights included the century against Australia

Kilmarnock Cricket Club team 1946

in 1956, 106 not out against South Africa in 1947 and 190 not out against Ireland in 1959, the last being then a Scottish record. In its first postwar season, the Club won the Western District Union Championship for the first time, and from then on proved a formidable force in Scottish cricket. In 1969 KCC won every competition

Kilmarnock Cricket Club team 1969

in which they competed, winning the Western Union Championship, West League Cup, Rowan Cup and Ayrshire Cup. Hugh Fulton, Secretary and Treasurer in this period, was responsible more than anyone else for the high standard of cricket in the 1950s and 1960s.

Success on the playing fields was largely a barometer of the town's fortunes in the 1970s and 1980s. In their heyday, many of the great industrial concerns, such as Saxone and Glenfield, had thriving cricket teams, and there were also excellent clubs in the surrounding district, such as Dunlop CC (founded in 1930) and Caprington CC.

In 1982 BMK was taken over by an English businessman, John Logue who transformed an ailing family company into a thriving, dynamic concern once more. The following year Logue came to the rescue of Kilmarnock CC whose membership had shrunk from 250 to 150; by merging it with the BMK Social Club (membership 156) Logue breathed new life into the Club and, in addition, some 80 new members joined shortly after the merger took place.

Today Kilmarnock Cricket Club is still playing in the Western Union.

Curling

Curling probably had its origins in the Netherlands, but it was well-established in Scotland by the fifteenth century and the game, in its modern form, was very much a Scottish invention. In Kilmarnock the earliest reference to curling occurs in 1644, the minister of Fenwick, the Rev. William Guthrie being described in his biography as a keen player. Because it depended on the presence of thick ice, curling tended to be a more ephemeral sport than others, but when the weather conditions were right it was taken up enthusiastically. The curlers of one district would challenge those of another, and persons of all ranks, young and old, would join in the bonspiel. The favoured venues for curling were the mill dams in the vicinity, but it was customary also to flood the level ground around the Cross and use it as a rink when it froze over. McKay records that, in the hard winter of 1740, curling took place at the Cross on 23 consecutive days. The water was raised from a well and the rink was dammed to prevent it escaping till it froze. Later a pond near Craufurdland Castle was regularly used. New Farm Loch takes its name from an artificial pond created each November by deliberate flooding to provide the

Curling at New Farm Loch

curlers with a large rink. In March, when the ice melted, the water would be drained off till the following winter. New Farm Loch was used by the curlers from 1845 until the 1950s.

The early curling stones were large, clumsy and rough pieces of granite. An ancient stone, said to have been used by William Guthrie, was preserved at Craufurdland Castle. The game took a quantum leap in 1864 when Andrew Kay of Mauchline used a water-powered lathe to polish the stones. In the winter months the local curlers competed in the Eglinton

County Curling Game for the Earl of Eglinton Plate, introduced in 1851. By the turn of the century the Kilmarnock curlers were organised into a number of clubs. There was the Kilmarnock Union Curling Club, Kilmarnock Townend (founded in 1810), Kilmarnock Juniors, Howard de Walden and Glenfield. Other trophies included Mrs Craufurd's Gold Model Curling Stone, for which the Union and Townend curlers competed at Craufurdland, the Gairdner Silver Stone, instituted by the banker Charles Gairdner in 1863, the Eglinton Jug and the Finnie Kettle.

Since the opening of the Galleon Centre in 1987, curlers have been able to enjoy the game indoors throughout a much longer season, with the rink

The Galleon curling rink

available for curling on average four days a week, extending from September through to the end of March each year. While early problems were encountered in precisely controlling the condition of the ice for the sport, recent advances have resulted in consistently keener ice, and curling has reached new heights. In February 1992, the Royal Caledonian Curling Club staged the Finals of both the men's and ladies' Scottish Junior Championships at the Galleon Centre as part of the 'Kilmarnock 400' celebrations. Such was the organisation of the event, and the quality of facilities laid on for the visiting curlers, and the response from the local populace who spectated, that it has already been confirmed that the same tournament will return to the Galleon Centre, and Kilmarnock, in 1993.

Association Football

'At the present time (1879), the game of Foot-ball is a favourite pastime in the town and neighbouring districts,' wrote McKay, an understatement if there ever was one. Some kind of game in which a ball was kicked around must have existed for centuries—one is reminded of the atrocity from the Covenanting period when poor James White's head was used as a football. The game played for centuries involved enormous teams—usually one side of the town against the other—and handling the ball was quite permissible. These monster matches were a way of letting off steam, not to mention paying off old scores! By the 1820s more formalised games were beginning to emerge and this led to the controversy between the 'hand' and 'no hands' schools of thought. In 1848 the Cambridge Rules were formulated, leading to the emergence of Rugby football as played by the great English public schools; but elsewhere it was still largely a free-for-all game. The 'no hands' movement gradually coalesced to form the English Football Association in 1863. Soccer came to Scotland in 1867, when Queen's Park FC were formed. The following year the boys of Kilmarnock Academy formed a team with the title of Kilmarnock Football Club which played a 'hands' game, not unlike modern Rugby Union, at Barbadoes Green. This was a disorganised game which only got proper direction when the Cricket Club took it up as a way of filling the winter months. The Academy boys joined the cricketers and the Kilmarnock Football Club was formally inaugurated in 1869. At this time the game conformed to Rugby, which is how the football ground came to be called Rugby Park. In those days the Club rented the field for £5 the half-year. It was not, in fact, till after October 1872 (when the Club acquired a copy of the rules of Association Football) that it embraced Soccer. The first match under the new regime was against Queen's Park. The result is unknown—clearly the newspaper report did not consider that as important as telling readers that both teams enjoyed a highly convivial evening afterwards 'the auspicious event celebrated afterwards in smoke and pewter'. This inaugural game took place at Grange Farm, Rugby Park being unsuitable at the time for the new rules. When approached, the farmer gave the Club permission to use his field with the words, 'Aye, lads, play awa. The grass is a' the better for being trampit a bit'. The present of a bag of meal as compensation for any damage done had the old farmer saying 'Thae fitba players are fine laddies'.

Eventually a growing conflict of interest led to a split between the cricketers and the footballers. About 1876 both factions used ground at Holm Quarry, but a dispute over the rent led to a rupture between the two groups. Football was now overtaking cricket as a spectator sport, and the cricketers felt that the footballers could shoulder much more of the burden of the rent, thus enabling them to enjoy the use of the ground in summer at relatively little cost. The footballers decamped and returned to Grange. In June 1877 the Kilmarnock Football Club first voted to rejoin the cricketers, then rescinded this decision and voted to carry on alone. The cricketers retaliated by bringing in new players and reconstituting themselves as the Kilmarnock Cricket and Football Club, later renamed Kilmarnock Athletic. This club ceased to exist in 1886 but was later briefly revived.

Meanwhile Kilmarnock FC went from strength to strength. In 1873 the Scottish Football Association was formed and Kilmarnock were one of the fifteen original members competing for the Scottish Cup in the season of 1873-4. Kilmarnock were knocked out by Renton in the first round. In the following season they beat Vale of Leven but lost to Eastern in the next round. What

Kilmarnock lacked in facilities—players had to change behind a discreet hedge—was made up for by the lavish hospitality and good sportsmanship. In the 1870s, as McKay commented, football swept the district and many other clubs were formed. At this period there were at least nine first-class teams in the town: Kilmarnock Arthurlie, Kilmarnock Dean, Kilmarnock Academicals, Kilmarnock Athletic, Kilmarnock Hawthorn, Kilmarnock Portland, Kilmarnock Star and Kilmarnock St Andrew's in addition to Kilmarnock FC which was the premier club; the best players from Portland, St Andrew's and Hawthorn tended to gravitate towards it. A more professional approach crept in, and players began meeting to exercise and practise together under the redoubtable Robert 'Cutler' Russell. In this period Kilmarnock returned to Rugby Park, the ground was modernised and a clubhouse, designed by Robert Ingram, was erected. The field was roped and a gate installed so that the public now had to pay to watch matches. The original ground was actually some way to the east of the present location, on

President—DANIEL GILMOUR, Esq.
Vice-President—MATTHEW R. D. ROBERTSON, Esq.

A. M'Gregor & Sons, Photo.
Hon. Treas.—A. L. WILSON, Esq.   Hon. Secy.—WM. MUNRO, Esq.

Our First Trophies, 1883-84.

Kilmarnock FC office-bearers and trophies 1883-84

the other side of South Hamilton Street, where Charles Street now stands.

Because Saturday was a normal working day in the 1870s, football matches could not begin till late in the afternoon and darkness had generally fallen before time was called. Bob Rankin, the team's captain and goalie, used to recount how, in one match which was continuing in pitch darkness, the attacking side were charging towards his goal. With great presence of mind he ran on to the bye-line between a goalpost and the corner flag and shouted to his backs for better cover. The ruse worked and the enemy forwards, following the sound of his voice, charged right past the goal in the darkness and missed what would otherwise have been the winning shot. This problem was overcome on 8th November 1878 when Kilmarnock became the first club in Scotland to introduce floodlighting. The *Standard* later reported this novelty, in a game between Kilmarnock and Portland. 'The lighting apparatus was supplied by E. Paterson, a London electrical engineer. There were three lights, the motive power for which was provided by a traction and two portable engines of six and eight horse power.' A large light of 6,000 candlepower was installed above the goal at one end, while two smaller lights, each of 1,200 candlepower, illuminated the corners at the other end, the power being generated by a Siemens gynamo (as dynamos were then known). As carbon filament lamps had only recently been invented by Joseph W. Swan who did not give a large-scale demonstration of his invention in England till October 1880, Kilmarnock's innovation was all the more remarkable. While the large lamp produced a brilliant light throughout the match the smaller lamps only worked intermittently owing to problems with the engines. There was a want of diffusion, with the result that parts of the field were in deep shadow which made it difficult for spectators

to follow the play. It could not have been too easy for the players either! Kilmarnock lost 3-1, so the experiment was not repeated. In that match two fine Kilmarnock players, Bailie Miller and ex-Provost J.B. Wilson, were so badly injured that they never played again.

In the 1880s further improvements at Rugby Park included a running track. In 1884 Kilmarnock FC won the Ayrshire Cup, then took the Kilmarnock Charity Cup in the same year. Players and supporters from Athletic and Portland thereafter switched their allegiance. In the season of 1887-8 Kilmarnock beat Ayr 5-1 to win the Ayr Charity Cup, then defeated the mighty English team, Preston North End 4-1. Of 40 matches that season Kilmarnock won 27 and drew 7, with 159 goals for and 53 against. Success, however, spelled near-disaster, as wealthy English clubs began poaching away the best players. This was a controversial issue, exacerbated by the acrimonious debate over professionalism which was then beginning to emerge. The English FA bowed to the inevitable and recognised professionals in 1885, but the SFA strenuously resisted because so many good players were being wooed away to the south. Kilmarnock, which had suffered more than most, backed the SFA; but this stance was in vain, though it was not till 1893 that the SFA gave way. Reluctantly Kilmarnock joined the new Scottish Alliance formed in 1894. In March that year the first international to be played at Rugby Park took place between Scotland and Wales. Previously J. 'Bummer' Campbell had played in the Scottish team against Ireland (1891) and Wales (1892), but now John Johnstone, Kilmarnock's brilliant half-back, played for his country on his home ground.

This was a turning point in the Club's fortunes. In 1896 it took the Ayrshire Cup and the Kilmarnock Charity Cup and entered the Second League

Opening of Rugby Park on 26th August 1899, league match Kilmarnock v Celtic

competition for the first time, ending in third place. In 1896-7 they beat Motherwell for the Scottish Qualifying Cup and reached the Scottish Cup semi-final, losing 4-3 to Dumbarton. The following season they won the Second League Championship and reached the final of the Scottish Cup for the first time, losing 2-0 to Rangers. Kilmarnock also made history that season, being the first club to take their players for special training at the seaside. The season of 1898-9 was even better and Kilmarnock won the Second League Championship again, as well as the Ayrshire and Kilmarnock Charity Cups, and only lost to St Mirren in the Scottish Cup final. They finished fourth equal in the Second Division and narrowly missed promotion in the play-off which Renton won 2-1. All their hard work paid off in 1899 when, having become Second League Champions for the third time, they finally won promotion to the First Division in place of Partick Thistle who were relegated.

Kilmarnock started their career in the First Division in fine style. In August 1899 the pitch at Rugby Park was lengthened and a covered stand erected. Again the Club made history by holding the first ever benefit match—for 'Bummer' Campbell who earned £120 as a result (about two years wages for a working man at that time). In 1906 the Club became a limited liability company, as Kilmarnock Football Club Ltd, with a share capital of £3,000 and a board of directors headed by Robert Dunlop and other local businessmen. One of the directors, Alexander Gibson, was also a member of the SFA Council. This was a golden era, when players like Jimmy Mitchell, Bobby Templeton and Andy Cunningham made Kilmarnock a force to be reckoned with. In 1914 Rugby Park underwent further improvements, including new dressing rooms and bathrooms, costing about £1,600. The First World War was a major setback to Soccer in general, but Kilmarnock managed to keep going, and when the Club celebrated its Golden Jubilee in 1919 a spirit of optimism was in the air. Reviewing the first half century showed that Kilmarnock had produced seventeen international players; but twice that number had left Kilmarnock for other clubs in Scotland and England. Too often Kilmarnock was regarded as a nursery from which the star footballers of the wealthiest teams were drawn. Crowds of up to 20,000 flocked to Rugby Park for the more important matches, bringing in gate money of up to £600 (about £100,000 in modern currency) on each occasion. Yet the Club was run on a shoestring, and its officials had no regular salaries.

In many respects the inter-war period was the heyday of football; with few counter attractions, it was *the* great spectator sport. It was a family game, without the hooliganism and rowdy behaviour which unfortunately marred Soccer in later years. Against all

Scottish Cup Final
at
Hampden Park, Glasgow
Saturday 6th April 1929
Kilmarnock 2 Rangers 0
Attendance 114,708

Photos courtesy of *Daily Record*

the odds, Kilmarnock battled through to the final of the Victory Cup in 1920; a record crowd of 95,000 turned out to see Killie matched against Albion Rovers at Hampden. After an exciting ding-dong struggle Kilmarnock won 3-2 and took the Scottish Cup for the first time. This success, however, was followed by nine lack-lustre years during which Killie narrowly averted relegation (1922) and seldom rose above the mid-point in the League table. In the season of 1928-9 the Club finished tenth in a field of twenty, but this, the Club's 75th anniversary, was celebrated magnificently when Kilmarnock beat the mighty Rangers in the Cup final before a crowd of 114,708 at Hampden. From the beginning Kilmarnock were very much on the defensive, facing the relentless onslaught of Rangers. Goalkeeper Sam Clemie played the match of his life, but all seemed lost when a foul on a Rangers player in the seventeenth minute resulted in a penalty kick by Tommy Craig. Clemie's superhuman save electrified his team-mates and from then on they never looked back. By half-time the score was nil-nil. In the second half, with the wind and the sun at their backs, Kilmarnock went on the attack. Jock Aitken scored the solitary goal of the match and Killie won the Cup for the second time; but Sam Clemie was undoubtedly the man of the match and received a hero's welcome when the team returned to Kilmarnock.

Throughout the 1930s Kilmarnock's league record was mediocre, only rising above tenth place in five of the ten years and again narrowly avoiding relegation in 1938. In the Cup, however, the Club did better, getting to the semi-final in 1931 and the final in 1932 when Rangers avenged their 1928 defeat—but only in the replay after a 1-1 draw first time round. Kilmarnock's fortunes were at a low ebb in succeeding years, culminating in the 1936 Scottish Cup defeat by Second Division Brechin City. Things began to look up again in December 1937 when James McGrory, the Scotland and Celtic centre-forward, took over from Hugh Spence as team manager. Under McGrory the team turned round what had until then been its most disastrous season and won a series of matches which kept them in the First Division by the skin of their teeth.

In the Cup, however, they battled through to the quarter-finals; ironically, they now found themselves up against McGrory's old team, Celtic, who were at that time enjoying a run of fifteen successive League matches without defeat. The last time Kilmarnock had met Celtic (in December 1937), they had been defeated by a humiliating 8-0. Now, three months later, would history repeat itself? Killie attacked from the outset and no one was more surprised than they were when Felix McGrogan scored. When Kilmarnock went ahead 2-0 before half time the Kilmarnock supporters went wild. In the second half Celtic counter-attacked and Kilmarnock held on grimly. A penalty to Celtic was taken by Malcolm MacDonald and the score was now 2-1. This setback would have unnerved most players, but Kilmarnock rallied and played like a team possessed, brilliant in defence and still dangerous up front, eventually winning the match. Celtic, on the other

hand, finished the season on a high note by winning the League championship for the nineteenth time—a fitting celebration for their jubilee. In the semi-final at Hampden Park Kilmarnock beat Rangers 4-3. Meanwhile East Fife, a Second Division side, had an even more sensational battle, beating Aberdeen in a replay, slogging it out three times with St Bernards before reaching the final by the odd goal in three. Kilmarnock were the favourites to take the Cup, after knocking out the Old Firm so spectacularly. But the severe strain of keeping up the momentum now began to tell. The first match ended in a 1-1 draw. A crowd of 92,000 witnessed the nail-biting replay which was only resolved in extra time when Miller and McKerrell scored the goals that gave East Fife a 4-2 victory. This brought the last prewar season to a sensational climax.

Following the outbreak of war Rugby Park was commandeered by the War Office and the pitch became an Army camp. The ground was de-requisitioned in 1945 and Kilmarnock was back in business in time for the Scottish League season of 1945-6. Towards the end of the war Kilmarnock had resumed play, using Blair Park in Hurlford, but the Club was virtually starting from scratch when League football recommenced. Jimmy McGrory left in 1945 to return to Celtic as manager, and his place was taken by Tom Smith who had a distinguished career with Kilmarnock FC, earning international recognition before finishing his playing career with Preston North End. Kilmarnock had a poor season, the team composed of young, immature players and ex-servicemen now past their best. The Club could not afford to buy the key players needed to keep them in the premier division. At the end of the 1946-7 season Kilmarnock were relegated, after an unbroken run of 48 years. Demoralised by relegation, Kilmarnock now found themselves up against very stiff competition from the clubs of B Division, and ended the 1947-8 season in sixth position. The road to promotion was long and hard, but under the management of Malcolm MacDonald (appointed in 1950) the team clawed its way up the ladder and by the end of the 1954 season had played 30 games, won nineteen and drawn four to earn 42 points and second place in the table. Kilmarnock was once more elevated to the First Division.

In their first postwar season in the First Division Kilmarnock ended in tenth place with 26 points. In 1955-6 they finished eighth with 34 points and in 1956-7 ended third with 42 points. On 20th April 1957 Kilmarnock were once more in the Cup final, this time against Falkirk. They drew 1-1 but lost 2-1 after extra time in the replay. MacDonald resigned soon afterwards to go to Brentford, and in July that year Willie Waddell took over. The ex-Scotland and Rangers right-winger gave Kilmarnock a new image and set it on the track to even greater things. League results improved steadily thanks to his strategic planning and in 1959-60 Kilmarnock (with 50 points) finished second behind Hearts. Killie had had a fantastic run of 21 unbeaten matches before conceding a goal and the match to Dunfermline, and the League Championship. In April 1960 Kilmarnock met Rangers in the Cup final and were unlucky to lose 2-0, having drawn 1-1 with Rangers in a League match only the previous week. But under Waddell Kilmarnock were forged into a full-time team and trained harder than before. Kilmarnock became a by-word for direct football, fitness and team spirit. Rangers beat them 2-0 in the League Cup final in October 1960, and in the League Championship Kilmarnock finished second to Rangers. In the early 1960s Kilmarnock were runners-up in both the League and the Cup. Indeed, the club which had been runners-up in major tournaments nine times were beginning to earn the reputation of 'second best'. In the League Cup final of 1962 they were pipped by Hearts 1-0, a goal in the closing seconds by Frank Beattie being disallowed. The controversy over the referee's decision reverberates to this day.

goal in the 52nd minute and then, with only eight minutes left, Jackie McInally scored a fourth, which gave Kilmarnock the equaliser. Miraculously, in the closing seconds, Ronnie Hamilton scored the goal which gave Kilmarnock the outright victory. Although Kilmarnock were later ousted by Everton, nothing could rob them of their moment of glory in defeating Germany's mightiest.

In the season of 1964-5 Kilmarnock slogged it out with Hearts, the two teams being neck and neck most of the time. With the last match of the season to be played at Tynecastle in April 1965, Hearts had 50 points and a goal average of 1.91, whereas Kilmarnock had 48 points and an average of 1.81. To take the championship Kilmarnock had to win by two goals. Against all the odds and a very spirited Hearts attack

Kilmarnock FC - Scottish League Champions, season 1964-65

After so many near misses and heartaches, however, Kilmarnock's time had come again, an opportunity to show their mettle arising in the Fairs City Cup. On 22nd September 1964 Kilmarnock played Eintracht of Germany, a formidable team whose awesome international reputation had been enhanced by defeating Real Madrid at Hampden in the final of the European Cup. Having previously lost 3-0 to this team in the first leg at Frankfurt, Kilmarnock started the second badly by conceding a goal in the opening minutes. Then Kilmarnock struck back and scored two goals in quick succession. Kilmarnock scored a third

in the first half Kilmarnock pulled it off, with goals by Davie Sneddon and Brian Milroy. It was a fitting climax for Willie Waddell who resigned at the end of that season to concentrate on football journalism. Malcolm MacDonald then returned as manager. The town went wild when the team returned in triumph with the Cup. But little did anyone realise then that Kilmarnock had reached their zenith, and would never again attain such heights.

This was a golden era of international fixtures in which Kilmarnock acquitted themselves well in the New York Tournament (1961-3). Now, with the League title of 1964-5 under their belts, Kilmarnock faced an even greater challenge, the European Cup. Their first essay in this tournament was a 0-0 draw against Nendori of Albania at Tirana in September 1965—a score that belies the brilliant football and spirited playing on both sides. In the second leg, at Rugby Park, they beat Nendori 1-0. In the next round, however, Kilmarnock drew 2-2 with Real Madrid at Rugby Park but went out 5-1 in the second leg. Defeat by this team was no disgrace, for it included the Hungarian Ferenc Puskas, arguably the greatest football player of all time.

In succeeding years there was another lull. In the season of 1965-6 Kilmarnock dropped to third place in the League table with 45 points, but dropped to seventh in 1966-7 and 1967-8 with 40 and 34 points respectively. In the Fairs Cup Kilmarnock fared rather better, beating Royal Antwerp and La Gantoise of Belgium and Leipzig Lokomotiv in the 1966 tournament. At the end of the 1967-8 season Malcolm MacDonald was succeeded as manager by Walter McCrae, who had been trainer since 1956. McCrae had impeccable credentials, having been trainer to Scotland's under 23 team since 1960 and trainer of the Scotland squad for the 1966 World Cup. He relinquished this post on becoming Kilmarnock's manager.

The Club celebrated its centenary in 1969 with a note of optimism, despite a lack-lustre performance since 1966. Alas, Kilmarnock remained in the doldrums throughout the 1970s and 1980s. There were now too many other attractions and forms of recreation to interest the up-coming generation. This, coupled with the tarnished image of Soccer in general and the effects of rising unemployment, combined to put a damper on the game. It was a vicious circle: dwindling gates meant less money in the kitty to pay players, far less afford expensive transfer fees. The situation by the early 1980s had got to the point where amateurs

Alan Robertson has made 581 team appearances for Kilmarnock FC over almost 20 years.

called up one week were playing First Division football the next. Crowds of 850 against Meadowbank on a Wednesday evening and 1,300 against Airdrie on a Saturday were risible. The supporters clearly showed what they thought of the fare being served up to them. Managers came and went in quick succession, and still the Club's fortunes continued to slip. By 1987 the Club was trailing at the bottom of the First Division, and after losing 2-0 to Queen of the South that September some 300 fans met the board of directors to hammer out a salvage operation.

By May 1988 Kilmarnock was narrowly escaping relegation from the First Division again. The 1988-9 season was even more disastrous and this time the

Club was ignominiously demoted to the Second Division. More seriously than this humiliation, the Club itself was now in dire trouble, faced with mounting debts of £295,000. Rival takeover bids were mounted by Robert Fleeting and Alex Ingram who headed two consortia, but they failed to agree to pool their efforts. Fleeting's offer was at first rejected by the Kilmarnock directors, a decision widely slated at the time as unwise, as the Club needed a massive cash injection to put it back on its feet and resume full-time football. Fleeting's offer of £500,000 was supported by the travel firm, A.T. Mays, and the American Laurel Chadwick; and its rejection led the Club's supporters to mount their own demonstration backing the bid. Over 1,100 fans registered their protest at a special meeting in the

Tommy Burns signed from Celtic in 1989 appointed manager in 1992.

Grand Hall in June 1989 and called for the resignation of the board. The sorry saga dragged on till the end of the year, with four Extraordinary General Meetings in October-November alone, including one cancelled only 90 minutes before it was due to take place. The negative and intransigent attitude of the directors was thoroughly demoralising for players and supporters alike. In the end, however, sanity was restored and Robert Fleeting became chairman of a Management Committee, unique in Scottish football, which even included a representative of the supporters' clubs which themselves now formed the Association of Kilmarnock Supporters to co-ordinate action in the future. Already, under the new regime, Kilmarnock FC are seeing an upturn in their fortunes, on and off the pitch, and it is to be hoped that this trend continues.

Kilmarnock Football Club is not all the football in Kilmarnock by any means. Kilmarnock Amateurs were regarded as the nursery team for the First Division team and in 1956 were League champions and winners of the League Cup, scoring an astonishing 257 goals in 45 games. In the heyday of the game district leagues were formed from teams such as Riccarton, Newton Rovers and Netherton. The big industrial concerns fielded first-class teams in an inter-works league which included BMK, Barclay's, Glenfield and Johnnie Walker's. Glenfield's, with over 2,000 employees at one time, even had their own works league, with teams representing the different departments. There was also a Churches League involving teams from Kilmarnock and neighbouring villages. While

KILMARNOCK

Kilmarnock FC playing squad 1992

Kilmarnock FC played on Rugby Park, the Academicals played on Lesser Rugby Park (the original site east of South Hamilton Street), but this was eventually redeveloped and is now a car park.

Ayrshire's Junior League was formed at Kilmarnock, when a group of enthusiasts met in the Bakers' Arms pub on 23rd November 1888 to form the Kilmarnock Junior Football Association, two years after the Junior SFA was founded. The following month seven teams affiliated: Kilmarnock Roslyn, Shawbank, Barkip Rangers, South Western, Kilmarnock Caledonia, Galston Athletic and Stewarton Cunningham. In the first Cup tie Roslyn beat Shawbank 4-1. Kilmarnock JFA was short-lived, making way on 26th April 1889 for Ayrshire JFA, with a membership of 28 clubs. The first Junior League was formed at Irvine in July 1902, followed in 1905 by a separate North Ayrshire League. However, seven teams formed their own Kilmarnock and District League. These and other local leagues were criticised for 'their selfish and unsportsmanlike behaviour', but larger groups were impracticable at the time.

Before the First World War there were no fewer than 46 junior teams in the county, and of these a round dozen were based in Kilmarnock, competing for the *Kilmarnock Standard* trophy and the Kilmarnock District shield. Later the Western League included such teams as Riccarton Bluebell and Kilmarnock Juniors who shared Kirkstyle Park. Walter McCrae started his football career as goalie with the Juniors and later became president and physiotherapist of the club. Bluebell eventually closed in

1953, and their great rivals went out of existence three years later. The mantle of junior football in subsequent years fell on Hurlford United at Blair Park, whose impressive record over the years has included Ayrshire Regional League winners in 1972-3, winning the South section of the league without losing a game and then defeating Irvine Meadow Western/Ayrshire League Cup winners of the North section and Scottish Cup holders by 4-1 at Winton Park Adrossan to become overall Ayrshire champions as well as the Junior Challenge Cup (1969, 1973 and 1974), the Ayrshire District Cup (1969), the Western League Cup (1941 and 1945), the Irvine District Cup (1945 and 1966), the Ayrshire League Cup (1972 and 1975) and the Moore Trophy (1939-40, 1940-41, 1944-45). In more recent years Hurlford Juniors and Hurlford Thistle AFC have kept the ball rolling.

Hurlford United unbeaten Ayrshire league champions 1973

It should also be noted that Kilmarnock has been home to several football personalities who made their name outwith the local Club. Ally MacLeod, Scotland's manager in 1977-8, retired to run a pub in the town, while Hugh Alexander of Annanhill graduated from amateur football to refereeing and between 1972 and 1986 refereed internationals in nineteen countries. John Doyle, one of Celtic's most promising players, lived in Jasmine Road and it was there that he was accidentally electrocuted by faulty wiring in October 1981 at the age of 30. He was capped for Scotland against Rumania in 1976.

Rugby Football

In 1973 the late Jock Thomson, commissioned to write the history of rugger in Kilmarnock, discovered that the handling game had a much longer history than had been suspected. In fact, the Rugby Club should have been celebrating its centenary in 1968. The confusion over the early years of the game is perfectly understandable, as the distinction between the different styles of football was not at all clear. The origins of the handling game in Kilmarnock go back to 1868 when the boys of the Academy formed a club with the title of the Kilmarnock Football Club. This developed into the soccer club formally inaugurated the following year, but in 1868 the game, described 'as an indisciplined rout' was definitely closer to the English public school rules formulated in 1848. John Wallace and Councillor Thomas Ferguson were the chief exponents of the handling game played on Barbadoes Green. At that time the only Rugby clubs in Scotland were Glasgow Academicals and the West of Scotland club in Glasgow and Edinburgh Academicals on the east coast, so Kilmarnock formed two teams, under the Captain and Vice-Captain, and played each other. Between 1868 and 1873 was a period of dissension within the Kilmarnock Football Club and it was not till 1874 that it dropped the Rugby rules and concentrated on the SFA rules. The Rugby rules were not clarified till 1877, the year in which the soccer players finally broke free from the Cricket Club.

On 25th October 1872 a meeting was held in the George Hotel and agreed to adopt the Rugby code. For a further year the Rugby players continued to belong to Kilmarnock FC but at a meeting on 16th December 1873, when the rugby faction failed to stop the Club from deciding that henceforth only soccer would be played, the Secretary, J.W. Railton resigned. There was an uneasy truce till 1877 when amalgamation with the Cricket Club was defeated. The final split came on 9th August that year when G.H. Lipscomb, William Douglas and Tom Ferguson resigned from Kilmarnock FC and joined the Cricket Club which already had the other rugger men. In this curious manner, not unlike the religious schisms of old, Kilmarnock Rugby Football Club came into existence. The hard core of the Cricket Club's football players continued as Kilmarnock Athletic FC and, in fact, won the Ayrshire Challenge Cup in 1878-9, but ceased to exist in 1885.

It was not until 1895 that rugby emerged as a separate force, free of the football and cricket clubs. This was signalled by the acquisition of a separate pitch that September.

In the inaugural game Kilmarnock beat Partick by three goals and three tries to nil. By 1898 a second XV was also playing, joined by a third XV a year later. In 1899 Kilmarnock joined the Scottish Rugby Union.

The game was played at Holm Quarry till 1903 when it transferred to Rugby Park (confusingly, the home of soccer).

The distinctive strip, with its Maltese Cross insignia, was adopted in February 1899. In 1901 Alex Frew was the Club's first international player, being capped against all three Home Countries. In 1924 Drew Ross was capped against Wales and France and two years later was picked to play for the British Lions. In September 1928 the Club moved to the playing fields on the south side of the River Irvine. Seven-a-side rugby began at Langholm in 1931 and spread to Kilmarnock two years later.

In more recent years the highlights have included the first floodlit rugby match at Rugby Park against a Glasgow Select team in March 1954. This experiment was repeated in March 1956 against a combined Glasgow-Edinburgh Select team. In 1961 Kilmarnock donated the Ayrshire Challenge Cup; in 1965 came the first tour of Armagh. On 5th September 1970 Bellsland was opened for play and the Kilmarnock-Ayrshire

Kilmarnock Rugby FC new field inaugural match v. International Select, September 1970.

team was formed. This was a brave attempt to give greater strength to North Ayrshire rugby and drew on members from Dalry and Ardrossan; but from the outset Kilmarnock provided the bulk of the players. Eventually Dalry and Ardrossan dropped out, leaving Kilmarnock to go it alone, but the joint name was retained in the hope that some day it would again become a reality. In 1971 W.B.N. Rose was capped for the B International team and the following year Kilmarnock-Ayrshire entered the First division of the Glasgow District League. Kilmarnock-Ayrshire won every trophy competed for by the rugby clubs in Ayrshire and was admitted to the Third Division of the Scottish Rugby Union League in 1973. Two years later it was promoted to the Second Division and ended that season as top team. In 1976 it was promoted to the First Division but had difficulty in maintaining its position there and subsequently dropped back to the Second Division. Like Kilmarnock FC, the Rugby Club has had its ups and downs in more recent times, but it has also featured some star players, such as Bill Cuthbertson. First capped for Scotland in the season of 1976-77, he has since played more than twenty times for his country and is the most capped player to play for Kilmarnock.

Golf

Kilmarnock's golfers were in the curious position of not having a course of their own for many years. In 1887 the Kilmarnock Golf Club was formed and played on land at Holmes Farm and other farms on the southwest side of the town. Relations with these farmers were mixed, to put it mildly. One farmer insisted on compensation for any cows injured by golf-balls, while another maintained his rights to spread manure on the fairways. This was an unsatisfactory situation which •was only remedied when the Club obtained permission to play on the course at Barassie near Troon. Plans for a municipal golf course matured in 1908 when the Town Council obtained the lease of land at Caprington. Umberlie House was included in the lease at a rental of £12 a year and this was used as a clubhouse. Rules and fees were drawn up early the following year: men paid 12s6d a year and women only 7s6d. David Kinell, golf professional at Prestwick St Nicholas, supervised the laying of the course. David Kilpatrick, greenkeeper at Barassie, was appointed superintendent, a job which he held from 1909 till 1947. The course was formally opened on 1st May 1909 by Councillor H.S. Dunn, JP. In the same year Loudoun Gowf Club near Galston was re-activated and has gone from strength to strength ever since.

In 1929 the Town Council bought 127 acres of land at Annanhill, using the profits of the electricity service for this purpose. It was intended that this land would be used for a golf course but this was delayed by red tape for many years. Plans were interrupted by the Second World War but in 1949 the Council resumed negotiations with the Scottish Home Department to create a golf course. This dragged on until 1956 when permission was finally obtained. In the meantime the

mansion house on this estate was used for various purposes and latterly (1950-4) was let to Massey Harris as a social club.

The course was laid out by Messrs John R. Stutt Ltd at a cost of £11,600, and was formally opened by Provost Daniel Cairns in April 1957. As part of the official opening a four-ball match was played involving Eric Brown, W. S. Macdonald, John Panton and John McLean. After the round Eric Brown, the Scottish Professional Champion, claimed that Annanhill had 'one of the best finishes we have ever played on'. Miniature golf or pitch and putting greens were also provided as part of the facilities in several of the parks in and around the town: in the Kay Park, at Bellfield, and north of the Annanhill golf course on the Irvine Road.

Jim Milligan sinks his putt to give
Britain's Walker Cup team a win over USA

The best known local golfer of recent years is Jim Milligan, a member of Loudoun and Kilmarnock Barassie. He was in the Walker Cup team which beat the United States in 1989; Jim playing against J. Seagle turned his game around from 3 down with 4 to play to half the match and give the British Team a vital half point for victory.

Other sports

Quoiting was a very popular sport for centuries, long before 1893 when the Dowager Lady Howard de Walden donated a cup for competition by the Kilmarnock Union Quoiting Club. Kilmarnock Thistle and Riccarton were the other clubs in the district who competed for this trophy until 1934.

Dog-racing has long been a traditional pastime in

mining communities and Kilmarnock had a dog track from the 1920s till 1971 at Queen's Drive where the champion whippets of the town and surrounding villages were put to the test.

Founded in 1927, Kilmarnock's Wallacehill Cycling Club is one of Scotland's premier cycling clubs, and has

Professional Cycling Championships, 1992 organised by
Kilmarnock's Wallacehill Cycling Club

produced many international competitors and Scottish champions. In the 1950s the Kinnear brothers, Robert, Billy, Gordon and Ian were to the fore in time trialing, then in the 1960s George Clare won national titles at schoolboy, junior and senior—the only competitor ever to win all three championships, In the 1980s Graham O'Bree won record after record before taking the British one-hour record at Meadowbank Velodrome. The club has for twenty-five years run the prestigious Girvan three-day race and has promoted British Amateur and Professional Championships.

As befits a town in a rural setting, Kilmarnock has had a traditional interest in horses. There is a record of steeplechasing in the surrounding countryside as late as 1845. Interest in horses declined in the early years of this century but has made a remarkable come-back since the Second World War and there are now several riding schools in the vicinity. Dallars was visited by Princess Anne in July 1989, giving prominence to the work done in encouraging handicapped riders. Kilmarnock could even boast of several show-jumpers—

David Landsborough, Hon. President
of the Glenfield Ramblers

David Moore and his sisters Helen and Debbie—who achieved some notable successes in this sport in the late 1970s.

A Ramblers Society was formed in 1871 by Archibald Adamson but this owed a great deal to his forceful personality and when he emigrated to the

United States in 1883 it looked as if it would fold. In March 1884, however, the Glenfield works took up this challenge and formed their own club, their inaugural foray being a visit to Bellfield. The Saturday rambles continue to this day, alternating with Wednesday evening lectures in the Technical College on a wide range of topics. For many years the historian and naturalist, the Rev. David Landsborough, was Hon. President of this society.

A municipal swimming pool was first proposed in November 1930 but it was rejected by the Town Council who felt that those depressed times were hardly propitious. As the economic situation improved,

Kilmarnock Baths

however, the idea was revived and won approval on 21st May 1937. Plans by Alexander Dunlop were submitted the following October and work began the following year on a site in Titchfield Street. Despite the outbreak of the Second World War the pool was completed at a cost of £37,322 and formally opened on 5th October 1940 by the wife of Provost G. H. Wilson. It was the second largest pool in Scotland with a length of 100 feet, a width of 42 feet and a capacity of 215,000 gallons. An innovation, however, was the wave-

The 'wave' making machine in action

making machine donated by Glenfield and Kennedy. This firm had developed these machines for the testing tanks used in naval architecture, but this was the first recreational use in the United Kingdom. The machine created a nine-foot wave which must have been sensational for swimmers, but eventually put enormous strain on the structure of the pool itself. For this reason the machine was not transferred to the new swimming pool in the Galleon Centre. The most outstanding swimmer Kilmarnock has produced is Margaret McDowall who dominated British women's backstroke swimming in the 1950s. At the age of fourteen Margaret was a member of the Scottish team which won the Bologna Trophy. Subsequently she won the junior and senior championships (1951) and a silver medal at the Helsinki Olympics (1952), was the first woman to win the British 100 yards championship in three consecutive years (1950-2) and Scottish senior 100 yards champion for eight successive years (1951-8).

Margaret McDowall

Kilmarnock Harrier and Athletic Club was founded in 1887 and got off, quite literally, to a flying start when its star performer J. McWilliams began entering national events. In 1889 he won the Scottish harriers-union championship. In more recent years Gregor Grant won nine consecutive Ayrshire senior cross-country championships between 1978 and 1987, a feat without parallel. Since then the high standards of the Club have been maintained by such athletes as Mary McClung and Alan Murray. Today it functions as the Johnnie Walker Kilmarnock Harriers and Athletic Club and boasts over 150 members who train at Scott Ellis Playingfield. Cameron Sharp attained international success as a sprinter and reached the semi-finals at the Moscow Olympics of 1980. Two years later he won three bronze medals at the Commonwealth Games in Brisbane, and was a member of the 400m relay team which won the gold medal. At the Crystal Palace meeting he won the 200 metres in 20.64 seconds, the fastest time set by a British athlete that season. His career was prematurely ended through injuries sustained in a car

Cameron Sharp

crash in the Borders in 1991.

Kilmarnock and Loudoun Amateur Boxing Club in London Road and the Witchknowe Boxing Club south of the river keep up the interest in pugilism. In recent years, however, the Oriental martial arts have attracted a large following and Kilmarnock now has clubs devoted to judo, karate, aikido, kung fu and taekwondo. Members of Kilmarnock's Kisan Karate Club took part in the world championships in Australia in 1986. Pat McKay was the leading exponent of karate, having been world light heavyweight champion in 1982 and 1984. David Coulter was European champion in 1978 and 1983 and Tom Gibson held the same title in 1988. McKay and Coulter have both been members of British teams which took world titles. David and his cousin Michael Coulter, both of Kilmarnock Sakai Club, have dominated the Scottish lightweight championship, David having won it from 1980 to 1983 and Michael every year since. The Sakai Club was founded by John Kerr who had previously been a member of Kilmarnock's Cluarankwai Judo Club formed in the 1950s. The name, a compound of Gaelic and Japanese words, means 'the way of the thistle'. Cluarankwai's Eddie Cassidy was five times Scottish champion, three times British champion and held the European championship till 1972 when he retired from competitive judo. Eddie still practises and teaches at the club and attained his sixth dan in 1984.

Kilmarnock has flourishing tennis and badminton clubs, an amateur weightlifting club. Arguably the most spectacular sport currently practised is hanggliding, given prominence by Club Secretary Jim 'Potty' Potts who has established a number of national records

Jim Potts

in recent years, including an epic cross-Channel flight with John Pilkington (1981). For his Irish Sea crossing the same year he won the title of 'Most Notable Flight of the Year', awarded by *Glider Rider* magazine of America.

The Galleon swimming pool

Reception area

Recreational facilities

Various industrial concerns in Kilmarnock pioneered recreational facilities for the use of their employees. Among these were the Clark memorial halls which provided a wide range of indoor sports facilities for the workers at the Saxone shoe factories in Titchfield Street next door to the Corporation swimming baths. In the 1950s the Apple Mini Sports Centre was opened in this location but it was demolished twenty years later to make way for a leisure complex at a cost of £140,000. This was the forerunner of the present-day Galleon Centre, an ambitious project which was first mooted in 1985. The Walker construction group of Livingston submitted plans in November that year and the £4.5 million scheme on the site of the former Saxone factory and Clark halls was completed in May 1987— four months ahead of schedule. The former Corporation swimming baths were then closed and the site redeveloped to provide a car park for the Galleon. The name is a curious one, for an inland town without maritime connections, but it was devised by William Armstrong in a prize competition, and derived from the Gallion Brae and Gallion Burn nearby. From the outset the Galleon Centre proved to be a powerful rival to the mighty Magnum Centre in Irvine and attracted 186,562 visitors in the first five months alone. In the inaugural week there were 20,000 visitors, of whom 9,880 were swimmers and 684 users of the fitness room. The Galleon has a leisure pool, children's pool and flume, attractively laid out with poolside tables and chairs. The ice-rink is used for skating, curling, ice hockey and ice discos, while there are also facilities for bowls, squash, badminton, soft tennis, football, the martial arts, gymnastics, aerobics and weightlifting.

This magnificent recreation complex was preceded by the Hunter Centre in Ardbeg Avenue, serving mainly the northern and western districts of the town. It was opened in September 1985 by John Hunter and named in recognition of his 21 years service on the Council. It has a large games hall with seating for 100 spectators, and three badminton courts, a conditioning room and a modern multi-gymnasium. The North-West Youth Centre in the former Onthank Community Centre serves the Kola Kids (an acronym from the four districts of Knockinlaw, Onthank, Longpark and Altonhill) providing recreational facilities for the 14-25 age group.

Football pitches and a running track are to be found in Scott Ellis Park, which is also the proposed site for Kilmarnock FC's new ground. There are a skate-boarding facilities and a cycle route in the Kay Park.

The Galleon Centre

13 LEISURE AND RECREATION

How did people spend their spare time in bygone times? For one thing, they had precious little time for themselves. The picture of the Cotter's Saturday night conveyed by Burns, though sentimentalised, was an accurate one. Country people—the peasantry—worked all the hours God made, and then some, from dawn till dusk, in the relentless struggle to wrest a living from the soil. The methods of agriculture practised in the era

'The Cotter's Saturday Night' by John Faed, R.S.A. engraved by I. Horsburgh

before the great improvements of the late eighteenth century, and the lack of farm machinery, meant that labour was the most important element in farming. Even small children were pressed into service almost as soon as they could walk. The lot of the urban labourer was little better. In the burgeoning coalmines of the eighteenth century, men, women and even quite young children laboured at the coal face. The collier's daughter in Burns's poem was happy to labour all day long, six days a week, to win her fivepence a day (about 2p in decimal currency); but even the most skilled miners seldom exceeded three shillings (15p) a week— the price of the Kilmarnock Poems. Miners were indentured to the coal-pits, a form of serfdom which continued well into the nineteenth century, although it exempted them from the hardships and miseries of impressment into the Royal Navy.

Much of the industry in the towns was conducted on a cottage basis, but the labour was no less sweated on that account, for payment was by the piece or the amount of yarn, in the weaving and spinning trades. Weavers spent twelve to sixteen hours at their looms, working by lamp or candle-light in the long winter nights. They were regarded as the aristocrats of labour and the best of them could earn £20 to £30 a year.

Working on their own, with plenty of time to think, they tended to develop independent minds and a taste for learning. From their ranks came many of the leaders of radicalism which eventually transformed the country. The other trades, the bonnetmakers, leather workers, flax-dressers, shoemakers and the like, worked just as hard for lesser amounts. After a long and poorly paid apprenticeship the most they could hope for was to ply their craft for a pittance which would enable them to raise a family. Only the very determined few managed to rise above this, becoming employers of labour themselves, or acting as agents, the middlemen who negotiated the sale of the finished goods to the 'manufacturers' (a misnomer for the middlemen farther up the scale who dealt with the wholesalers). The result was that people had precious little disposable income and even less time in which to spend it. Drink was very cheap, however, and alehouses proliferated, much to the disgust of the ministers who railed against the drunkenness, dissipation and lax morality of their parishioners. The pubs and drinking dens, however, probably afforded the only social intercourse—for the menfolk at least. Women and children had few outlets.

The chief sources of amusement were the fairs. The second *Statistical Account* mentioned that, in addition to the Friday market each week, three great fairs were held in the course of the year: on the second Tuesday in May for the sale of cattle, another on the last Thursday of July for horses, black cattle and wool, and the third, on the last Thursday of October, for the sale of horses. Kilmarnock, as the most flourishing town in North Ayrshire, was a magnet to all kinds of hawkers, pedlars and many odd characters who congregated on these occasions to offer their wares for sale, or to procure, by less honourable means, one or two days' livelihood. Tinkers, ballad-singers, wheel-of-fortune men, 'slight-of-hand blackguards', card-sharps, magicians, sword-swallowers and many others too numerous and varied to detail thronged the market-place and other neuks of auld Killie; and sometimes a scene of riot would ensue in consequence of a collision of these adventurers with the townspeople, or from the freaks of John Barleycorn, which frequently ended in blood-letting.

The Cattle Market, on the south-west side of the town, was the venue of the annual Grozet Fair which spilled over into stalls and side-shows in Waterside Street. By the turn of the century this had all the excitement of the fairground, with a switch-back, helter-skelter, gondola rides and the cake-walk. Baker's Circus was one of the major attractions, as was Clark's ghost illusion using a system of mirrors to create that hardy annual 'The Collier's Dying Child', a dramatic performance which nowadays would be called a three-hankie weepie. A menagerie and Green's variety show vied with fortune-tellers, midgets and shooting galleries.

Paterson reminds us that, early in the nineteenth century, the magistrates had no police force, but a guard of tradesmen belonging to the burgh was formed under the command of the two town officers to preserve order and tranquillity. The burgesses then undertook the charge of the place, so many being called out in rotation from each district. A captain and sergeants were elected by ballot. While all burgesses were liable for this service the older men usually found substitutes. For the younger men the fun and novelty of the duty was sufficient inducement for them. The Town Hall was the place of rendezvous, one division remaining inside, so as to answer any call that might be made upon their services, while the other perambulated the streets. The supply of food and drink was usually abundant, the captain for the night being in honour bound to stand a handsome addition to the common stock. It frequently happened, in consequence, that the peace-keepers were the most noisy towards morning, and next day was generally given to frivolity. McKay had the recollections of the elderly inhabitants who recounted with glee the difficulties they encountered in keeping the land-loupers and other clamjamphrie that attended the fairs from getting the upper hand. The Guard, or Fair-keepers as they were termed, were supplied with ale at the expense of the town. Even the itinerant pipers who came to the fair were sometimes paid from the town's funds for their services, and every encouragement was given to harmless mirth and innocent amusement.

Kings birthdays, too, were then commemorated with great spirit and provided the inhabitants with yet further opportunity for suspending labour and meeting in the ale-houses. The civic authorities assembled at mid-day in all due pomp and circumstance at the Court-house and pledged His Majesty's health in flowing bumpers, while the crowd outside responded to the toast by repeated cheers. The juvenile section of the community amused themselves in the evening by kindling bonfires on the streets with coals supplied by the town, and sometimes with wooden casks, crates and other scraps stolen from private property for the purpose of prolonging their noisy and enthusiastic manifestations of loyalty. Not everyone enjoyed these rowdy spectacles. The kill-joys were known as Blacknebs who, if they could not suppress the jollity, did their best to show their contempt and derision. On one occasion, one of their number got hold of a horse's head which he garlanded with flowers (nettles, thistles, hemlock and other deadly weeds) and placed it in his window in opposition to those displaying the fairest of flowers. Talk of 'cutting one's nose to spite one's face'—the dead head must soon have stunk out the house! The burgh records contain numerous references to sums disbursed for coals, ale, porter, rum punch, wine, raisings (sic) and almonds, ribbons and bonnets, and payments to pipers, the town drummers, bell-ringers and the burgh barber (whose duties included

the serving of punch to the bailies and councillors on such occasions).

At one time Kilmarnock, in common with other burghs, had an annual Riding of the Marches. This custom was probably very ancient, but it was formally instituted by an ordinance of the Town Council in 1710 which decreed that the last Monday of May should be set aside for this ceremony.

> *Twelve young men, who with such a number of the*
> *burliemen in town, or the most old men as the bailies*
> *also shall condescend upon, shall visit and take*
> *inspection of the Marches in and about the whole*
> *lands to the town pertaining and belonging, and that*
> *what marches are wanting be set up and keeped in*
> *memory from tyme to tyme.*

The 'burliemen' were men appointed to hold Burlaw or Byrlaw (burgh law) courts for the sole purpose of delineating the town boundaries as well as the boundaries of each property within the town. The Byrlaw courts, in effect, settled property disputes between neighbours. These arbitrators were also responsible for seeing to it that the townspeople knew where the burgh ended and the landward areas of the parish began. The townspeople who wished to witness the inspection generally formed a procession and proceeded to the various landmarks, accompanied by the magistrates and the town drummer. The old men pointed out the marches and as they did so it was usual to give some of the boys present a hearty drubbing, so that they might remember in later life the location of the boundaries. It is not known when this quaint custom died out, but James Reid, who died in 1822 at the age of 82, could recall these inspections from his boyhood, which would therefore place them in the middle of the eighteenth century.

Processions of the Trades were also common in the eighteenth century and afforded occasional relaxation from labour, as well as some amusement, in a period when statutory holidays were unheard of. The most impressive of these displays was that of St Crispin's Society, as the shoemakers' craft was known. A king for the day was chosen from among their number and, arrayed in regal robes with a dazzling crown on his head, he walked majestically in front, with several smart little pages bearing up his train. Other officials appointed for the occasion were the lord mayor, an alderman, an Indian king and a champion clad in a coat of chain-mail. This custom of the shoemakers began about 1773; at least that was the date when the robes and other articles were purchased at a cost of £23 14s 5d. The last parade of the shoemakers took place on 10th March 1863 to celebrate the marriage of the Prince of Wales (later King Edward VII) and Princess Alexandra of Denmark. On that auspicious occasion the other trades of the town also processed, together with the magistrates and councillors, justices of the peace, commissioners of police, the local militia, the freemasons, the Oddfellows, the letter-carriers and other postal employees and many other bodies. In the afternoon Provost Archibald Finnie dined with the magistrates and other influential citizens at the George Hotel, and a free dinner was served to about 200 old men in the market of the Corn Exchange. Tea was served to about 600 poor people, chiefly females, in St Marnock's Church. The day was rounded off with a grand ball in the hall of the George Hotel, while a large bonfire blazed at the Cross and the Council Chambers, some of the churches and other prominent buildings, were brilliantly lit.

Fastern's E'en

One of the most important days of amusement was Fastern's E'en (Shrove Tuesday) which derived its local name from the fact that it was the evening preceding the first day of the Fast of Lent. This holiday should have been abolished at the Reformation, along with all the other holidays rooted in the observances of the Catholic Church (such as Christmas and Easter), but it survived in many parts of the country till the eighteenth or early nineteenth centuries, long after the original reason for the holiday had been forgotten. In Kilmarnock, this holiday survived till 1831 when it was formally discontinued by order of the magistrates and Council. In the spring of 1858 there was a campaign to revive this ancient holiday and a field to the east of the town was accordingly provided for the festivities which consisted mainly of athletics, pony-racing and assorted sideshows. This revival, however, lacked the popularity of its predecessor and survived for only a couple of seasons. McKay, who vividly remembered the celebration in his youth, describes the event thus.

> In the forenoon the fire-engines of the town were brought to the Cross, filled with water, and the management of the pipes intrusted to some expert individual, who all of a sudden began to pour the cooling liquid in all directions; and the Cross being by this time thronged with the inhabitants and people from the country, a scene of disorder and confusion ensued, to the infinite delight of those who had the good luck to escape with a dry skin.

John Ramsay, the poet of Kilmarnock, has left this vivid description of the 'water sports':

> Out-owre the heighest house's tap,
> He sent the torrent scrievin;
> The curious crowd aye nearer crap,
> To see sic feats achievin:
> But scarcely had they thicken'd weel,
> And got in trim for smilin,
> When round the pipe gaed like an eel,
> And made a pretty skailin
> 'Mang them that day.

McKay continues:

> This part of the day's sports continued for about an hour. Preparations were then made for a foot race. The officers or beadles of the town, accompanied by a drummer and a fifer, marched through the principal streets bearing a halberd, from the top of which were suspended a cloth pouch, a pair of leather breeches, a pair of shoes, and a broad blue bonnet. These represented the particular trades of the town, and were (or their value in money) to be awarded as prizes to the respective winners... This, though an annual affair, always attracted universal attention. After going their rounds the officers halted at the Town-house, where the Bailies and Councillors formed into procession in front of the crowd, and all marched off at the sound of the drum and the fife to the race-ground, which was usually the Ward's Park in the vicinity of Kilmarnock House. In a local poem, the odd characters that joined in the procession about the beginning of the nineteenth century, are thus alluded to:

> And queer auld chaps I trew were there,
> Pye Robin, wi his lang tied hair,
> Snap Tam, Bird Will, and twa three mair
>   O sic degree,
> A' marching out wi proud-like air
>   The sports to see.

> Two or three races were run; and, as the competitors were generally from the moorland districts and swift of foot, remarkable feats of running were often displayed. These pastimes, though not the most rational that might have been devised, may have had their advantages; but some of the day's proceedings were marked by acts of cruelty, revolting to reason, religion and humanity. We allude to the fiendish and disgraceful practice of cock-fighting. Two or three dozens of individuals , having the external form of human beings, but devoid of the finer feelings, engaged in that work in different parts of the town; nor was the practice confined to young men alone; the aged also mingled with the others in the arena of cruelty, and eyed the contrast with as much interest as if the fate of nations had been about to be decided by the feathered combatants. The youths attending school, too, had their cock-fights on Fastern's E'en; and in some instances the schoolmaster, forgetting his position in society and duty to the rising generation, encouraged the barbarous practice by presiding over the scene of action; and every biped that was killed he greedily claimed as a sort of reward for the service he had rendered.

It should be noted that cock-fighting associated with Fastern's E'en was a pretty widespread custom in Lowland Scotland and a similar practice obtained in Dumfries for centuries, the schoolmaster there regarding the birds thus slaughtered as his perquisite also.

This holy day, which eventually became a holiday, was often attended by rioting and public disturbance. The worst incident, however, occurred in 1755 when a tumult arose in which the town magistrates were insulted by the mob and the dykes of the town green were demolished in the affray. The Town Council afterwards raised a prosecution at Ayr Sheriff Court against Mathew Fairservice, John and William Muir, and John Thomson, all glovers, who were alleged to have been the ringleaders.

Other customs

McKay also mentions Hogmanay and the ancient custom of first-footing on New Year's morning, 'another custom that prevailed here to a great extent during the last century, but which is now almost abolished.' From

'Auld Lang Syne' by J.M. Wright engraved by J. Rogers

this it may be inferred that Ne'erday revelry—then, as now, accompanied with a great deal of drunkenness—had all but died out in Victorian times, thus reflecting the puritanical atmosphere of the period. It began to make a come-back at the turn of the century and is now too well-established to deserve comment, far less the lengthy description which McKay gave to it a century ago.

> As soon as the town clock had numbered twelve, hundreds of persons of both sexes sallied forth from their domiciles to greet their friends and acquaintances, and treat them with intoxicating liquors. The town immediately assumed the appearance of some vast rendezvous of bacchanalians, rather than the peaceful abode of beings gifted with reason.

Nowadays Communion is taken quarterly in the Scottish churches but until the late nineteenth century this was an annual sacrament. In those days it was preceded by a Fast Day, generally the Wednesday preceding Communion Sunday. All shops and places of work and business were closed and the churches open. In an earlier era the Holy Fair which attracted crowds of thousands to the preaching tents and field pulpits of the various ministers of the district often degenerated into yet another excuse for a day's outing and consequently had something of a carnival

atmosphere, beautifully captured in Burns's great poem. Latterly the Fast Days, too, degenerated considerably, most people treating them as a holiday. One newspaper commented sadly (1872) that the religious aspect of the day seemed to have disappeared. 'We listened to one lad going along the street whistling, which among the youth in days gone past was held to be a very great profanation.' In 1882 the churches of the Synod bowed to the inevitable and Fast Days were abolished because of the 'increasing tendency on the part of many to disregard it as a day of preparation for the observation of the ordinance of the Lord's Supper'.

Cultural events

Not surprisingly, many of the cultural events of Kilmarnock have had a Burns flavour. In addition to the specific events previously mentioned, Burns has always played a prominent part in the annual celebrations of more recent years. Kilmarnock Week started in June 1967 with a grand fête organised by the Rotarians, a Festival of Music in the Grand Hall, a football tournament in Howard Park, moonlight bathing, an Oxfam Concert in the Palace Theatre, an exhibition by the Townswomen's Guild and WRVS, and a Carnival Parade on the closing day. This soon became a popular annual event, drawing visitors to the

town from a wide radius. In more recent years it has been transformed into the Kilmarnock and Loudoun Festival, held in September on an even larger scale, augmented and given a cosmopolitan flavour by the addition of performers from Kilmarnock's twin towns.

In 1951 the Festival of Britain was staged to mark the centenary of the Great Exhibition, and although most of the limelight fell on London, local authorities all over the country were encouraged to put on their own celebrations. In Kilmarnock a wide range of events were staged during the third week of June, the highlights being the Kilmarnock and District Choral Union's staging of Mendelssohn's *Elijah* and the performance of Ramsay's *Gentle Shepherd* by the Saxone Dramatic Club in the Exchange Theatre (as the Corn Exchange was briefly known before its transition to the Palace Theatre).

Parks and open spaces

Early maps indicate a place called Hawket Park just north of the town, but despite its name this was in fact a private house. The earliest field set aside for the recreation of the young people of the burgh was Barbadoes Green south of Kilmarnock House and originally forming part of the Kilmarnock estate. No place of recreation is mentioned in either of the two early *Statistical Accounts*, nor is this field marked on the maps of 1783-1831, probably because the Town Council, for some inexplicable reason, had sold the land to the Earl of Glencairn on 22nd June 1749 and thereby relinquished the people's rights to it. By the 1840s, however, the Ward Park was in public use and during the cholera epidemics of 1832-49 was the site of the temporary isolation hospital. This area was divided into the Heich and Laigh Wards by a small stream which is now carried under Dundonald Road. The only part of it which now survives is the small triangle at the junction of Grange Street and Irvine Road, used in the nineteenth century as a bleaching green. In the early 1850s Barbadoes Green was again being used as a playground and in 1879 it was greatly beautified by the planting of trees along its boundaries and the west bank of the Kilmarnock Water on which it abutted. At the same time the Lady's Walk from St Marnock Street along the riverbank was greatly improved, ornamental shrubs being planted and park benches installed, together with a handsome drinking fountain. This became a favourite recreational spot for those living on the western side of the town.

Contemporary with the Burns Monument was the Kay Park in which it was located. Alexander Kay, a

Kay Park with Burns Monument in distance.

native of Kilmarnock who had made his fortune as a Glasgow insurance broker, died in 1866 and left a considerable sum of money to the town. Some £6,000 was applied to erecting and endowing two schools, but £10,000 was used to purchase about 31 acres of land from the trustees of the Duke of Portland. This tract of land lay north of the railway line not far from Braehead House and the home of Tam Samson, and extended from the Kilmarnock Water at Blackwood's Dam to the Grassyards Road at the gate of the New Cemetery. The park embraced the romantic Clerk's Holm and the steep and heavily wooded riverbank, extending up to the Townhead Bridge from which, through the wood to the main body of the park, some attractive walks were laid out. From one of these walks at the riverside a fine view could be obtained of the natural waterfall over the Black Rock when the river was in spate.

In addition to the Burns Monument, a large and highly elaborate fountain was erected in the Clerk's Holm nearby. This cost about £800 and was donated by Mrs James Crooks of Wallace Bank, a member of a well-known tannery family in the burgh. On the day of the inauguration of the Burns Monument the drinking fountain was similarly initiated. Thomas Stewart, the ironmonger responsible for its erection, formally handed over the fountain to the civic authorities. Mrs Robert Fleming, sister of Mrs Crooks, turned on the water, to the cheers of the many thousands assembled. Mrs Crooks managed to attend the ceremony but was too ill to take an active part in the proceedings and, in fact, died three weeks later. From the outset, the park had several entrances, one from London Road past the front of Braehead House and along the side of the old bowling green, one from Holehouse Road near Parkhead farm, and one from the Townhead Bridge. A broad carriage drive was laid out round the park and a pedestrian pathway was laid out at the eastern extremity of Strawberry Bank, near the cemetery. The Kay Park is on rising ground from which splendid views of the surrounding countryside can be obtained, as far as Loudoun Hill in the east and Arran in the west. In 1885 Lord Rosebery unveiled a fluted Corinthian column, dedicated to the martyrs of the Reform struggles of 1816-20, on a promontory in the park. Later a bandstand was erected in the Holm near the fountain and in 1890 a boating pond was laid out on the eastern side of the park. A pitch and putt course was laid out in the 1960s. Additional ground on the north side was subsequently acquired and now forms Strawberrybank Gardens.

George Buchanan, a prosperous Glasgow merchant, had three unmarried daughters who died in 1869, 1871 and 1875 respectively. The Misses Buchanan made a generous bequest to Kilmarnock and Riccarton in the form of the 254-acre Bellfield estate lying between the latter village and Hurlford. The River Irvine formed the northern boundary of the estate, which included the farms of Kaimshill and Riccarton Mill. The fine eighteenth century mansion of Bellfield, together with its contents (including fine family portraits and a library of 1500 volumes) was incorporated in the bequest. Part of the trust came into effect as soon as

Elizabeth Buchanan, last of the three sisters died, but the chief portion did not come into force till Martinmas 1885. In the meantime, the rents from the estate were applied to various charities in and around the town, including the Kilmarnock Infirmary and the Ragged School. Riccarton was the chief financial beneficiary, a substantial sum being laid aside as salary for a missionary to the parish, as well as money for the 'deserving poor'. The terms of the bequest stipulated that, as soon as convenient, Bellfield House was to be opened to the public as a library 'for consultation and reference only', and the policies and garden were to be

Bellfield House

opened as a place of recreation. The trust also envisaged the conversion of the mansion into an asylum for aged and infirm persons not on the parish Poor Roll, but who had been for at least ten years resident in Kilmarnock or Riccarton parishes. The inmates were to be clothed and fed and all costs of maintaining and staffing the asylum met from the rentals of the estate and its mineral rights. The trustees, however, were given the discretion to abandon the asylum scheme if the revenues were insufficient. This being the case, the estate was from the outset used solely for recreational purposes. Bellfield Park was formally opened to the public in 1888. For many years it boasted a beautiful rock garden with ornamental pools, as well as a walled garden where exotic soft fruits could be grown, a conservatory and a play area. In its heyday Bellfield was the most popular picnic spot in the locality. The house itself continued to be used for a wide range of cultural activities until the 1960s when escalating costs of repairs and maintenance forced the trustees to demolish it, along with the walled and rock gardens. At the same time some of the land was feued to the Town Council for development, and some 1,800 council houses were subsequently erected in what is now the Bellfield district. A substantial portion of the original estate

has survived, despite the encroachment of housing and the Hurlford Road and Kilmarnock By-pass, and the area now has very extensive playing fields, a pitch and putt course, bowling green and tennis courts, a children's playground and a community centre.

The original Barbadoes Green, which was mainly used as a football pitch from 1879 onward, was considerably extended in 1894 when Baroness Howard de Walden gifted land lying to the south. This was

Howard Park

transformed into the Howard Park and had a total extent of 18 acres. Footbridges were erected to provide access to the park from Douglas and West Netherton Streets, while West Shaw Street, continued by a road bridge across the Water to McLelland Drive, formed the southern boundary of the park. A memorial was unveiled in the park in 1896 to mark Dr Alex Marshall's 42 years of service to the burgh.

Beautifully situated on the north-east side of the town is the wooded valley now forming the Dean Castle Country Park. The nucleus of this was the tract of 13 acres presented to the town in 1974 by Lord

Dean Castle Country Park

163

Howard de Walden, later added to by the purchase of the rest of the policies in 1977. The ninth Baron gifted the Castle itself, together with its contents, to the District Council in 1975. The Country Park has extensive woodlands along both banks of the Kilmarnock Water and its tributaries, the Fenwick and Craufurdland Waters, parkland and picnic areas, and a wide range of walks of varying lengths to suit people of all ages. The Dean Bridge provides access to the Castle from Judas Hill, while just south of Dean Road is the Lauder footbridge opened in 1905 and named in memory of Hugh Lauder who raised the funds for its erection. The suspension bridge had an unfortunate and ignominious beginning when, shortly after the opening ceremony was performed by Mrs Margaret Lauder, the bridge collapsed under the weight of the sightseers gathered for the occasion. Fortunately no injuries were sustained and the bridge was soon replaced. The Children's Corner has many kinds of birds and animals, and a variety of play equipment. The Riding School has facilities for adults and children, experts and beginners alike. The park extends across Assloss Road in the north and is bounded by the By-pass on the east, Glasgow Road on the west and Dean Road on the south with free access to parking facilities on Dean and Assloss Roads. Admission to the grounds, car parks, tea room, visitor centre (formerly the Dower House), Children's Corner, special summer exhibitions and gift shop is free, but a small admission charge is made for the guided tour of the Castle itself, renowned for its magnificent collection of arms and armour, tapestries, furniture, early musical instruments, family history and Burnsiana.

For a town of its size, Kilmarnock is remarkably well-served by parks and recreation areas. In addition to those described earlier, there are the seven-acre Riccarton Park opened in 1909, the four-acre Bonnyton Park (1925), the six-acre Piersland Park (1927), the three-acre Victoria Drive Park (1927), the two-acre Hill Street Playground (1928), the two-acre Loanhead Gardens (1937) and the Scott Ellis playing fields, extending to 29 acres (1939). The largest of the prewar accretions to the leisure and recreation amenities was the Annanhill estate, comprising 125 acres and providing a golf course, children's playground, pitch and putt course and playing fields on the south side of the Irvine Road. With the development of new housing schemes in the postwar period parks and recreational areas were laid out at Altonhill, Longpark, Hillhead and New Farm Loch.

Music, theatres and concert halls

In the eighteenth century Kilmarnock appears to have been a place pretty well devoid of music, other than that produced by the human voice. The church organ, or 'kist of whistles', was denounced as the Devil's instrument and shunned by the fiercely Calvinistic churches of the period. It was not until the middle of the nineteenth century that this ban was gradually lifted. The High Church was the first Presbyterian church in Kilmarnock to acquire an organ, built by Hunter of London at a cost of £275. St Marnock's organ, presented by John Gilmour of Elmbank, cost £350 and was built by Foster and Andrew of Hull. The Laigh Kirk organ, by Harrison and Harrison of Durham, cost about £500. The best organ in the burgh was that presented by W.H. Houldsworth to Holy Trinity Episcopal Church at a cost of £1,000. Hurlford Parish Church got a Foster and Andrew organ as a result of the munificence of William Weir of Kildonan. The Winton Place Church and St Joseph's were also among the first churches to acquire mechanical music which raised the standard of choral worship significantly.

This more liberal approach to sacred music went hand in hand with the cultivation of an interest generally in vocal and instrumental music which culminated in 1845 with the foundation of the Kilmarnock Philharmonic Society. In its heyday, the Society had about 70 members of both sexes and although its prime object was the development and mutual improvement of its members' talents, it regularly gave public concerts. Here again, McKay could not resist a patronising comment:

they not only extend beyond the sphere of the society those higher influences which peculiarly belong to choral harmony, and which tend to ameliorate the moral and social feelings, but also alleviate in some degree the wants and necessities of the poorer classes of the community.

At one of these concerts in April 1848, Handel's oratorio *Judas Maccabaeus* was brought before the public for the first time in Ayrshire. To encourage the Society still further, the Town Council presented them with the musical parts for Handel's oratorio *Joshua* and this, together with the *Messiah* and *Samson* by Handel and the *Creation* by Haydn were staged with great success. At the turn of the century the Burgh Brass Band was formed and gave excellent concerts of light classical music in the Kay Park, as well as heading formal processions and other ceremonies. Later, both the burgh and the constabulary boasted excellent pipe bands.

Kilmarnock's earliest theatre and concert hall was a block of stables which were converted to a higher purpose early in the nineteenth century. This building stood on a site behind what is now British Home Stores in King Street. Edmund Kean (1787-1833) and his son Charles (1811-68) performed here in 1829 during their highly acclaimed Scottish tour, giving the citizens of Kilmarnock the opportunity to see classical Shakespearean acting at first hand. Gustavus Brooks, another fine tragedian, made his debut on this stage as a boy. Many celebrated performers gave concerts here in the second half of the nineteenth century, probably the most outstanding *virtuoso* being the great violinist and composer Paganini who was more or less hi-jacked into giving a private recital in 1855 when his journey to Glasgow was delayed here. Later that year the old theatre was acquired by the Commercial Bank and converted to a more commercial role.

For several years Kilmarnock was without a purpose-built theatre or concert hall and had to make do with the hall of the George Hotel which was used for all manner of purposes, from Burns Suppers to religious services while breakaway congregations were seeking more permanent accommodation. On 16th September 1863, however, the suite of buildings making up the Corn Exchange was opened and appropriately the Philharmonic Society gave two performances in its hall of that old stand-by of its repertoire, *Judas Maccabaeus*.

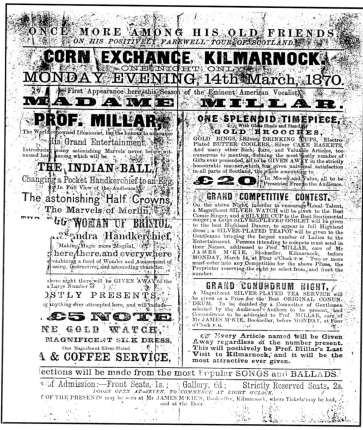

Adjoining the Corn Exchange the Corporation erected a large Agricultural Hall which subsequently doubled as the drill hall for the Volunteers. This was completely refurbished and restructured in 1927 and emerged as the Grand Hall, together with Nos. 1 and 2 Art Halls and the Under Art Hall. The Grand Hall had seating for 1,500 while the total seating accommodation of the Halls was 2,700. The Grand Hall was used for concerts but after the Second World War it was mainly employed for public dances in the big-band era, both Joe Loss and Ted Heath performing here on various occasions. As the vogue for ballroom dancing declined the Council used this hall for roller skating. Pop stars, such as Sweet, the Hollies, T Rex and David Bowie among many others, played at the Grand Hall in 1960s and 1970s.

In 1874 the Theatre or Opera House was built in John Finnie Street and opened in March of the following

year. The foundation stone was laid by John Gilmour of Elmbank in the presence of a number of the shareholders and other gentlemen who afterwards repaired to the George Hotel for a social afternoon. The building was predominantly Italianate, but its architect James Ingram, could not resist the customary eclectic touches. It had seating for 1,500 people and cost about £7,000 to erect, Andrew Calderwood being the builder. The first lessees were Messrs Glover and Francis, long-connected with Glasgow's Theatre Royal, and the first production was a dramatised version of Scott's *Guy Mannering*. It was too lavish and ambitious for a town of the size of Kilmarnock and it seldom operated at a profit. It struggled for half a century before closing; but then re-emerged as St John's United Free Church. Later it was secularised and became auction salerooms and latterly was a public house. It came to an inglorious end in 1989 when it was gutted by fire, though the façade still stands.

Early this century Kilmarnock got not one but two new theatres. The Palace opened in 1903 and the King's Theatre the following year. The Palace, together with the Grand Hall, were created out of the former Agricultural Hall previously noted. The proprietor was Mr. John Cummings who provided a wealth of stars from that era, including Florrie Forde, Little Tich, Harry Lauder and Billy Walters. It is reported that Billy Walters, in one revue called 'Risk It,' was upstaged by a little known second comedian, one Will Fyffe, who was then earning the giddy sum of £7 per week! The Palace and the Grand Hall were also used for concerts, soirees, musical evenings, lectures, magic-lantern shows and dramatic performances given by touring companies, but like their grandiose predecessor they were not a commercial success.

In 1911 Clerk's Lane Church was converted into the town's first cinema, the Electric. Two years later the purpose-built Empire Picturehouse was opened in Titchfield Street and Kilmarnock was consumed by a craze for the movies. Both the Palace and the King's Theatre were forced to fall into line and became cinemas, although they continued to cater to live stage performances from time to time, as the occasion demanded. The King's Theatre, which in its heyday had been the town's principal music-hall, struggled on until 1934, doubling as a picturehouse and having the honour of putting on 'The Jazz Singer', the first talking picture in the town (1929). Eventually, however, it conceded that there was little scope for the legitimate stage and on 17th December 1934 was converted into the Regal Cinema. The Scotia Cinema opened in Union Street in 1920, later changing its name to the Savoy and ultimately becoming the Imperial. The Forum Picturehouse opened soon after the Scotia, and stood a site at the corner of Titchfield Street now occupied by the Food Giant supermarket. The George Hotel closed in 1920 but three years later part of the building was converted into the George Picturehouse.

The seventh of Kilmarnock's cinemas was the Plaza which opened in 1940. In their heyday, during and just after the Second World War, the six cinemas then in existence had a combined seating capacity of 7,000. The Regal and Plaza, with 2,000 seats in each, were in the first rank of provincial cinemas and showed newly released films which attracted large audiences from Kilmarnock and the surrounding district; the other, smaller cinemas were mainly patronised by local people.

Even the cinemas had a rather chequered career, long before television and video sounded their death-knell. The Electric disappeared in 1938, making way for a car park. The Imperial eventually became a dance-hall before closing in the 1950s. The George operated as a bingo hall and latterly as a disco/night club. The Empire burned down in 1965 and the Plaza was demolished in 1971 to make way for road-widening and the construction of Marks and Spencer's department store. Today, only the King's, later re-incarnated as the ABC (3 in 1) and now the Canon Cinema, survives for devotees of the silver screen.

On the other hand, the Palace Theatre, after a lengthy history in the dual role of cinema and theatre received a gift of £5,000 in 1947 to make the Palace into a Civic Theatre and in 1951, following £30,000 spent on alterations, it re-opened as the 'Exchange Theatre.' The venture was however doomed to failure, and the theatre closed again. Mr. William Cummings, the son of the earlier proprietor John Cummings took up the challenge, and started by changing the name back to 'The Palace Theatre' and he achieved some success when, during 1954, the theatre housed no fewer than eighteen weeks of repertory from May to September, and finished the year with a Christmas Pantomime. However, this success was not sustained but as a result of Community Drama Festivals in the immediate postwar years there was a marked improvement in the standard of production. At that period there was, in addition to the Kilmarnock Dramatic Club, the Kilmarnock Operatic Society, Saxone Dramatic Club, a Green Room Club and several other groups associated with the churches and youth clubs, all of which provided a firm basis for theatrical progress.

In 1956 control of the theatre passed to the Arts Guild, which body carried on until the building was severely damaged by fire in 1979.

The new era for the Palace dawned on 4th September 1982, when the then Convener of Leisure, Councillor Tom Ferguson, re-opened the building as a civic theatre, mainly due to the efforts of the District Council to provide a theatre-venue of which the town could be proud. The refurbishment of the theatre was completed in two phases, the first being the modernising of the auditorium for 1982, the second phase consisting of the construction and modernisation of the bars, toilets, foyers and workshops. All was completed in time for the official re-opening, on 31st August 1985, by Billy Connolly.

The Theatre is now able to stage quality productions with upgraded technical facilities including a

Scenes from Palace pantomimes

The Palace Theatre

the addition of two libraries, previously separate, belonging to the Philosophical Institution and the Kilmarnock Athenaeum. By 1880 this library numbered over 10,000 books. A bequest by the bookseller and publisher Robert Crawford (1800-46) provided the library with an annual income of over £100 which was used exclusively for the purchase of new titles. At that time the library operated on a subscription basis, with an entry fee of 10s and an annual charge to each subscriber of 5s, which tended to limit its usefulness to the wealthier classes. The Kilmarnock Library was eventually housed in part of the Corn Exchange Buildings, which also accommodated the Philosophical Institution and the Athenaeum.

computerised lighting system and top quality sound system.

The Stage Door Café and Bar has further enhanced the reputation of the Palace as a venue with a warm and friendly atmosphere and the highly successful Palace pantomime is now an annual event attended by thousands of people, young and old, during the month of December. Local amateur groups such as Kilmarnock Amateur Operatic Society, Loudoun Musical Society, Kilmarnock Dramatic Club and Laigh Kirk Dramatic Club also provide a wealth of entertainment.

The Palace Theatre has survived the redevelopment of the inner town area and today enjoys better prospects, both real and metaphorical, than ever. The clearance of the old congested buildings opposite now reveals the Palace Theatre, the Grand Hall and the Albert Tower to much better advantage.

At a time when theatres in general are suffering the effects of recession, the Palace under its enterprising manager Bruce Gilmour has been forging ahead and after almost 130 years of uncertainty, it can confidently look forward to a bright future as one of Scotland's top provincial theatres.

Libraries, Museums and Art Galleries

'In a moral and intellectual point of view, the inhabitants of Kilmarnock are not inferior, we believe, to those of any other town in Scotland,' wrote Archibald McKay. The most important of the town's literary institutions in the nineteenth century was the Kilmarnock Library, founded in 1797 by a few of the wealthier inhabitants. By 1811 it boasted 840 volumes, but by 1862 the book stock had risen to upwards of 3,000. In that year it was considerably augmented by

The cultural hub of the town was reinforced in 1901 with the opening of the Dick Institute a short distance along the London Road, to which the book stock of the old Library was subsequently transferred. The Public Libraries Act was passed in 1850 to give local authorities the power to establish free libraries within their boundaries. The act, sponsored by William Ewart (after whom the library in Dumfries is named) was extended to Scotland in 1853, but for many years

Dick Institute

thereafter it was a dead letter as few burghs had the funds to implement it. In 1900, however, Andrew Carnegie launched his scheme providing the towns of Britain with public libraries or furnishing a substantial proportion of the necessary funds. In Kilmarnock the prime mover in the campaign for the adoption of the Public Libraries Act was David Mackay, and it was mainly due to his influence that James Dick of Greenhead, Glasgow, a native of Kilmarnock, gifted the Dick Institute to the town in memory of his brother Robert. The Institute, located in the grounds of the former mansion of Elmbank off the London Road, was opened in 1901. Prior to that the Library and Museum were inaugurated in the house itself in 1895 but the Institute was built after the mansion was demolished in 1898. Only eight years after it opened, however, it was gutted by fire and most of its collections destroyed. Various local organisations and companies rallied round and when it re-opened in 1911 its book stock had been considerably expanded as a result of the generosity of both individuals and local firms. In 1917 the Institute was requisitioned by the War Office and converted into a military hospital but two years later it reverted to its normal peacetime role. Today it comprises a museum and art gallery, library, reading-room and lecture hall. Since 1980 the building has been extensively renovated and modernised, a process which continued for more than a decade.

Part of Dick Institute library

The Art Gallery was completely refurbished and air-conditioning, light control, security system and advanced display facilities introduced. The Gallery contains important Scottish works by Raeburn, Hornel and Colquhoun, as well as paintings by Constable, Millais, Brangwyn, Teniers and Corot. Some of the finest works by Leighton and Alma Tadema, and sculpture by McGill, are included in the collection. The Museum has sensibly concentrated on subjects of local interest, and includes comprehensive collections of geology, archaeology, natural history and the history and development of local industries.

The Library, which now has a separate Children's Library, boasts a large collection of books, pamphlets, manuscripts and ephemera of Ayrshire interest, a reference section of 3,000 volumes and a lending section of over 70,000 books. The former Department of Cultural Services for Kilmarnock and Loudoun District had its administrative offices in the Dick Institute and was responsible for the branch libraries opened at Riccarton in 1934, and in more recent years at Dean and Tourhill, as well as those at Crosshouse, Darvel, Fenwick, Galston, Hurlford, Kilmaurs, Stewarton and Newmilns. The Riccarton library was subsequently closed and replaced by that at Bellfield. Fenwick library has also been closed and the village is now served by a mobile library from Kilmarnock. Under the aegis of the Dick Institute, the Bute County Libraries were established in 1946 with branches in Brodick, Millport and Rothesay.

Clubs and societies

The oldest cultural association in Kilmarnock was the Burns Club, founded in January 1808. The Kilmarnock Philosophical Institution, formed in 1823, also had a rather chequered history and for many years was in limbo; but after the Second World War it was revived to provide a wide range of lectures on topics of general interest by distinguished speakers. The Forensic Society, founded in 1831, met weekly for several years. At each meeting an original paper on some important subject was read, after which a debate ensued on the sentiments it contained. Several of the members afterwards rose to distinction as authors, including James Paterson, the statistician F.G.P. Neison, Hugh Craig and Dr John Taylor. The last named was the leading light of the society and as an extempore speaker he had few equals. The Eclectic Club was formed in 1857 in order 'that persons of liberal tastes and studies might have opportunities of meeting together socially and of enjoying the benefits which such intercourse, under judicious regulations, necessarily confers'. Like its predecessor, it laid emphasis on the reading of papers of wide-ranging interest and the subsequent lively debates thereon. The poet, Alexander Smith, and the landscape painter, Horatio McCulloch were members of this club.

These clubs and societies, appealing principally to the more leisured classes, flourished in an era when people had to make their own amusements. The music-hall and the cinema, however, led to the decline of such bodies in the early years of the present century. An art club was restarted in 1889 but lapsed during the Second World War. In the 1940s, however, despite the counter-attractions of radio and the cinema, soon to be overtaken themselves by television, there was a determined revival in the cultural sphere. The art club was the first to benefit from this renaissance, being reconstituted in 1947 as the Kilmarnock Art Club and continuing to this day, with exhibitions under civic auspices at the Dick Institute. Similarly the Philosophical Institution was revived in 1948 to provide public lectures along traditional lines. By the time of the third *Statistical Account* (1950) Kilmarnock could boast a wide range of musical organisations, including the Lyric Choir, the Aeolian Male Voice Choir and the Choral Society, all of which held annual concerts at which prominent vocalists sang. A Society of Musicians flourished at the turn of the century and confined itself to the operettas of Gilbert and Sullivan. It was succeeded by the Kilmarnock Amateur Operatic Company with a special interest in musical comedy. The Kilmarnock Music Club brought to the town a variety of chamber music. The Kilmarnock and District Arts Guild was formed in 1969 to promote and encourage the study, practice and knowledge of the arts, drama, literature, music and culture in all its aspects.

Many of the factories in Kilmarnock had clubs and societies for their employees, but none ever surpassed the Glenfield Ramblers, founded in 1884, for the study of natural history through lectures in the winter months and outings in the summer. This body, which flourishes to this day, has over the years collected numerous specimens of fauna and flora, fossils and geology which now grace the collections of the Dick Institute. There have been no fewer than nineteen Burns clubs in and around the town. In addition, the 1950 *Account* mentioned the Kilmarnock Club, essentially a businessmen's organisation which was founded in the mid-nineteenth century and held its meetings in a building in John Finnie Street. The local branch of the YMCA was formed in 1903 and is still going strong. The Rotary Club was established in 1927 and the Junior Chamber of Commerce in 1963. Hobbies of all kinds were catered for by the Photographic Club, the Society of Model Engineers, the Chess Club, the Anglers' Club, the Rifle Shooting Club, Toc H, the Kilmarnock Magic Circle and several Bridge Clubs.

Women's organisations included the guilds associated with the various churches, but in addition there are, or were, the Women Citizens' Association, British Women's Temperance Association, Soroptimists, the Business and Professional Women's Club. The numerous youth groups and organisations have already been mentioned in Chapter 8.

Besides the many recreational associations there

Kilmarnock dog breeder Mrs Morag Bolton with her 2 year old whippet Pencloe Dutch Gold, Crufts Supreme Champion 1992.

was a large variety of other bodies of different kinds. Kilmarnock has had four Masonic lodges. The oldest is Kilmarnock Kilwinning St John's No. 22, instituted in 1734 and one of the oldest lodges in Ayrshire. St Andrew's, No. 126 was instituted in 1771. Lodge St Marnock was originally founded in 1767 but was dormant for many years before being revived in its centenary year and flourishing from then onwards. St James Nethertonholm was another old lodge which was eventually dissolved. St Clements, No. 202 originally met in Riccarton but later transferred to Kilmarnock itself. A new Masonic Temple for the use of all four lodges was opened on London Road in December 1927.

The Loyal St Marnock Lodge of Odd-fellows was instituted in January 1841 and within forty years boasted a membership of 969. It existed primarily as a benefit society, providing sickness

The Glenfield Ramblers

benefits and funeral money in an age when such help was not provided by the State. McKay noted that

while many friendly societies have ceased to exist during the last twenty or thirty years (1850-80), this institution, by judicious and economical management, continues to be prosperous and bids fair to be as beneficial in years to come as it has been in those that are past.

Though primarily philanthropical, this body, like the Co-operative, had a flourishing social side. At the turn of the century its membership had risen to over 1,200 and it had a strong juvenile membership. The Oddfellows Hall occupied a handsome suite of buildings on the east side of John Finnie Street. Other bodies of a similar nature, with a strong charitable,

philanthropic and moral flavour, which were still flourishing in the middle of the present century, were the Gardeners, Foresters, Rechabites and Good Templars. In addition to the social clubs run by the various political parties there was a local branch of the Fabian Society which organised weekly lectures. Then there was the Kilmarnock Trades Council with all the local affiliated trades union branches, the Kilmarnock branch of the Scottish Council for Educational Advance to which were attached the Trades Council, the Kilmarnock Workers' Educational Association and the local Educational Institute of Scotland. The Kilmarnock and District Chamber of Industries founded in 1946, later reformed in 1964 as the Ayrshire Chamber of Industries, is now part of the Ayrshire Chamber of Commerce and Industry.

A popular visitor attraction—the Great Hall in the Keep at Dean Castle

14 HOUSING AND PUBLIC SERVICES

As an appendix to his book Archibald McKay gave a brief account of the town since 1816. Though written from memory, he believed that it was fairly accurate.

To begin at the head of the town. There were then no houses at Beansburn except a little row of thatched cottages, some of which are still there. The Townholm, which is now nearly filled with buildings, was then a corn-field. The only houses near it were the old Foundry buildings at the head of the field, and a little cottage, which still stands at the foot of it. The road to the Foundry went round by Tam's Loup, and thence along the edge of the water. Various buildings, especially public works, have likewise been erected at the head of High Street and in Menford Lane. Dean Street was not so large as it now is. There were no houses in Witch Road, and none in Hill Street, save one or two where Witch Road joins it, and an old tollhouse and another building which stood at the head of what was then called 'Kilmaurs Brae'. Neither was there a single dwelling where Buchanan Street, India Street and Henrietta Street branch off from Hill Street, or where Park Place or Montgomery Street stands. Several of the houses in Wellington Street were not then built. The site of Henderson Church was a garden stocked with old fruit trees, and the site of the houses near it, on the east side of Portland Street, was also garden ground attached to the houses in Back Street. Union Street, in the same quarter, was opened up about eighteen years ago [1860]. West George Street, at the head of which was a bowling-green, was not formed till after 1819; neither was East George Street. Langlands Street, West Langlands Street, North Hamilton Street, Kadikoi Place [named after an

engagement in the Crimean War, 1854] and Bonnieton Square occupy ground which was then under the tillage of the husbandman, and considered by the townspeople as in the country. The most of the houses in Morton Place, including the Observatory, and also the whole of those in Park Street and Park Lane have been built since that time.

To return to Portland Street: The George Inn was not erected, and there were some empty steadings between it and the Cross. The Cross also has a more spacious and improved appearance by the opening of Duke Street and the erection of its elegant buildings. The most of the villas and houses in London Road are comparatively modern. King Street itself—our principal street—was not completed for some time after 1816. About 1818 a weaver's shop and a few old rickety structures stood on the Sandbed side of it, near the present Bridge Lane, and on the other side some feus were unoccupied. St Marnock Street, St Marnock Place, Dundonald Road, Portland Terrace, South Hamilton Street and Grange Terrace are all modern, and at the time to which we refer there was no building in that direction except Kilmarnock House and its offices, and a few little huts or cottages which stood between the policies of the mansion and Kilmarnock Water, and where the celebrated Haw's Well was situated.

The additions which have been made to the town on the east side of King Street are no less remarkable. Mill Lane, or 'Between the Dykes', as it was then called, from two tall hedges with which it was enclosed, had no houses in it except a smithy, a barn, and one or two old structures which stood near the site of the present Reformed Presbyterian Church, where we recollect seeing the spinning of thairm [animal gut twisted for use as cord] carried on in our boyhood. Clark Street was then without a single house, and was the site of gardens or a nursery. The populous street called Robertson Place, together with Welbeck Street, was not formed, and no habitation was in that direction, save the house of the late Mr James Hamilton, gardener, which stood on the rising ground near Mr Dick's park. The ground on which Fowlds Street stands was a nursery, possessed by Mr Fowlds, whose name it bears. The site of Princes Street and part of that of Queen Street were in the same nursery. St Andrew's Street, or the 'Back Road', as it was then termed, is in a great measure a new street, an at the time of which we speak, two tall trees, probably the remains of some ancient plantation, grew at the head of it, near the foot of King Street. Bentinck Street is comparatively modern; so is West Netherton Street; and in East Netherton Street several new houses have been erected. In short, so numerous are the additions which have been made to Kilmarnock since about

The Sandbed

the year 1816, that it may now be considered an entirely new town compared with what it was at that period.

An anonymous manuscript now preserved in the Dick Institute is a lengthy essay on Victorian Kilmarnock. The writer began his schooldays in 1887, the year of Queen Victoria's Golden Jubilee. He walked a mile to the Grammar School, twice a day in each direction, from his home in Dean Street to Dundonald Road, and had vivid memories of the houses along the route. The toll-house was still standing, opposite the entrance to the Dean Park. Prior to 1883 Beansburn had been a separate village but in that year cottages and villas were erected along the road linking it with Kilmarnock. The first house beyond the tollgates was 'Degu', the home of Alexander Robertson who owned the Kilmarnock Forge at Townholm. Dean Terrace was occupied mainly by businessmen who had their premises in the town. Beansburn village itself consisted of a cluster of small grey cottages, a smithy, a joinery and a little grocery cum general store. Several villas, including Dean House, stood between Beansburn and Knockinlaw Road. Near the Castle was Turner Place, a row of single-storey cottages occupied by retired estate workers. On the steep slope opposite Dean Terrace stood the large villas of Deanhill (Hugh Craig of Craig's Brickworks and Potteries in Kilmaurs Road and his brother-in-law Mr Taylor) and Deanside.

Several tenements were erected about that time south of the toll. 'Gillsburn' was a large villa in its own grounds, owned by the Blackwood family of the High Street woollen mills. Across the street stood cottages occupied by some of the smaller shopkeepers as well as the foremen in the new High Street factories. At the end of this road were four two-storey villas, one of which was occupied by Hugh Highet, manager of Craig's Brickworks.

Orchard Street and its hinterland, stretching to Thomson Street, had been a market garden till the 1870s when a local joiner erected four tenements there. In the closing decades of the nineteenth century this site was developed by Messrs Boyd and Forrest. William and Blair Streets and the northern half of Thomson Street were developed in the 1890s and early 1900s. At the foot of Orchard Street, about this time, John Ford built four three-apartment flats, all with inside bathrooms, the first venture of its type in this part of the town. The southern end of Dean Street was originally Cotton Street, where the cotton weavers lived. This short stretch of street housed over 60 families and two of the old grey-stone tenements had backlands of a much earlier period. Remarkably, this street also boasted three dairies supplied from cows which grazed in fields north of William Street, near the Toll or Hill Street, but they were herded into byres in the street.

Similar dairies, with haysheds and byres adjoining, were dotted all over the town till the turn of the century.

Beyond Dean Street was Dean Lane and Witch Road. Until King Street was opened, Dean Lane was on the way from Glasgow to the Cross. It was a narrow lane with a steep incline, too steep for houses to be built on it. Two old tenements with outside stairs stood at the corner of Wellington Street and nursery gardens were developed on the brae face, providing the town with rhubarb, gooseberries and vegetables. Opposite was Boyd Street, a row of old houses. Dean Lane led to High Street which ran parallel to the Water. Houses had once stood on its right bank, but these gave way by the mid-nineteenth century to a row of factories stretching to Union Street: woollen mills, a carpet works, bonnetworks and McCall's wheelwright premises. Witch Road was open ground till 1820 when its western end was opened up with the building of artisans' cottages as well as the villas of the town's industrialists, such as Bailie Ritchie of Messrs Grant and Ritchie of Townholm. The High Church manse was farther along this road. The eastern end of the road was developed in the 1870s when the land, previously the garden of 'Mansefield', a villa in Wellington Street, was purchased by James Rome who built eight tenement blocks, each of eight flats, with indoor toilets but only cold-water plumbing. Wellington Street, named after

High Street looking towards Fore Street

the victor of Waterloo, consisted of two parts. The lower part was developed many years earlier, but the street was not completed and named till 1820. Opposite Rome's tenements was 'Galahill', a Georgian house which eventually became a hostel for working girls during the Second World War.

'Mansefield' bordered on 'Springbank' which fronted on The Avenue serving Wallace Bank where a row of villas had been built by some of the town's businessmen. Across the road were two cottages and a villa, which was converted into flats in the 1880s.

Next to this stood the Kay School, one of the two donated by Sir Alexander Kay. This school closed in 1898 and the second Kay School was then renamed Bentinck School after the street in which it stood. The lower part of Wellington Street consisted of houses erected in the second half of the eighteenth century. On the east side it gave opening to Fulton's Lane, a street of mean little houses and garrets, connected by Morris Lane to High Street. Among these congested tenements was a laundry, the first in the town. The washing was done in the backyard and the ironing in a dwelling-house facing the street. In this area, containing some of the oldest houses in the town, lived many of the miners employed at the Hillhead Pit.

Portland Street, opened between 1816 and 1820, led on to Union Street occupied by workmen's cottages, and this led to High Street and the new factories. At the High Street end was the old meal market and alongside Union Street School which disappeared in 1899 on the opening of the new Academy. Opposite Union Street was Garden Street, providing a shortcut to the railway station. Seven streets converged on the Cross and most of the shops were located in this area. In this congested area there were no back greens, but the occupiers had the right to dry their weekly washing on the Town Green, facing the Sun Inn in Green Street. Duke Street was developed in the 1850s, a vast improvement over the congested slums of the Foregate, Soulis, New and Regent Streets. Once the home of Kilmarnock's well-to-do classes, this area degenerated during the Industrial Revolution. By the 1880s it had 140 slum dwellings, 31 shops (some open 24 hours a day), six pubs, a coalyard and six common lodging houses. Cheapside, dominated by the Laigh Kirk, alludes to the chapmen or merchants who congregated in its vicinity on

Low Glencairn Street

market days. Opposite the Crown Inn was the entrance to Sandbed, on the line of the main road to Ayr. King Street was a well-paved highway which carried the main Glasgow-Ayr traffic, leading on to Titchfield Street, still in the 1890s a street of single-storey weavers' houses, but from the mid-nineteenth century onwards the area to the south carried the new factories and heavy industries of the town. From King Street, St Marnock Street led to the Grammar School on Dundonald Road. Across the road was Waterside Street leading to the Cattle Market.

Municipal Housing

Kilmarnock continued to develop in a rather haphazard, piecemeal fashion. It was left to private individuals to erect dwelling-houses and tenements for rent to the vast influx of workers who came to the town during the Industrial Revolution, and there was little or no control by the burgh authorities, nor provision for sanitation. Bucket latrines and privies were the rule till the middle of the nineteenth century; although water closets gradually came into use from about 1840 onwards (invariably debouching straight into the river and its tributaries) it was not until the Burgh Police (Scotland) Act of 1892 that the Town Council had the authority to levy rates for the erection and maintenance of sewers. A main drainage scheme, extending well beyond the burgh boundaries, was created in the 1880s and 1890s.

The first attempt at public housing was the formation, in 1824, of the Kilmarnock Building Company with the object of erecting houses on a uniform plan for its members. Each member paid £3 entry-money and ten shillings a month until the cost of building was defrayed. As a result of this company's endeavours Robertson Place was added to the town. So far as can be ascertained, this was the earliest example of a co-operative housing project anywhere in

Corner of Duke Street

Britain. Sadly, once the scheme was completed, the idea was allowed to disappear, and by the end of the century Roberston Place had degenerated into slums which continued to be an eyesore until they were demolished in the 1960s and replaced by modern three-storey flats.

By the early years of this century many of the industrial towns of Scotland were overcrowded and ridden with slums. Recruiting officers for the armed forces were alarmed at the number of ill-nourished, under-sized and chronically sick recruits, a high percentage of whom had to be rejected. Bad housing was at the root of the problem, and in 1912 a Royal Commission was appointed to examine the housing situation in Scotland. This body published its report in 1918 and came up with the startling facts that 235,990 houses were required, of which 121,430 were needed immediately to relieve overcrowding and take the place of dwellings unfit for habitation. Various Housing Acts gave powers and financial assistance from central government to local authorities to build cheap rental housing for the working classes. In 1919 the Town Council embarked on a programme of building cheap housing to replace slum properties which had long been condemned. Three years later the Corporation even unveiled the house of the future, a house in Middleton Park which was hailed as the first all-electric dwelling. Thousands of people flocked to

marvel at the gadgetry (including a dishwasher) which came to life at the touch of a switch. It was to be many a long year before the wonders of electricity became a commonplace. In the two decades up to the outbreak of the Second World War more than 3,000 new houses were erected, mainly in new schemes. The term 'scheme' arose from the fact that each development had to be sanctioned by a separate Act of Parliament.

Under the 1919 Act the scheme provided for 190 houses: in Holehouse Road (156) and the first phase of Scott Road (30). As an experiment four steel dwellings, known as Thomson's Patent Houses, were also erected. Rents fixed under this Act ranged from £23 a year for a three-apartment flat to £29 a year for a four-apartment cottage. Under the Act of 1923, the second, third and fourth phases of the Scott Road scheme were developed, providing 84 houses. Fulton's Lane (24), Townholm (12) and the first phase of the Longpark rehousing project (24) completed the scheme, whose rents varied from £23 to £30 per annum.

The 1924 Act provided for smaller dwellings, including two-apartment flats at £16 10s a year. The 1925 Slum Clearance Act reduced the rents even further, two-apartment flats costing £10 or £12 a year and three-apartment flats costing £13 or £15 a year. Under these Acts council housing embarked on a truly ambitious programme in Bonnyton (182), Yorke Place (48), Annanhill (82), New Mill Road (20), Ayr Road (88),

Craigie Road (150), Stoneyhill (90), Longpark second and third phases (60), New Street (4), London Road (162) and Granger Road (46), making 936 new houses erected in a five-year period. The 1930 Rehousing Act reduced the rents of some two-apartment flats to £9 10s a year and even six-apartment flats were only £15 a year. New houses and flats were erected in Townholm (152), Riccarton (144), Longpark (316), Longpark Hostel (16), Knockinlaw (581), New Street and Hurlford Road (77) and High and Boyd Streets (36), totalling 1,322 dwellings. Longpark Hostel provided one-room apartments at £13 a year, which included rates, lighting and cleaning. The 1933 Act provided for 160 dwellings at a rental of £15 12s to £16 18s erected in Bellevue. The last of the prewar Acts, passed in

Grange Street

1935, provided flats and cottages ranging from £19 10s for three-apartments to £24 for five-apartment dwellings. A total of 490 dwellings were constructed in Bellevue, Nursery Avenue, Maxholm and Kilmaurs Road. In addition, the 1935 Act sanctioned the erection of houses under a non-subsidy scheme (i.e. without a grant from central government) which meant that slightly higher rents had to be charged, ranging from £19 10s for a three-apartment flat to £22 for a four-apartment flat or a three-apartment cottage. Under this scheme 322 dwellings were erected at Stoneyhill, Longpark, Witchknowe, Kilmaurs Road, Bellevue and Melville Street. By the time work on this scheme was completed, shortly before the outbreak of the Second World War, Kilmarnock had built 3,564 council dwellings. On 15th March 1939 Mrs A. McTaggart, wife of the Housing Convener, unveiled a plaque on the wall of the 3,000th council house. This building programme was considerably assisted by the Municipal Extension Act of 1935 which extended the burgh

boundaries and added almost 2,000 acres to its area.

In the decade from 1939 to 1948 almost 1,000 additional houses were erected, although these included, in the immediate postwar years, 257 temporary houses known as 'pre-fabs'. Many of these prefabricated houses, at Altonhill, Hillhead and Burnpark, were still in use twenty years later, their original metal fabric being reinforced with brick cladding. The Scottish Special Housing Association (SSHA) added some 500 houses in this period. By 1948 there were 11,427 dwelling houses in the burgh, of which almost half (4,874) had been erected since 1919, 4,430 by the local authority and 444 by private enterprise. The population of Kilmarnock at the 1951 Census was 43,500. In the 1950s and 1960s there was further expansion of municipal housing, at Shortlees, Onthank and Bellfield; and Burnpark, Witchknowe, Samson Avenue and Wallacehill were also developed in this period. Swedish timber houses appeared at Altonhill.

In addition to Corporation housing, the SSHA erected 919 houses at Shortlees, 54 at Onthank and 56 at Bellfield, making 1,119 in all. Between 1960 and 1972 the vast New Farm Loch scheme was developed in fourteen phases. By 1970 the total number of houses built by the Town Council since 1919 totalled 10,780. Since then there has been a great deal of in-filling and redevelopment, often by private builders, in various parts of the town. Many of the large villas of the nineteenth century have been modernised and converted into flats or office accommodation. Architecturally the council housing of the interwar period was not particularly exciting; but in recent years there have been some excellent schemes which are visually appealing. One may cite in this context the maisonettes in Dean Street and the

New Farm Loch

sheltered housing in Bonnyton, nicknamed 'the Pyramids' on account of their startling sloping frontage.

While the bulk of the new building in the course of this century took place on the periphery of the town, the inner area was subject to redevelopment on several occasions. Hand in hand with the programmes of municipal building in the new schemes went a systematic process of clearing the slums north of the railway line towards Townholm and westwards in Bonnyton or south through Netherton. The increase in motor traffic in the interwar period, however, made road-widening top priority, but so long as the main Glasgow-Ayr road continued to cut across the town any measures became inadequate to the volume of traffic before they could be completed. In 1929, for example, the Cross was widened and the statue of Jimmy Shaw, erected in 1848, was dismantled and relocated on a site opposite the Dick Institute at the corner of Elmbank Avenue and London Road, well away from the town centre. A roundabout was installed at the Cross in the 1950s to regulate the flow of traffic and in 1966 a north-south one-way system was adopted, but these measures merely tinkered with the problem.

Law and order

The Rev. James Mackinlay observed (1790) that the inhabitants of Kilmarnock were, in general, 'as sober and industrious as the people of any town of its size in Scotland. Nay, to their praise, it must likewise be observed that the ruinous practice of dram-drinking has of late been, in great measure, laid aside.' Under the manorial system the Earls of Kilmarnock and their predecessors had the power of pit and gallows, which meant that they could imprison malefactors in a pit— the aptly named Thieves' Hole—or hang those found guilty of the more serious crimes. From the existence of such placenames as Gallowsknowe in Kilmarnock and Judgment Seat in Riccarton it appears that both the judicial process and the execution of the sentence were carried out in public as an object lesson and deterrent to the populace.

Law and order were maintained by the baron bailies, acting on behalf of the Lords and Earls of Kilmarnock. Their power passed to the town bailies in 1747 and from them descended the police magistrates and justices of the peace of more modern times. The Tolbooth and Town Gaol were in Cheapside Street, with the Thieves' Hole on the edge of Kilmarnock Water. Both male and female lawbreakers were confined in this cell; the passageway is still there and is known locally as the Hole in the Wall. An Act of 1802 provided for a new Town Hall and Guard House, and the enlargement of the Tolbooth. The new Town Hall and Guard House was erected in King Street three years later, the cost of maintenance being defrayed by rates (known as Conversion Money) levied on the inhabitants. A further Act, in 1810, provided for 'paving, lighting, cleansing, and watching the Burgh of Kilmarnock and for regulating the Police and Markets'. In 1823 the Town Guard during fairs and public markets was

discontinued, but three years later Special Constables were enrolled, as and when required, to suppress rioting by the meal mobs. In 1828 the library of the Town Hall was converted into an office for use by the Commissioners of Police, Conversion of Monies, Surveyor of Police and Collector of Road Money. An Act of 1840 empowered the establishment of county constabularies, but the policing of burghs was left in the hands of town councils. The Rev. Andrew Hamilton (1839) stated that 'the police establishment, though not extensive, is kept by the commissioners of police in vigorous operation, and is very efficient. There is perhaps no town of the same size in Britain, where the persons and property of the inhabitants are more secure than they are in Kilmarnock.' He also observed, as Mackinlay had done half a century earlier, that the inhabitants in general were industrious and well behaved, kind and hospitable.

For some years after 1840, however, the burgh continued to be governed without the aid of policemen in the modern sense. Two town officers were all the force deemed necessary, assisted on fair days and other special occasions, by a roster of the burgesses. On exceptional occasions the bailies and town officers were responsible for quelling disorder. In the case of the great radical demonstrations of 1816-20, they could call out the military if required; but at other times two or three civic functionaries sufficed to bring the unruly citizens to heel. In the early nineteenth century Bailie Fulton of Greenhill wielded his authority with undue officiousness and earned the hatred of the populace for his high-handedness during the radical disturbances. To this worthy magistrate fell the responsibility of dealing with a band of housewives who rioted in 1829 when the local farmers tried to force up the price, or rather reduce the measure, of sour milk sold from carts at the Cross. Milk jars were smashed and carts overturned. Bailie Fulton was assisted by the town officer, Moses Wyllie (known locally as Mosie Dabbie), but their appearance merely inflamed the mob who set the milk barrels running down the slope. The bailie and his officer were squirted with buttermilk till they were totally drenched in the acrid liquid. The Sour Milk Rebellion continued until the old measures were restored. This was but the best remembered of a serious of meal mobs and bread riots which took place periodically in the early years of the nineteenth century.

Wyllie was joined in due course by a second town officer, an old soldier named Sergeant Paton, formerly of the Scots Greys. According to Paterson, Paton was a rather portly, well-formed man above middle age, who kept his head erect, the breast well forward, and walked with a measured military step. 'Clad in his new official dress, he had a swaggering appearance, which not only eclipsed his non-military colleague, but threw the very magistrates into the shade, as they were wont to parade to church on Sundays.' The town officers were sheriff-officers and burgh bellmen as well, in all of which capacities Sergeant Paton performed his duties in a style altogether his own.

On Wyllie's death, his place was taken by John Cook, a former sergeant from a foot regiment. Their duties gradually became more ceremonial, following the appointment in 1846 of a burgh police force, consisting of a sergeant and four constables. They had their headquarters at the Town Hall and in addition to patrolling the town they were responsible for guarding the felons and miscreants lodged in the lock-up cells in the basement. These cells formed the most objectionable part of the old Town-house, being low-roofed, almost without light or air, 'and such, in short, as would, in all likelihood, have called forth the disapprobation of the philanthropic [John] Howard, had he, in Providence, been permitted to visit them,' added McKay. In one of these grim cells, about 1840, a prisoner on remand awaiting his transfer to Ayr to stand trial on a charge of forgery, committed suicide by cutting his throat. During the Great Flood of 1852 the burgh police exhibited considerable bravery in risking their own lives to wade through the swirling waters, to open the cell doors with the greatest difficulty, and lead to safety the 21 prisoners then incarcerated.

The first Superintendent of Police was William Blane, appointed in 1846. On one occasion he discovered a number of local dignitaries drinking after hours and ordered them out of the public house. The bigwigs retaliated by bringing so much pressure to bear on the superintendent that he became insane and was confined in the county asylum, dying soon after his release. He was succeeded in 1855 by Superintendent D.R. Craig. By the 1860s the burgh constabulary consisted of one superintendent, one inspector, three sergeants and thirteen constables. Superintendent George Willison, a law clerk aged 29, was appointed in 1868 and ten years later became the first Chief Constable. Under the Police Act of 1892 half the cost of the police force was borne by central government and half by the rate-payers. By this time the police were responsible for the prevention and detection of crime, public safety, traffic control, the inspection of closed premises, protection of private property, keeping the peace and the control of public lighting. The police were responsible to a Watching Committee, appointed by the Council, and this body met on the last Tuesday of each month.

George Hill was appointed Chief Constable in 1898, the year in which the new Burgh Police Chambers were opened in Sturrock Street. As the town grew in size, so the need to expand the constabulary became more acute. By 1935 the Kilmarnock Constabulary, under Chief Constable Charles Roy, MBE, had 54 all ranks. After the Second World War continued growth in the force led to severe overcrowding, so a new administrative headquarters were opened at 82 Dundonald Road in 1954. The Kilmarnock Constabulary amalgamated with Ayr Burgh and the Ayrshire Constabulary on 15th May 1968. This force (numbering a Chief Constable, one superintendent, six inspectors, fourteen sergeants, 89 constables and eight policewomen) became part of Strathclyde Police in 1975. The old burgh police station in Sturrock Street was demolished in 1972 and the station in Bank Street

Sturrock Street Police station

became the principal office of the Kilmarnock force. The administrative headquarters remained at Dundonald Road until 1978 when the present Divisional Headquarters at St. Marnock Street were officially opened. A short distance away from Divisional Headquarters can be found Kilmarnock's new Sheriff Court House. Located on the corner of St. Marnock Street and Dundonald Road the new Court House, opened in 1986, faces its predecessor which now serves as the Procurator Fiscal's office.

Military Forces

Since time immemorial the able-bodied citizens were expected to turn out with whatever weapons they could muster in times of national unrest and civil war. The actions of the Kilmarnock men during the Jacobite Rebellions of 1715 and 1745-6 have already been mentioned in Chapter 2, while the exploits of the Covenanters and their persecutors were recounted in Chapter 7. It will have been seen that neither during the Killing Times, when government dragoons were forcibly quartered upon them, nor during the second Jacobite Rebellion when Prince Charlie's army threatened to descend on Kilmarnock, did the citizens take kindly to military oppression.

Following the outbreak of the French Revolutionary War in 1793 the government raised a number of fencible regiments. These, as their name suggests, were intended primarily for the defence of the country, as opposed to the regular regiments which could be despatched overseas. The fencibles relieved the regular troops of home defence duties. Many of them were raised in the Highlands, and in 1794 the Sutherland Fencibles did garrison duty at Kilmarnock. Memories of the Highland Host which pillaged the south-west of Scotland in 1678 would have died out long before that time, but there was a certain antipathy towards the Highlanders with their kilts and uncouth speech. The fencible regiments were raised on a county basis, and the local force was the County of Air (sic) Militia to which the burgesses of Kilmarnock, among others, had to contribute both men and cash. This body continued for several years after the threat of invasion disappeared. The Dick Institute preserves a list of March 1824 which gives the names of eight militiamen from Kilmarnock.

By Colonel ANDREW DUNLOP, Commanding the Regiment of AIRSHIRE Fencible Cavalry.

THESE are to certify, that the bearer hereof *John Dughorn* in the Regiment aforesaid, and in *Capt. Thomas White's Troop* hath served honestly and faithfully for the space of *four years & Ten months*.

but as the Regiment is to be disbanded is hereby discharged, having first received a full and true account of all his clothing, pay, arrears of pay, and all demands whatsoever, from the time of his enlisting, to the present day of his discharge, as further appears by his receipt on the other side hereof.

Given under my hand, and Seal of the Regiment, this *seventeenth* day of *April* 180 *0*.

To all whom it may concern.

AIR, Printed by J. & P. Wilson.

A third line of defence was provided by the local Volunteers who were raised from 1794 onwards as a part-time force. They drilled in the evenings and at weekends and would have been mobilised had 'Haughty Gaul invasion threatened'. In Kilmarnock two units were raised. The Kilmarnock Rifles or Sharpshooters were under the command of Captain James Thomson, while the Royal Kilmarnock Volunteers came under Major William Parker of Assloss. In addition, many men from Kilmarnock and district enlisted in the regular army or were hi-jacked into the Royal Navy if they were unlucky to be caught by the press gangs which roamed the seaports.

In the late eighteenth century Kilmarnock was one of the principal recruiting stations for North Ayrshire and it was thither that twenty year-old Charles Ewart tramped over the moors from Elvanfoot in Lanarkshire to enlist in the Scots Greys. The story of his capture of the eagle standard is too well known to need repeating here, but some of the facts were later distorted by Sir Walter Scott and subsequently repeated by others more for its romantic appeal than historical accuracy.

The two regiments of Volunteers stood down at the end of the Napoleonic Wars, but a similar body, derisively known as the Dandies from their gaudy uniforms, was re-activated in 1820 when radical insurrection was feared. When actual trouble broke out in 1816, however, it was the Edinburgh Yeomanry which had to be summoned to quell the disturbances. In 1860 there was a war scare, when Napoleon III of France threatened to emulate the ambitions of his famous uncle. The Volunteer movement was revived and many men joined the Ayrshire Yeomanry, a cavalry regiment, or the Volunteer battalions of the Royal Scots Fusiliers. The Agricultural Hall attached to the Corn Exchange was used as a drill-hall. The Volunteers were re-organised in 1908 as the Territorial Army and three years later regiments from all over the south-west of Scotland converged on Kilmarnock. At the turn of the century the main camp for the weekend soldiers was at Gailes near Irvine, but for two weeks in July 1911 the Territorials were concentrated at Woodhead, Riccarton. War fever was at its height that summer, due to the Agadir incident when a German warship tried to oppose the French takeover of Morocco, and the Territorials were on constant alert. The crisis subsided, but three years later the country was engulfed in the First World War. The young men of Kilmarnock responded to the call to arms, and sadly many of them gave their lives. In 1917-18 the Dick Institute was commandeered as a military hospital and the library was moved to the Corn Exchange temporarily.

The Second World War

The Second World War differed from all previous conflicts in that everyone, including the civilian population, was affected. This was the era of Total War, when aerial bombardment and gas attacks were expected. In May 1935 the government had instituted a Civil Defence Department and the following year Parliament passed an Act compelling local authorities to set up their own Air Raid Precautions Committees. In Kilmarnock, Provost George Wilson himself became Convener of the ARP Committee. By 1941 some 500 Air Raid wardens had been trained, as well as 180 First Aid workers. Municipal workmen, mainly from the Cleansing Department, were trained as decontamination squads to cope with mustard gas attacks and rescue squads to retrieve air raid victims from the rubble of destroyed buildings. Fortunately these preparations were only called upon on one occasion, during the Clydebank Blitz of 1941 when a German bomber accidentally released its load over Kilmarnock, hitting Grassyards Cemetery and a house in Culzean Crescent.

Kilmarnock also had a unit of the Royal Observer Corps, while many women enrolled in the Women's

KILMARNOCK DURING THE SECOND WORLD WAR

1. Breech mechanism for six-pounder anti-tank guns made in Kilmarnock
2. London Underground emergency floodgates made and installed by Glenfield and Kennedy
3. The Provost takes the salute as the Home Guard marches past
4. Rugby Park taken over by army as training ground
5. R.A.F. balloon winches made by Andrew Barclay & Co
6. Visit of King George VI and Queen Elizabeth, June 1942.

12000 pounder bombs codenamed Tall-Boys, machined and fitted in Glenfield Works, being loaded on to a Lancaster bomber

eight chief inspectors, each in charge of a division corresponding to the burgh's wards, with 34 inspectors and 235 constables. In 1942 the 17/21st Lancers, by that time a tank regiment, was stationed at Stewarton. The Territorials consisted of units of the RSF and Ayrshire Yeomanry (now Royal Artillery) and in the postwar period this tradition was continued by the Kilmarnock Battery of 279 Ayrshire Field Regiment RA. At the time of Dunkirk civilians in reserved occupations or over military age were enrolled in the Local Defence Volunteers, shortly afterwards reconstituted as the Home Guard, under the command of Colonel Wilkie. 600 men and six women eventually formed the 4th Battalion of the Ayrshire Home Guard. After D-Day, when the threat of Nazi invasion disappeared, the Home Guard stood down, after a ceremonial parade in the playground of James Hamilton Central School on 3rd December 1944.

Ordinary civilians also played their part, gathering salvage and surrendering their pots and pans to build aircraft. Iron railings were also scrapped, a wanton act of vandalism which did little for the war effort and destroyed a great deal of fine wrought ironwork. On a more positive note Kilmarnock raised half a million pounds in Warship Week and £1.5 millions during Salute the Soldier Week. War Savings in Kilmarnock, under the dynamic leadership of Alex Goldie, Chairman of the North Ayrshire Local Savings Committee, outpaced any other town in the county, per head of population, and in 1943 savings exceeded their target by 50 per cent. At the peak of war activity individuals were saving nearly a third of their disposable incomes. This had a two-fold effect: by taking money out of general circulation inflation was curbed, and by lending the money to the government, the costs of conducting the war could be met to a large extent.

After the war Civil Defence continued as the Cold War intensified, but after 1967 it was gradually run down. The first royal visit to Kilmarnock took place in June 1942 when King George VI toured the town and

Voluntary Service and also served with the St Andrew's Ambulance Association. Lieutenant Colonel D.M. Wilkie, OBE was appointed Chief Warden and had his ARP headquarters in Bank Street where a staff of 73 women and 88 men worked under Controller James A. Scott. At the height of the Blitz the burgh had 634 volunteer wardens and 26 full-time salaried wardens. Inspector Donald McLeod of the Kilmarnock Constabulary was seconded to ARP as liaison officer.

Charles Roy's regular police force had risen to 64 all ranks in 1939, but this was augmented by the Special Constabulary, a part-time force which consisted of

Royal inspection of Kilmarnock Civil Defence Services in Howard Park, June 1942

Henry Gardner, M.D. of Glenfield and Kennedy, is presented to
Queen Elizabeth and the Duke of Edinburgh during the royal visit, 1956.

was remarkably low. Gas lamps, intermittently used since the 1830s, became more common after 1850 and continued well into the present century, although from 1905 onwards electric lighting was gradually introduced. The burgh continued to be partly lit by gas lamps as late as the 1950s. In 1939 the burgh had 148 court lamps, 199 electric lamps and 1,111 gas lamps. From 1936 onwards, however, much was done to improve the public lighting system and by 1938 certain streets even had the Mercury Vapour Discharge lamps.

reviewed the local Civil Defence services in Howard Park. Queen Elizabeth and The Duke of Edinburgh visited Kilmarnock in 1956 and again in 1962 when they spent half an hour touring the burgh. They were accompanied on their car ride by Bailie (later Provost) Daniel Cairns, the senior magistrate and one of the most prominent local figures of this century.

Public services

Street lighting was non-existent before the middle of the nineteenth century and the 'neuks and corners' of Kilmarnock must have been a hazard to pedestrians after dark. Nevertheless, the incidence of street crime

Keeping the streets clean was originally a police responsibility but as the town grew in size and the task of maintaining the streets in a salubrious condition became much more complex, the problem passed to a separate Cleansing Department, headed by an inspector and a staff which, in 1939 numbered 67 permanent and seven temporary men. This body was responsible for 38.52 miles of streets in the burgh, and keeping them clean cost an average of £102 10s 11d a mile per annum. The Cleansing Department had two horses, four carts, five refuse wagons, two lorries and, from 1937 onwards, various forms of specialised equipment, including a mechanical refuse destructor, a mechanical sweeper and a dual-purpose sludge cleaner and gulley emptier.

As long ago as 1753 the Town Council maintained a voluntary fire brigade and in that year expended £40 on a water machine for extinguishing fires. With this pump-action water cart went 40 feet of leather hosepipe which pumped water from an on-board tank and projected it at the fire. Horse-drawn water carts of this type continued to be used well into the present century, manned by

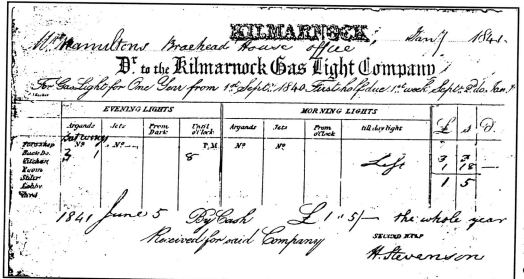

part-time volunteers. In an era when many buildings had thatched roofs and were crowded together, the risk of fire was very great indeed.

Provision of more adequate fire services began in 1863 when new sheds were erected in Green Street to house the fire engines, and fire hydrants were installed in Waterloo Street. In 1871 a Powder House and Fire Engines Committee was formed and five years later the Committee increased the Fire Brigade from six to ten men. The firemen worked part-time and were paid £2 10s a year, plus 5s for each fire attended. In 1876 a slater named James Yuille was appointed the first Superintendent, with a salary of £5 per annum plus the customary 5s bonus for each fire. At this time the Committee decided to procure helmets in order to 'distinguish them from the Police and other members of the public'. The firemen got their helmets, but had to wait for thirty years before the Committee's decision to acquire a steam fire-engine could be implemented. In 1884 part of Riccarton Toll-house was converted into a fire station to cover the area south of the river. Statutory powers to levy a rate for the maintenance of a fire service were given under the Special Burgh Police Act of 1892 and, as a result, a new hand pump and a 36-foot ladder were purchased the following year. A third station, at Calcutta Lodge, was set up in 1896. The number of hydrants was steadily increased over the years, but it was not till 1911 that the burgh got its first steam fire-engine.

A full-time firemaster, Archibald McMillan, was appointed in 1905 with a salary of £85 a year, and when the Brigade took delivery of its Halley engine six years later it was the first provincial town in Scotland to have a motor fire engine (costing £985—an enormous sum for that time). Kilmarnock continued to rely on a largely voluntary, part-time force and in this respect was probably no better and no worse than any other town, to judge by the report of the Royal Commission

on Fire Prevention established in 1923. This body recommended a drastic tightening up of the measures taken by burghs to cope with fire. In 1935 the Kilmarnock force of five full-time firemen responded to 60 calls, but by 1937 its men were dealing with an average of 107 calls a year. On 22nd November that year, the Fire Brigade became a fully professional force and a new station on Titchfield Street was erected on a site adjoining the Corporation Cleansing Depot at Calcutta Lodge, was inaugurated on 22nd November. Under Firemaster David Inverarity the firemen lived 'on the premises' and were on 24 hour call. Kilmarnock in 1939 had 474 fire plugs and 36 valve hydrants, while the brigade had just completed a modernisation programme and now had five motorised appliances, including a 90 hp Dennis fire engine with turbine pump and a capacity of 750 gallons per minute. Shortly before the Second World War this service was augmented by a unit of the Auxiliary Fire Service comprising two mechanic drivers and eight firemen. These were part-time volunteers, liable to call-out on rosters from their own homes. During the war, however, the AFS expanded considerably and at one point had 165 volunteers.

In 1937 the Scottish Office prepared a scheme for a nationwide emergency fire brigade organization, and this was implemented in 1940, Kilmarnock being placed in the Ayrshire and Renfrewshire Area of the Western District. The brigade now came under the Area Office at Paisley. The following year the administration of fire services was transferred from the local authorities to the Secretary of State and the Kilmarnock brigade became part of the National Fire Service. David Inverarity retired and his duties were taken over by the Area fire force commander. After the War the Kilmarnock brigade came under the South Western Area Joint Board covering Ayrshire, Dumfriesshire, Kirkcudbrightshire and Wigtownshire. In the post-war period the standard of equipment and the conditions of service improved considerably. Mobility was increased, but radios were not fitted till the 1970s. When the new fire station was opened at Ayr in 1963 Area headquarters moved thither from Kilmarnock, but two years later the Kilmarnock station was restructured and refurbished. In May 1975, as a result of regionalisation, the South Western Area Fire Brigade was re-organized and now forms D Division of Strathclyde Fire Brigade.

15 HEALTH AND SOCIAL SERVICES

In these modern times, when it has become fashionable to criticise the NHS and DSS, it comes as a salutary shock to realise that the medical, health and social services which we take for granted have only been in existence for 80 years, a relatively short period in human history. Before the inception of the Welfare State by the Liberal government in 1909-10 provision of services depended almost entirely on what people could afford, often through the medium of friendly societies, masonic lodges and the Co-operative movement, and very little was provided by charity. Over the centuries the provision of health and social services, such as they were, lay in the hands of the Kirk and later the civic authorities.

The Poor

Only as a last resort would the Kirk treasurer disburse small sums of money to the most needy. The books of the Kirk Session reveal the nature and amounts of these payments. Thus we find such entries as 'Given to a paralytic man, a stranger, 15s Scots' (1712), 'To a lame seaman, by ye 2 ministers, app., 18s Scots' (1713), 'To Baylie Moris, for drugs to the poor lad's arm that was cut off, £10 1s 1d Scots' (1714), 'To Baylie Tough, upon ye same account, £6 16s Scots' (1714) and 'To the poor Lad himself, the remainder that was left, £12 6s Scots (1714). Other payments relate to blankets or coffins for paupers who had died. The Session Records show that between 15th June 1701 and 22nd June 1705 payments to the poor of the parish totalled £2,711 5s 8d Scots (£225.91 sterling). This amounted to an annual average of £56 9s 9d or little more than a pound a week for the entire district. Individual payments must have been very small indeed, but probably made all the difference between life and death in many instances. By 1880 the annual assessment for the support of the poor was about £5,000 sterling—a hundred-fold increase over the level of 175 years earlier.

The first *Statistical Account* sheds light on the situation towards the close of the eighteenth century when Kilmarnock was feeling the first effects of the agricultural and industrial revolutions. 'The poor, in such a large and populous parish, it is to be expected, must be very numerous,' wrote James Mackinlay, 'and would require a considerable sum for their support.' At that period the industrious classes had begun to practise self-help, and the various trades, societies and incorporations were assiduous in maintaining their indigent and distressed members and thereby keeping them from being a burden on the public. These trade and crafts societies annually disbursed about £180. In addition the number of poor on the pension list of the Kirk Session, and in receipt of weekly alms, was 80, besides some others who received occasional supplies. The contributions at the Laigh Kirk and the chapel of ease (the High Church) amounted to £100 a year. This was augmented by bank interest and occasional donations and bequests, but it represented the sum total available for disbursement to the needy, who got sixpence or a shilling a week in this manner.

'Although it may assist them a little,' wrote Mackinlay, 'it is by no means able to support them in their own houses, even when joined to the profits of any little labour which some of them may have strength to perform. Begging, therefore, is allowed, and is a very great burden on the inhabitants.' Mackinlay felt that the poor would never be suitably nor permanently provided for, until the local landowners agreed to assess themselves in a sum that would be adequate for this purpose.

When it is considered that the greater part of the heritors are non-residing, that they contribute nothing to the maintenance of the poor by their own personal charity, and that the value of their property is greatly increased by the manufactures and population of the place; such a measure, must appear, to every humane and benevolent heart, to be highly equitable and proper; and it is to be hoped, will be soon carried into effect.

Mackinlay's recommendations, of course, were ignored and the poor were left to the tender mercies of Kirk charity and whatever they could beg from the general public. The Rev. Andrew Hamilton (1839), however, noted a vast improvement thanks, in part, to the growth of friendly societies (of which there were then 37 in the town and parish) and the compulsory system of assessment. But he felt that the compulsory system had actually led to an increase in pauperism. The main cause of the increase, however, was the influx of 'natives of the sister isle' (Ireland) who had acquired a residence in the parish and were therefore on the pauper's roll. 'Notwithstanding noble exceptions,' he added, 'there is much more, than once there was, of a disposition among many of our own poor to look upon parochial relief as a right rather than a painful resort.' By that time the lowest amount allowed to any pauper was 2s a month, the highest 8s, unless in very peculiar circumstances. House rents were paid for paupers to the amount of about £120 a year. At that time there were 277 paupers on the roll, and as many of these cases included families or more individuals than one, the number of persons directly or indirectly receiving aid was perhaps 500.

The year's assessment averaged £1,500. When this system was introduced in 1837 the assessment was raised in equal proportions from the town and country heritors, but shortly afterwards it was revised, so that four-tenths was furnished by the country heritors and six-tenths by the town. This was inequable, but the Court of Session in 1839 decided that the assessment should be applied, one half on the whole heritable property, and the other on the means and substance of the whole inhabitants of the town and parish. As the town rental considerably exceeded that of the country, the proportion was altered to rather more than seven-tenths to the town and less than three-tenths to the landward part of the parish. Under the voluntary system the chief part of the town's share was made up of collections at the church doors; but as matters now stood, an assessment was laid on the means and substance of the inhabitants by stent-masters, appointed to estimate the ability of each ratepayer.

Kilmarnock was unusual in that it never had a poorhouse or workhouse. From 1862 paupers who were in need of attention were sent to the Cunninghame Combination Poorhouse in Irvine. In 1865 it was suggested that Kilmarnock should have a poorhouse of its own as it was felt that the contribution to the Combination Poorhouse was too high in relation to the number of people sent there. This suggestion was rejected, and it was agreed that the paupers should still be sent to Irvine as they had been in the past. In general, the people consigned to the poorhouse were habitual beggars and 'foreign poor' (another jibe at the indigent Irish). In other words, the poorhouse was used as a deterrent as well as a social dustbin. The law governing the sending of poor people to such an institution was the Act of 1579 'for the punishment of the strong and idle beggars and relief of the poor and impotent' but the emphasis was always on the suppression of beggary and vagrancy rather than a charitable attitude towards the genuinely poor. It was not until 1845 that Scotland had a more humane law, following the lines of the English Act of 1834, and by this poorhouses were instituted, administered by parochial boards and supervised by Inspectors of the Poor. The very word 'poorhouse' sent a shudder through the 'respectable working classes'. It is impossible nowadays to appreciate the stigma attaching to having a close relative in this institution, far less the shame of being sent there oneself. The same philosophy was at the heart of the decision, in 1855, to create the Certified Industrial School. The fact that this, in common with similar institutions elsewhere, was popularly known as the Ragged School is an indication of people's attitudes.

The poorhouse was a place of last resort, applied in extreme cases. Most people who were down on their luck were helped financially, even if the sums were derisory, by remaining in the parish. The parochial poor boards were abolished in 1894 and replaced by parish councils under the control of the Scottish Board of Health. A peculiarity of the Scottish law, however, was that, until 1921, an able-bodied pauper had no legal right to relief of any kind. The Poor Law Emergency Provisions Act of that year partially remedied this desperate situation. The situation only began to improve after the passage of the Local Government Act of 1929 and the new Poor Law Act of 1930 which paved the way to a more humane and just treatment of the poor. In January 1880 McKay recorded 426 registered poor in Kilmarnock, with 240 dependants, and seventeen casual poor with ten dependants; but including all classes of poor, 1,209 were relieved in 1879, a reduction of the number (1,357) listed in his edition of 1864. Of these, only one-third were natives of Ireland, so the problem of 'foreign poor' was not as great as some writers suggested.

The Corporation, conscious of the evils which resulted from the overcrowding of travellers and vagrants in the various lodging-houses in the town, opened a Model Lodging House in Ladeside Street in July 1878. McKay noted that

the superior comfort gained in this establishment, compared with that offered by the old lodging houses, caused its benefits quickly to be appreciated by the poorer classes, with the result that the building is now self-supporting, and has an average of four hundred sleepers weekly.

A second building was erected shortly afterwards in Soulis Street which in later years served as a college of further education. Both buildings were demolished in the early 1970s.

Besides the parochial assessment, the local authorities of the nineteenth century relied to a large extent on individual acts of charity. At one time two boards hung on the wall of the Laigh Kirk listing public benefactors and the amounts of their bequests; these ranged from 1675 to 1759 and were mainly expressed in merks (two thirds of a pound Scots and latterly worth only 13.3 pence in sterling). The interest from these bequests yielded about £100 a year in 1790, as much as the annual amounts raised by church-door collections. The large bequests began in 1844 with Robert Crawford's bequest of £2,650 towards a town library, but the first gift to benefit the poor directly was the trust of £1,000 made by John Fulton in February 1864 'towards the maintenance of a Soup Kitchen... the soup to be sold at not more than one-half of the cost price'. The original soup kitchen was opened in Nelson Street and continued there till 1883, but another soup kitchen was opened the following year and continued

Nelson Street, 1890

intermittently till the Second World War. For many years James Arbuckle (appointed a bailie in 1878) operated this philanthropic project with the aid of Hugh Paton and two ladies. He was a forceful personality who begged, borrowed and brow-beat his fellow citizens, especially the butchers, bakers and grocers of the town, into providing him with the scraps and left-overs which were turned into a really good thick Scotch broth. This was accompanied by two thick slices of bread, the meal being originally provided free of charge, though later a charge of one penny was made and raised to twopence in 1923.

As late as the late 1940s when the postwar Labour government laid the foundations of the present system of social security, public assistance was administered by the Town Council. In 1936 there were 338 poor and 253 dependants classified as ordinary outdoor poor (i.e. continuing to live in their own homes), 17 poor and 27 dependants classed as destitute able-bodied unemployed and a further 49 indoor poor, held in the Combination Poorhouse. By 1939 the numbers of ordinary outdoor had risen sharply to 451 poor and dependants but the destitute unemployed had dropped to three poor and five dependants. Indoor poor, however, had risen to 63 by 1938 but dropped to 58 the following year. By 1939 just over £20,000 was being spent on public assistance, which worked out at a cost of about 10s per head of the population.

Medical Services

The first *Statistical Account* made no mention of medical facilities of any kind and certainly there was no hospital in Kilmarnock at that time. By the time of the second *Account*, however, some progress had been made. It was still the practice for those who could afford it to be treated in the comfort of their own homes by the local doctors. In 1827, however, some provision was made for the relief of the sick poor. A dispensary was established for those who were unable to pay for medical attendance and advice. 'It is patronised by most of the medical practitioners in town, who attend in regular rotation, and cheerfully render their gratuitous assistance,' wrote Andrew Hamilton. 'The expenses incurred by medicines, house rent, etc are defrayed by subscriptions among the inhabitant at large. The subscriptions have usually covered the expenditure. These facts demonstrate, that there exists in the mind of the public a conviction of the utility of the institution.' Kilmarnock was divided into fourteen districts, apportioned among the various doctors as near as possible to their residences. This service cost about £50 a year to run, and the voluntary subscriptions just about covered the modest expenses. In 1835 no fewer than 243 patients were treated which was somewhat above the average annual figure since the service started. The figures were distorted by the cholera epidemic of 1832 when a temporary isolation hospital had to be erected in Ward Park, near where the Cholera Monument now stands. In 1831 there were 105 cases of 'fever', but it rose sharply to 246 the following year. In 1833, however, it dropped to 43 and in 1834 only fifteen cases were treated. In 1835 there were 45 fever cases, of which five were fatal.

Smallpox was one of the dread diseases of the eighteenth and nineteenth centuries, but there were

Early ambulance, the 'fever wagon', at Kilmarnock Cross, c1895

only five cases in 1835 and none of them was fatal. By the early nineteenth century the practice of vaccination was becoming well-established, but it did not become compulsory till 1863.

It seems incredible that Kilmarnock lacked proper hospital facilities until 1868. Agitation for an infirmary started in 1865 and in September 1867 the project had advanced far enough for the foundation stone to be laid on a site between Portland and Hill Streets north of the railway line. In October 1868 the Infirmary was inaugurated. The cost of the site and the development of the building as a 24-bed hospital totalled £4,146. At the outset the Infirmary was staffed by a matron assisted by two nurses. The original mansion house of Mount Pleasant was retained as a dwelling house for administrative staff. Extensions were made in 1881 and 1893, substantially adding to the number of beds. In 1891 the Children's Block (later used as kitchens) was opened, together with the Nurses' Training School funded by the Dowager Lady Howard de Walden, and an anaesthetist (described as a 'chloroformist') was appointed. In the same year, however, Kilmarnock Infirmary agreed to take 25 fever cases from Ayrshire County Council and facilities for this were provided in the Fevers Block opened in 1899 at a cost of £4,000. Most of the funds for this were raised by a Great Bazaar. In its inaugural year the Infirmary handled 101 cases; this rose to 420 a year by 1878 and 1,481 by 1919. Further extensions were planned in 1912-14 but work had to be curtailed on the outbreak of the First World War during which the Dick Institute was used as a temporary war hospital. In 1919 the expansion programme recommenced, but costs had risen during the war and the Infirmary incurred a bill of £44,000. Once more, its supporters resorted to bazaars and sales of work, and raised £53,800. By that time the costs of projected improvements had escalated to £111,715, but voluntary workers redoubled their efforts and eventually raised £87,372. This work was carried out in the early 1920s and the Infirmary expanded to 130 beds theoretically (but by various ingenious methods 147 beds were crammed in), together with an operating theatre, x-ray facilities and a physiotherapy unit. The Fevers Block and Mount Pleasant were demolished to make way for the new wings. In 1926 the Infirmary

Dick Institute in service as an auxiliary hospital 1917

installed wireless facilities for the patients, one of the first Scottish hospitals to do so.

Annual expenditure of running the hospital was £14,000 by 1925, but it rose to £17,000 by 1935 and then £20,000 in 1939. By 1935 it was realised that a much

Ambulance, driver and nurse

larger hospital was required and the directors entered negotiations with Ayr County Hospital for the creation of a single large hospital, to be located at Symington, but these plans came to nothing. Eventually a fresh site

Kilmarnock Infirmary

was earmarked in Grassyards Road north of St Joseph's and negotiations with the Howard de Walden estates were in train when the Second World War broke out and the project was shelved for the duration. After the war the directors were more concerned to improve the existing Infirmary in preparation for the handover to the National Health Service in 1948. As a result a pathology laboratory and diet kitchen were opened in 1946, and ophthalmic, diabetic and blood clinics added in 1947. It seems astonishing, however, that, as late as 1948 when the Infirmary was nationalised, it had no facilities whatsoever for out-patients. Under the NHS various improvements were made. When fire severely damaged the upper floor of the administrative block in May 1955 the opportunity was taken to rebuild and add another storey. Even under nationalisation, the Infirmary continued to rely to some extent on charity. In the 1950s the Infirmary benefited from generous bequests by two sisters, Miss Finnie (who left her house

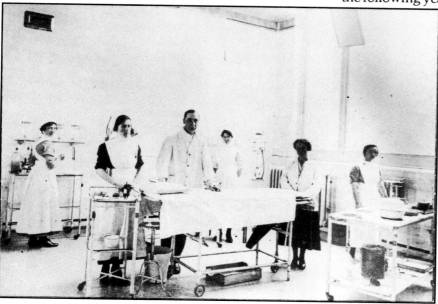

Dr Frew and Miss Inglis in the operating theatre

in Hill Street to the hospital) and Mrs William G. Sturrock, who gave £15,000 and Thorntoun House for use as a nurses' home. These bequests enabled much new development to take place. In addition, Torrance House came to the health board as a legacy and was subsequently converted into a convalescent hospital, enabling a greater turn-round of surgical patients.

Separate facilities for fevers and infectious diseases were provided when the Kilmarnock Burgh Infectious Diseases Hospital was opened at Kirklandside on 11th September 1909. The fever hospital was suitably remote, yet not too inconvenient, being a ten-minute walk from the Hurlford tram terminus. It occupied a spacious 27-acre site and had seven blocks, each 40 feet apart. These included administrative buildings and laboratories as well as three wards—a 24-bed scarlet fever pavilion, an 18-bed enteric ward and a 6-bed diphtheria unit. Each ward had male and female units with single bedrooms for the isolation of serious cases. The hospital was built

by Archibald McCrone to designs by James Hay and cost £20,000. By 1940 this hospital had been expanded to 116 beds. A sanatorium for the treatment of tuberculosis was established in 1917 and by 1940 had 33 beds. A VD clinic and a smallpox reception house were added in 1920. With the exception of the Infirmary (which was maintained by voluntary subscriptions) the hospital and health facilities were the responsibility of the Town Council's Public Health Committee.

Maternity facilities were non-existent till 1919 when a modestly equipped child welfare centre opened in Titchfield Street. At that time, and for many years thereafter, most confinements took place at home. In November 1924 Mr and Mrs William Murchland gave the Town Council a house in Green Street, next to Dick's Garage and one of the oldest residential buildings in the town, together with the money necessary to install electric light and modern plumbing. This opened the following year as the Maternity and Child Welfare Centre with three beds; but in 1926 it was expanded to twelve beds. From three births in 1924 it rose to 426 deliveries in 1936. In that year, however, there were 984 births in Kilmarnock as a whole, so that more than 50 per cent were still taking place at home, although quite a few babies were born at the private Kilmarnock Nursing Home in Richardland Road.

A major breakthrough came in 1937 when the Dairy School for Scotland moved from its original location at Holmes Farm to Auchencruive. The Town Council purchased the building for £2,000 and converted it into a 32-bed maternity hospital which was opened by Councillor Henry Blackwood on 11th October that year. Bailie Climie made a speech on this occasion saying that it was hoped that the new hospital would encourage a rise in the birthrate! The Maternity Hospital was designed to cope with 700 births per annum. In 1987 it celebrated its golden jubilee, but shortly afterwards, in May 1988, it was announced that it was scheduled for closure. Dunlop House, formerly the home of Mrs Frances Wallace Dunlop, the friend and correspondent of Robert Burns, had been acquired for use as a hospital for the mentally handicapped, but it was too remote and inconvenient to serve a really useful purpose.

In 1974 the Scottish Health Service was re-organised and local hospital services became the responsibility of the Ayrshire and Arran Health Board. By this time Kilmarnock boasted a 700-bed general hospital, a geriatric hospital (Torrance House), four old people's homes (Barbadoes House and Mount House in Dundonald Road, Lainshaw House, Stewarton and Springhill House in Portland Road), two children's

Crosshouse Hospital

homes, two day nurseries, a centre for the physically handicapped (Dunlop House, Dunlop), two adult training centres (the Glebe Centre, Kilmarnock and at Cessnock Road, Hurlford) and a centre for the mentally handicapped (Kerrmuir Hostel). In 1988 Ayrshire and Arran Health Board proposed the closure of the Maternity Hospital and decided that eventually maternity cases would be concentrated on Ayrshire Central Hospital in Irvine. This was greeted with dismay in Kilmarnock where a petition with 8,000 signatures was soon gathered. Despite this opposition, the Board went ahead and closed the Maternity Hospital at the end of March 1989. Since then it has been refurbished and converted for use as a residential and respite centre for the handicapped, taking over this role from Dunlop House. There is also a residential respite care centre in Moscow. The remaining maternity facilities and ante-natal clinic were transferred to the clinics on Old Irvine Road and Treeswoodhead.

The biggest upheaval in the hospital services affected the Infirmary. If it had seemed to be overcrowded by 1935, the situation had only got worse by 1965. In that year the local health board grasped the nettle and began planning an entirely new hospital on a site near Crosshouse, at a projected cost of £7,056,350. Matters proceeded at a very leisurely pace and plans were not submitted until 1971. Three years later responsibility for the project passed to the new Ayrshire and Arran Health Board and work was by that time well in hand. It was hoped to open the new hospital in May 1977, but the scheme was subject to interminable delays and unforeseen technical problems. The ventilation system, designed to purify the air every twelve minutes, caused

many headaches, and then it was discovered that the water system had an unacceptably high level of copper in it. These and other problems set back the progress of construction by several years. In the meantime the Board were forced to spend £129,000 on re-equipping the obsolescent Infirmary. A further £3,000,000 had to be spent on additional work in the new hospital because of changes in the building regulations *during* the period of construction. For three years the hospital stood empty while these defects were remedied, thus earning the nickname of the 'ghost hospital'.

By the time the hospital opened, seventeen years after it was projected, the costs had risen to an astronomical £26,000,000. By November 1980 the College of Nursing and Midwifery (on a separate site within the hospital grounds) was ready. In 1981 Robert Taylor had the privilege of being the first out-patient treated in the physiotherapy department. Other departments opened in the course of 1981-2 with the first in-patient being admitted in August 1982. A month later the old Kilmarnock Infirmary was closed down, Crosshouse Hospital was by this time fully operational as an accident and emergency reception centre. On 1st August 1983 the children's wards opened, thus completing the range of medical services. The 706-bed hospital was ceremonially inaugurated by George Younger, Secretary of State for Scotland, on 2nd June 1984—nineteen years after it was first projected. It occupies an area of 50,000 square feet— enough for nine football pitches—and has a staff of 2,000. Boissevain and Osmond of Glasgow were the architects while Melville, Dundas and Whitson were the main contractors.

Since then Crosshouse Hospital has continued to expand, and improve its facilities. A major breakthrough in otology (ear surgery) was made on 23rd March 1989 when Mr R.S. Singh performed Scotland's first cochlear implant operation, enabling a patient, who had been deaf for 23 years following a head injury, to hear again. The surgeon, Mr Raj Singh was one of the first otologists worldwide to have performed this operation. A haematology unit was added in 1989, a £500,000 Computed Tomography (CT) scanning facility in September 1990, a diabetics day centre in December 1990 and most recently the John Stevenson Lynch Renal Unit. The Renal Unit, opened in September 1991 was purpose built at a cost of £420,000, £250,000 of which was donated from Ayrshire-based builders Lynch Homes. This state of the art renal technology means that Ayrshire kidney patients will no longer have to travel to Glasgow for dialysis.

Meanwhile the Kilmarnock Infirmary had been standing empty since 1982 and was costing a fortune in maintenance and security. At one point it was considered as an alternative (and much more convenient) site for the treatment and care of the mentally handicapped instead of Dunlop House, but some councillors felt that it should be kept for geriatric cases. By August 1989, however, repairs to the structure were estimated at £250,000 and permission was given to demolish it. This was vetoed by the Secretary of State in January 1990 on the grounds that the Infirmary and the neighbouring Nurses' Home were List B buildings. By 1991 a proposal by Stakis to convert it into a 90-bed private nursing home was being considered.

Mr Singh and some of his young patients who have benefitted from cochlear surgery

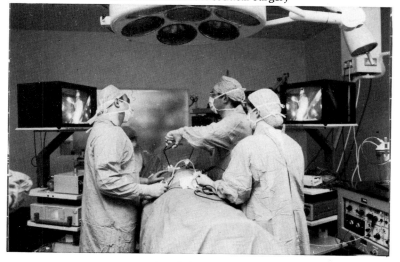
'Keyhole' surgery

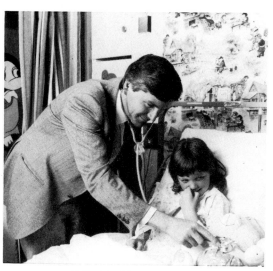
G.P. visits his young patient

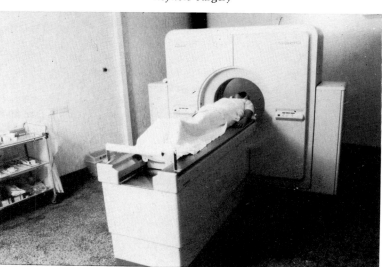
CT scanner in operation

16 KILMARNOCK IN THE WORLD

Kilmarnock cannot claim to have been particularly prolific in the number of men and women it has produced who have made their name in the world.

Sandy Allan, cousin of Robert Burns, was born at Old Rome Ford or Rumford in Dundonald parish but lived in Kilmarnock from 1792 till 1800 while serving his apprenticeship as a shoemaker. Later he went to Galston and then took to the sea. From operating a coastal smack out of Saltcoats he founded the Allan Line which evolved from a one-man operation to become the seventh largest shipping line in the world and the largest privately owned fleet.

Kilmarnock can even claim a connection with two Nobel Prize winners. **Sir Alexander Fleming** (1881-1955), who won the Nobel Prize for medicine in 1944 for his part in the discovery of penicillin, was born at Lochfield near Darvel but received his secondary education at Kilmarnock Academy. Another Darvel man educated at the Academy is **Dr J. Morton Boyd**, CBE, a prolific writer on natural history and Scottish Director of the Nature Conservancy from 1971 till his retirement in 1985.

John (later **Lord**) **Boyd Orr** (1880-1971), born at Kilmaurs and educated at the parish school there, however, went in the opposite direction, receiving his secondary education at Bellahouston Academy, Glasgow before going on to the University to study medicine. A brilliant record in the First World War (DSO, MC and mentioned in despatches) was followed by a long list of important appointments which included Professor of Agriculture at Aberdeen University and MP for the Scottish universities. He was awarded the 1949 Nobel peace prize for his work as Director General of the United Nations Food and Agricultural Organisation.

Farther afield, within the area of the present Kilmarnock and Loudoun District, **John Fulton** (1800-53) of Fenwick was a self-taught genius who mastered the mysteries of astronomy, mechanics and botany and is best-remembered for the orrery which he constructed for the Kilmarnock Philosophical Society.

Robert Dunsmuir (1825-89) was born in Hurlford but educated at the Academy and later married a Kilmarnock girl, Joanna White. His father James owned coalmines at Barleith and Skerrington and Robert started work at the coal-face of one of his father's pits on leaving school. In 1850 he and his wife emigrated to Canada and settled on Vancouver Island where Robert amassed a fortune developing the rich coal and mineral resources of the area. He is remembered today for Craigdarroch Castle, a Scottish baronial mansion which he built on the outskirts of Victoria, British Columbia and now a major tourist attraction.

Below are summarised the careers of men of Kilmarnock who achieved fame, and sometimes fortune as well, individuals for whom Kilmarnock can take credit for nurturing and giving their earliest start. Artists and writers of local origin have been discussed in Chapter 10.

Famous Kilmarnockians

The **Rev. Dr Robert Findlay** was born in Bank Street in 1721, the son of a merchant named William Findlay and his wife Barbara Hodgeart, who was the daughter of Robert Hodgeart, surgeon. Robert Findlay was educated at the Universities of Glasgow and Leyden where he originally studied medicine but then switched courses and entered the ministry. In 1744 he was ordained minister of Stewarton and a year later moved to Galston. Later he moved to Paisley and in 1782 was appointed minister of the North West Church, Glasgow and elected Professor of Theology. He was highly regarded in ecclesiastical circles in his day and wrote a number of ponderous tomes with appropriately lengthy titles of which *A Vindication of the Sacred Books, and of Josephus against Voltaire* was a typical example. He died in 1814.

James Shaw was born at Mosshead, the son of a farmer in Riccarton parish, in 1764. Shaw senior died bout 1769 so his widow and young family moved into Kilmarnock. Here Jimmy was educated at the old grammar school under the unfortunate John Graham. At the age of seventeen Jimmy went to America at the behest of his elder brother David who held a position in the commissariat and through his influence obtained a post in the commercial house of George and Samuel Douglass of New York. He spent three years in their employ, which means that he must have been there during the closing years of the American War of Independence. About 1784 he returned to Britain and in a short time became a junior partner in the same firm's London office. He soon made his mark in the City and moved in wealthy and influential circles. In 1805 this real-life Dick Whittington became Lord Mayor of London and in his official capacity led the funeral of Nelson after Trafalgar. Four years later he became a baronet and from 1806 till 1818 was also a Member of Parliament for one of the London seats. After retiring from the House of Commons he continued as one of the Aldermen of London till 1831 when he was raised to the office of Chamberlain of the City. He resigned this office in May 1843 and died the following October after a long illness. He was a tall and commanding figure, possessed of great integrity and personal courage. When the mob stormed the Royal Exchange in 1816 Sir James seized one of the ring-leaders and also captured one of the radicals' flags. He used his position wisely to help many of his fellow countrymen. He took a leading part in raising funds for the widow of Robert Burns and it was by his exertions that Robert Junior secured a position in the Stamp Office and his two younger brothers obtained cadetships in the East India Company's service. Sir James also raised £310 for the illegitimate daughters of the poet by Elizabeth Paton and Ann Park. As the 'local boy who made good' Sir

James Shaw was soon remembered by his former townsfolk who subscribed almost £1,000 for the erection of his statue at the Cross on 4th August 1848. The statue, of Ravaccione marble, was carved larger than life-size by James Fillans and showed the late baronet in the dress costume of Lord Mayor of London. Jimmy Shaw continued to gaze down benignly on the traffic at the town centre for 80 years. When Jimmy stood at the Cross he was the focal point for Hogmanay revelry as the chimes rang out the old year. On 28th March 1929, however, Jimmy had to yield to the burgeoning traffic. His statue was carefully dismantled and re-assembled in more tranquil surroundings on Elmbank Avenue opposite the Dick Institute and alongside the War Memorial. Many people mourned the ignominious transfer of the burgh's most famous son to such an out-of-the-way spot; but there are hopes that Jimmy can be restored to his rightful place at the now pedestrianised Cross.

F.G.P. Neison was born early in the nineteenth century and educated at the Academy. He trained as an accountant and played a leading role in the literary institutions of the town, delivering lectures on mathematical subjects. In 1840 he left Kilmarnock to take up an appointment as actuary to the Medical, Invalid and General Life Assurance Society of London and thereafter developed a keen interest in statistics. His first paper on the subject was delivered before the Statistical Society of London in January 1844, in reply to a paper at the previous meeting given by Edwin Chadwick, then Secretary to the Poor Law Commissioners. Neison's paper was subsequently published in the *London Statistical Journal*. In March 1845 he published *Contributions to Vital Statistics* which was very favourably noticed in the national press. This work was based on four years' research and analysis of the many thousands of returns submitted by friendly societies throughout the country and was hailed as the most valuable contribution to the laws of sickness and mortality. It placed Neison immediately in the front rank of statists. A third and greatly enlarged edition of this seminal work appeared in 1857. *Statistics of Crime* covering England and Wales (1842-4) was published in September 1846, with a supplementary report at Oxford the following year. These works excited considerable interest among sociologists and penal reformers both in Britain and on the Continent. Subsequently Neison turned his attention on India, publishing *Vital Statistics of the East India Company's Armies in India, European and Native* in 1847. Neison later was employed by the Home Office in drafting the Act for the Regulation of Friendly Societies (1848). He died at London in June 1876.

Thomas Y. McChristie was born at Townhead in 1797 but soon afterwards the family moved to Beansburn where his father opened a pub called the Rising Sun and Compass. Thomas was educated at a school in the Foregate but one day he was hit by a stone ball in the playground and badly crippled. He was bed-ridden for three years but gradually recovered to the extent that he could hobble around on crutches.

Despite this handicap he later attended the Academy and became so proficient that William Henderson made him his assistant. At the age of fifteen or sixteen he opened a school of his own in Ayr but gave this up and decided to seek his fortune in England. A Yorkshireman who happened to be in the Beansburn inn one day and saw him there was sufficiently impressed by Thomas that he invited him to go thither. Encouraged by this he boarded a carrier's cart one day, and he made his way to Yorkshire. Three weeks later he arrived at his destination with only a shilling and twopence halfpenny to his name. Luckily he soon located his benefactor who gave him a job as a clerk, and by sheer hard work and ability he rose to be the principal of the establishment. Eventually he branched out on his own, but the insolvency of his business partners left him penniless. By this time he had acquired skill in shorthand writing and resolved to go to London to seek employment as a newspaper reporter. At first he had no luck, and in desperation he called one day on Sir James Shaw. Sir James received him sympathetically and, having no work to give him, pressed a gold sovereign on him to meet his immediate needs. With the help of this little gift, which he husbanded with miserly care, he was able to persevere a little longer and at length, when taking notes one day in the Court of Chancery where he had gone to practise, he was engaged by a solicitor to report a case of importance which was about to come to court. For this work, which he accomplished in a satisfactory manner, he received upwards of £5, which was then to him a little fortune. One of his first acts was to call on Sir James Shaw and repay the sovereign. Sir James was so impressed by this that ever afterwards he kept a close eye on his young friend's progress.

From this time he daily rose into notice and reputation as a court reporter, and was soon, and for many years, considered to be one of the most expert shorthand writers and parliamentary reporters in London, being employed by *The Times* and other leading newspapers. Later he was also employed by *The Lancet* to furnish reports on the principal medical lectures. While thus engaged he became a medical student and in 1829 obtained his diploma from the Royal College of Surgeons. He now practised as a surgeon, while continuing to act as a parliamentary reporter and continued his studies for the degree of doctor of medicine. It should be added that, by a mixture of physiotherapy and the invention of an ingenious contraption, he eventually overcame his handicap and could get by without crutches. He was awarded his MD degree in 1833, and then studied law for five years at Lincoln's Inn and was called to the Bar in 1838. In this career he excelled, as in everything else he put his mind to. As an instance of his forensic abilities, it may be stated that in 1845 he received 1,000 guineas as a retainer, plus other fees and expenses, to go to Ceylon (Sri Lanka) to conduct a case for the recovery of a large estate on that island. This sum would represent about a quarter of a million pounds in today's currency. He was appointed Revising Barrister for the City of London in 1842 and this brought him a great deal of official and government work. In 1857, for example, he went to Australia on an important mission. Although he accomplished this task with his customary skill the arduous journey home impaired his health and he died on 7th December 1860 at his residence in Great James Street, London.

In Chapter 2 mention was made of the radical reformer, James Johnston. While in Paisley, his wife gave birth to a son, christened **James Johnston**. Later the family returned to Kilmarnock where the boy was educated at the Academy. He was something of an infant prodigy, contributing articles to the *Ayrshire Miscellany* while still a schoolboy. Later he entered the University of Glasgow with the intention of studying for the ministry, and put himself through college by giving English lessons. He also taught during the University vacations, and in 1822 was back in Kilmarnock teaching English composition. He eventually became a preacher of the gospel, but by now he was inclined to the study of geology and chemistry. He headed south and opened a private school in Durham, but in 1833 was appointed Reader in Chemistry and Mineralogy at the new University in that city. In 1843 he was appointed chemist to the Agricultural Society of Scotland. His text-book on agricultural chemistry and geology ran to 33 editions and was translated into many languages. He was a prolific writer on many subjects and contributed numerous articles to the *Edinburgh Review* and *Blackwood's Magazine*. Professor Johnston died at Durham in September 1855.

The brothers **Robert** (1820-91) and **James Dick** (1823-1902) were born in very humble circumstances in Kilmarnock. In 1828 the family left the burgh and settled in the Gorbals district of Glasgow. Robert served his apprenticeship as a watchmaker but his younger brother drifted in and out of several jobs and was unemployed at the time when they stumbled across something which was to change their lives utterly. In 1843 Dr William Montgomery, a medical missionary, brought back to Glasgow from Malaya some lumps of a strange dirty grey material. This was gutta percha, the evaporated latex of the palaquium tree. Unlike indiarubber latex, no practical use had been found for this substance, although the Malays had used it in fashioning the handles of knives and whips. Montgomery tried to promote gutta percha as a substitute for leather in footwear and in 1846 he sold his samples to the Dick brothers. They melted the lumps in a frying pan in the wash-house of their tenement in Crown Street, causing consternation and annoyance among their neighbours with the terrible stench, but they succeeded in producing 'pancakes' of gutta percha. That night James soled and heeled three pairs of shoes, and when their experiment worked Robert put his savings into the lease of a shop at 12 Gallowgate where James could develop the gutta percha business. From this small building grew a mighty empire with a huge factory at Greenhead near the Templeton carpet factory. By 1885 Dickbelt, conveyor

belting made from balata (a cheaper substitute for gutta percha which the Dicks obtained from South America), was used all over the world and the Dick brothers had become millionaires. James Dick never forgot his roots and when Robert died he decided to make a gesture to Kilmarnock in his brother's memory. From this came the Dick Institute, opened barely months before James himself died. Provost David Mackay, who had been largely responsible for the negotiations with James Dick over the project, later married James's widow as his second wife.

William Reid was born in the parish of Riccarton on 1st September 1822, one of a family of twelve born to a tenant farmer. A sickly child, he was considered unfit for farm-work on leaving school and the parish doctor recommended that he emigrate to a warmer climate. With £5 from his father, William set off to Spain and Portugal. He obtained a berth as a cabin boy and worked his passage to Madeira. Here, in 1836, when he was barely fourteen, William Reid settled. He worked for a German bakery; the hours were long and the pay was low, but somehow he managed to scrape together enough capital to start up, in 1846, as a wine merchant, exporting the wine for which the island is world famous. Within a few years, by dint of hard work, he had become the largest vintner on Madeira. The profits from the wine business were invested in property, just as Madeira began to enjoy a boom in tourism. From renting villas to the rich visitors, William expanded into the hotel industry and eventually owned four first-class hotels and a number of lodging-houses. His ultimate ambition, however, was to create a luxury hotel on a special site. In 1886 he succeeded in buying a headland offering fabulous views, and work on the construction of Reid's New Hotel began the following year. Sadly, William died in 1888 before his dream was realized. The hotel opened in November 1891 under the management of William's two sons. The Reid family retained ownership of the hotel till 1925. At the turn of the century Reid's was regarded as one of the top hotels of the world, ranking with Shepheard's in Cairo and the Raffles in Singapore as a haunt of wealthy tourists. Its centenary was recently celebrated by an extensive programme of refurbishment. William Reid's tomb may be seen in the cemetery at Funchal, but his chief memorial is the great hotel which is one of the island's major landmarks.

James Thomson was born in Kilmarnock in 1823, one of twelve children of a poor bootmaker. James had no proper schooling but through his own endeavours secured a good job in Glasgow. He studied geology at evening classes in the Andersonian College. He worked as a travelling salesman for a tea company, and this enabled him to gather fossil specimens as he travelled all over Scotland. Eventually he revolutionized the classification of fossil corals and became the world authority on the subject. In 1892 he donated his collection of fossils and geological specimens to the town, but was too ill to attend the ceremony in 1899 at which he was given the freedom of the burgh. James died the following year.

Born in the same year as Thomson, **James Blackwood** came from a totally different background, being the son of a prosperous wool-spinning millowner. By 1866 he was a councillor and three years later became a magistrate. He played a large part in the establishment of the new Academy and the Infirmary. Despite all these public duties he became an accomplished scientist, with an intense interest in optics, light and photography. In 1863 he produced the first electric light, in a room on the upper floor of a building overlooking the Cross. He also built his own geological cutting equipment and microscope.

Andrew Fisher was born in Orr's Land, Crosshouse on 22nd October 1862, the second of a family of six sons and a daughter born to Robert and Jane Fisher. At the age of ten he joined his father down the local pits and worked there for nine years. Robert Fisher was a founder member of the Crosshouse Co-operative Society, founded in the year of Andrew's birth. Andrew had no education beyond the basic elementary level, but he was an avid reader and acquired an articulacy which led him, in his teens, into the political arena. At the age of seventeen he was appointed district secretary of the Ayrshire branch of the Miners' Union. As such, he played a major role in the bitter miners' strike of 1881, for which he was blacklisted. Unable to obtain work, he used his enforced leisure to further his education. Eventually he got work, but was again blacklisted in 1885 and decided that there was no future for him in Scotland. In June that year he emigrated to Australia and settled in Queensland where he obtained employment in the coal-mines of Gympie. In his spare time he studied economics and social science and worked as a union leader. In 1893 he was elected to the Queensland Legislative Assembly as member for Gympie. In December 1899 Queensland had a Labour government for all of several days and in the short-lived Dawson administration Andrew Fisher was Secretary for Railways and Public Works.

At the first elections for the Federal Parliament in 1901 Fisher was returned to the House of Representatives as member for Wide Bay, a seat he held till his retirement fifteen years later. When J.C. Watson formed the first Labour Ministry in April 1904 Fisher became Minister for Trade and Customs. Watson, defeated four months later, resigned in 1907 the leadership of the party and Fisher was elected in his place. In November 1908 he withdrew the support he had been giving to Alfred Deakin's administration, and became Prime Minister and Treasurer. He was displaced by the Fusion Government of Protectionists and Free-traders in June 1909, but at the general election of April 1910 Labour secured a majority of the House and Fisher returned to power as Prime Minister and Treasurer. During his three years in office more than a hundred measures were passed, ranging from the establishment of the Commonwealth Bank to the introduction of maternity allowances. Fisher's social revolution introduced the Welfare State to Australia. In 1911 he attended the Coronation of King George V and represented Australia at the Imperial Conference where he was created a Privy Councillor. In the general election of June 1913 Labour was narrowly defeated, but at the double dissolution of September 1914 Fisher was returned with a working majority. It was during this election that he made his famous declaration that Australia would assist the Empire to 'her last man and her last shilling'. In October 1915 Fisher resigned as Prime Minister, being succeeded by W.M. Hughes. He now became Australian High Commissioner in London, a position which he held until 1921. After a visit to Australia he returned to Britain and in 1923 tried to get adopted as Labour candidate for the Kilmarnock Burghs in the general election of 1924, but was rejected by the constituency selection committee because his views were not in conformity with the programme and policy of the National Labour Party. He retired to London where he died on 22nd October 1928, survived by his wife Margaret, five sons and a daughter. Three times Prime Minister, he served longer than any other Australian Prime Minister prior to the time of Bob Hawke, but the many and sweeping measures initiated by this warm-hearted man have left their mark on Australia to this day. It is interesting, but idle, to speculate on how he might have changed the course of British politics had he been elected as Kilmarnock's MP in the 1920s.

James Stevenson was born at Kilmarnock on 2nd April 1873 and educated at the Academy. On leaving school he became a travelling salesman for John Walker and worked his way up to become joint managing director of the company. It was he who coined the slogan used by the whisky firm to this day. On the outbreak of the Second World War in 1914, Stevenson offered his services to the government. The following year he was appointed director of area organization in the Ministry of Munitions, a post which he held till 1917 when he was appointed vice-chairman of the Munitions Advisory Committee and in 1918 a member of the Munitions Council for Ordnance. After the war he became chairman of the Munitions Council committee on demobilization and reconstruction and from 1919 to 1921 was surveyor-general of supply to the War Office. He held a succession of important posts in the Army Council, the Air Council and the Committee on Civil Aviation, and in 1922-3 was adviser on commercial affairs to the Colonial Office, helping to save the rubber industry of Ceylon (now Sri Lanka) and Malaya. His immense organizational skills were latterly employed in managing the great British Empire Exhibition held at Wembley in 1924-5. For his public services Stevenson became a baronet in 1917 and GCMG in 1922. Two years later he was raised to the peerage as Baron Stevenson of Holmbury. Though twice married he was childless, so the barony became extinct on his death on 10th June 1926.

Kilmarnock and Loudoun on the world map

If you drive south-east from Fredericksburg, Virginia along State road number 3, you will pass through King George, Westmoreland, Northumberland, Richmond and Lancaster counties. Seven miles east of the county town of Lancaster you will come to the rocky coast of Chesapeake Bay and there, nestling at the head of a picturesque inlet, is the village of Kilmarnock (population 927). How the town got its name is not known for certain, but it was probably named by a homesick immigrant. The town celebrates St Marnock's Day (25th October) as a local holiday, and caused some embarrassment on this side of the Atlantic when Fred Burke of the Kilmarnock Community Council wrote in May 1990 to his counterpart in Kilmarnock and Loudoun District Council seeking information on how the saint's day was celebrated here! In July 1949 Walter Harvey, mayor of Kilmarnock, paid a visit to the Ayrshire town and exchanged civic gifts and greetings with Provost Daniel Cairns in the Town Hall. This returned a visit which Provost Cairns had previously made to his Virginia counterpart. Boydton, Virginia and Boyd Lake in Canada's North West Territories may also have a Kilmarnock connection. Then there is Loudon (*sic*) in Malawi, Loudon (Tennessee), Loudounville (New York State) and Loudonville (Ohio) in the United States, and Riccarton in the South Island of New Zealand. Darvel Bay was at one time an important coalmining area in North Borneo (now Sabah) which presumably was developed by miners from the Irvine Valley.

Town twinning

The informal visits between the mayor and provost of the two Kilmarnocks, 3,000 miles apart, more than 40 years ago, have their modern counterpart in the practice of town twinning. This charming custom began in 1947 when Hanover in Germany twinned with Bristol in England. Forty years later no fewer than 408 towns and cities in Britain had twinned with German towns and *Jumelage* as it is known in France has grown enormously over the same period, involving links between towns in every European country. While most towns are content to find a link with just one other, some German towns have up to six twins. Kilmarnock, with four twins, ranks high in the British league and has even earned a rebuke from the Scottish Development Department, no less, for overdoing things. This impertinence came with a refusal to allow Kilmarnock to erect road signs proudly naming its twins. The SDD would only allow two names on the sign, and therefore the scheme had to be abandoned.

Kilmarnock, in fact, was comparatively late in the twinning business. Informal links between individuals as far back as 1956 led to Kilmarnock twinning with the French town of Alès in March 1974. A gala performance in the Palace Theatre was held on 29th March in honour of the Mayor of Alès and the following day the twinning charter was signed in the Grand Hall. Alès, in the

Cevennes region, is not unlike Kilmarnock in many respects. With a population of 31,000, it is the centre of an agricultural district, famous for its cheeses and silk industry. Formerly coal was worked in the region but this is now in decline. The steelworks were recently modernised and there is a wide range of light industry, including a piano factory and an IBM plant. Since 1974 there have been numerous cultural exchanges between the two towns, ranging from school parties and rugby matches to civic delegations.

In 1974 Kilmarnock twinned with Kulmbach in the province of Upper Franconia in north-eastern Bavaria. Georg Hagen, *Oberbürgermeister* of Kulmbach, visited Kilmarnock as far back as 1956 and Provost Cairns paid a reciprocal visit to Kulmbach two years later. These civic visits forged links which steadily increased over the years and culminated in the signing of a twinning charter in Kulmbach on 27th June 1974, ratified

ceremonially at Kilmarnock on 30th October. This town of 74,000 is, like Kilmarnock, an industrial town in an agricultural setting, famed for the manufacture of agricultural and farming machinery, woollens, hosiery and cotton, clothing and textiles, mainly fabric for upholstery. Just as Johnnie Walker put Kilmarnock on the global map, so the Kulmbach brewery has made the name synonymous with good beer the world o'er. Another link is that Kulmbach was a centre of the Reformation and staunchly defended its beliefs during the Thirty Years War. Kulmbach's Evangelische Kantorei (church choir) gave performances in Kilmarnock in May 1989. The town's castle, the Plassenburg, stands on a rock and dominates the town. Kulmbach was also a centre for the manufacture of *zinnsoldaten* and the town museum boasts an enormous collection of painted model figurines. Passage Kilmarnock in Kulmbach's shopping precinct was inaugurated in 1982, along with similar

streets honouring Kulmbach's other twins, Rust (Austria) and Lugo (Italy).

Alès twinned with Herstal in Belgium in 1969 and it was at a meeting in Alès in 1974 that Kilmarnock's civic leaders first met their Belgian counterparts. This led to the twinning of Kilmarnock and Herstal on 9th April 1977. Again, there are close similarities between the two towns. Herstal (77,000), on the outskirts of Liège, is an industrial town with a tremendous history for Pepin II, King of the Franks was born here and his grandson Pepin the Short died there in 768. The town also claims to have been the birthplace of the Emperor Charlemagne—a claim disputed by Aix la Chapelle (Aachen). The name comes from *Heerstelle* meaning a permanent Army camp. In the nineteenth century it grew rapidly as an iron and steel town, but these industries have since declined. The main employer is Fabrique Nationale which began as a cannon foundry and now manufactures small arms for the NATO armies. Kilmarnock Way in Herstal was inaugurated in 1981.

On 14th December 1985 Valery Pilaya and a delegation from Sukhumi, capital of the province of Abkhazia in the Soviet republic of Georgia, visited Kilmarnock and agreed to twin with the town. This was duly ratified the following year. Sukhumi (114,000), on the shores of the Black Sea, is a holiday resort with an agricultural hinterland, raising crops of tobacco, citrus fruits and tea.

Kilmarnock and Loudoun Twin Towns' Association is affiliated to the United Towns' Organisation which co-ordinates the cultural co-operation of twinned towns throughout Europe. In 1980 Kilmarnock was awarded the prestigious European Flag of Honour in recognition

Award of Council of Europe Flag of Honour 1980

of the work which it had done in fostering mutual activities with its twins. Parties of school pupils have gone to the twin towns while groups from them have stayed in Kilmarnock. The Kilmarnock Chess Club conducts postal chess with enthusiasts in Kulmbach and Alès. The Police Pipe Band has performed in the twin towns during their civic celebrations, while 160 citizens from Herstal alone attended Kilmarnock's Civic Week in 1980. In 1981 it was estimated that there were over a hundred different links between Kilmarnock and its twins. Kilmarnock Rugby Football Club and Colts have regularly played in Alès and Herstal, and there have been numerous reciprocal visits of dancers and musicians which have considerably enlivened civic celebrations. But mainly it has been the interchange of visits by the ordinary men, women and children of Kilmarnock and its twin towns which have helped to foster and strengthen goodwill and understanding, giving practical meaning to the immortal words of Burns 'That man to man the world o'er, shall brithers be for a' that.'

BIBLIOGRAPHY

All publications are from Kilmarnock, unless otherwise stated.

Adamson, Archibald R. *Rambles round Kilmarnock, with an introductory sketch of the town* (Kilmarnock Standard, 1875).

Aitchison, Rev. James *One Hundred Not Out: Kilmarnock Cricket Club* (1952).

Aiton, William *General View of the Agriculture of the County of Ayr* (Ayr, 1811).

Anderson, E.M. *The Economic Geology of the Ayrshire Coalfields: Kilmarnock Basin* 1st ed. 1925, 2nd ed. 1930.

Blackwood, Morton and Sons Ltd *From Loom to Lathe and back again* (1946).

Beattie, Frank *Kilmarnock in Old Picture Postcards* (1984).

Begg. M.T. (ed.) *Kilmarnock Glenfield Ramblers Society: Annals, 1898-99 and Jubilee Number, 1884-1934* (1934).

Boyle, Andrew *The Ayrshire Book of Burns-Lore* (Alloway Publishing, Darvel, 1985).
Ayrshire Heritage (Alloway Publishing, Darvel, 1990).

Bryden, Robert *Etchings of Ayrshire Castles* (Bryden, 1889-1908).

Caldwell, Kay *The Strathclyde Story: Kilmarnock, Loudoun and Cunninghame* (n.d. [1990]).

Christie, A.V. *Brass Tacks and a Fiddle.*

Cochrane, Drew *The Story of Ayrshire Junior Football* (John Geddes, Irvine, 1976).

Deans, Brian T. *Green Cars To Hurlford.*

Department of Agriculture *The Soils of the Country round Kilmarnock* (DoA, Edinburgh, 1956).

Dick, Adam M. *The Story of Dick Brothers (Motors) Ltd, 1895-1945* (Dunlop and Drennan, 1945).

Donachie, Bill *Who's Who of Kilmarnock FC* (Mainstream, Edinburgh, 1989).

Foster, Rev. John *An Account of the Behaviour of the Late Earl of Kilmarnock, after his Sentence, and on the Day of his Execution* (London, 1746).

Fulton, William *Views of Kilmarnock* (Fulton, n.d.).

Gallagher, Nisbet *The Golden Years, 1952-1976* (Kilmarnock Cricket Club, 1976).

Glenarthur, J. *The Parliamentary History of Kilmarnock* (n.d. [1928]).

Gregory, James S. *Vital Statistics of the District or Parish of Kilmarnock, 1858* (1859).
Digest of the Census of Kilmarnock with Registration Statistics (1861).

Hamilton, Rev. Andrew *Kilmarnock Parish* [1790] (in Statistical Account of Scotland, vol 2. Creech, Edinburgh, 1792).

Hamilton, James *Extracts from Old Burgh Records of Kilmarnock* (Kilmarnock Standard, n.d.[1881]).

Hunter, James *History of the Old High Kirk* (n.d.).

Hunter, James and Thomson, J.F.T. *Dean Castle* (Kilmarnock and Loudoun District Council, 1976).

Hunter, John Kelso *Retrospect of an Artist's Life.*

Johnston, W.T. *Kilmarnock Printing in the Eighteenth Century* (1982).

Kilmarnock Burgh Council *The Residential and Industrial Advantages of Kilmarnock* (several editions, undated).

Landsborough, Rev. David *Contributions to Local History* (Kilmarnock Standard, n.d. [1879]).

McKay, Archibald *A History of Kilmarnock*: 1st edn. 1848, 2nd edn. 1858, 3rd ed. 1864, 4th edn. 1880; 5th edn. revised and updated by J. Findlay 1909.

Mackay, James A. *The Burns Federation, 1885-1985* (Burns Federation, 1985).

Mackinlay, Rev. Dr James and Robertson, Rev. John *Kilmarnock Parish* [1839] (in Statistical Account of Scotland, Blackwood, Edinburgh, 1842).

Malkin, John *Andrew Fisher, 1862-1928* (Alloway Publishing, Darvel, 1979).
Pictorial History of Kilmarnock (Alloway Pubishing, Darvel, 1989).

Millar, A.H. *The Castles and Mansions of Ayrshire, with historical and descriptive accounts* (William Paterson, Edinburgh, 1885).

Morris, James A. *A Romance of Industrial Engineering* (Glenfield and Kennedy, 1939).

Morrison, Ian O. *The Physical Influences on Kilmarnock's Development and History* (typescript of lecture, 15th October 1974).

Morton, Jocelyn *Three Generations in a Family Textile Firm* (Routledge, London, 1971).

Munro, William *Some Kilmarnock Celebrities* (Kilmarnock Standard, 1924).

Paterson, James *History of the County of Ayr* 2 vols. (Dick, Ayr, 1847-52).
Autobiographical Reminiscences (Ogle, Glasgow, 1871).

Pont, Timothy *Cunninghame Topographized, 1604-8* (Tweed, Glasgow, 1876).

Railton, J.S. *Kilmarnock Old High Kirk, its Management and its Ministers, 1739-1939* (1940).

Robertson, George *Topographical Description of Ayrshire, more particularly Cunninghame* (Cunningham Press, Irvine, 1820).

Robertson, William *Historic Ayrshire* 2 vols. (Thomson, Edinburgh, 1891-4).*Ayrshire, its History and Historic Families* 2 vols. (Dunlop and Drennan, 1908).
Kilmarnock Equitable Co-operative Society: A Fifty-Year Record, 1860-1910 (KECS, 1910).

Scott, James A. *Burgh of Kilmarnock Civil and Financial Information* (Kilmarnock Standard, 1941).

Scott, Stephen *Letter to Mungo Campbell regarding the Glasgow and Kilmarnock Road* (Glasgow, 1830).
Report as to a Railway between Glasgow and Kilmarnock (Glasgow, 1836).

Shaw, James Edward *Ayrshire, 1745-1950: a social

and industrial history of the county (Oliver and Boyd, Edinburgh, 1953).

Simpson, Anne T. and Stevenson, Sylvia *Historic Kilmarnock: the Archaeological Implications of Development* (Glasgow University, 1981; serialised in *Kilmarnock Standard*, July-August 1982).

Smellie, Thomas *Sketches of Old Kilmarnock* (Dunlop and Drennan, 1898).

Smith, Sheriff David B. *Curling: An Illustrated History* (1981).

Stewart, Alan *Kilmarnock (Barassie) Golf Club* (1987).

Strawhorn, Dr John *Ayrshire: A Social and Industrial Survey* (Ayr, 1950).
Farming in Eighteenth Century Ayrshire (Ayr, 1955).
The Background to Burns (Ayr, 1958).
Industry and Commerce in Eighteenth Century Ayrshire.
Ayrshire, the Story of a County (Ayr, 1975).
The History of Irvine (John Donald, Edinburgh, 1985).

Strawhorn, John and Boyd, William *Ayrshire* (Third Statistical Account, Oliver and Boyd, Edinburgh, 1951).

Taylor, Hugh *Go, Fame... The Story of Kilmarnock Football Club* (1969)

Thomson, J.F.T. and Malkin, John *Kilmarnock in Times Past* (Countryside Publications, Chorley, 1979).

Walker, James *Old Kilmarnock: character sketches* (Brown, 1895).

Wilson, M. *The Ayrshire Hermit and Hurlford* (1875).

Maps

Town plans of 1808, 1819, 1879, 1928.
Plan of traffic proposals (1963).
Grange Farm, Kilmarnock, (Peter Sturrock 12 inches to 1 mile).
Kilmarnock Cross at the end of the Eighteenth Century.
Map of Environs (R. Aitken, 1828).
Parliamentary Boundaries, 1832.
Ordnance Survey maps, various editions (1857-1963).

Periodicals in the Dick Institute

Auld Killie (August 1898).
Cunninghame Calls (monthly journal, 1937).
Kilmarnock Mirror and Literary Gleaner (October 1818 to January 1820).
Kilmarnock Standard (June 1863 to date: indexed 1863-1930).
Kilmarnock Standard Annual (1959-1966, indexed).
St Marnock (October 1898 to September 1900)

Miscellaneous

Boyd Papers (partly in Register House, Edinburgh, but mainly at Dean Castle, Kilmarnock).
Beattie, Frank Album containing press cuttings of articles (in Dick Institute).
152 files of cuttings, manuscripts and ephemera of local interest arranged thematically, from General History (1-6) to Folk Music (152) (in Dick Institute)

INDEX

202